Modes of Production and Archaeology

UNIVERSITY PRESS OF FLORIDA

Florida A&M University, Tallahassee
Florida Atlantic University, Boca Raton
Florida Gulf Coast University, Ft. Myers
Florida International University, Miami
Florida State University, Tallahassee
New College of Florida, Sarasota
University of Central Florida, Orlando
University of Florida, Gainesville
University of North Florida, Jacksonville
University of South Florida, Tampa
University of West Florida, Pensacola

# MODES OF PRODUCTION AND ARCHAEOLOGY

Edited by Robert M. Rosenswig
and Jerimy J. Cunningham

University Press of Florida
Gainesville · Tallahassee · Tampa · Boca Raton
Pensacola · Orlando · Miami · Jacksonville · Ft. Myers · Sarasota

Printed in the United States of America on acid-free paper

This book may be available in an electronic edition.

22 21 20 19 18 17 6 5 4 3 2 1

A record of cataloging-in-publication data is available from the Library of Congress.
ISBN 978-0-8130-5430-8

The University Press of Florida is the scholarly publishing agency for the State University System of Florida, comprising Florida A&M University, Florida Atlantic University, Florida Gulf Coast University, Florida International University, Florida State University, New College of Florida, University of Central Florida, University of Florida, University of North Florida, University of South Florida, and University of West Florida.

University Press of Florida
15 Northwest 15th Street
Gainesville, FL 32611-2079
http://upress.ufl.edu

# Contents

# Figures

# Tables

# 1

# Introducing Modes of Production in Archaeology

ROBERT M. ROSENSWIG AND JERIMY J. CUNNINGHAM

It is an understatement to observe that historical materialism has had a profound influence on the social sciences. In fact, the proposals of Marx and Engels are so fundamental to how social scientists, including archaeologists, analyze societies that the insights have moved to the realm of disciplinary common sense (Gilman 1989; Kohl 1981; Patterson 2003, 2009). Processual archaeologists adopted evolutionary concepts from historical materialism through the writings of White, Wittfogel, Service, and Polanyi—who were all Marxists—that were depoliticized in the writings of Steward and Binford (McGuire 1993:114; Trigger 2003:13–16). Some of the early post-processualists (e.g., Shanks and Tilley 1987a, 1987b; Spriggs 1984) advocated an idealist reformulation of Marxism, inspired by the French structural Marxists.[1] And everyone has internalized the Marxist-inspired analytic program of Childe (1936, 1950) to some degree, especially his Neolithic and Urban revolutions. The basis of some theoretical debate is therefore not a matter of whether to employ Marxist insights, but a product of the different ways that they have been fragmented and incorporated into archaeology, often without these ties being explicit.

Our proposal, emphasized in this book, is that historical materialism, as originally described by Marx and Engels, remains relevant to archaeologists. There are many different forms of materialism, but the one defined by Marx and Engels is particularly relevant to explain long-term patterns in human history. The analytic system laid out by Marx and Engels assumes that economic organization is rooted in a web of social relations (Wolf 1999:288). *Homo sapiens* is a social species whose history is not a passive response to natural processes. More than social animals, our ancestors were also political animals and became more so as population density increased. Even among the biological sciences, there is increasing realization that human evolution was embedded within a political economy (e.g.,

Hicks and Leonard 2014). In fact, proposals for a niche construction theory (Odling-Smee et al. 2003), when brought to their logical conclusion for *Homo sapiens,* are to define the cultural niche that humans have created and subsequently adapted to for thousands of years.[2] Such a nonreductive materialism reaffirms the long-standing Marxist belief that technology, social organization, and political realms form a cohesive holism.

Our assumption in writing this introduction is that many readers (and especially those English speakers under ~50 years of age) primarily employ secondhand knowledge of the writing of Marx and Engels. Basic Marxist concepts that structure analysis (such as mode of production) have been filtered through the writings of anthropologists and understood under different names and are now attributed to scholars of the second half of the twentieth century. McGuire et al. (2005:356) observe "that many contemporary archaeologists, positivists, postmodernists, and feminists alike simply do not know that many of their key concepts and perspectives derive from Marxism." We therefore begin by reviewing key concepts from Marx and Engels' original writings and define basic Marxist terms.

Fundamental to a historical materialist analysis is the mode of production that describes how sociopolitical organization and economic relations are integrated and how surplus is deployed. As Saitta (1994:226) notes: "That all societies produce surplus labor was one of Marx's key insights, and this basic idea has been developed by anthropologists." How this surplus labor is organized and "spent" provides the engine for social developments (but see Clark [2007] for a contrary opinion).[3] In the collection of essays that follows, modes of production are employed to understand a wide range of societies. We adhere to a basic tenet in mode of production analysis, which is that different production systems have their own economic and political "logics." This does not mean that economic decisions are irrational; rather, that rationality is expressed differently according to particular social and political organization as well as ideological traditions that structures decision making. We accept that "rational" decisions underlie all economic organization and decisions of individual actors. However, the structure of sociopolitical relations (especially differences between those that are egalitarian and hierarchical) affects how economic rationality is expressed (Hirth 1996:205; Patterson 2003:25–27; Saitta 1994:207). As discussed at greater length below, we describe Eric Wolf's (1982) three distinct "logics" that can be discerned based on different modes of production (i.e., kin-ordered, tributary, and capitalist). These are not necessarily the only modes of production (and authors in this volume describe a range of modes) but they are inclusive and simple so as to focus attention on historical process rather than classification.

Modes of production are used in a variety of ways by authors in this book but all employ the framework as an analytical tool to explore the reproduction of society. Each author provides examples of how one or multiple modes of production (in succession or simultaneously) promotes distinctive questions and new insights about the past. The aim of the volume is not to (re)affirm the value of mode of production analysis to those already convinced of its utility but instead to suggest to a broader audience that such analyses can provide insights that are not available through conventional archaeological approaches. As a group, we follow Marx's analysis of capitalism in making our cases for the utility of mode of production analysis by working through concrete examples. Changing modes of production—and combinations of modes (Cunningham, chapter 8; Ensor 2000:20–21, Ensor, chapter 10; Gailey 1987:34–38; Gailey and Patterson 1988; Patterson 1986:56–57; Patterson, chapter 2)—should resonate with all archaeologists who collect diachronic data and try to infer changing economic organization, social relations, political structure, and associated forms of social consciousness (also known as culture).

It is worth emphasizing that modes of production, by their very definition, do not refer to a stable form of organization (either through time or over space). Marx and Engels defined various modes of production as abstractions played out in the historical contingencies of actual societies. Ancient societies were described as having Germanic, Slavic, Asiatic, and Teutonic Roman modes of production, defined in the ethnic terms of social science at the time. Such early modes were further contrasted with a capitalist mode of production that was spreading during the 19th century and a feudal mode that was waning in Western Europe at the time. Precapitalist modes were often vaguely modeled and/or inconsistently defined (Gilman 1984:115, 1995; Roseberry 1989:155; Wolf 1982:75). Marx's definitions of noncapitalist modes are thus not always directly transferable for archaeologists to adopt (Rolland 2005; but see Anderson 2010:198). However, it does not matter whether Marx "should have postulated two or eight or fifteen modes of production, or whether other modes should be substituted for those suggested by him. The utility of the concept lies not in classification but in its capacity to underline the *strategic relationships* involved in the deployment of social labor by organized human pluralities" (Wolf 1982:76, emphasis added). It is these strategic social relations that transform labor into political capital that concern us in this volume.

There is a risk of reifying a series of modes of production into a set of types and the classification of society as providing a goal in itself. A classification-focused research agenda for pigeonholing modes of production would parallel the limited utility of processualist evolutionary typologies, epitomized in identifying chiefdoms as a research end in itself (Yoffee 1993; Pauketat 2007). Soviet scholars and the so-called vulgar materialists[4] were criticized for this very thing. We accept this critique as valid and endorse a more nuanced historical materialism such as that proposed by Wolf (1982), Roseberry (1989), Haldon (1993), Trigger (1993, 1998, 2006), and Patterson (2003, 2009), among others. We agree that ideal evolutionary types (devoid of historical specificity) provide limited interpretive insight. However, non-reified modes of production can instead be used to comparatively explore historical (or prehistorical) processes.

Studying mode(s) of production is to ask questions about how social labor is organized, how surplus is deployed, and how this can either maintain or change an existing political system. Surplus labor is work undertaken beyond that required to maintain the life of those working and their dependents. Archaeologists generally identify the material residue of surplus labor in exotic or labor-intensive objects as well as monumental architecture. Surplus can be produced by egalitarian foragers and ranked horticulturalists as well as socially stratified ancient empires and modern nation-states (or any other social plurality). A key question in mode of production analysis is how surplus is directed to maintain or transform a social and political status quo that can be egalitarian, hierarchical, or both. Put simply, the mode of production concept provides a set of heuristic concepts that can focus attention onto specific processes and actions in a social and historical context and develop a framework to compare the structural logics and organizations of a wide range of societies. It thus provides the potential for archaeologists to comparatively investigate changing human organization (Chapman 2003:29–31; Trigger 1993:167–169, 1998:89–91). Modes of production focus attention on how social labor is deployed to facilitate the reproduction of society, and how political motivations result in the appropriation of surpluses by those in power. McGuire (1986:253) notes, "It does not seek to specify universal causes but rather to identify the key structural relations we should examine in any given instance of change." Archaeologists have long acknowledged that understanding a society's political economy provides a powerful framework through which to explore the economic foundations of political evolution (Cobb 1993; Feinman and Nicholas 2004; Hirth 1996). The mode of production does one better by emphasizing specific linkages between the economy and the realms of politics and ideology. In the nineteenth-century context in which they were writing, Marx and Engels agreed with the political economy framework (advocated by Adam Smith, etc.) as a description but one that failed to "see" who benefited from the value-laden, taken-for-granted concepts embedded in industrial society. The mode of production framework helps us to explore a "politicized political economy"—both today and in the past.

In the remainder of this introductory chapter, we first review the mode of production framework as it was originally defined by Marx and Engels. We then examine two influential uses of the term *mode of production*, specifically, the Asiatic mode of production (Polanyi 1957; Wittfogel 1957) and the household mode of production (e.g., Sahlins 1972). We observe that Wittfogel and Polanyi's work caused much disagreement (and spurred much new research) by their particular view of how ancient non-Western societies were organized. Sahlins' definition of a "domestic" mode of production is a neo-Marxist redefinition of the term based on ontologically idealist assumptions that are fundamentally antithetical to what Marx and Engels actually wrote (Trigger 1993:177). A domestic mode of production would more accurately have been called a domestic "type" or "form" of organization.[5] We end our introduction by describing Eric Wolf's (1982) formula of kin-ordered, tributary, and capitalist modes of production. Our intention throughout this chapter is not to squabble about the historiography of Marxist theory, or with those who draw inspiration from it. Instead, we provide a simple definition of modes of production that is amenable to making cross-cultural comparisons.

## Marx and Engels' Modes of Production

As noted, our goal is to begin with what Marx and Engels wrote about modes of production to provide a historical context for the terms. Rather than being synonymous with a "type" or "form" of production, modes of production are the social relations that permit the existing technology, environmental conditions, etc. to generate surplus that is then employed to perpetuate, reproduce, or alter existing social and political relations (and associated forms of social consciousness). The social/political system can be egalitarian or hierarchical (or both), but those in decision-making positions generally strive to maintain the culture norms that have placed them in decision-making roles.

### *The German Ideology*

In the 1846 coauthored volume *The German Ideology*, Marx and Engels critique the idealist Hegelian tradition in which they were themselves educated. If at times the vehemence of their materialist position seems overstated, it is because they were reacting to what was, in their minds, the intellectual norm of their day. Like all theoretical propositions, Marx's historical materialism is anchored in a particular intellectual history, in this case, in a rejection of Kant's and Hegel's idealist understanding of humanity and its history (see Kolakowski 1978:132–138). Hegel thought that humanity's essence was spiritual consciousness and that history was the result of processes that objectified that consciousness in the world and reabsorbed that externalized consciousness through sublation. History was thus a series of steps toward self-awareness. Marx wanted to set Hegel "right side up" by suggesting that humanity's nature was not a metaphysical spiritual essence but lay in human interactions with the natural world through the process of labor. They begin, in a section titled "Feuerbach: Opposition of the Materialistic and Idealist Outlook," by stating: "As we hear from the German ideologists, Germany has in the last few years gone through an unparalleled revolution. The decomposition of the Hegelian philosophy . . ." (Marx and Engels 1978:147). They critique the Young Hegelians (see Breckman 1999; Stepelevich 1990), who were also criticizing the traditional Hegelian position as being politically conservative and serving to bolster the German state. However, the Young Hegelians were firmly wedded to the idealist ontology of the Hegelian tradition. Marx and Engels make their materialist critique of this absolutely clear:

> Since the Young Hegelians consider conceptions, thoughts, ideas, in fact all the products of consciousness, to which they attribute an independent existence, as the real chains of men (just as the Old Hegelians declared them the true bonds of human society) it is evident that the Young Hegelians have to fight only against these illusions of the consciousness. Since, according to their fantasy, the relationships of men, all their doings, their chains and their limitations are products of their consciousness, these Young Hegelians logically put to men the moral postulate of exchanging their present consciousness for human, critical or egoistic consciousness, and thus of removing their limitations. . . . The Young Hegelian ideologists, in spite of their allegedly "world-shattering" statements, are the staunchest conservatives. . . . It

> does not occur to any of these philosophers to inquire into the connection of German philosophy with German reality, the relation of their criticism to their own material surroundings. (Marx and Engels 1978: 149)

For Marx and Engels, politically progressive ideas are fatally undermined if the idealism of the Hegelian tradition is maintained. This means that twentieth-century French structural Marxists (as well as their post-structuralist and post-processualist brethren), with their idealist ontology, are the intellectual heirs of the Young Hegelians rather than Marx and Engels. It is on this point that Trigger (1993:186) long ago argued "that idealist explanations, and therefore much (but not all) of what passes as neo-Marxism, forfeit the right to bear the name." But neither were Marx and Engels proposing economic reductionism. In a letter to Joseph Bloch written in 1890 (after Marx's death and *after the entire corpus of their writings had been set to paper*), Engels makes this clear:

> According to the materialist conception of history, the *ultimately* determined element in history is the production and reproduction of real life. More than this neither Marx nor I have ever asserted. Hence if somebody twists this into saying that the economic element is the *only* determining one, he transforms the proposition into a meaningless, abstract, senseless phrase. The economic situation is the basis, but the various elements of the superstructure: political forms of the class struggle and its results . . . and even the reflexes of these actual struggles in the brains of the participants, political, juristic, philosophical theories, religious views and their further development into systems of dogmas, also exercise their influence upon the course of the historical struggles and in many cases preponderate in determining their *form*. (Tucker 1978:760, italics in original)

Rosenswig (2015) has recently discussed ultimate versus proximate causation (or "determined elements in history"—to use Engels' words above) in the context of Mesoamerican food production. He argues that ultimate causes associated with climate change (with resulting environmental, demographic changes) affected the economic organization of Late Archaic and Early Formative period (5000–1000 cal BC) Mesoamerican societies, but, crucially, that these changes played out through proximate causes that were defined by the historical details of the superstructure (see also

Rosenswig 2012). To frame ultimate causality in terms of the economy is the essence of Marx and Engels' insight as is the necessity that the economy is embedded in social relations.

The nuanced materialism of Marx and Engels is defined in terms of the mode of production concept in *The German Ideology*. They argue:

> The way in which men produce their means of subsistence depends first of all on the nature of the actual means of subsistence they find in existence and have to reproduce. This mode of production must not be considered simply as being the reproduction of the physical existence of the individuals. Rather it is a definite form of activity of these individuals, a definite form of expressing their life, a definite *mode of life* on their part. As individuals express their life, so they are. What they are, therefore, coincides with their production, both with *what* they produce and with *how* they produce. The nature of individuals thus depends on the material conditions determining their production. (Marx and Engels 1978:150, italics in original)

Again, they emphasize that social relations are fundamental to the mode of production because that is "how they produce" and how they generate a surplus. This is also the passage that has led Bate (1977, 1998) and others in Latin America (Benavides 2001; Patterson 1994) to define a *Modo de Vida* as the mode of life that can define differing peoples that share the same mode of production (Acosta, chapter 4; Ensor 2000). As with the position advocated here, scholars in many parts of the Spanish-speaking world reject the functionalism and idealism of the French structural Marxists for the nuanced historical materialism of the original texts (Chapman 2003:18–31; McGuire 1993:110–111).

### Preface to *A Contribution to the Critique of Political Economy*

In his 1859 preface to *A Contribution to the Critique of Political Economy*, Marx succinctly and unambiguously laid out the position that would guide his future analysis. We quote it at length here, as it is foundational to historical materialism and the generations of subsequent scholars' discussions of modes of production. Marx begins:

> My investigation led to the result that legal relations as well as forms of state are to be grasped neither from themselves nor from the so-called general development of the human mind, but rather have their roots in the material conditions of life, the sum total of which

> Hegel . . . found combines under the name "civil society," that however, the anatomy of civil society is to be sought in political economy. (Marx 1978:4)

His materialist ontology is consistently presented in explicit contrast to Hegelian idealist philosophy when defining the organization of society. One sentence later, he continues:

> The general result at which I arrived and which, once won, served as a guiding thread for my studies, can be briefly formulated as follows: In the social production of their life, men enter into definite relations of production which correspond to a definite stage of development of their material productive forces. The sum total of these relations of production constitutes the economic structure of society, the real foundation, on which rises a legal and political superstructure and to which correspond definite forms of social consciousness. The mode of production of material life conditions the social, political and intellectual life process in general. It is not consciousness of men that determine their being, but, on the contrary, their social being that determines their consciousness. (Marx 1978:4)

While this passage gives us what might be considered the key "components" of a mode of production, it is important to stress that the concept was not formulated as a "model" of society, but was part of a distinct philosophical system that sought to explore humanity as a product of its material existence. Labor was the most fundamental concept because, as physical beings, humans transformed nature to produce the nutrients that they needed to survive through labor and came to understanding consciousness through actions in the world. Many of the key concepts, such as means of production or relations of production, relate to this fundamental question about how humanity produces its existence through labor. For example, the means of production is the dominant technology (e.g., stone tools, metal plow, factory) along with knowledge and organization of its use. In addition, the relations of production are the social relations (e.g., kinship, serfdom, private property) that allow for the means of production to operate. These are framed by associated forms of social consciousness that provide a meaningful context for the deployment of labor and reproduction of the social system. Together the means and relations of production, as well as the political and jural superstructure, provide the elements that establish a holistic and dialectically intertwined mode of production. New forms of technology and new social relations have the potential to produce contradictions that lead to the emergence of new modes of production, just as preceding modes of production remain as "survivals." The point is not to get bogged down in Marxist terminology but to emphasize that the mode of production is the overarching organization of Marx and Engels' analysis and the way they expanded the political economy perspective of Adam Smith and others.

Marx continues with an explanation of how change occurs:

> At a certain stage of their development, the material productive forces of society come in conflict with the existing relations of production, or—what is but a legal expression of the same thing—with the property relations within which they have been at work hitherto. From forms of development of the productive forces these relations turn into their fetters. Then begins an epoch of social revolution. With the change of economic foundations the entire immense superstructure is more or less rapidly transformed. (Marx 1978:4–5)

The mode of production concept is the most fundamental part of Marxist analysis and why we focus on it in this collection of essays. Changing modes of production provide yet untapped potential for archaeologists with our diachronic data. We cannot overemphasize that what distinguishes historical materialism from other forms of materialism is that the engine of change is internal to society itself. While environmental conditions and population levels can provide the ultimate potential for change to occur, it is the specific, historically determined changes in social relations that are the proximate causes that explain how change actually happened. Marx continues by emphasizing his ontological frame of explaining such changes:

> Just as our opinion of an individual is not based on what he thinks of himself, so can we not judge of such a period of transformation by its own consciousness; on the contrary, this consciousness must be explained rather from the contradictions of material life, from the existing conflict between the social productive forces and the relations of production. (Marx 1978:5)

Marx clearly and consistently lays out a materialism that is based in social relations and is therefore not reductive to simple economic or environmental causes. There are those (e.g., Stalin) who quote Marx to say that the economic base determines ideology and other aspects of the superstructure in a simple and direct manner (i.e., vulgar materialism). There are others, like the French structural Marxists or post-processual archaeologists, who argue that social relations and ideology determine the economic base (i.e., vulgar idealism[6]). Both are at odds with what Marx and Engels actually wrote, as Roseberry (1989) has so cogently argued. Marx and Engels' original writings were more nuanced than often given credit and therefore worth returning to (Patterson 2003:19–20). When economic relations change they can come into conflict with ideological principles, laws, etc. and create tensions within society. This antifunctionalist proposal—that conflict and negotiation internal to society explain cultural change—is one of the single most significant contributions of historical materialism for archaeologists. Marx and Engels focused on specific historical instances of change. That is, on how capitalism was displacing feudalism in Europe and how European royalty with their divine right to rule and ownership of all national lands was quickly (by the mid-1800s) being displaced by various forms of parliamentary and republican rule justified by democracy and with new private property laws (Meillassoux 1972:93–94). Elected houses of government, private property, and democratic ideals that justify them were not what ultimately caused change; these changes were wrested from the monarchy by an emerging capitalist class based on their newfound economic power. Marx and Engels' theoretical proposal therefore needs to be understood in terms of the concrete and historically specific political environment of nineteenth-century Europe.[7]

In the final passage from *A Contribution to the Critique of Political Economy* we will quote, Marx elaborates his view of both change and modes of productions. He observes that

> mankind always sets itself only such tasks as it can solve; since, looking at the matter more closely, it will always be found that the task itself arises only when the material conditions for its solution already exist or are at least in the process of formation. In broad outlines Asiatic, ancient, feudal, and modern bourgeois modes of production can be designated as progressive epochs on the economic formation of society. (Marx 1978:5)

Again, the cause of change is internal to society, and the manner in which it occurs is therefore culturally specific and historically determined. This second mention of modes of production could be read as a mechanical, unilineal evolutionary typology that all societies pass through, and this is precisely what Stalin did (see Currie 1984). However, Marx is simply describing what he knows to have happened, and this is only to the best of his mid-nineteenth-century knowledge of the past. It is worth emphasizing that the point of this review is not to argue that everything Marx ever wrote was correct. His writings are filled with the nineteenth-century taken-for-granted sexism and Western ethnocentrism that we disagree with today. The point is instead to elaborate the insight provided by his materialist analysis of history and social change through the specific definition of modes of production.

## Anthropology's and Others' Modes of Production

The mode of production concept continues to figure prominently in social science analysis. Lately, some argue that modes of production should be reengineered to define modes of exchange (Foster 2014; Karanti 2014) or how surplus production articulates with social relations (Graeber 2006:77). Others, particularly in relation to development of the Indian subcontinent, continue to argue for the importance of the classical mode of production concept (Banaji 2012), but this is not universally accepted (see Bernstein 2013; Campling 2013). The mode of production literature is immense, and we do not attempt to summarize or distill it here. Instead, we observe that idiosyncratic and incomplete uses of modes of production (and reactions to them) led to theoretical ennui among many anthropologists by the 1980s (see Roseberry 1989:129, 145). Further, arguments about modes of production can descend into detailed histories of Marxist theory that is off-putting to archaeologists not politically inclined or unfamiliar with nineteenth-century terminologies and intellectual history. Our contention in putting this book together is that as originally conceived by Marx, and updated by Wolf (and others) for precapitalist societies, the mode of production has continued value for the interpretation of archaeological data. We critically discuss two examples of anthropological uses of modes of production to provide clarity as to the processes and social relation that are entailed. Simply put, mode(s) of production provide a framework to explore the organization of surplus production and appropriation and how this is employed to maintain the social and political status quo of existing kin and/or class relations. As an inclusive framework, it is ideally suited for making cross-cultural and cross-temporal comparisons.

## Wittfogel and the Asiatic Mode of Production

During the middle of the twentieth century, considerable effort was expended in defining precapitalist modes of production. The Asiatic mode received particular attention and was dissected from the Western academic tradition (Krader 1975) as well as from within the Soviet tradition (Dunn 1982; Wittfogel 1957:6–7). Polanyi's (1957) Marxist-inspired work, with its divide between capitalist and pre-capitalist society, assumed absolute and unchanging power of Eastern dictatorships and was influential for many archaeologists. However, Wittfogel (1957:6) notes "that Marx, far from originating the 'Asiatic' concept, had found it ready-made in the writings of classical economists" (see also Wittfogel 1957:372–386).[8] Arguably the single most relevant formulation of the Asiatic mode of production for archaeologists was Wittfogel's (1957:369–412) detailed treatment in *Oriental Despotism*, where he reviews how Marx, Engels, Lenin, and Stalin each defined the Asiatic mode of production. Wittfogel's perspective, that irrigation infrastructure was crucial to monopolizing political power, was so influential that it launched a sustained treatment of the concept (e.g., Bailey and Llobera 1981; Currie 1984; Dunn 1982; O'Leary 1989).

Our purpose here is not to review or add to debates concerning the Asiatic mode of production. The simple fact that so much research was conducted to both support and critique Wittfogel's (and Polanyi's) Marxist-inspired ideas is a tribute to their importance in structuring the current academic landscape of various disciplines, including archaeology. However, that the control of irrigation infrastructure does not explain state power in, for example, Hawaii (Kirch 1994) or Mesoamerica (Feinman and Nichols, chapter 10; Offner 1981; but see Wittfogel 1972) as Wittfogel hypothesized, says little about the mode of production framework itself. Instead, it simply indicates that Wittfogel's conception is not confirmed by empirical evaluation. Further, when processual archaeologists (e.g., Carneiro 1970:734; Flannery 1972:418) evaluated Wittfogel's ideas, it was as a depoliticized version that did not address the political nature of surplus production but rather simply the importance of irrigation facilities for state control (and so the processual archaeologists provided examples of a political economy approach rather than of historical materialism). Likewise, Goody's (1990) critique of the Asiatic mode of production is of Wittfogel's formulation—not of the analytic framework but of a specific application. This distinction between Marx's mode of production concept and Wittfogel's application is important. Currie (1984:259) convincingly argues that what Marx actually proposed was that in arid environments, rather than the emergence of despotic states being caused by the control of irrigation facilities, the link was instead "between conditions of irrigation agriculture and the *extension* of state control" (Currie 1984:259, italics in original). Therefore, rather than making a generalizable rule about the origins of state power, as Wittfogel advocated, Marx himself was making an observation of specific historical instances of already established states with existing funds of surplus labor using irrigation agriculture facilities to expand or cement existing power. Control of irrigation infrastructure was not a cause but *an effect of state power*. Marx observed a historical correlation, and Wittfogel inverted the causal arrow (see argument in Haldon 1993:2–4).

### Sahlins' Domestic Mode of Production

Marshall Sahlins' (1972) discussion of underproduction defined in terms of a "domestic" mode of production is well-known to archaeologists. Within the context of traditional societies' reactions to colonial powers, Sahlins (1972:86) proposed that the domestic mode of production "harbors an anti-surplus principle. Geared to the production of livelihood, it is endowed with the tendency to come to a halt at that point. Hence if 'surplus' is defined as output above the producers' requirements, the household system is not organized for it. Nothing within the structure of production for use pushes it to transcend itself." This is not a mode of production in the Marxist sense, as should be clear after our review in the previous section. Sahlins' "mode" is instead a Chayanovian description of subsistence production of conquered peoples resisting a capitalist mode of production. This discrepancy is made clear when Sahlins (1972:86) claims: "Work is accordingly unintensive: intermittent and susceptible to all manner of interruption by cultural alternatives and impediments ranging from heavy ritual to light rainfall. Economics is only a part-time activity of the primitive societies, or else it is an activity of only part of the society." Economic activity and the production of surplus can most certainly not be separated from the cultural or ritual realm according to the analysis proposed by Marx and Engels.

Sahlins' analysis is explicitly framed within the French structural Marxist tradition, and uses its terms. For example, he cites Engels and presents a table contrasting the relationships of the *means of production* between chiefly and *bourgeois ownership* on the very same page where he proposes the economic rule that "there is no class of landless paupers in primitive society. If expropriation occurs it is accidental to the mode of production itself, a cruel fortune of war for instance, and not a systematic condition of the economic organization" (Sahlins 1972:93). How could appropriation of surplus labor possibly be accidental to a mode of production? That is precisely what defines it!

In Sahlins' second complete chapter devoted to defining his domestic mode of production, the structural Marxist revisionism is clear. Sahlins (1972:102) claims: "The determination of the main organization of production at an infrastructural level of kinship is one way of facing the dilemma presented by primitive societies to Marxist analyses, namely, between the decisive role accorded by theory to the economic base and the fact that the dominant economic relations are in quality superstructural, e.g., kinship relations (see Godelier 1966; Terrey 1969)." His first problem is citing the French structural Marxists rather than what Marx and Engels actually wrote (Roseberry 1989:160–161; and see Gailey 1987:6). Second, as presented clearly in the previous section, the superstructure (religion, laws, kin relations) certainly do structure the political economy. Just because a historical materialist perspective assumes the economic factors are causative (in an ultimate sense) does not mean that ideology is irrelevant to historical analysis. A materialist straw man is erected so as to present an idealist solution to a problem that never existed. We soon learn just how deeply antimaterialist Sahlins' view of culture was. He claims:

> Hawaiian kinship is a more intensive economic system than Eskimo kinship. Because, simply, the Hawaiian system has a greater degree of classification in the Morganian sense: a more extensive identification of collateral with lineal relatives. . . . All other things equal, then, Hawaiian kinship will generate a greater surplus tendency than Eskimo. (Sahlins 1972:123)

To argue that kinship terms (and the relationships they reflect) develop independently and then result in differing propensities to intensify economic production is squarely Hegelian, precisely what Marx and Engels railed against in *The German Ideology*. The basis of Marx and Engels' argument (and ours) is that kinship relations come to reflect (and reinforce) the conditions under which surplus is produced and deployed. Kinship relations may evolve slowly in traditional societies, and shifting standards may not seem abrupt to those living through periods of transition. Over dozens of generations kinship terms and obligations can be transformed dramatically, or, as Gailey (1987) documents for the Pacific during the nineteenth century, such changes in kinship can occur very rapidly in response to economic transformation.

Sahlins' idealist redefinition of the mode of production has resulted in much confusion. This very critique was long ago leveled against Sahlins' appropriation of Marx and Engels' terminology (e.g., Friedmann 1980), and it is not our purpose here to propose it as an original observation. Instead, we wish to clearly differentiate the historical materialism we describe from Sahlins' much-cited book. A Google Scholar search indicates that *Stone Age Economics* is Sahlins' most cited work, with 6,447 citations as of January 23, 2016. Sahlins' domestic mode of production thus persistently contributes to definitional cloudiness and impedes what we are trying to lay out in this volume. Furthermore, Meillassoux (1981), also inspired by the Marxist tradition, employed a "domestic mode of production" but defined it in different terms than did Sahlins. Equally muddying is Wilk's (ed. 1989) use in the subtitle of his edited volume *Household Economy: Reconsidering the Domestic Mode of Production* that follows neither Sahlins' nor Meillassoux's definition. In this volume the domestic mode of production is used to understand not societies' political economies but instead how households: "manage and combine their production, exchange, investment, inheritance, sharing, minding, pooling, preparing, and consuming" (Wilk 1989:25). In fact, only one paper, of the dozen assembled in the volume, cites anything written by Marx, only three cite Sahlins (1972), and two cite Meillassoux (1981). Wilk's edited volume is thus primarily interested in exploring "domestic production" rather than a mode of production (e.g., Cunningham, chapter 8; Donham 1999). Domestic mode of production has been so variably used by anthropologists that we feel it could be retired for the sake of definitional clarity.

## Wolf's Modes of Production: A Streamlined Trinity

As we detail in this chapter, modes of production describe how social labor is deployed for economic pursuits, usually with political motivation and consequences. It is "a specific, historically occurring set of social relations through which labor is deployed to wrest energy from nature" (Wolf 1982:75). Wolf (2001 [1981]:342–352 and see 1982:75–100, 400–404) defines a capitalist, tributary, and kin-ordered mode of production. Wolf's elegantly simple trinity of modes has been employed by many archaeologists influenced by the Marxist tradition (e.g., Arnold 2000; Gilman 1995; Ensor 2000; Kristiansen 1998; McGuire 1986; Rosenswig 2012; Saitta 1994, 2005; and see McGuire 1992:152–153; Muller 1997:30–37; Patterson 2003:18–25). Such modes are not proposed as being all-encompassing, universally applicable, or mutually exclusive. Instead, as Wolf (1982: 76–77) observes, the goal of structuring analysis with modes of production is in:

> revealing the political economic relationships that underlie, orient, and constrain interaction. Such key relationships may characterize only a part of the total range of interactions in a society; they may comprehend all of a society; or they may transcend particular, historically constituted systems of social interaction. Used comparatively, the concept of mode of production calls attention to major variations in political-economic arrangements and allows us to visualize their effect.

A capitalist mode of production is defined by the ability to appropriate surplus value of production and to sever the tie between producers and the means of production (i.e., tools, land). Once this happens, the holders of wealth can dictate the terms under which they will allow workers to operate the means of production in exchange for a wage with which workers can then pay for what they need to sustain themselves. Workers produce more than their wage (and the operating costs of a farm or factory or shop) to generate a surplus, which is the profit for the holders of wealth. Such holders of wealth (aka capitalists) can increase profits either by lowering the wages of employees or by increasing their productivity, and the latter is usually achieved through improving the technology of production (more mechanized factories or farming practices, more efficient types of material like iron or plastic, as well as more productive species of plants and animals). Ever more surplus is accumulated by capitalists who reinvest part into increasingly efficient technology, which continues to increase profits. Importantly, wealth is not capital until it is reinvested into the system and so defines the engine that increases surplus production. In this way, the Marxist notion of capitalism does not describe a synchronic state (and certainly not a philosophy) but describes instead a dynamic set of relationships. The manner in which surplus is extracted by capitalists is economic and not (directly at least) through political mechanisms. Taxes are not levied by the capitalist class but instead are levied to support political administrators and other state functionaries who facilitate, but do not directly contribute to, the capitalist's surplus production. Politicians facilitate wealth acquisition by the capitalist class domestically by maintaining infrastructure and enforcing private property laws and internationally by sustaining an army to protect foreign investments.

The tributary mode of production, in contrast, characterizes economic organization where producers are not separated from the means of production. This mode of production does not set up a self-perpetuating system of technological development that increases the surplus (and thus profit) of those who control the means of production. Instead, surplus is extracted directly from producers (who continue to own the means of productions such as their tools and land) through military and political coercion. This is the basis of a feudal system where serfs work the land and owe the lord a proportion of their crops and/or a number of days' work per month. Noncompliance is generally enforced by threat of violence and, when necessary, actual violence. The organization of a tribute-extracting elite depends on whether there is a strong central ruler or if local lords hold more sway. Diachronically, there would be a continuous struggle between the central and local interests that make the system dynamic and fluid. Central authorities are more powerful if they command standing armies or if they can control a strategic element of the means of production (e.g., irrigation canals). As we have seen, such a system of powerful, centralized organization is what Marx called the Asiatic mode of production. Local authorities are more powerful when they control the means of coercion and/or elements of the process of production. In such cases, local elite can limit the flow of tribute that reaches the central authorities (and this is how the feudal mode of production was defined). As Wolf (2001 [1981]:347) observes, rather than different organizational logic, with the Asiatic and feudal modes of production "we are dealing, rather, with variable outcomes of the competition between classes of non-producers for power at the top" (and see Gledhill 1981:26). Modeling a variety of precapitalist societies that all possess exploitive relations is a significant contribution of Wolf's formulation (Haldon 1993:63–139). Kristiansen (1998:89) interprets European prehistory as cycling between these two ends of the tributary mode of production, and Gilman (1995:249) proposes that a Germanic mode (with even weaker central rulers) should also be considered on this continuum (see Ling et al., Chapter 9). As we previously emphasized, modes of production are not functional types but instead describe the creation and distribution of surplus in a dynamic and ever-changing manner. Local and regional elites are continually vying for the upper hand, and archaeologists have approached such intrapolity struggles using terms such as *factional competition* and *heterarchy*.

The kin-ordered mode of production is defined by its use of kinship relations as the key to mobilizing resources rather than economy/technology of the capitalist mode or political/military means of the tributary mode.

As Wolf (2001 [1981]:349) describes it: "Kinship thus involves symbolic constructs that place actors into social relationships which permit them to call on shares of social labor from others so as to effect the necessary transformations of nature." This is a materialist definition of kinship as the organizational system used to produce material goods. Far from being egalitarian, unequal relations in societies organized by the kin-ordered mode of production are based on seniority within the structure of kinship, and so elders, higher-ranking lineages, and the descendants of first settlers dominate juniors, lower-ranking lines, and newcomers. Kinship ties determine who can direct the labor of others, decide marriages, have access to land, etc. Political hierarchy and economic egalitarianism are characteristics of many prehistoric societies in North America that operate according to a kin-ordered mode of production. What distinguished this mode from the other two is that "the kin-ordered mode regenerates itself and its oppositions by particularizing tensions and conflicts" (Wolf 2001 [1981]:351). Social classes do not exist, and so conflict arises not between classes but among individuals. However, conflicts frequently cannot be resolved in such societies, and social fissioning results, which provides a mechanism for social change. Egalitarian foraging peoples as well as what some would call tribes, big-man societies, and simple chiefdoms are all organized according to this mode of production, as it was through kin relations that surplus was controlled (Ensor, chapter 10; Patterson 1986). Marx called this "primitive communism" or the "primordial mode of production," and it subsumes what some have begun to call a ritual mode of production (Cunningham, chapter 8; Rappaport 1984:410; Spielmann 2002). The kin-ordered mode of production also describes the organization of societies on the Pacific coast of North America discussed by Patterson (chapter 2) and Angelbeck (chapter 3), as well as those in Latin America presented by Acosta (chapter 6) and Alvarez and Briz (chapter 5).

## This Volume

Chapters in this volume employ the mode of production concept to enhance understanding of archaeological, ethnographic, historical, ethnohistorical, and cross-cultural data from a wide range of societies. We do not try to generate conceptual uniformity but instead seek to showcase the ways that a mode of production analysis can be employed to analyze past human organization. Most authors (re)introduce their understanding of the mode of production concept and its relevance for archaeological interpretation. Some redundancy is folded into this volume, as authors cover ground plowed by this introduction. However, each chapter plants the seeds for its own analysis. Further, the careful reader will note that we do not all completely agree with how modes of production are to be used; nor would we want theoretical homogeneity. As is generally the case when archaeologists get together, there are as many opinions as scholars present.

As we have already stated, our aim in this volume is not to get buried in typological quibbling. Some authors subdivide what Wolf calls the kin-ordered mode and Marx originally referred to as the primitive mode of production (e.g., Angelbeck, chapter 3; Alvarez and Briz, chapter 5). Others define a plantation mode of production as being a variety of the capitalist mode (Delle 2014, chapter 13). The assumption of these contributors is that each form of economic organization should be differently named with a distinct mode. Ensor (chapter 6), citing Patterson (1986), calls such distinctions "forms of production" within a single mode. If modes of production are defined as the all-encompassing political, economic, social and ideological manner in which surplus production is organized and deployed, then a variety of economic strategies can be subsumed within an overarching mode. Each mode of production can contain a variety of means and relations of production so that seasonal variations of resource extraction, the tools used, and the social relations employed can change (and/or coexist). Therefore, to some degree, the number of modes recognized depends on whether one is inclined to be a lumper or a splitter. Regardless of these inclinations, each contribution in this volume engages the mode of production framework to better understand how past societies were organized through the deployment of surplus labor.

Whatever value this collection of essays provides will not be derived from this introductory chapter. Instead, the utility of modes of production depends on whether new insights can be provided through their use. We therefore hope you agree that the value of this framework is contained in the essays that follow. We also hope that these papers provide an open-ended invitation to engage with the classical Marxist tradition generally and, in particular, with a mode of production framework.

## Acknowledgments

This essay has benefited from the detailed and thoughtful comments of Tom Patterson.

## Notes

1. Trigger (1993:174–178) provides a succinct introduction to the archaeological implications of neo-Marxism, defined largely by the rejection of Marx's idea that economic relationships form the basis of cultural change.

2. Niche construction theory has been used by archaeologists to examine small-scale societies (Smith 2007, 2011) but is equally relevant to more complex ancient pluralities. In fact, a Marxist niche construction theory could be defined as the economic adaptation to a culturally constructed political niche. That is, the main existential threat driving human evolution is not getting enough to eat but getting on with others.

3. Dunn (1982:12) argues that the term *mode of production* refers only to the economic base and that '"order" is the broader term that Marx used to incorporate both base and superstructure. While this may be correct, it is not how the term has been used (see Jessop 1990 for a good introduction). We employ *mode of production* to necessarily incorporate both the social organization of labor and corresponding political, jural, and other ideological elements that constitute the superstructure (Wolf 1982:74–75).

4. *Vulgar materialism* was used by Friedmann (1974) to describe what today we would call economic or ecological reductionism, that is, that environment, ecology, or economy dictates cultural form. Such vulgar materialism includes today's cultural materialists, cultural ecologists, selectionists, etc., who place the engine of cultural change external to human society. Because cultural evolution is assumed to be driven by forces external to human society, it is therefore external to human control. Among other things, this has the effect of naturalizing the status quo and absolving those that exploit the labor of others. Vulgar materialism is contrasted with the materialism of the classical Marxist tradition that we advocate, where both base and superstructure are dialectically linked. Operating within environmental and technological constraints, this historical materialism posits that cultural evolution is driven by the social cleavages (and related interests) within society. Again, among other things, those exploiting the labor of others create forms of consciousness that support this economic arrangement. Whether these new forms of consciousness are false or not, their creation does not alter the fact that economic interests generate justifying ideologies (Rosenswig, chapter 7).

5. As Haldon (1993:53) notes, such nonmaterialist redefinition of Marxism "does not help us to see either how the relations of production, appropriation and distribution of social wealth are achieved, nor how the production, accumulation and redistribution of surplus wealth is integrated into a process of social reproduction of the society in question as a totality."

6. As Trigger (1993:175) points out, Jack Goody (1980:17) uses the term *vulgar idealism* to describe French structural Marxists such as Godelier (1977, 1984), who rejects Marx's core proposal that economic relations are the cause of change and instead argues that politics, kinship, and religion organize the relations of production. This is the position that Sahlins (1972) popularized in the English-speaking world, and it is addressed at greater length below.

7. *The Eighteenth Brumaire of Louis Bonaparte* is arguably Marx's ([1998][1869]) most substantive work with an extended application of his materialist theory of history to understanding the 1848 French coup. Anyone inclined to argue that Marx's analytic

framework was economic reductionism cannot have read this analysis, which is rich in historical detail and its exploration of the role of ideology in political drama. However, as Marx argues, political intrigues conceal the class struggle and so must be stripped away to truly understand history (see Tomba 2013).

8. To criticize the ethnocentric orientalism of calling a mode of production "Asiatic" (Said 1979:153–157) is precisely what Stalin did at the 1931 Leningrad conference when the term was stricken from twentieth-century communist theorizing (Currie 1984). This was part of the reason why Wittfogel (1957:2–3) opted to drop the term but maintain the idea of total state power that "Asiatic" had been employed to denote. Hindess and Hurst (1975:180), among many in the latter part of the twentieth century, critiqued the ethnocentrism of the unfortunate word choice. However, to use the racialization of concepts and the Western-centrism of nineteenth-century scholarship as a justification for the dismissal of analytical ideas behind the label, as Blanton and Fargher (2008:8–10) recently have, displays a lack of historicism. As Currie (1984:263) notes, "The rejection of the term, however, does not necessarily entail negation of the mode." Anderson (2010:208–224) has recently documented how Marx's sympathies lay squarely with those resisting European colonialism and explicitly responds to Said's critique (Anderson 2010:17–20).

## References Cited

Anderson, Kevin B.

2010 *Marx at the Margins: On Nationalism, Ethnicity, and Non-Western Societies.* University of Chicago Press, Chicago.

Arnold, Jeanne E.

2000 Revisiting Power, Labor Rights, and Kinship: Archaeology and Social Theory. In *Social Theory and Archaeology*, edited by M. B. Schiffer, pp. 14–30. University of Utah Press, Salt Lake City.

Bailey, Anne M., and Jesop R. Llobera

1981 *The Asiatic Mode of Production: Science and Politics.* Routledge, London.

Banaji, Jairus

2012 *Theory as History: Essays on Modes of Production and Exploitation.* Haymarket, Chicago.

Bate, Luis F.

1977 *Arqueología y materialismoistórico.* Ediciones de Cultura Popular, Mexico City.

1998 *El proceso de investigación en arqueología.* Crítica, Barcelona.

Beckman, Warren

1990 *Marx, the Young Hegelians, and the Origins of Radical Social Theory.* Cambridge University Press, Cambridge.

Benavides, O. Hugo

2001 Returning to the Source: Social Archaeology as Latin American Philosophy. *Latin American Antiquity* 12:355–370.

Bernstein, Henry

2013 Historical Materialism and Agrarian History. *Journal of Agrarian Change* 13:310–329.

Blanton, Richard, and Lane Fargher
2008 *Collective Action in the Formation of Pre-Modern States*. Springer, New York.
Campling, Liam
2013 Debating Modes of Production and Forms of Exploitation: Introduction to the Symposium on Jairus Banaji's Theory as History. *Historical Materialism* 21:3–10.
Carneiro, Robert L.
1970 A Theory of the Origin of the State. *Science* 169:733–739.
Chapman, Robert
2003 *Archaeologies of Complexity*. Routledge, London.
Cheal, David
1989 Strategies of Resource Management in Household Economies: Moral Economy or Political Economy? In *The Household Economy: Reconsidering the Domestic Mode of Production*, edited by Richard Wilk, pp. 11–22. Westview, Boulder, Colorado.
Childe, V. Gordon
1936 *Man Makes Himself*. Watts, London.
1950 The Urban Revolution. *Town Planning Review* 21:3–17.
Clark, John E.
2007 In Craft Specialization's Penumbra: Things, Persons, Action, Value, and Surplus. In *Rethinking Craft Specialization in Complex Societies: Archaeological Analysis of the Social Meaning of Production*, edited by Rowan K. Flad and Zachary X. Hruby, pp. 20–35. Archeological Papers No. 17. American Anthropological Association, Arlington, Virginia.
Cobb, Charles R.
1993 Archaeological Approaches to the Political Economy of Nonstate Societies. *Journal of Archaeological Method and Theory* 5:43–100.
Currie, Kate
1984 The Asiatic Mode of Production: Problems of Conceptualizing State and Economy. *Dialectical Anthropology* 9:251–268.
Delle, James A.
2014 *The Colonial Caribbean: Landscapes of Power in Jamaica's Plantation System*. Cambridge University Press, Cambridge.
Donham, Donald L.
1999 *History, Power, Ideology: Central Issues in Marxism and Anthropology*. University of California Press, Berkeley.
Dunn, Stephan P.
1982 *The Fall and Rise of the Asiatic Mode of Production*. Routledge and Kegan Paul, London.
Ensor, Bradley E.
2000 Social Formation, Modo de Vida, and Conflict in Archaeology. *American Antiquity* 65:15–42.
Feinman, Gary M., and Linda M. Nicholas
2004 Archaeological Perspectives on Political Economy. University of Utah Press, Salt Lake City.

Flannery, Kent V.

1972 The Cultural Evolution of Civilizations. *Annual Review of Ecology and Systematics* 3:399–426.

Foster, John Bellamy

2014 *The Theory of Monopoly Capitalism: An Elaboration of Marxian Political Economy*. Monthly Review Press, New York.

Friedmann, Harriet

1980 Household Production and the National Economy: Concepts for the Analysis of Agrarian Reformations. *Journal of Peasant Studies* 7:158–184.

Gailey, Christine Ward

1987 *Kinship to Kingship: Gender, Hierarchy and State Formation in the Tongo Islands*. University of Texas Press, Austin.

Gailey, Christine Ward, and Thomas C. Patterson

1988 State Formation and Uneven Development. In *State and Society: The Emergence of Social Hierarchy and Political Centralization*, edited by John Gledhill, Barbara Bender, and Mogens Trolle Larsen, pp. 77–90. Unwin Hyman, London.

Gilman, Antonio

1984 Explaining the Upper Paleolithic Revolution. In *Marxist Perspectives in Archaeology*, edited by Matthew Spriggs, pp. 115–126. Cambridge University Press, Cambridge.

1989 Marxism in American Archaeology. In *Archaeological Thought in America*, edited by C. C. Lamberg-Karlovsky, pp. 63–73. Cambridge University Press, Cambridge.

1995 Prehistoric European Chiefdoms: Rethinking "Germanic" Societies. In *Foundations of Social Inequality*, edited by T. Douglas Price and Gary M. Feinman, pp. 235–251. Plenum, New York.

Gledhill, John

1984 The Transformation of Asiatic Formations: The Case of Late Prehispanic Mesoamerica. In *Marxist Perspectives in Archaeology*, edited by Matthew Spriggs, pp. 135–148. Cambridge University Press, Cambridge.

Godelier, Maurice

1977 *Perspectives in Marxist Anthropology*. Cambridge University Press, Cambridge.

1984 To Be a Marxist in Anthropology. In *On Marxian Perspectives in Anthropology*, edited by Jacques Maquet and Nancy Daniels, pp. 35–57. Undena, Malibu, California.

Goody, Jack

1980 Slavery in Time and Space. In *Asian and African Systems of Slavery*, edited by James L. Watson, pp. 16–42. Blackwell, Oxford.

1990 *The Oriental, the Ancient and the Primitive: Systems of Marriage and the Family in the Pre-Industrial Societies of Eurasia*. Cambridge University Press, Cambridge.

Graeber, David.

2006 Turning Modes of Production Inside Out, or, Why Capitalism Is a Transformation of Slavery. *Critique of Anthropology* 26: 61–85.

Haldon, John F.
1993 *The State and the Tributary Mode of Production.* Verso, London.
Hicks, Kathryn, and William R. Leonard
2014 Developmental Systems and Inequality: Linking Evolutionary and Political-Economic Theory in Biological Anthropology. *Current Anthropology* 55:523–550.
Hindess, Barry, and Paul Hirst
1975 *Pre-capitalist Modes of Production.* Routledge and Kegan Paul, London.
1977 *Mode of Production and Social Formation.* Macmillan, London.
Hirth, Kenneth G.
1996 Political Economy and Archaeology: Perspectives on Exchange and Production. *Journal of Archaeological Research* 4:203–239.
Jessop, R.
1990 Mode of Production. In *Marxian Economics*, edited by John Eatwell, Murray Milgate, and Peter Newman, pp. 289–296. Norton, New York.
Karanti, Kojin
2014 *The Structure of World History: From Modes of Production to Modes of Exchange.* Duke University Press, Durham.
Kirch, Patrick
1994 *The Wet and the Dry: Irrigation and Agricultural Intensification in Polynesia.* University of Chicago Press, Chicago.
Kohl, Philip L.
1981 Materialist Approaches in Prehistory. *Annual Review of Anthropology* 10:89–118.
Kolakowski, Leszek
1978 *Main Currents of Marxism.* Vol. 1, *The Founders.* Oxford University Press, Oxford.
Krader, Lawrence
1975 *The Asiatic Mode of Production.* Van Gorcum, New York.
Kristiansen, Kristian, and Larsson, Thomas B.
2005 *The Rise of Bronze Age Society: Travel, Transmission and Transformation.* Cambridge University Press, Cambridge.
Marx, Karl
1978 Preface to *A Contribution to the Critique of Political Economy.* In *The Marx-Engels Reader,* 2nd ed., edited by Robert C. Tucker, pp. 3–6. Norton, New York.
1998 [1869] *The Eighteenth Brumaire of Louis Bonaparte.* International, New York.
Marx, Karl, and Frederick Engels
1978 *The German Ideology.* In *The Marx–Engels Reader.* 2nd ed., edited by Robert C. Tucker, pp. 146–200. Norton, New York.
McGuire, Randall H.
1986 Economics and Modes of Production in the Prehistoric Southwestern Periphery. In *Ripples in the Chichimec Sea: New Considerations of Southwestern-Mesoamerican Interactions,* edited by Frances Joan Mathien and Randall H. McGuire, pp. 243–269. Southern Illinois University Press, Carbondale.

1992 *A Marxist Archaeology*. Academic, New York.

1993 Archaeology and Marxism. *Archaeological Method and Theory* 5:101–157.

2008 *Archaeology as Political Action*. University of California Press, Berkeley.

McGuire, Randall H., Maria O'Donovan, and LouAnn Wurst

2005 Probing Praxis in Archaeology: The Last Eighty Years. *Rethinking Marxism* 17:355–372.

Meillassoux, Claude

1972 From Reproduction to Production: A Marxist Approach to Economic Anthropology. *Economy and Society* 1:93–105.

1981 *Maidens, Meal and Money: Capitalism and the Domestic Community*. Cambridge University Press, Cambridge.

Muller, Jon

1997 *Mississippian Political Economy*. Plenum, New York.

Odling-Smee, F. John, Kevin N. Laland, and Marcus W. Feldman

2003 *Niche Construction: The Neglected Process in Evolution*. Princeton University Press, Princeton.

Offner, Jerome A.

1981 On the Inapplicability of "Oriental Despotism" and the "Asiatic Mode of Production" to the Aztecs of Texcoco. *American Antiquity* 46:43–61.

O'Leary, Brendan

1989 *The Asiatic Mode of Production: Oriental Despotism, Historical Materialism, and Indian History*. Blackwell, Oxford.

Orser, Charles E., Jr.

2011 *Race and Practice in Archaeological Interpretation*. University of Pennsylvania Press, Philadelphia.

Patterson, Thomas C.

1986 La creación de cultura en las formaciones sociales pre-estatales y no-estatales. *Boletín de Antropología Americana* 14:53–61.

1994 Social Archaeology in Latin America: An Appreciation. *American Antiquity* 59:531–537.

2003 *Marx's Ghost: Conversations with Archaeologists*. Berg, Oxford.

2009 *Karl Marx, Anthropologist*. Berg, Oxford.

Pauketat, Timothy R.

2007 *Chiefdoms and Other Archaeological Delusions*. AltaMira, Lanham, Maryland.

Polanyi, Karl

1957 *The Great Transformation*. Beacon, Boston.

Rappaport, Roy A.

1984 *Pigs for the Ancestors: Ritual in the Ecology of a New Guinea People. New, enl. ed.* Yale University Press, New Haven.

Rolland Calvo, Jorge

2005 "Yo [tampoco] soy marxista": Reflexiones teoréticas en torno a la relación entre marxismo y arqueología. *Complutom* 16:7–32.

Roseberry, William

1989 *Anthropologies and Histories: Essays in Culture, History and Political Economy*. Rutgers University Press, New Brunswick.

Rosenswig, Robert M.
2010 *The Beginnings of Mesoamerican Civilization: Inter-regional Interaction and the Olmec*. Cambridge University Press, New York.
2012 Materialism, Mode of Production and a Millennium of Change in Southern Mexico. *Journal of Archaeological Method and Theory* 19:1–48.
2015 A Mosaic of Adaptation: The Archaeological Record for Mesoamerica's Archaic Period. *Journal of Archaeological Research* 23:115–162.
Sahlins, Marshall
1972 *Stone Age Economics*. Aldine, New York.
Said, Edward W.
1979 *Orientalism*. Random House, New York.
Saitta, Dean J.
1994 Agency, Class and Archaeological Interpretation. *Journal of Anthropological Archaeology* 13:201–227.
2005 Dialoguing with the Ghost of Marx: Mode of Production in Archaeological Theory. *Critiques of Anthropology* 25:27–35.
2007 *The Archaeology of Collective Action: American Experience in Archaeological Perspective*. University Press of Florida, Gainesville.
Shanks, Michael, and Christopher Tilley
1987a *Social Theory and Archaeology*. Polity, Cambridge.
1987b *Re-constructing Archaeology: Theory and Practice*. Cambridge University Press, Cambridge.
Smith, Bruce D.
2007 Niche Construction and the Behavioral Context of Plant and Animal Domestication. *Evolutionary Anthropology* 16:188–199.
2011 General Patterns of Niche Construction and the Management of "Wild" Plant and Animal Resources by Small-Scale Pre-industrial Societies. *Philosophical Transactions of the Royal Society* 366:836–848.
Spielmann, Katherine A.
2002 Feasting, Craft Specialization, and the Ritual Mode of Production in Small-Scale Societies. *American Anthropologist* 104:195–207.
Spriggs, Matthew
1984 *Marxist Perspectives in Archaeology*. Cambridge University Press, Cambridge.
Stepelevich, Lawrence S. (editor)
1999 *The Young Hegelians: An Anthology*. Humanity, New York.
Tomba, Massimiliano
2013 Marx as the Historical Materialist: Re-reading *The Eighteenth Brumaire*. *Historical Materialism* 21:21–46.
Trigger, Bruce G.
1993 Marxism in Contemporary Archaeology. *Archaeological Method and Theory* 5:159–200.
1998 *Sociocultural Evolution: Calculation and Contingency*. Blackwell, Oxford.
2003 Introduction: Understanding the Material Remains of the Past. In *Artifacts and Ideas: Essays in Archaeology*, edited by Bruce G. Trigger, pp. 1–30. Transaction, New Brunswick.

2006 *A History of Archaeological Thought. 2nd ed.* Cambridge University Press, Cambridge.

Tucker, Robert C.

1969 *The Marxian Revolutionary Idea.* Norton, New York.

1978 *The Marx–Engels Reader.* 2nd ed. Norton, New York.

Wilk, Richard R.

1989 Decision Making and Resource Flows within the Household: Beyond the Black Box. In *The Household Economy: Reconsidering the Domestic Mode of Production*, edited by R. Wilk, pp. 23–52. Westview, Boulder, Colorado.

Wilk, Richard R. (editor)

1989 *The Household Economy: Reconsidering the Domestic Mode of Production.* Westview, Boulder, Colorado.

Wittfogel, Karl A.

1957 *Oriental Despotism: A Comparative Study of Total Power.* Yale University Press, New Haven.

1972 The Hydraulic Approach to Pre-Spanish Mesoamerica. In *The Prehistory of the Tehuacán Valley*, vol. 4, edited by Richard S. MacNeish, pp. 59–80. University of Texas Press, Austin.

Wolf, Eric R.

1982 *Europe and the People without History.* University of California Press, Berkeley.

1999 *Envisioning Power: Ideologies of Dominance and Crisis.* University of California Press, Berkeley.

2001 [1981] The Mills of Inequality: A Marxian Approach. In *Pathways of Power: Building an Anthropology of the Modern World*, edited by Eric Wolf, pp. 335–352. University of California Press, Berkeley.

Yoffee, Norman

1993 Too Many Chiefs? (or, Safe Texts for the '90s). In *Archaeological Theory: Who Sets the Agenda?*, edited by Norman Yoffee and Andrew Sherratt, pp. 60–78. Cambridge University Press, Cambridge.

# 1

# HUNTER-GATHERER STUDIES

# 2

## Modes of Production in Southern California at the End of the Eighteenth Century

THOMAS C. PATTERSON

This chapter is concerned with the dynamics of sociohistorical change. It suggests that a mode of production analysis of social formations in Southern California during the late eighteenth and early nineteenth centuries may afford new insights into the dynamics of those societies as well as raise new questions about the analytical categories and concepts now used to reconstruct and interpret them. While the chapter deals with reconstructions and interpretations of the archaeological and ethnohistorical records, it does not present or analyze new data. Its focus instead is (1) to examine interpretations of those records in Southern California, especially the Santa Barbara Channel region, and the implications of the analytical categories and presuppositions used; (2) to suggest an alternative: modes of production analyses that explore the significance of contradictions—the structurally based antagonisms or tensions (class struggle) that may actually impede processes of social stratification and class formation; and (3) to use both lines of analysis to enhance or clarify current interpretations of those communities.

### Increasing Societal Complexity in the Santa Barbara Channel Region and Beyond

The importance of archaeological and ethnohistorical research in the Santa Barbara Channel region owes in large part to the efforts of authors to produce superb databases and theoretically sustained arguments to account for the dynamics of sociohistorical development of communities in the region (e.g., Arnold 2001; Arnold and Graesch 2004; Gamble 2008; Johnson 1988; King 1976 [1971], 1981). By building their evidence and propositions in this systematic fashion, they have opened the way for further theoretical exploration.

In the early 1970s Chester King (1976 [1971], 1981) employed a social evolutionary framework derived from Herbert Spencer's writings to characterize the articulation of the economic, political, and religious systems of Chumash society, their differentiation, and their interactions as reflected by changes in the diversity and abundance of particular artifact types—in this case, varieties of shell beads. He followed several of Spencer's (1876–1896) prescriptions in *The Principles of Sociology.* First, King (1981:14) notes that "increases in the complexity of human social systems . . . were seen by Spencer as a structural trend in societal evolution"; that differentiation and diversification were directional and constituted one criterion for measuring increasing complexity; that increasing complexity in one part of the social system was not necessarily accompanied by increases in the complexity of the other parts; that complex (internally differentiated) societies were more stable than homogeneous ones; and, finally, that phases of increasing and decreasing complexity may operate simultaneously or sequentially, driving the totality as a whole toward some kind of increasing equilibrium with even denser and more numerous interconnections between the components. Second, King (1981:12) also remarks that Spencer believed that changes in dress were responsive to changes in political organization, that "money often took the form of body ornaments," and that the value of these ornaments when they became currency was the amount of labor expended in making them. Third, King (1978:61) asserts that "monetized economies are more efficient in decreasing the influence of fluctuations in available food supplies where there are many variable resources (both geographical and seasonal)," and that "political regulation is more efficient for decreasing the influence of fluctuations when there are relatively few important variable resources." Fourth, King (1981:185–186) argues that there was a greater array of resources available in the Santa Barbara area, and that trade provided its inhabitants with more opportunities to accumulate wealth than in other parts of California. Fifth, King (1981:1) writes that "shell beads were the basic unit of exchange value" (King 1981:1). Sixth, King (1981:186–187, 250–251, 323–325) suggests that the accumulation of wealth began before 3500 BC, that the gradual evolution of a centralizing political system meant that less effort was spent in maintaining the economic system than before or after AD 600, and that more effort went into the accumulation of wealth (valuables), judging by large quantities of shell beads in some graves and relative scarcity in others. Seventh, he argues that, after 600 BC, less wealth was being placed in graves, which suggests "a shift to a more centrally organized society with inheritance of political and economic power," and that, in contrast to exchanges of stone bowls, more energy was "being invested in the manufacture of beads which were a portable form of wealth and could be traded" more easily to groups living farther away (King 1981:241–253). Finally, he indicates that a differentiation of the political and secular economies occurred after AD 1150; that there was also differentiation in the types of political economies, access to which was largely hereditary; that these processes were accompanied by a proliferation of bead types used in the various economic subsystems; and that, by inference, hereditary chiefs organized the production of certain kinds of shell beads, appropriated and accumulated the finished products, and controlled their circulation (King 1981:323–325).

Jeanne Arnold has conducted considerable research on archaeological sites created by Island Chumash communities in the Channel Islands during the Transitional and Late Periods—roughly ca. AD 1150–1350 and 1350–1800, respectively. First, she suggests that

> the emergence of sociopolitical complexity should be marked by clear economic reorganization, including a restructuring of labor and newly centralized manipulation of that labor (or its products), *and* the emergence of hereditary leadership. . . . Associated with these changes—because they deeply affect other spheres of life—we would expect to see substantial technological innovations, new capital investments, and changes in the ways people do many things, including how they subsist, produce, trade, organize ritually, and bury their members. It is important to note that the emergence of sociopolitical complexity in the Chumash past is *not* constituted by a search for the first appearance of specific Chumash "traits." . . . Rather, it is a search for major organization changes, particularly in the political and economic spheres, with clear implications for formal leadership, hereditary ranking, and the complex organization of labor. (Arnold 2001:287)

In her view, a cluster of organizational changes occurred between AD 1150 and 1350 and persisted into the historic period (the late 1700s and after). She lists 15 developments and discusses their implications. Let us consider seven of them:

1. Plank canoes (*tomols*) "constituted the largest capital investment." Chiefs and the other elite owners of the canoes supported a high-ranking and wealthy guild of canoe makers. The canoes were essential for cross-channel trade, and their owners promoted or constrained the flow of goods and information between the islands and mainland; they also provided access to highly prized, deepwater fish and cetaceans. In a phrase, "each factor was important to sociopolitical evolution in the region. The *tomol* stood as the most powerful symbol in Chumash society of the ability to command resources and labor" (Arnold 2001:288).

2–3. Changes in the organization of bead production. Small-scale craft production of beads for personal use expanded in several subregions of the Chumash homelands toward the end of the first millennium AD; however, neither the manufacture of the microlithic chert tools used to make shell beads nor bead-making itself was centrally organized, and the artisans were not specialists. This changed about AD 1150 with the emergence of craft specialists in the islands—chert tool and shell-bead makers who controlled their production and formed "islands-centered monopolies in their crafts, creating new economic relationships within the islands and throughout the region," along with the plank canoe owners who controlled their distribution; this shift was accompanied by the appearance of new forms of shell-beads that "required superior drilling tools and overall greater labor investments" and "substantial increases in the quantities of beads and ornaments manufactured" (Arnold 2001:288–289).

4. The rate of exchange between the islands and the mainland accelerated greatly between AD 1150 and 1350, judging by the quantities of beads found in various stages of manufacture and by the quantities of beads found in some mainland burials. This suggests that "more canoes could be financed by a possible expanding pool of elites," and that "the opportunity to manipulate many people's labor and products through control of cross-channel trade was seized by canoe owners" (Arnold 2001:289).

5. New labor-intensive types of shell beads appeared about AD 1200 and were still in use in 1800 as "standards of value, or currency." Economic and political control over the production and/or release of currency was essential in order to ensure "its value if

counterfeiting is rampant or even a serious threat." While the production of tools and the beads was relatively widespread, the canoe owners controlled the distribution of currency (Arnold 2001:289).

6–7. Social stratification and social hierarchy were well established by AD 1200–1300. The production of labor-intensive, symbolically status-marking goods increased after AD 1350, and these were typically found in high-status households—i.e., those associated with wealthy or powerful people (Arnold 2001:289–290).

Arnold (2001:289) notes that human burials in the Chumash homelands dating to the period from AD 1000 to 1300 showed higher incidences of poor health and trauma; she also notes that a significant number of Chumash relocated their settlements at this time, "likely because of unfavorable climatic conditions." This, of course, corresponds to two prolonged periods of persistent drought in Southern California—AD 890–1100 and 1210–1350 (Davis 1998:21–23). She implies that they may have been one motor driving the pulse of innovations she observes in the archaeological record. In sum, she argues that emergence of a managerial elite, social inequality, community-level craft specialization, shell-bead money, and trade were animated in order to buffer food shortages through new or intensified exchange relations.

Lynn Gamble (2008) reconstructs what mainland Chumash society was like when a handful of Franciscan priests, soldiers, and neophytes from Mexico came to Alta California in 1769. There were large villages, some with a thousand or more residents and as many as three or four captains, one of whom was first among equals; some chiefs wielded power in communities beyond the boundaries of their own villages. The priests and soldiers were also impressed by the wealth of some individuals as well as by feuding and raiding that took place. There were trade networks linking mainland and island communities: "The chiefs were the nexus of a far-reaching exchange network that used shell beads as money" (Gamble 2008:2). However, in contrast to Arnold, Gamble argues that the networks were forged by:

> powerful individuals [who] gained ever-increasing control over exchanges as the demand for prestige goods [rather than staples or subsistence goods] in the burgeoning mainland settlements increased. . . . An important component of network power is a system of wealth finance, which involves the exchange of prestige goods, many of which have established values. These are often used to finance

> political officials and other individuals that maintain the system. . . . I also believe that this strategy was not a recent development but had existed for centuries in the region. (Gamble 2008:13–15)

She also writes, "I believe that the Chumash in many ways were close to being a capitalist society despite the fact that they were non-agriculturalists and lacked a state-level political organization" (Gamble 2008:234).

John Johnson (1988:1) provides a succinct summary of how missionaries, soldiers, and settlers viewed Chumash society:

> [They] regarded Chumash culture as possessing unique characteristics which set it apart from that of other Native California societies. Features of Chumash society that most impressed early observers included settlement permanence, relatively high population density, political integration among some communities, emphasis on economic exchange, fine craftsmanship, and unusual technological achievements (e.g., the *tomol* "plank canoe").

Subsequent writers added to this list, noting that the Chumash spoke languages unrelated to those of communities living to the south in the Los Angeles Basin and the inland valleys to the east and that they were matrilineal and uxorilocal or matrilocal in contrast to their patrilineal and patrilocal southern neighbors. Anthropologists have described the latter in different terms. They were autonomous village communities—"tribelets" in Kroeber's (1925:474) terms. These patrilineal villages were composed of men who were close kin, the women from other villages who married them, and their children. What made them a community was their shared participation in the activities of the group—burning, harvesting, cooperative hunting, and participating in fiestas and ceremonies sponsored by a village or its neighbors. Women also owned property—e.g., oak trees or groves—in their natal communities. The villages were bound together by kinship, marriage, and exchange relations—sometimes involving gifts like shell beads, sometimes sharing knowledge, and sometimes participating in the mourning rituals of their neighbors. While headmen often inherited the position from their fathers, those unacceptable to the community were passed over in favor of others. A good leader was a man who shared his wealth with his kin and neighbors and who represented their interests with other communities. He was not a man who hoarded wealth or used it solely for his own benefit; such men were ignored or worse (Gayton 1976:219).

## Modes of Production

Marx's mode of production concept has been called the skeleton upon which society and culture are built. Modes of production have often been described in terms of an architectural or structural metaphor consisting of an economic base or foundation with superstructures. It was also railroad slang used to describe railroad tracks and the trains that moved on them. Marx's (1970 [1859]:20–22) depiction derives from a one-paragraph summary published in the preface to *A Contribution to the Critique of Political Economy* in 1859. It is also the kind of comment that appears in abstracts or overtures to longer, more detailed works—for example, *Grundrisse* or *Capital*—that he was either writing or conceptualizing at the time. A more dynamic metaphor than a building might be a large freight yard with trains picking up and dropping off freight and switching back and forth on tracks that parallel one another, merge, cross, and separate en route to their destinations. Marx described several modes of production in a sentence toward the end of that paragraph: "In broad outline, the Asiatic, ancient, feudal and modern bourgeois modes of production may be designated as epochs marking progress in the economic development of society."

Some writers have portrayed this list as a linear succession of stages in the evolution of human society from some primitive stage (i.e., initial, beginning, or fundamental to the human condition) to a modern capitalist society populated by rational individuals seeking to optimize their pleasures and minimize discomforts. Others have followed Marx's (1973 [1857–8:472) comment in the *Grundrisse* that the passage merely represents a list of alternative pathways out of an unnamed communal stage based on sharing (Hobsbawm 1964). In their view, these trajectories reflect the distortion and dissolution of social relations of societies marked by "the communal appropriation . . . and utilization of land" (Marx 1973 [1857–1858]:472). They express different forms of individuation and property relations developing in particular socio-historical circumstances from the primitive condition. In the mid-1860s Marx (1964 [1878–188]:68) called this collectivity "the communal body as a whole." Subsequently, Morgan (2003 [1881]:63) called it "communism in living" or "primitive communism," in which "several families, related by kin, united as rule in a common household and made common stock of the provisions acquired by fishing and hunting and by the cultivation of maize and plants." More recently, Siskind (1978) and Wolf (1982:88–100) referred to it as the "kin-ordered mode of production." It is important to note that Marx, at least in his later writings, did not begin with the family as some kind of primordial social unit that subsequently agglomerated into logically and temporally later communities, as Émile Durkheim (1964 [1893]) or Julian Steward (1938) did. On the contrary, both he and Engels (1972 [1884]) began with the community and viewed families as logically later developments that occurred within the community. One thing that distinguished Marx's and Engels' writings was that the latter adopted Morgan's distinction between kin-based and territory-based societies—*societas* and *civitas*—and incorporated it "wholesale . . . into historical materialism through the notion that biological reproduction (reflected in kinship) rather than material reproduction (reflected in property) was the basis of primitive communism" (Asad and Wolpe 1976:473).

For Marx, what distinguished social formations (societies producing and reproducing themselves) manifesting different modes of production was:

> the specific economic form in which unpaid surplus labour [or goods] is pumped out of the direct producers. [It] determines the relationship of domination and servitude, as this grows directly out of production itself and reacts back as a determinant. On this is based the entire configuration of the economic community and hence also its specific political form. (Marx 1981 [1864–1894]:927)

Subsequent writers in the Marxist tradition have brought three concepts to the fore, all of which are useful to archaeologists, historians, and ethnologists. The first is the theory of uneven and combined development. What Marx, Engels, and their successors observed in the late nineteenth and early twentieth centuries was (1) that capitalism was developing in various ways in different places; (2) that the various manifestations of capitalist development were interrelated in complex ways; (3) that some capitalist states were more or less advanced or developed than others; (4) that there were complex linkages within capitalist states between their industrializing and nonindustrial (i.e., backward) regions, economic sectors, and populations as well as with their colonies and the nations they dominated. These overlapping processes were taking place simultaneously in the capitalist and noncapitalist worlds. While there was uneven development among the capitalist nation-states, there was combined development within capitalist states, their colonies, and subordinated countries on their peripheries. Marx recognized this as early as the 1870s, but these ideas remained largely inchoate until Trotsky (1969 [1906], 1980 [1932–1933]:5–6) crystallized them. He was the first of several writers—for example, Gramsci (1977 [1917])—who noted their importance. Trotsky's theory was a breakthrough. It identified relative changes in the power relations between capitalist nation-states and in the structural inequalities that existed between them and the colonies and countries they dominated. It explained what happened when the overleaping processes or skipping of stages of historical development took place in the colonial or backward countries. It laid the foundations of the core-periphery and world-systems theories of the 1970s onward (e.g., Amin 1974, 1976 [1973]; Wallerstein 1974:347–357; see also Herrera 2005).

The second concept was the interrelationship or articulation of capitalist and precapitalist modes of production (Anderson 2010:196–236). He made three relevant remarks in passing. One was that capitalism reproduces itself on a continually expanding scale that involves enmeshing, dissolving, and ultimately destroying the social relations of the precapitalist mode of productions (Marx 1977 [1863–1867]:874, 931–932). A second remark was that industrial capital may, using the money form of capital, acquire raw materials and other means of production from social formations manifesting precapitalist modes of production as long as the latter produce commodities (e.g., Marx 1981 [1865–1885]:189). The third was that precapitalist social formations that integrated agricultural and industrial production—like China and the village communities of India—were quite resistant to the corrosive influence of commerce (Marx 1981 [1864–1894]:451–452). The theme of articulation was elaborated by later writers, including a number of anthropologists in the 1970s. For Rey (1979, 1983 [1979]) articulation is a collision and an ongoing battle between precapitalist and capitalist modes of production that is both a process and a relation of transformation that specifies the nature of underlying contradictions and tensions, confrontations, and alliances they define. Articulation, in Wolpe's (1980:41) view, is "the relationship between the reproduction of the capitalist economy on the one hand and the reproduction of productive units organized according to precapitalist relations and forces of production on the other."

The third concept, closely related to the other two, is the transition from one mode of production to another. In *Capital*, Marx (1977 [1863–67]:873–942) sketched what he saw as the process of social historical development in Western Europe—the transition from the ancient and feudal modes of production to industrial capitalism. Marx outlined two theories to account for the simultaneous dissolution of the tributary relations typical of feudal society and the consolidation of capitalist social relations. The first, sketched in the 1840s, argued that the rise of industrial capitalism resulted from merchants in towns who spread commercial networks, promoted commodity production, dissolved the natural economy (i.e., non-market economy) that dominated the countryside by restructuring labor processes and organizing a rural putting-out system, and removed production from the guild-imposed limits of the towns, eventually transforming class and power relations of the old feudal order. In this iteration, capital first appeared in the form of the monetary wealth of the merchant and usurer; it presupposes the production of commodities, whose values are realized through exchange with money. Money is the lubricant for the exchange of different products; an item is sold for money, which is then used to purchase a second item. The circuit is C-M-C—i.e., commodity, money, and different commodity (Marx 1977 [1863–1867]:247–248; 1981 [1864–1894]379–390). Two decades later, he proposed an alternative that focused on property relations rather than exchange relations. It occurs when small producers begin to produce goods for exchange (commodities) rather than goods for use and become both merchants and capitalists in the process (Marx 1981 [1864–1894]:453–454). In this form, the circuit is M-C-M' and money is capital that is converted into a larger amount of money (profit) after the commodity is sold; it involves the production of value through the appropriation of labor power (surplus value). The first line of analysis has been pursued in recent years by core–periphery theorists like Wallerstein; the second by analysts like Bois (1984 [1976]), Brenner (1976, 1977), or Hilton (1985).

In *Capital*, Marx described the motor driving the rise and expanded reproduction of the industrial capitalist mode of production: (1) the expropriation of the agricultural population from the land and the simultaneous creation of a home market and potential wage-labor force separated from their means of production and reproduction; (2) legislation that reduced wages; (3) the formation of a class of capitalist farmers who produced for the domestic market; (4) the separation of agricultural and industrial production and the genesis of the industrial capitalist; (5) the historical tendency for the capitalist accumulation through the appropriation of surplus value from workers who were separated from the means of production and were increasingly forced to rely on wage labor to acquire the commodities they needed to satisfy their needs and to secure their cultural, social, and demographic reproduction; (6) the reproduction of itself on an expanding scale; (7) the subsumption and subordination of existing of noncapitalist social relations; (8) the concentration and centralization of capital in steadily smaller numbers of increasingly large, capital-intensive firms; (9) the tendency of the rate of profit to fall; and (10) the movement of capital from one economic sphere or department to another in search of a higher rate of profit. These were not smooth processes, since there was opposition and resistance to them. However, in the *Grundrisse*, written in the late 1850s, Marx had already outlined a different argument, in which different trajectories of historical development underlay the formation of what he unfortunately labeled "Asiatic" societies (e.g., Mexico and Peru as well as China and India). He continued this line of inquiry in the 1870s, reading voluminously about the historical development of colonies and the anthropological literature about the evolution of human society that was appearing at the time. These *Ethnological Notebooks* remained in manuscript, virtually unknown until the 1970s, when a portion of them was published for the first time (Marx 1974 [1880–1882]; Anderson 2002, 2010; Gailey 2006).

Marx (1973 [1857–1858]:472–474; 1977 [1863–1867]:478–479) described social formations manifesting the Asiatic mode of production in two different ways (Krader 1975). The first was in terms of self-sufficient, rural village communities existing independently side by side. It is strikingly similar to his unnamed communal social form based on sharing rather than exchange relations or to the tribal form of property in which "the division of labour is . . . very elementary and is confined to the natural division of labour existing in the family" (Marx and Engels 1976 [1845–1847]:32). In the second, several self-sufficient, rural villages become enmeshed in a hierarchical form of organization in which some headman or overarching entity attempts to assert authority but does not necessarily succeed in claiming ownership, extracting tribute, or reducing the villagers to mere possessors of their means of production. Marx (1973 [1857–1858]:494, 1977 [1863–1867]:479) described the Asiatic forms as relatively impervious to change. They were resistant to the formation of private property; the communities retained ownership or control of land, resources, and the goods they produced; they did not develop distinctions between food production and manufacture or between towns and countryside; and the social relations of the hierarchical forms were unstable or fragile because of resistance or foot-dragging by the autonomous communities that had become enmeshed in those relations (Patterson 2009:96–98). While this concept did not preclude the existence of exchange networks, it presupposed that commodity exchange was external to the communities and was connected mainly with excess production. To return to the freight-yard metaphor for a moment, social formations manifesting articulations of the two forms of the Asiatic mode of production are analogous to trains with squeaky wheels that do not run smoothly in the same direction, often stop, frequently back up, and pick up or shed "baggage" as they proceed on their way. Archaeologists and cultural anthropologists have repeatedly described the dynamics resulting from this form (e.g., Burger and Salazar 2012; Clastres 1987 [1974]:189–218; Gailey 1987:248–266, 1993; Leacock 1982; Leacock and Gailey 1992; Lee 1992, 2005; 2005; McGuire and Saitta 1996; Price 1975; Trigger 1990; Woodburn 1982, 1998, 2005).

## Social Formation in Southern California

An image created from archaeological and ethnohistorical studies is that of a somewhat stratified Chumash society surrounded by less stratified neighbors. In this portrait, exchange (circulation) is the motor of historical development. A few high-status Chumash chiefs held sway over supravillage groups or districts, whereas the influence of headmen in neighboring communities was limited to the villages where they and their kin resided. Both participated in a wider, monetized economy in which shell beads manufactured in the Santa Barbara Channel region, whose distribution was controlled by Chumash chiefs, were simultaneously measures and stores of value as well as media for economic exchange and generalized symbolic communication. The question is how best to account for the simultaneity of stratified, territorially based society in the midst of a sea of kin-communal societies.

When viewed in these terms, the situation is reminiscent of Edmund Leach's (1954) description of the Kachin communities in his *Political Systems of Highland Burma.* This was a region where Marx's two forms of the Asiatic mode of production existed simultaneously. Leach describes it not as a mini–world system held together by exchange, but rather as an oscillation between the two forms: "a village of four households which asserted its right to be considered fully independent" and the Shan state with forty-nine districts, some of which had more than a hundred separate villages.

> The political organisation of the area has been very unstable. Small autonomous political units have often tended to aggregate into larger systems; large-scale feudal hierarchies have fragmented into smaller units. There have been violent and very rapid shifts in the overall distribution of political power. It is therefore methodologically unsound to treat the different varieties of political system . . . as independent types; they should be thought of as part of a larger system in flux. (Leach 1954:6)

Briefly, his argument is that individuals have status positions in several different social systems at the same time; and, given the ambiguities and inconsistencies of their circumstances, they collectively have the potential to manipulate those conditions. As a result, Kachin communities appear to oscillate between two polar types—a relatively anarchistic, democratic, and egalitarian (*gumlao*) form on the one hand and a hierarchically organized autocracy on the other. He proceeds to point out that the majority of the Kachin communities (*gumsa*) are neither but rather fall between the two ideal types; that these intermediate communities are not static; that "temporary stability can only be achieved by political and military expedients"; and that headmen who try to make themselves into chiefs lose the support of their kin and thus the basis of their power (Leach 1954:8–9, 290; Friedman 1998 [1972]:273).

The oscillations between social formations described by Leach are also evident in the inland valleys east of Los Angeles. At least seven multivillage alliances (the hierarchical form) formed quickly after the arrival of the missionaries and soldiers. One attacked, looted, and destroyed part of the San Gabriel Mission as it was being built in 1771–1772. A second was a plot organized by a woman and her relatives to destroy the mission in the mid-1780s. A third erupted in the San Barbara missions in 1824. A fourth looted and destroyed in the mission's San Bernardino cattle ranch in San Bernardino in 1834. These multivillage forms were short-lived. Three other multivillage alliances unified under single leaders were forged quickly as native peoples were "pushed into the rocks" following the Mexican government's closure of the missions and redistribution of property to its supporters; their lands and their resources had been appropriated from many villages by the colonial government during the preceding seven decades (Phillips 1975; Shipek 1987). These were of longer duration than the four mentioned above. In these instances the hierarchical forms of organization were situational responses to contradictions, antagonisms, and tensions within the social formation and the kinds of alliances that could be forged under historically contingent conditions. The shift and transition from one form to another were quick. At the same time, their durations were quite variable, perhaps a few months to a decade or more. From this perspective, two questions about social formation in Southern California might be: Why did the hierarchically organized Chumash chiefdoms last for such a long period of time, and how were the structures reproduced?

Clearly, the Southern California social formation was transformed in the late eighteenth century when the Spanish colonial government established missions, presidios, and settlements after 1769 to prevent perceived threats by the Russian and English merchants and land seizures. Initially these were sustained by irregular shipments from Mexico; however, it quickly became apparent to priests, soldiers, and settlers that they could not rely on the ships for food and other necessities, and that they had to become self-sufficient. In practice this meant dispossessing the indigenous communities, destroying their food and other resources, appropriating their labor, and resettling a slowly increasing number of their members on missions and in the newly established city of Los Angeles. These conditions were further complicated from the 1780s onward when Russian and New England merchant ships skirted the California coast in search of sea otter pelts destined for the lucrative market in China. While the colonial government viewed this as an illegal activity, priests, soldiers, settlers, and First Nation peoples in coastal communities all bartered furs for more than 40 different items proffered by the ships' captains (Patterson 2014). Thus, by the end of the eighteenth century, the social formation consisted of the articulation of communities manifesting forms of the Asiatic mode of production, a plunder economy, and a colonial sector that was attempting to become self-sufficient but was dependent for both labor and goods on native peoples, many of whom moved back and forth between the missions and nascent city on the one hand and their natal communities, on the other.

What was happening was that the indigenous communities were being slowly enmeshed in the social relations characteristic of merchant capital and a frontier province of New Spain. Events at the Santa Barbara Mission provide an informative example of how this ensnarement occurred. A number of Island Chumash came to the mission after the 1812 earthquake. The priest who understood the Chumash language and customs actively promoted and sponsored their traditional ceremonies at the mission in order to attract neophytes and potential converts; he also encouraged gift exchange within and between the communities. As a result, the demand for shell beads increased steadily, while the supply declined. By the end of the decade, Chumash chiefs were complaining about the costs of the ceremonies; the fiestas were draining their communities of foodstuffs and other products. The priest's response was to establish a mission-supported guild of shell-bead makers, mostly older men and women, to fill the demand that he had helped to create. The kind of beads they made required less labor time to produce than the types they manufactured earlier.

The capitalist mode of production was not the dominant one in Southern California in the 1810s; however, when the priest at the Santa Barbara

Mission gave shell beads manufactured by the guild he had created to the Chumash chiefs, he was actually reinforcing their power at the same time that the missions were distorting, dissolving, and reconstituting the native communities and integrating them into an emerging social-class structure and economic system that was dominated increasingly by the expansion of capitalist property and social relations. What this indicates is (1) that capitalist relations never immediately or completely eliminate the precapitalist modes of production they seek to replace; (2) that they are not always the dominant mode of production in a social formation; and (3) that forms of production and social relations associated with the precapitalist modes of production may be absorbed or subsumed into the emergent articulation and social formation.

The social formation of Southern California was an amalgam of different modes of production from the 1770s onward. It was also unevenly developed. The influence of the colonial government—centered on the missions, the Santa Barbara Presidio, and the city of Los Angeles—did not extend more than 30 miles inland until the turn of the century, when the governor began giving land grants to a handful of retired soldiers. The number of ranches grew slowly, and by 1840 there were about 40 extending from the coast inland to the San Bernardino area. The rancheros were soon engaged in exchange relations with New England merchant ships seeking to purchase cowhides for the burgeoning leather industries of the Northeast. What the ranches also introduced were wage-labor relations in which wages were usually paid in kind—for example, alcohol—instead of currency. The combination and differential penetration of different forms and modes of production were fragile and sources of inbuilt social instability. They were bundles of the contradictions associated with each as well as new ones that were forged by the articulation. New alliances and balances of power have their beginnings in these arrays of contradictions, relations, and historically contingent conditions.

Charles Bettelheim (1975 [1968]) coined the term "economy of transition" to conceptualize those moments where there is a relative balance of force among the modes of production or they exist in some sort of quasi-equilibrium. In his view these circumstances provide the conditions for the emergence of a new mode of production and the erosion of others. The dissolution of the dominant mode of production in a social formation merely creates the conditions for the emergence of something new; however, it does not guarantee that a new social formation will appear. The conditions for transformation and transition are determined by the totality of economic, political, social, political, and ideological relations, as well as by the associated forms of social consciousness. Economies of transition involve a difficult problem of periodization in which history and the dynamics of social formations appear as opposite sides of the same coin. We understand the former as the flow of events conceived both as a linear progression and as changes in the balance of force; we understand the latter by analyzing what is happening beneath the surface in order to comprehend the whole. The totalities of these economies or moments of transition are historically contingent, multilevel unities of contradictions characterized by the interaction and interpenetration of forces and relations from different levels, the coexistence of opposing principles that shape interaction, positive and negative feedback, and spontaneous activity. The various elements of the totality as well as totality itself are continually changing, though at different rates. At any given moment, one element might appear fixed in relation to the others, and new elements appear while others wither.

Economies of transition are unstable and fragile, with unpredictable outcomes. There is no motor necessarily driving development in one direction or another but rather a dynamic emerging from the contradictions, tensions, and alliances they create. The dynamics are not fixed laws of history with preordained teleological outcomes; they are forged instead under historically contingent circumstances and may appear as teleological only when the balance of force has shifted and particular courses of action have been set in motion. Marx described social formations manifesting the Asiatic mode of production as particularly resistant to change—the reasons being that the direct producers retained control of the means of production and were self-sufficient; tribute and *corvée* labor were appropriated only after production to satisfy their own needs. As a perceptive student once remarked, "chiefs don't starve the people who are making them wealthy and powerful through the circulation of the goods manufactured by the direct producers."

In this chapter I have emphasized Marx's and some Marxian analytical categories of mode of production, social formation, articulation, uneven and combined development, and contradiction. Collectively, they provide the basis for alternative understandings of social formation in Southern California as well as a critique of explanations that employ explicitly or implicitly notions of universal (teleological) progressions of historical stages; that naturalize the exchange relations specific to industrial capitalist mode of production; that use linear historical narratives as a basis for describing and analyzing social formations exhibiting articulations of modes of production and uneven and combined development; and that show unreflective empathy for the victors in struggles for power (the potential to make things happen or not).

## Acknowledgments

An earlier version of this chapter was prepared in a session, "Modes of Production in Archaeology," that was organized by Jerimy Cunningham and Robert Rosenswig for the 79th annual meeting of the Society of American Archaeology, held in Austin, Texas, April 23–27, 2014. I want to acknowledge the thought-provoking work of Jeanne Arnold, Lynn Gamble, John Johnson, and Chester King. I also want to thank Wendy Ashmore, Felipe Bate, Richard Burger, Christine Gailey, Christina Halperin, Richard Lee, Randy McGuire, Bob Paynter, Dean Saitta, Lucy Salazar, Mario Sanoja, Karen Spalding, and Iraida Vargas for thought-provoking questions, comments, and clarifications over the years.

## References Cited

Amin, Samir
1974 *Accumulation on a World Scale: A Critique of the Theory of Underdevelopment.* Monthly Review Press, New York.
1976 [1973] *Unequal Development: An Essay on the Social Formations of Peripheral Capitalism.* Monthly Review Press, New York.

Anderson, Kevin B.
2002 Marx's Late Writing on Non-Western and Precapitalist Societies and Gender. *Rethinking Marxism* 14(4):84–96.
2010 *Marx at the Margins: On Nationalism, Ethnicity, and Non-Western Societies.* University of Chicago Press, Chicago.

Archibald, Robert
1978 *The Economic Aspects of the California Missions.* Washington: Academy of American Franciscan History.

Arnold, Jeanne E.
2001 Social Evolution and the Political Economy in the Northern Channel Islands. In *The Origins of a Pacific Coast Chiefdom: The Chumash of the Channel Islands*, edited by Jeanne E. Arnold, pp. 287–296. University of Utah Press, Salt Lake City.

Arnold, Jeanne E., and Anthony P. Graesch
2004 The Later Evolution of the Island Chumash. In *Foundations of Chumash Complexity*, edited by Jeanne E. Arnold. Perspectives in California Archaeology, 7:1–16. Cotsen Institute of Archaeology, University of California, Los Angeles.

Asad, Talal, and Harold Wolpe
1976 Concepts of Modes of Production. *Economy and Society* 6(4):470–506.

Bettelheim, Charles
1975 [1968] *The Transition to Socialist Economy.* Harvester Press, Hassocks.

Bois, Guy
1984 [1976] *The Crisis of Feudalism: Economy and Society in Eastern Normandy c. 1300–1550.* Cambridge University Press, Cambridge.

Brenner, Robert
1977 The Origins of Capitalist Development: A Critique of Neo-Smithian Marxism. *New Left Review* 104:25–92.
1985 [1976] Agrarian Class Structure and Economic Development in Pre-Industrial Europe. In *The Brenner Debate: Agrarian Class Structure and Economic Development in Pre-Industrial Europe,* edited by T. H. Aston and C. H. E. Philpin, pp. 10–63. Cambridge University Press, Cambridge.

Burger, Richard L., and Lucy C. Salazar
2012 Monumental Public Complexes and Agricultural Expansion on Peru's Central Coast during the Second Millennium B.C. In *Early New World Monumentality*, edited by Richard L. Burger and Robert M. Rosenswig, pp. 339–430. University Press of Florida, Gainesville.

Clastres, Pierre
1987 [1974] *Society against the State.* Zone Books, New York.

Davis, Mike
1998 *Ecology of Fear: Los Angeles and the Imagination of Disaster.* Metropolitan Books, New York.

Durkheim, Émile
1964 [1893] *The Division of Labor in Society.* Free Press, New York.

Engels, Frederick
1972[1884] *The Origin of the Family, Private Property and the State: In the Light of the Researches of Lewis H. Morgan.* International, New York.

Friedman, Jonathan
1998 [1987] *System, Structure, and Contradiction: The Evolution of "Asiatic" Social Formations.* 2nd ed. AltaMira, Walnut Creek, California.

Gailey, Christine W.
1987 *Kinship to Kingship: Gender Hierarchy and State Formation in the Tongan Islands.* University of Texas Press, Austin.
1993 Egalitarian and Class Societies: Transitions and Transformations. In *From Labrador to Samoa: The Theory and Practice of Eleanor Burke Leacock*, edited by Constance R. Sutton, pp. 67–76. Association for Feminist Anthropology, Washington, D.C.
2006 Community, State, and Questions of Social Evolution in Karl Marx's *Ethnological Notebooks*. In *The Politics of Egalitarianism: Theory and Practice*, edited by Jacqueline Solway, pp. 31–52. Berghahn Books, New York.

Gamble, Lynn H.
2008 *The Chumash World: Power, Trade, and Feasting among Complex Hunter-Gatherers.* University of California Press, Berkeley.

Gayton, Anna H.

1976 Yokuts-Mono Chiefs and Shamans. In *Native Californians: A Theoretical Perspective*, edited by Lowell J. Bean and Thomas C. Blackburn, pp. 175–224. Ballena, Menlo Park, California.

Gramsci, Antonio

1977[1917] The Revolution against "Capital." In *Selections from Political Writings, 1910–1920*, edited by Quentin Hoare, pp. 34–37. International, New York.

Herrera, Rémy

2005 Theories of the Capitalist World-System. In *Critical Companion to Contemporary Marxism*, edited by Jacques Bidet and Stathis Kouvelakis, pp. 209–224. Haymarket Books, Chicago.

Hilton, Rodney

1985 *Class Conflict and the Crisis of Feudalism: Essays in Medieval Social History.* Hambledon, London.

Hobsbawm, Eric

1964 Introduction. In *Karl Marx: Pre-capitalist Economic Formations*, edited by Eric J. Hobsbawm, pp. 9–65. Lawrence and Wishart, London.

Johnson, John R.

1988 *Chumash Social Organization: An Ethnohistoric Perspective.* Ph.D. dissertation, Department of Anthropology, University of California Santa Barbara. University Microfilms, Ann Arbor.

King, Chester D.

1971/1976 Chumash Inter-village Economic Exchange. In *Native Californians: A Theoretical Perspective*, edited by Lowell Bean and Thomas Blackburn, pp. 289–318. Ballena, Menlo Park, California.

1978 Protohistoric and Historic Archaeology. In Handbook of North American Indians, vol. 8, *California*, edited by Robert F. Heizer, pp. 58–68. Smithsonian Press, Washington, D.C.

1981 *The Evolution of Chumash Society: A Comparative Study of Artifacts Used in Social System Maintenance in the Santa Barbara Channel Region before A.D. 1804.* Ph.D. dissertation, Department of Anthropology, University of California, Davis.

Krader, Lawrence

1975 The Asiatic Mode of Production: Sources, Development and Critique in the Writings of Karl Marx. Van Gorcum, Assen.

Kroeber, Alfred L.

1925 *Handbook of California Indians.* Bureau of American Ethnology Bulletin 78. Government Printing Office, Washington, D.C.

Leach, Edmund

1954 *Political Systems of Highland Burma: A Study of Kachin Social Structure.* Cambridge University Press, Cambridge.

Leacock, Eleanor B.

1982 Relations of Production in Band Societies. In *Politics and History in Band Societies*, edited by Eleanor Leacock and Richard Lee, pp. 159–170. Cambridge University Press, Cambridge.

Leacock, Eleanor B., and Christine W. Gailey
1992 Primitive Communism and Its Transformations. In *Essays in Honor of Stanley Diamond*, vol. 1, *Civilization in Crisis*, pp. 73–74. University Press of Florida, Gainesville.

Lee, Richard B.
1992 Demystifying Primitive Communism. In *Essays in Honor of Stanley Diamond*, vol. 1, *Civilization in Crisis*, pp. 95–110. University Press of Florida, Gainesville.
2005 Power and Property in Twenty-First Century Foragers. In *Property and Equality*, edited by Thomas Widlok and Wolde Gosse Tadesse, vol. 2, *Encapsulation, Commercialisation, Discrimination*, pp. 16–31. Berghahn Books, Oxford.

Marx, Karl
1964[1857–58] *Pre-capitalist Economic Formations*. Lawrence and Wishart, London.
1970[1859] *A Contribution to the Critique of Political Economy*. International, New York.
1973 [1857–1858] *Grundrisse: Foundations to the Critique of Political Economy*. Vintage Books, New York.
1974[1880–1882] *The Ethnological Notebooks of Karl Marx*, edited by Lawrence Krader. Van Gorcum, Assen, Netherlands.
1977[1863–1867] *Capital: A Critique of Political Economy*. Vol. 1. Vintage Books, New York.
1981[1865–1885] *Capital: A Critique of Political Economy*. Vol. 2. Vintage Books, New York.
1981 [1864–1894] *Capital: A Critique of Political Economy*. Vol. 3. Vintage Books, New York.

Marx, Karl, and Frederick Engels
1976 [1845–1847] *The German Ideology*. In *Karl Marx, Frederick Engels: Collected Works*, vol. 5, pp. 19–452. International, New York.

McGuire, Randall, and Dean Saitta
1996 Although They Have Petty Captains, They Obey Them Badly: The Dialectics of Prehispanic Western Pueblo Social Organization. *American Antiquity* 61(2):197–216.

Morgan, Lewis H.
2003 [1881] *Houses and House-Life of the American Aborigines*. University of Utah Press, Salt Lake City.

Patterson, Thomas C.
2009 *Karl Marx, Anthropologist*. Berg, Oxford,.
2014 Shell-Bead Money and the Mission Period Economy of Alta California. *Journal of Social Archaeology* 14(1):112–127.
2015 *From Acorns to Warehouses: Historical Political Economy of Southern California's Inland Empire*. Left Coast Press, Walnut Creek, California.

Phillips, George H.
1975 *Chiefs and Challengers: Indian Resistance and Cooperation in Southern California*. University of California Press, Berkeley.

Polanyi, Karl
1957 The Economy as Instituted Process. In *Trade and Market in the Early Empire:*

*Economies in History and Theory*, edited by Karl Polanyi, Conrad M. Ahrensberg, and Harry W. Pearson, pp. 243–269. Free Press, Glencoe, Illinois.

Price, John A.

1975 Sharing: The Integration of Intimate Economies. *Anthropologica* 17(1):3–27.

Rey, Pierre-Philippe

1979 Contradiction in Lineage Societies. *Critique of Anthropology* 13–14:41–60.

1982 [1973] Class Alliances. *International Journal of Sociology* 12(2):1–120.

Shipek, Florence C.

1987 *Pushed into the Rocks: Southern California Indian Land Tenure, 1769–1986.* University of Nebraska Press, Lincoln.

Siskind, Janet

1978 Kinship and Mode of Production. *American Anthropologist* 80(4):860–872.

Spencer, Herbert

1876–1896 *The Principles of Sociology*, 4 vols. Williams and Norgate, London.

Steward, Julian H.

1938 Basin-Plateau Aboriginal Social Groups. *Bureau of American Ethnology Bulletin* 120. Government Printing Office, Washington, D.C.

Trigger, Bruce G.

1990 Maintaining Economic Equality in Opposition to Complexity: An Iroquoian Case Study. In *The Evolution of Political Systems: Sociopolitics in Small-Scale Sedentary Societies*, edited by Steadman Upham, pp. 119–145. Cambridge University Press, Cambridge.

Trotsky, Leon

1969 [1906] Results and Prospects. In *The Permanent Revolution and Results and Prospects*, pp. 29–122. Pathfinder, New York.

1980 [1932–1933] *The History of the Russian Revolution.* Monad, New York.

Wallerstein, Immanuel

1974 *The Modern World-System: Capitalist Agriculture and the Origins of the European World-Economy in the Sixteenth Century.* Academic, New York.

Wolf, Eric

1982 *Europe and the Peoples without History.* University of California Press, Berkeley.

Wolpe, Harold

1980 Introduction. In *The Articulation of Modes of Production: Essays from* Economy and Society, edited by Harold Wolpe, pp. 1–43. Routledge and Kegan Paul, London.

Woodburn, James

1982 Egalitarian Societies. *Man* 17(3):431–451.

1998 "Sharing Is Not a Form of Exchange": An Analysis of Property-Sharing in Intermediate Return Hunter-Gatherer Societies. In *Property Relations: Renewing the Anthropological Tradition*, edited by Chris Hann, pp. 48–63. Cambridge University Press, Cambridge.

2005 Egalitarian Societies Revisited. In *Property and Equality*, edited by Thomas Widlok and Wolde Gosse Tadesse, vol. 1, *Ritualisation, Sharing, and Egalitarianism*, pp. 18–31. Berghahn Books, Oxford.

# 3

## Applying Modes of Production Analysis to Non-State, or Anarchic, Societies

### Shifting from Historical Epochs to Seasonal Microscale

BILL ANGELBECK

For some time, modes of production have been a very effective form of analysis for archaeologists. Archaeologists have deployed such analyses, developed by Marx, since the time of V. Gordon Childe. As a theoretical tool, modes of production provide a way for archaeologists to examine material items in the archaeological record, and to interpret from the patterns of those materials some understandings of sociopolitical relations. Some even extend it further, toward ideology and the hegemonic practices associated with it. By using modes of production, we can move from this base in material items toward the superstructure, involving the sociopolitical relations that guide and structure how labor is deployed and resources are distributed, as well as a sense of ideologies and symbols that concern such relationships. For such reasons this is a useful theory for archaeologists. We mainly have material remnants, and many of us are more comfortable with keeping interpretations of these artifacts close to the artifact, which is a more scientific approach, wary of speculation. Yet Marx viewed his method as scientific as well, just deployed toward human economies and social structures. This body of theory allows for forms of interpretation concerning social relations, political organization, and ideology that remain tied to the material record. In this way Marxist archaeologies found a niche that went well beyond processualist positivism toward post-processualist concerns, although without abandoning a materialist orientation.

Yet the utility for archaeologists working with non-state, or anarchic, societies can be quite generalized, mainly useful for broad temporal scales of analysis. These include any societies that are decentralized in sociopolitical organization and lack formal institutions of government; typically, these societies involve small-scale societies of hunter-gatherer bands or horticultural villagers and many pastoralist groups, as opposed to centralized chiefdoms and states. Within the sociopolitical organization of such societies, chiefdoms and states also centralize their mode of production, whereas non-state societies lack such central political control. To apply modes of production to these anarchic or non-state societies, I reorient the analysis from broad-scale historical epochs to a focus on the micro-scale, evaluating the seasonal shifts of activity throughout the annual round. For complex hunter-gatherers, such as the Coast Salish of the Northwest Coast, modes of production shifted constantly season by season, as they adjusted their subsistence strategies toward the availability of varied resources. In so doing they implemented distinct means of production and varying relations of production to harness those resources most effectively. Some involved small-scale formations, with dispersed families (egalitarian and autonomous), while others involved corporate multifamily groups (hierarchical with ranks of authority), for instance, to process fish during annual salmon runs. In this way Salish individuals engaged in multiple modes of production throughout the year, each varying in degrees of autonomy, which they often pursued. By focusing on particular micro-modes of production, we can track the micro-scale revolutions that occur within broader historical epochs.

First, I briefly recap modes of production analysis, for the sake of argument. Next, I address its inapplicability for much of the Northwest Coast, as typically handled, and this would be true for its utility toward hunter-gatherers, fishers, or foraging peoples in general. Then, I propose a way to use modes of production analysis for the Northwest Coast and other non-state, anarchic, or decentralized societies. In the process, I draw upon the theory of anarchism, which emphasizes the self-organization of society, politically, socially, and economically (Angelbeck and Grier 2012). Here, I highlight the emphases upon individual and local group autonomy, voluntary forms of association, and decentralized forms of organization.

## Modes of Production concerning Non-State Societies

Karl Marx developed the concept of modes of production in 1859 in his *Contribution to the Critique of Political Economy*. He used this to assess the immense variability throughout human history by keeping a material focus on the economy and how societies were politically and socially managed. He provided general categories for numerous types of modes of production, ranging from the Asiatic and feudal modes of production to capitalist and communist ones—the latter he intended to be an ultimate political goal for humanity in general (Rosenswig and Cunningham, chapter 1). For Marx, human evolutionary history began, accordingly, with primitive communism. This mode of production applied to foraging bands as well as to horticultural or pastoralist tribes that generally practiced egalitarianism and exhibited few authorities. In these cultures peoples organized their societies in decentralized formations, often structuring their relationships in networks of interaction. The more complex forms of such societies exhibited numerous authorities, some with "big men" or others with numerous chiefly individuals. With wide local variation, these typically had authorities, or those authorities that they recognized for their leadership, judgment, craft, knowledge, wisdom, or spiritual power; such natural authorities were sought for decision making, dispute resolution, advice, or their skills. These societies have been described as heterarchies (Crumley 1995). The concept of heterarchy helps to distinguish such societies as differently structured than those with centralized hierarchies, or even from egalitarianism, where there are far fewer distinctions of authority or differential treatment. It is this mode of production that I address throughout, particularly in the case study of the Coast Salish, complex hunter-gatherer-fisher societies of the Northwest Coast.

After primitive communism, Marx outlined the Asiatic, ancient, or feudal modes of production, among others, which were various forms of oligarchical or monarchical chiefdoms and states; another way to describe those is as centralized political formations. The industrial period developed into capitalist and socialist modes of production, both state-backed political economies. Marx also envisioned a communist mode of production—although that has never happened historically—which would be a way to promote egalitarianism and its equal access to resources that was generally operant among primitive communist societies but to develop that within contemporary post-industrial societies.

For some, Marx had produced a somewhat arcane taxonomy. When Eric Wolf (1982) sought to analyze European colonialism in *Europe and the People without History*, he simplified Marx's categories of modes of production (MoP) for anthropological and historical analysis into three forms: kin-ordered MoP, a tributary MoP, and the capitalist MoP. Since he was dealing with European colonialism through the 1800s, he had no need to include a socialist mode of production. Wolf's treatise was a singular analysis of how European colonialism affected indigenous cultures. It was not just that Europeans introduced new technologies or that they incorporated indigenous peoples into European mercantilist economies. Rather, his point is that they incorporated indigenous peoples within a new mode of production, initially tributary in some cases, then capitalist. And this new mode of production, with its new productive forces and differently structured relations of production, had destabilizing effects on peoples that generally operated within a kin-ordered mode. His analysis is a detailed chronology and analysis of how changes in the mode of production can be very detrimental for indigenous societies. Now it's worthwhile to turn back to Marx to review the concept itself.

## The Mode of Production as Applied to Epochs in History

According to Marx, the mode of production involves two primary components, involving the forces of production (or productive forces) and the relations of production. In this volume, others offer similar treatments, but I present this summarization here for sake of argument. *The productive forces* refers to the means of production and the labor power and skills applied. Archaeologists deal with the remnants of the material means of production. From the archaeological record, we begin with the physical, material artifacts and have to interpret those other aspects of the productive forces—labor, technique, craft—which are immaterial aspects of the archaeological record. Marx, however, regarded that all of those aspects are part of the material forces of history, including in a nonreductive manner the aspects of human agency in production. To modify for an archaeological application, the means of production should be emphasized (as opposed to productive forces), as we proceed to interpret labor, technique, and craft, and then the relations of production.

The means of production involve the tools used by people in their productive efforts. These are the concrete material items through which they apply their labor, whether a simple device such as a digging stick, cobble chopper, chert scraper, or arrow point. Fishing tools could include a bone fishhook, dip net, or weir, all of which are common means for Coast Salish peoples. Such means also include hunting rifles, factory machines, computers, or robots—any productive tool. For archaeologists, these means of production compose much of what we find as artifacts. It is the patterns in the artifactual means of production that allow us to interpret the other productive forces as well as the relations of production.

The relations of production involve the sociopolitical organization of people in their productive activities. These are the ways in which people implement the means for subsistence. Notably, for Marx, a subsistence strategy—whether foraging, horticulture, herding, agriculture, or industrialism—is never simply the extractive or subsistence strategy itself (even though as anthropologists or archaeologists we often speak of it in such limited ways). Rather, the subsistence strategy is always enmeshed in overarching sociopolitical relations that govern or structure how that subsistence activity is organized and enacted. Depending on the scale, these relations of production could be the nuclear family or the household, a guild or a company or could involve a hierarchy of one class over another (e.g., the bourgeoisie over the proletariat). A society organizes its economy in particular ways, not only for managing the extraction, production, and distribution of resources but also for conducting the human labor to carry out those practices. For some anthropologists, like David Graeber, social relations are the key aspect of a mode of production, in that it's important to consider modes of production "not as simply ways in which people produce and struggle over some kind of material surplus, but as, equally, about the mutual fashioning of human beings" (Graeber 2006:77).

In this way modes of production reflect not just social relations but political organization. For societies with a kin-ordered mode of production, these are often expressed (and archaeologically patterned) as egalitarian political forms or heterarchical ones. They maintain or steward their own lands and generally have similar access to their means of production; all the produce and surplus from their activities is theirs. For those within tributary modes of production, an aristocracy, oligarchy, or monarchy (essentially a class that is not involved with the actual productive or subsistence activity) extracts tribute or labor from others and controls the flows of economic resources in a society. Those peoples subject to a tributary mode of production maintain their own lands and means, but a portion is paid as tribute. The capitalist mode involves the dispossession of lands as well as its privatization, such that most people sell their labor for a wage to work on the land of those with capital and to be able to use their means of production. In all of these general examples, relations of production involves the organization of people in a society to structure how they implement their labor in productive activities.

It was important for Marx to make such a distinction within the mode of production between the means of production and the relations of production. Over time, according to a dialectical and historical materialism, contradictions and tensions develop between the productive forces and the relations of production, which build to a point of revolutionary climax in which the relations of production are reordered. These modes of production leave patterns in the archaeological record lasting throughout the continuity of such modes of production. These are disrupted by revolutions to new forms—marked by discontinuities. This was a way for Marx to explain the changes in history, and archaeologists have followed this as they identify different periods through continuities and discontinuities in regional culture histories.

This method was useful to Marx and Wolf, and to their readers, as these modes of production changed over time in history and allowed us to understand the basic societal structure and the main resource flows within a society or between societies. In this sense, these analyses by Marx or Wolf were quite useful to understand the changing nature of societal relationships in the past. Yet these modes of production were offered at large temporal scales, at the scale of the epoch. For Marx, his taxonomy of modes of production mainly was intended to understand complex and centralized societies, to better understand the formation of capitalism. For Wolf's application, this theoretical approach also had broad regional scale. Both have been more useful for analyzing so-called complex societies, or centralized chiefdoms or states that over centuries shift through various phases of political regimes and relations of production.

Applied to the complex hunter-gatherers of the Northwest Coast, however, these taxonomies are not very useful. For Marx, all of Coast Salish culture history (or all of the Northwest Coast) concerns the "primitive communist" mode of production. For Wolf, it would be the "kin-ordered" mode (Table 3.1). Anthropologists have identified similar categories for precapitalist societies. For Marshall Sahlins (1972), it's the "domestic" mode. For Richard Lee (1981), it's the "foraging" mode. Each is similar in conveying the primitive communist or kin-ordered mode of production. Accordingly, for these theorists, at such epochal scales all of Northwest culture history comprises one single mode of production.

As archaeologists, however, we know that regions, even watersheds and

Table 3.1. Central Coast Salish culture history as correlated with an epochal mode of production

| BP Thousands | Northwest Coast Chronology | Lower Fraser River Chronology | Mode of Production |
|---|---|---|---|
| 1 | Late Pacific | Late Period | Kin-Ordered MoP |
| 2 | | | |
| | Middle Pacific | Marpole | |
| 3 | | Locarno Beach | |
| 4 | | | |
| | Early Pacific | St. Mungo | |
| 5 | | | |
| | | Old Cordilleran | |
| 6 | | | |
| | Archaic | | |
| 7 | | | |
| 8 | | | |
| 9 | | | |
| 10 | | | |
| 11 | Paleoindian | (Clovis) | |
| 12 | | | |
| ... | | | |

various inlets, have complicated culture histories. How is it, then, that these represent one mode of production throughout the entirety of pre-European contact in the Northwest Coast? The problem is one of scale. For Marx and Wolf, who were concerned with large-scale and global processes of human history, their epochal modes of production served to illuminate the socio-economic structures at large regional and global scales.

Yet, for those of us working with kin-ordered societies, another scale of analysis is needed. As noted by Antonio Gilman (1984:116), this analysis works at the scale of larger, global interactions, but he questioned whether such a Marxist analysis would apply when thinking about hunter-gatherer or other non-state societies outside of their relationships to imperialist or colonial powers, remarking, "It is not so clear, however, that the contrasts and changes between and within kin-ordered societies can be subjected to an analysis which remains Marxist as such."

To do so, it is necessary to break down the concept of modes of production into an array of modes. Some have already raised this issue that modes of production need to be broken down. For instance, Althusser and Balibar (1970:307) detailed that such epochal modes of production often were a "a more general synchrony englobing several systems and their relations." Due to the variety of social relations within societies, there was a need to consider multiple modes of production operating at once, both in terms of the transitions (as from a feudal mode transitioning and competing with a growing capitalist mode) as well as within societies overall, where one form may predominate but other modes are working in smaller-scale or in marginal capacities. For instance, in one analysis, the Chinese economy can be seen to incorporate three modes: the socialist mode with state-owned factories; a capitalist mode oriented toward exports; and a peasant mode of production (e.g., Potter and Potter 1990:329).

For complex yet decentralized societies such as the Coast Salish, for other foragers, or for many non-state or anarchic societies, it is necessary to break down or decentralize the epochal notion of the mode of production and consider multiple modes of production. Consider that among non-state societies several subsistence activities will have their own means and relations of production. Thus, it's not just one mode but several modes of production throughout the foraging groups' seasonal round. There is no overarching political organization that governs the economy or its social relations. Rather, these modes of production are typically self-organized by local groups, and these can shift by the season toward particular subsistence activities. Among the Coast Salish of the Northwest Coast, peoples will voluntarily enter into variable relations of production throughout the year. Thus, there are not just multiple modes of production operating in conjunction within a society, as noted by some (discussed above), but Coast Salish individuals themselves enter into various modes of production throughout the year.

## The Multiple Modes of Production in the Seasonal Round: A Couple of Coast Salish Cases

To apply modes of production analysis to non-state societies, I offer that we need to reorient modes of production from historical epochs—with varieties of foraging, domestic, or kin-ordered modes of production—to smaller scales that help us break these down into more manageable tools for analysis. One avenue with potential is to evaluate the seasonal shifts of activity throughout the annual round and to consider that these are not timeless cycles (as such rounds often are conceptualized) but represent historically contingent seasonal activities as well as modes of production that structure them. That is, while some subsistence activities, such as fishing in early spring, may have long continuity, the means of production and the relations of production for that activity both may change over time.

For complex hunter-gatherers, such as the Coast Salish of the Northwest Coast, their modes of production shifted constantly season by season, as they adjusted their subsistence strategies toward the availability of varied resources. In some seasons, they operated as households containing several extended families or allied families as corporate groups, for instance, to assemble at spring salmon fishing camps. Then, the households may split into nuclear family groups to pursue various seasonal resources, whether roots, berries, or clams. Some modes are even engaged in as individuals or with partners.

As Coast Salish peoples shifted their subsistence strategies toward different resources by the season, they used distinct means of production (tools and infrastructure) as well as varying relations of production to harness those resources most efficiently. For instance, multifamily households dispersed in family groups to seasonal camps, where they predominantly operated in egalitarian groups, and at the other extreme they also gathered during salmon runs as multifamily households to organize their labor toward processing fish for storage. Yet they conducted these larger economic endeavors within hierarchical relations, with differential distributions of salmon by rank.

Wayne Suttles (1990) found that Coast Salish peoples engaged in various subsistence activities individually or as two-person or corporate groups (Table 3.2). Throughout much of the Coast Salish seasonal round, activities involved small groups or even one or two persons. These usually involved simple means, those that can be made or owned by most anyone, such as a

Table 3.2. Central Coast Salish subsistence activities as identified by scale of labor organization

| Type of Activity | One-Person Activities | Two-Person Activities | Group Activities |
|---|---|---|---|
| Gathering | Berrying | | |
| | Root gathering | | |
| | Shellfish gathering | | |
| FISHING | Fish harpooning | | Reef netting |
| | Gaff hooking | | Trawl netting |
| | Halibut fishing | | Weirs |
| | Dip netting | | Tidal pounds |
| | Basket trapping | | |
| Hunting | Land mammals (deer, elk, goat, beaver, squirrel, etc.) | Sea mammals (most; e.g., seal, porpoise) | Sea lion hunting[a] |
| | | Sturgeon fishing | Deer netting |
| | | | Duck netting |

*Note*: After Wayne Suttles (1990).
[a]Sea mammal hunting mainly practiced by Penelakut.

digging stick, gathering basket, or bow and arrow. Further, these one- and two-person subsistence activities involved use of common areas that are not owned, that for such activities there "were no restrictions on where you could fish or hunt by these methods" (Suttles 1990:148). These productive activities thus accorded a great deal of autonomy for families and individuals.

He found that the activities involving corporate groups were "generally more productive" (Suttles 1990:148), yet these happened to also involve the ownership of the means of production and often ownership of the land or resource. That is, these group activities involved different relations of production, including means of production that were not available to all as hierarchical relations about how the goods were redistributed.

In this way Salish individuals participated in different modes of production throughout the year, some that were egalitarian and others that were hierarchical. When we break down an epochal mode of production into the various modes that are engaged throughout seasonal rounds each year, we have the opportunity to assess socioeconomic changes and tensions at smaller scales. In the following sections, I present a couple of examples of changes in the means of production and the implications for the relations of production.

## Hunting Modes of Production: From the Atlatl and Dart to the Bow and Arrow

One example of a shift of mode of production regards hunting practices associated with the particular hunting tools. The shift from atlatl and dart hunting to bow-and-arrow hunting represents one such shift in mode of production. Ian Cameron and I have argued that this shift represents a change in the socioeconomic organization of labor that occurred in the Coast Salish area circa 1600 BP (Angelbeck and Cameron 2014). The mode of production associated with atlatl and dart technologies is largely associated with group-based forms of hunting. This premise is based upon ethnographic studies of spear-hunting groups throughout the world, as well as spear-based forms of hunting in the Coast Salish area, for instance, as in sea-lion hunting using the harpoon, which is essentially a compound form of spear.

The reason for group hunting with spear-based technologies is primarily that these are one-shot forms of hunting. A hunter may carry an additional dart or two, but the spears are light and require some additional time to set and prepare the next shot (Churchill 1993). Moreover, an atlatl requires substantial throwing space, and, thus, the throw itself is likely to startle game; it's not a tool with much capacity for stealth, a critical component of hunting (Yu 2006). So, for these reasons, a hunter's first throw toward the prey is likely the last. To compensate for this, hunters generally worked in groups, so as to maximize the number of shots at prey in quick succession. This is the case ethnographically among spear-based hunting groups, for instance, among those such as the Tyua of the northeastern Kalahari; there were protocols that governed spear-based hunts, which they conducted in groups; notably, these were hierarchical hunting teams (Hitchcock and Bleed 1997:355). Group hunting is also the case among Coast Salish groups whenever they resort to spear-based technologies when harpooning sea lions (Suttles 1987 [1952]).

To harpoon large sea lions, the Penelakut Coast Salish organized their labor, involving scouts and various canoe crews of rowers, with a harpooner in the bow of the canoe. Organized as crews, they were able to impale the sea lions, with each piercing representing the ranking priority for the distribution of the meat. The first to spear the sea lion got more than the second,

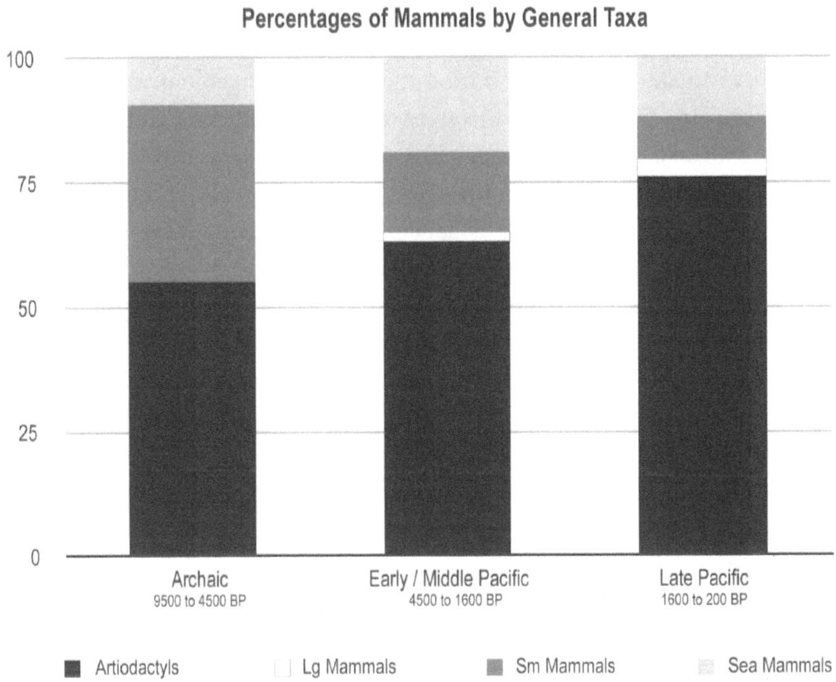


Figure 3.1. Percentages of general taxa by time period from the faunal archaeological record of 49 components throughout the Salish Sea for components before and after the widespread adoption of the bow and arrow ca. 1600 bp.

and so on. In turn the canoe crews divided the meat by a rank order from harpooner to rower to scout. In this way, through group efforts, they were able to effectively hunt sea lions, which would have been very difficult for a lone individual. So, most of these individuals voluntarily entered into hierarchical relationships to acquire some sea-lion meat, even if their proportion would have been less than those of the harpooners that controlled the main means of production, involving the canoe, harpoon, and floats. Also, relations of production were at play, often involving cultural prerogatives to lead such efforts.

The bow and arrow, however, as a multishot device is predominantly associated with individualist hunting in the Coast Salish area, as detailed by Suttles (1987 [1952]) and others (Barnett 1955:197; Elmendorf 1992 [1960]:92). However, this individualist form of hunting, this mode of production, was not likely to be operant prior to the introduction of the bow and arrow, which was widely adopted (if not necessarily first introduced or invented) circa 1600 BP.

To investigate this, we examined the faunal archaeological record of 49 components from 28 sites throughout the Salish Sea for differences in the general taxa both before and after this change in means of production. We primarily focused on the artiodactyls—deer, elk, mountain goat, moose—in comparison to other general taxa, involving large mammals, small mammals, and sea mammals. Notably, after 1600 BP, there was a marked (and statistically significant) increase in artiodactyl hunting (12.5 percent), which continued through to contact (Figure 3.1). Thus, with this new means of production, there was a greater focus on artiodactyl hunting. Plus, as ethnographers have described, this was an individualist pursuit. In this way this mode of production, with greater individual autonomy, was present after the bow and arrow, but was not the likely practice before, with the atlatl.

The main point for us here concerns the means and their indications for social organization. This shift in the mode of production first entailed a shift in the means of production (or tools) from atlatl and dart to the bow and arrow. Correspondingly, this is associated with a change in social organization from group hunting to individualist, which lasted until contact, the time of ethnographic documentation.

## Fishing Modes of Production: From Dip Netting to Reef Netting

Reef-net fishing provides another case in which the means of production shifted. For the Northwest Coast, reef-net fishing involves the largest form of labor organization for fishing in one specific locale. These were located in the Straits region of the Salish Sea, primarily in the San Juan Islands, as well as along the southern tip of Vancouver Island, along areas known for the annual or semiannual runs of salmon in near-shore passages. These reef-netting locales were owned by higher-status individuals with rights to those areas during the salmon fishing seasons.

Prior to reef netting, fishing was done predominantly with dip nets, fish spears, gaff hooks, often conducted by individuals or small family groups. There were also moderate-scale means, including fish traps, extended gill nets, and weirs. However, reef netting allowed for the extraction of the greatest number of fish of any method developed by Northwest Coast peoples.

As described by Wayne Suttles (1951), who observed this technique in practice, reef netting involved a crew working in two canoes with a large, V-shaped net (10 to 12 m long by 8 to 10 m wide) suspended between them in the reef, anchored in four places by stone piles set beneath on the seafloor, two of the anchor lines extending from each canoe's side (Figure 3.2). These were set in shallower waters filled with eelgrass. In many cases, they wove eelgrass into the net to mask the large net. As the salmon runs flowed into the eelgrass, the crew lifted the reef net. When the runs were dense, they could make a substantial catch. The canoes used were also a particular type, with a broader base, a wide bow, and a flat stern; these were stable for such activities and able to carry a lot of fish in their hold.

A reef net was manned by a crew of six to twelve men. In the stern of each canoe was a watchman. These two watched for the approach of the fish. The watchman in the offshore canoe was the captain; when he observed the fish pass over the mouth of the net, he directed the crew to pull at the net weights and net side lines. When the sides of the net were over the gunwales and the ends were out of the water, the fish were cut off. When the captain had made sure they were still in the net, he directed a man to pull one of the pins. The canoes then swung together, and the men pulled the net into the inshore canoe while dropping the fish into the offshore canoe (Suttles 1951:160).

Once the offshore canoe was full, they would load the catch into the inshore canoe, until both were filled. During dense fish runs, a crew was able to acquire "several thousand fish in a day" (Suttles 1951:161). They transported the fish to shore, where teams were ready to process them, preparing them for drying in the sun, on racks, or smoking. The owner of the reef-net location, who was generally also the captain (although a good fisherman might be hired as well, according to Boas [1890:568]), redistributed the fish to the crew members, generally 20 fish per round. The owner divided, or had his captain divide, the fish among the crew in this way after each day's fishing until they had received enough. Thereafter, the fish were his (Suttles 1951:180).

Reef netting salmon required a particular form of labor organization, without which such fishing was not possible. Fishers created particular means of production for this activity, which included the large reef net itself, the buoys, drilled-stone net weights, breast lines, anchor lines, anchor-stone piles, and special, flat-stern canoes for both stability and storage space in the hull. There were also the reef-netting camps on the shore, set

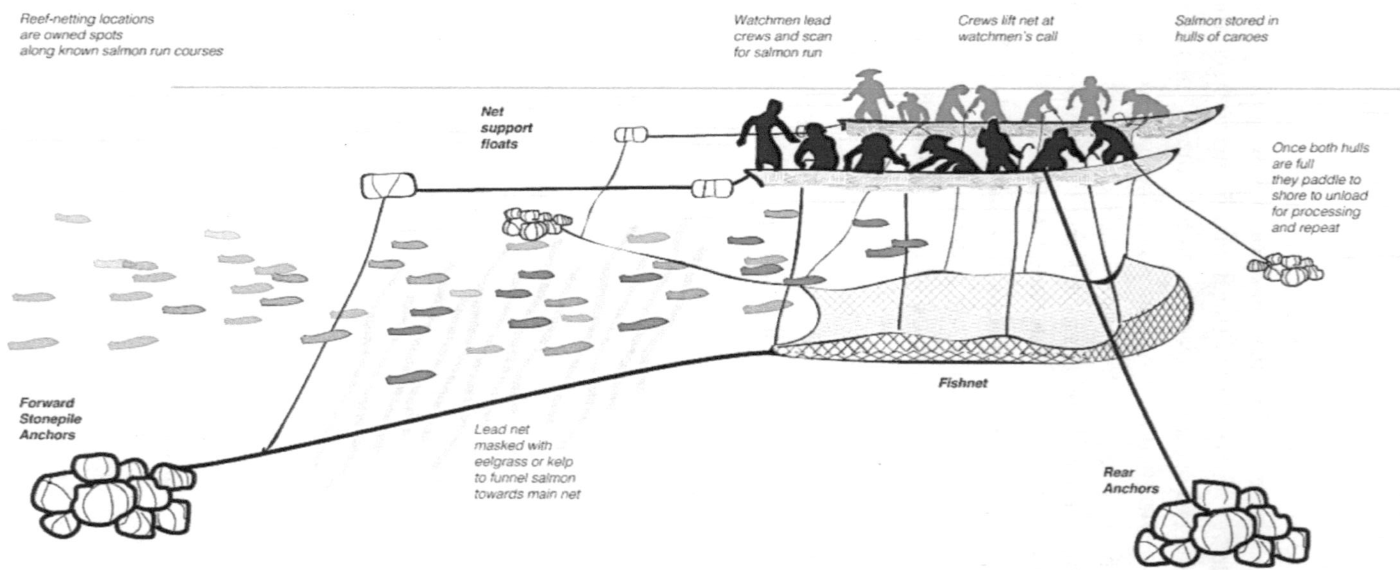


Figure 3.2. Depiction of offshore component of reef netting (after Hilary Stewart 1977).

up for processing, sun drying, and smoking salmon. Some of these tools were useful in other capacities, but most were applicable only for reef netting. That is, the use of the tools themselves relied upon the relations of production being in place. Such artifacts—anchor-stone piles, net weights, large nets, and ropes—are markers, then, not just of the means of production; they also indicate the social relations of production that were in place to use them.

Archaeologists have conducted surveys to document reef-netting sites throughout the Straits Salish area, in northwestern Washington state and southwestern British Columbia (Boxberger 1980, 1985; Rozen 1981). Charles Moore and Andrew Mason (2011) have used side-scan sonar to provide detailed surface maps of anchor stone piles at reef-netting sites. To date, the most intensive investigations have been conducted by Norman Easton (1985, 1990), who developed a method of estimating the age of reef-netting sites based on the size of the anchor-stone piles, which are renewed in the same area with each season of use. Archaeologists had estimated that reef netting was in place by the Marpole phase, beginning ca. 2000 BP, generally regarded as a period of cultural efflorescence. From his investigations, however, Easton estimated that Coast Salish peoples started to practice reef netting about 500 BP, or slightly earlier, to 600 BP, with estimates indicating a range from about AD 1400 to 1550.

Easton (1985) also argued that this change represented a change of mode of production. He viewed the reef netting equipment as means of production and recognized the labor organization as a particular relations of production. He also recognized that this mode of production was substantially different from those that preceded it, finding that the "logic of the apparent contradictions in Straits society, such as between owners of reef-net locations and non-owners [revealed] a transitional economic formation, one from a primitive communist to a proto-tributary mode of production" (Easton 1985:i–ii).

Easton used the term "proto-tributary" after Lee (1981), who did break down the epochal categories of kin-ordered and tributary into at least one more type that accounted for the transition between those two forms. One limitation in Easton's presentation, however, is that he extends the reef-netting mode of production as a characterization of Coast Salish society as a whole. This is not the case. Rather, the reef-netting season was limited to part of summer. The rest of the year, all of those involved, whether captain or crew, went on to participate in other modes of production as part of their seasonal rounds. I should note that this applies mainly to his framing of the discussion, as Easton (1985:198) also recognized competing forms, as "while reef-netting was the primary source of surplus production it was not the only available means of subsistence, and a location owner could not appropriate fish if he had no crew to catch them." Even further, he remarked that there were "major ideological contradictions" between the reef-netting relations of production and those that operated with most other subsistence activities (Easton 1985:189). Still, due to the high productivity of this fishing mode of production, the discrepancies were apparent both ethnographically and archaeologically.

## Discussion

In these two cases shifts occurred in the mode of production, although these changes were related to only one aspect of the seasonal round. Accordingly, in each case only one facet of the seasonal round revealed such a shift. Based on the change in means of production, we can interpret a change in the relations of production. Other subsistence activities, other modes of production, remained unaffected, continuing their mode of production as before. Berry gathering remained a family activity, while dip-net fishing spots continued to be associated with extended family households. Reef netting did mark an introduction of large crews, hierarchically arranged, with captains, owners, and others about 500 to 600 BP; yet this affected activities only in spring, among communities with reef-netting locations. In this way Coast Salish peoples shifted their modes of production from individualistic and family-oriented ones, which were generally egalitarian in structure, to those that were multi-household-based ones that were hierarchical in structure. The focus here is upon the structure of the mode of production, whether egalitarian or family structured as opposed to the hierarchical multi-household endeavors. The aim is not to advance that each tool corresponds to a particular mode of production, but rather that thinking through the means of production can help to interpret the relations of production, which is the real focus. It is not that tools or means determine the relations of production, since each mode of production is historically situated within its own cultural context. Yet mode of production analysis helps us to move beyond the specific artifact as a tool type, reminding us that the use of tools is enmeshed in social relations organized to implement them. Among the Coast Salish was a spectrum of modes

Table 3.3. A seasonal round of the Coast Salish portrayed as shifting modes of production, from family groups to hierarchical teams

| Resource/Activity | Means of Production | Relations of Production |
|---|---|---|
| **Spring** | | |
| Spring salmon fishing | Dip nets | Individual |
| Eulachon fishing | Nets | Households |
| Green-shoots gathering | Baskets | Individual/Families |
| Roots/Bulbs collecting | Digging sticks/baskets | Individual/Families |
| Sea-lion hunting | Canoes, harpoons, harpoon lines, floats | Hierarchical crew |
| **Summer** | | |
| Berry picking & drying | Baskets | Individual/Families |
| Salmon fishing | Nets/Dry-rack fishery | Households |
| Terrestrial hunting | Bow and arrow | Individual/Partner |
| Reef-netting salmon | Reef net/Anchors/Canoes | Hierarchical crew[a] |
| **Fall** | | |
| Late berries | Baskets | Families |
| Swamp-potato collecting | Digging sticks/Baskets | Households |
| Main terrestrial hunting (deer/elk) | Bow and Arrow | Individual/Partner |
| Waterfowl hunting | Duck nets | Cooperative to hierarchical teams |
| **Winter** | | |
| Clam digging | Digging Sticks/Baskets | Individual/Families |
| Sturgeon fishing | Sturgeon spears/Canoe | Two-person team |
| Bear hunting | Spears | Two-person team |
| Winter ceremonials: Potlatches and spirit dancing | Masks | Households/Village |

[a]Usually involved ownership of sites

in which they shifted from individualistic productive activities to family based to household based and to multi-household based, each of which was increasingly hierarchical. By decentralizing the epochal notion of the mode of production, it is possible to consider various modes of productions as parts of seasonal rounds and to get us beyond general concepts such as the kin-ordered mode.

Another point is that the preference generally was to favor and engage in productive activities that allowed for autonomy. Some individuals or families may have chosen not to participate in such hierarchical modes of production. Suttles (1990:151) emphasized this when he noted that if a "family also had, as most did, kin ties in other villages and the option of changing residence, they could still have been pretty independent of any would-be powerful chief in their own village." Thus, participating in a hierarchical group activity was an option they could choose.

In some sense, such forms appear as a trade-off, relinquishing a portion of autonomy in exchange for coordinated action, with the hopes of a better cut of the produce of such efforts than could be attained alone. In this way, among such hunter-gatherers, people do enter into social relations of their choosing, despite Marx's dictum that people find themselves "not in circumstances they themselves have chosen" (Marx 1964 [1851]). Suttles (1990:151) argued, "It is my guess that for people living like the Central Coast Salish to have become docile followers of powerful chiefs, there would have to have been greater rewards for organized activities and an increase in the hazards of independence."

Over periods of time, sometimes long, sometimes short, these freely entered relationships often do develop into increasingly hardened hierarchies, based on the inequality of distribution of the surplus. For Marx (1964 [1859]:713–714), this starts as the increasing expropriation of resources, a consolidation of capital, and this solidifies; or the "expropriation is accomplished . . . by the centralization of capital." Thereby, people do find themselves "under the given and inherited circumstances with which they are directly confronted" (Marx 1964 [1859]).

## Conclusion

The takeaway is that, for pre-contact Coast Salish peoples, there was no overarching mode of production. There were no centralized authorities in the past, and there was not a centripetal flow of resources, nor did commands descend from the apex of a societal or economic hierarchy. This applies as well to other complex hunter-gatherers and many non-state or anarchic societies, for any that do not have a formal political institution, generally centralized, that exists apart from forms of social organization. Instead, they had a heterarchy of leaders, each of whom could attract others to their endeavors, economic and otherwise. There was as well a great deal of local autonomy expressed on the part of households within a village, families within a household, and even individuals within families.

This pursuit is seen as a preferred form of socioeconomic interaction, even while there were circumstances in which individuals entered into relations of hierarchy, which initially was a trade-off for their portion of the produce that resulted.

This is a constant tension in history. This is what Peter Kropotkin (1987 [1898]) referred to as the ongoing tension between "the authoritarian and the libertarian impulses" in any society, between imperialist factions trying to concentrate and centralize power as opposed to collective efforts to resist such assertions of power. Kropotkin or Marx and others were typically describing tensions on the global scale, acting between large-scale classes within industrial countries. However, these tensions play out in the smallest scale of social organization as well. In the Coast Salish past, such tensions were expressed in very particular aspects of their seasonal round. These were not contradictions within one grand or epochal mode of production, but rather these involved specific tensions of hierarchy versus heterarchy, resulting in negotiations and contestations of each aspect of their seasonal round.

I have highlighted two examples whereby specific modes of production changed in Coast Salish archaeological history, with the atlatl-and-dart to bow-and-arrow transition, ca. 1600 BP, and with the shift from various small-scale fishing methods to a reef-netting mode of production, ca. 500 BP. Often archaeologists can regard these as simply technological changes, markers for a discontinuity in a region's culture history. However, as means of production these tools were the basis for specific relations of production. Coast Salish peoples implemented particular forms of labor organization often to harness those resources most effectively, and these are the relations of production. Some of these forms of labor organization involved small-scale formations, with dispersed families (egalitarian and autonomous), while others involved corporate multifamily groups (hierarchical with ranks of authority). In this way Coast Salish individuals engaged in different modes of production throughout the year, each varying in levels of autonomy, which they generally pursued. Such an analysis should be applicable to other non-state or anarchic societies, those that are complex and yet decentralized. By breaking modes of production into very particular modes, we can track the microscale revolutions that occur within broader historical epochs.

## Acknowledgments

I want to thank Colin Grier, Kurt Jordan, and an anonymous reviewer for their edits to this manuscript, as well as the questions, comments, and conversations about earlier forms of this work in presentations at Cornell University, Simon Fraser University, and the Northwest Anthropological Conference. I want also to thank the editors, Robert Rosenswig and Jerimy Cunningham, for their work with this volume and for the invitation to be a part of it.

## References Cited

Althusser, Louis, and Etienne Balibar
1970 *Reading* Capital. Pantheon Books, New York.

Angelbeck, Bill, and Ian Cameron
2014 The Faustian Bargain of Technological Change: Evaluating the Socioeconomic Effects of the Bow and Arrow Transition in the Coast Salish Past. *Journal of Anthropological Archaeology* 36:93–109.

Angelbeck, Bill, and Colin Grier
2012 Anarchism and the Archaeology of Anarchic Societies: Resistance to Centralization in the Coast Salish Region of the Pacific Northwest Coast. *Current Anthropology* 53:547–587.

Barnett, Homer
1955 *The Coast Salish of British Columbia*. University of Oregon Press, Eugene.

Boas, Franz
1890 The Lku'ñgen. *Report of the British Association for the Advancement of Science* 59:563–582.

Boxberger, Daniel L.
1980 The Lummi Indian Reef Nets. *Wassaja: The Indian Historian* 13:48–54.
1985 A Preliminary Underwater Survey of Legoe Bay, Lummi Island, Washington. *International Journal of Nautical Archaeology* 14:211–216.

Churchill, Steven E.
1993 Weapon Technology, Prey Size Selection, and Hunting Methods in Modern Hunter-Gatherers: Implications for Hunting in the Palaeolithic and Mesolithic. *Archeological Papers of the American Anthropological Association* 4:11–24.

Crumley, Carole L.
1995 Heterarchy and the Analysis of Complex Societies. *Archeological Papers of the American Anthropological Association* 6:1–5.

Easton, Norman A.
1985 The Underwater Archaeology of Coast Salish Reef Netting. Master's thesis, Department of Anthropology, University of Victoria, Victoria.

1990 The Archaeology of Straits Salish Reef Netting: Past and Future Research Strategies. *Northwest Anthropological Research Notes* 24:161–177.

Elmendorf, William W.

1992 [1960] *The Structure of Twana Culture*. Washington State University Press, Pullman.

Gilman, Antonio

1984 Explaining the Upper Paleolithic Revolution. In *Marxist Perspectives in Archaeology*, edited by Matthew Spriggs, pp. 115–126. Cambridge University Press, New York.

Graeber, David

2006 Turning Modes of Production Inside Out, or, Why Capitalism Is a Transformation of Slavery. *Critique of Anthropology* 26:61–81.

Hitchcock, Robert, and Peter Bleed

1997 Each According to Need and Fashion. In *Projectile Technology*, edited by Heidi Knecht, pp. 345–368. Springer US, Boston.

Kropotkin, Peter

1987 [1898] *The State: Its Historic Role*. (Originally, *L'Etat—son role historique*). Free Press, London.

Lee, Richard B.

1981 Is There a Foraging Mode of Production? *Canadian Journal of Anthropology* 2:13–19.

Marx, Karl

1904 [1859] *A Contribution to the Critique of Political Economy*. International, New York.

1964 [1852] *The Eighteenth Brumaire of Louis Bonaparte*. International, New York.

Moore, Charles D., and Andrew R. Mason

2011 Demonstration Survey of Prehistoric Reef-Net Sites with Sidescan Sonar, near Becher Bay, British Columbia, Canada. *International Journal of Nautical Archaeology* 41:179–189.

Potter, Sulamith Heins, and Jack M. Potter

1990 *China's Peasants: The Anthropology of a Revolution*. Cambridge University Press, New York.

Rozen, David L.

1981 Underwater Archaeology at Point Roberts, Washington, Preliminary Survey Results and Recommendations. *Midden* 13: 9–10.

Sahlins, Marshall

1972 *Stone Age Economics*. Tavistock, London.

Suttles, Wayne

1951 *Economic Life of the Coast Salish of Haro and Rosario Straits*. Ph.D. dissertation, University of Washington.

1987 [1952] Notes on Coast Salish Sea-Mammal Hunting. In *Coast Salish Essays*, by Wayne Suttles, pp. 233–247. University of Washington Press, Seattle.

1990 Central Coast Salish Subsistence. *Northwest Anthropological Research Notes* 24:147–152.

Wolf, Eric

1982 *Europe and the People without History.* University of California Press, Berkeley.

Yu, Pei-Lin

2006 From Atlatl to Bow and Arrow: Implicating Projectile Technology in Changing Systems of Hunter-Gatherer Mobility. In *Archaeology and Ethnoarchaeology of Mobility*, edited by Frédéric Sellet, Russell Dean Greaves, and Pei-Lin Yu, pp. 201–220. University Press of Florida, Gainesville.

# 4

# Early Agricultural Modes of Production in Mesoamerica

## New Insights from Southern and Central Mexico

GUILLERMO ACOSTA OCHOA

### Marxism and Latin American Social Archaeology

The historical materialism followed here has its philosophical roots in the social and economic theories proposed by Marx and Engels in the nineteenth century, as well as in the Latin American archaeology and anthropology of the 1970s, when Marxism took hold of the academic spaces after the political struggle of the Mexican Student Movement of 1968, the resistance against the dictatorships supported by the American government, and the ensuing government persecutions throughout Latin America. Within this context Mexico served as refuge for many exiles from the Spanish-speaking world whose ideas found their way into the local academic community.

Such circumstances set the stage in the 1980s for the ideas of anthropologists and archaeologists from Spain (José Luis Lorenzo), Chile (Felipe Bate and Julio Montané), Venezuela (Mario Sanoja and Iraida Vargas), the Dominican Republic (Marcio Veloz and Héctor Díaz), and Mexico (Eduardo Matos and Manuel Gándara) to be brought together and to evaluate the coherence of the current Marxist archaeology. Their first meeting in Teotihuacan (1979) was followed by meetings in Cuzco (1984), Caracas (1985), and Oaxtepec (1986), incorporating new participants from other Latin American countries such as Peru (Luis Lumbreras).

These first meetings served as the starting point for the creation of a workgroup known as Latin American Social Archeology (LASA). It has been defined as a time largely dominated by "statements of principles," but it was also a period of intense debate on the main concepts of the substantive theory (Acosta 1999; Bate 1977, 1978, 1998; Gándara 1990, 1992,

1994; Sanoja 1983; Vargas 1985, 1990; Veloz 1984; among others). During the 1980s and 1990s, social archaeology was focused mainly on defining general concepts rather than on providing empirical examples to evaluate proposals (i.e., too much theory and little practice).

In recent years some colleagues (including myself) have turned away from the excessive use of the categories commonly used a few decades ago (see a summary in Acosta 2000:24–26). Instead we describe the distinctive "modes of production" and "modos de vida" (Vargas 1985, 1989; Veloz 1984; Veloz and Vega 1987) in order to explain concrete instances of precolumbian societies, as well as the core processes of their history, such as their initial settlements, early agriculture, and emergence of social classes (Acosta 2000; Bate 1986; Bate and Terrazas 2006; Vargas 1987). Consequently, our research focuses on concrete case studies from the Mesoamerican area.

This chapter aims to illustrate the usefulness of analyzing the mode of production of the preceramic societies in Mesoamerica, particularly in assessing the transitional process of appropriating societies toward food-producing societies. Here, I emphasize the importance of pretribal hunter-gatherers in developing the first domestications in Mesoamerica, but this precedent itself does not trigger a shift to sedentism or social hierarchy. Instead, other factors could trigger this change toward "tribal revolution"; for example, in the Basin of Mexico, this change may have been triggered by a very productive environment that allowed fully sedentary communities at the Playa phase (ca. 6000 BCE). In other areas of the lowlands of Mesoamerica, such as Balsas or the Pacific Coast, possible implementation of more-intensive cultivation techniques such as slash-and-burn could intensify the mode of production and promote social complexity; however, this question is still under debate. Finally, I discuss other secondary aspects of the mode of production, particularly the exchange of raw materials at the end of the preceramic period, as important to understanding the interaction of these early agrarian communities. This interaction continued until the Formative period and should have triggered further changes in the mode of production during the Early and Middle Formative.

## Modes of Production and Economic Formation

In this chapter I highlight the fact that techno-economy cannot be used as the main criterion to characterize the socioeconomic formation (SEF) of a specific community. Concepts such as "hunter-gatherers" and "agricultural societies," rather than indicating a degree of historical development, are simply particular forms of subsistence. There may also be hunter-gatherer or food-producer communities at different stages of development.

On the other hand, I don't mean to use the term *mode of production* as a synonym for the degree of development of human societies (or as a sort of "classification" for the evolution of societies). Within social archaeology, we rather think of the concept of social formation as one that better characterizes the degree of historic development. The mode of production, though fundamental to productive social relations, is part of the social-economic formation, together with other categories such as the mode of reproduction[1] (both mode of production and mode of reproduction are the basis of an SEF) and superstructures.

In sum, social-economic formation is a category that allows us to consider human society, in every period of its evolution, as a single "social body" that includes within itself all social phenomena in their organic unity and their reciprocal action on the basis of mode of production. The material basis of this structure is determined historically and is integrated by the mode of production and the mode of reproduction. The first integrates all economic processes that allow the material reproduction of society (production, distribution, exchange, and consumption), while the second defines the forms that reproduce and restore a labor force.

This is the way in which I use the term *mode of production*. Likewise, I discuss the usefulness of analyzing modes of production associated with food production at different scales and try to explain through case studies why food production begins with the hunter-gatherer societies but that it is not until the appearance of tribal revolution that a gradual dependency on domesticated plants begins. Dependence on these domesticates are, then, associated with population growth and the transformation of the local environment for the construction of agro-ecosystems.

I assume that the material basis (mode of production and mode of reproduction) of an SEF constitutes the fundamental motor of history and reject other idealistic Marxist positions (such as Althusser's) that accept the causal primacy of the superstructure. I also reject the primitive-community/slavery/feudalism/capitalism/socialism sequence as universal. Historical changes should consider the particularity of local developments, that is, the multilinearity of social evolution (Childe 1964), since the developmental sequence of subsistence practices in the New World does not correspond to the development sequences of the Old World, where sedentism precedes agriculture.

The perspective of social archaeology described here recognizes at least four archaeologically observable social formations for Mesoamerican societies: 1) hunter-gatherer primitive communities, 2) egalitarian tribal societies, 3) hierarchical tribal societies (chiefdoms), and 4) initial classist societies (or tributary societies). These social formations have their own characteristic modes of production. For instance, hunter-gatherer primitive communities[2] are characterized by food appropriation, while tribal societies may or may not have a food production system, in the form of either agriculture or herding.

Before addressing the issue of early agriculture modes of production in Mesoamerica, I would like to clarify some concepts related to the associated archaeological indicators. First, the concept of *hunter-gatherers* in the anthropological literature refers to the techno-economical dimension of societies rather than to their sociohistoric development. According to Lee and Daly (2004:3), "hunter-gatherers are human groups whose subsistence is based on the hunting of wild animals and the collection of wild plants without their domestication and, with the exception of dogs, without domestic animals." Here we find the first issue: groups whose mode of production is based on hunting and gathering, and at the same time societies with a highly complex social structure that goes beyond the integration level of a band society. We will come back to this point. But why mention hunter-gatherer communities if the main subject here is modes of production related to agricultural societies? Well, because I consider the development of agriculture as a long-term process that has its origins in these kinds of societies.

A second concept has to do with "cultivation." *Cultivating* is the action of raising crops by artificially spreading seeds, slips, or roots, but also looking after plants, either wild or domesticated. Consequently, cultivation may precede domestication. In fact, hunter-gatherers usually practiced this method to a lesser or larger extent. It is different from domestication in that domestication implies handling a species up to a degree where genetic modification may occur by selective pressure (Smith 2001).

In contrast, *agriculture* is a cultural system based on domesticated plants. Agricultural production may be classified by two distinct methods: intensive and extensive. Extensive agriculture requires a relatively large piece of land and is defined by a system based on raising crops, followed by a fallow period of up to seven years (depending on the characteristics of the soil) to permit the recovery of nutrients. Intensive agriculture, on the contrary, implies the intensification of production by technical means, such as irrigation, manuring, and preparation of humidity retention systems (terraces), among others.

Finally, we must talk about *sedentism*. Sedentism implies a permanent human settlement, in contrast to nomadism, which implies constant moving from one place to another. Most archaeological and ethnographic cases of sedentism are associated with agricultural societies, but this is not universal (Rosenswig 2006). Particularly in Mesoamerica, sedentism is a very late process compared to the first domesticated plants, with exception made for the Basin of Mexico.

We must keep this in mind, because the hunting, cultivation, domestication, agriculture, and sedentism processes have been traditionally considered historically subsequent, even though they are independent and not necessarily consecutive.

## Hunter-Gatherer Primitive Communities and First Domestications

First, I would like to define the general features of a hunter-gatherer mode of production, and its links to the early processes of domestication in Middle America. Hunter-gatherer communities have been defined as "band societies" (Service 1962), "non-storage hunters" (Testart 1982), "immediate-return societies" (Woodburn 1982), or simply as "primitive communities of hunter-gatherers" (Bate 1998:83) to differentiate them from tribal hunter societies. These pretribal hunter communities were characterized by a social structure that has been compared with "primitive communism" (Lee 1988; Morgan 1981; Testart 1982), where the relations of production are based on the absence of territorial private property.

One of the core elements for this social formation is *economic precariousness* (Bate 1986). These societies rely completely on natural production, and their productivity is subject to the local availability of resources. Consequently, their producing–consuming cycles are short, with almost no social storage (Ingold 1983).[3] Domestic units create strong reciprocal relations to reduce the risks associated with such precariousness (Sahlins 1965), giving their members the right to receive assistance, and the obligation to give such assistance when needed (Bate 1998:84). This means that pretribal appropriation societies developed a mode of production that restricted the growth of population, except for the initial settlements in the New World, where the wild territory provided an unlimited reservoir of natural resources. Once the most productive environments were populated, including some marginal environments, a contradiction arose. This contradiction is similar to the one proposed by Binford (1968) in *Post-Pleistocene Adaptations* (the carrying capacity of the environment). In such cases, as Bate and Terrazas (2002:23) pointed out, the demographic explosion characteristic of the Neolithic Revolution described by Childe would have been the motor of change in the fundamental relations of production. This is because a more complex demographic structure cannot be sustained by pretribal hunter-gatherer societies.

In addition, high mobility and low demographic density are closely related. Low demographic density results not only from the restrictions in a system of production that depends on stationary productivity but also from the social strategies employed to preserve the natural resources from an excessive exploitation by means of different contraceptive measures. The lack of social storage (in the form of storage pits, cultivation plots or herds) provides high mobility, but the nursing periods tend to reduce it. Thus, longer intervals between births produce a lower rate of natality.

Even if economic precariousness generates strict social rules that are likely to reduce social differences (birth control and mating rules, the observance of sex and gender roles, or the observance of taboos), there is always space for human agency. Agency operates at an individual level, since there aren't true governments, not at a higher group level, where decisions are taken in a consensual and consulted manner by elders or people with a leading role. Consequently, hunter-gatherers "vote with their feet" (Lee and Daly 2004) to resolve conflicts within a community, as well as to generate sources of cultural and historical diversity. This kind of organization was present in Mesoamerica from when the earliest populations colonized the region to at least 6000–4000 BC.

The first domesticates were traditionally credited to groups of the so-called Mesoamerican Archaic period. However, according to recent studies, earlier domesticates date back to the limits of the Pleistocene–Holocene, up to 10,000 years for species like squash (*Cucurbita*) and bottle gourd (*Lagenaria siceraria*) (Erickson et al. 2005; Smith 1997, 2005). Based on genetic data and AMS dates, it has been proposed that dogs and bottle gourds came from Asia with the first American settlers (Erickson et al. 2005; Tito et al. 2011; van Asch et al. 2013).

By the end of the Pleistocene and the beginning of the Holocene, typical Paleoindian groups still had a hunter-gatherer social formation ("bands" in Service's terminology), but some groups were already changing to a way of life with a more "Archaic" pattern, resulting from particularities in their mode of production, which was more related to gathering and cultivation of plants. Grinding stones have been found in sites like Guilá Náquitz in Oaxaca and Cueva de Santa Marta in Chiapas dating back to 10,500 and 9800 uncal. BP (Acosta 2010; Flannery 1986). Remains of *Theobroma cacao* have also been recorded in Santa Marta at levels down to 10,050 uncal. BP, in addition to *Zea mays* pollen, and starch grains of species like *Phaseolus* (bean) and *Ipomoea batatas* (sweet potato) at the same levels (Figure 4.1).

It has been argued that the distinction between starches of domesticated and wild plants cannot be easily established, but species like teosinte (*Z. mays parviglumis*) suggest an early introduction and cultivation of this plant, as there are no reports of native teosinte. Another issue has to do with *Theobroma cacao*, whose South American origin has been generally accepted, in spite of the possibility of its early domestication in Mesoamerica (Cuatrecasas 1964; Motamayor et al. 2002).

Why should hunter communities need domesticated plants?[4] Many explanations have been suggested. For example, Braidwood (Braidwood and Willey 1962) assumed that agriculture was possible only when the knowledge of plants and technology was sufficient for their cultivation and domestication. However, Flannery (1968) points out in his proposal for Guilá Náquitz, Oaxaca, that this could not be the case, because hunter-gatherers already knew the reproductive cycle of plants on which they relied for their subsistence. The answer to this issue may be not in the mode of production, but in the mode of reproduction. The *mode of reproduction* is part of a society's material base, and it refers to *the material processes oriented toward the restitution of labor force*. It includes activities such as sex, leisure, recreation, classificatory kinship, and mating rules (Bate and Terrazas 2002). The need for a strong (political or matrimonial) alliance system through ceremonies involving the use of stimulating plants in domestic units would prevent endogamy and stimulate social interaction for the exchange of knowledge and products (including exogenous species). Consequently, the true cause for the meeting of macrobands during times of plenty or concentration of resources would be both economic and reproductive, and not only symbolic and superstructural.

In an earlier paper, I observed that many plant species recovered from Santa Marta at the Pleistocene-Holocene transition level, correspond to plants with stimulating properties, with radiocarbon calibrated dates from 10,400 BCE to 9,900 BCE (Acosta 2009). The findings include pollen of cacao (*Theobroma cacao*), *Zea mays* (teosinte?), chili pepper (*Calyptrantes chiapensis*), and damiana (*Turnera diffusa*), as well as starch grains from a

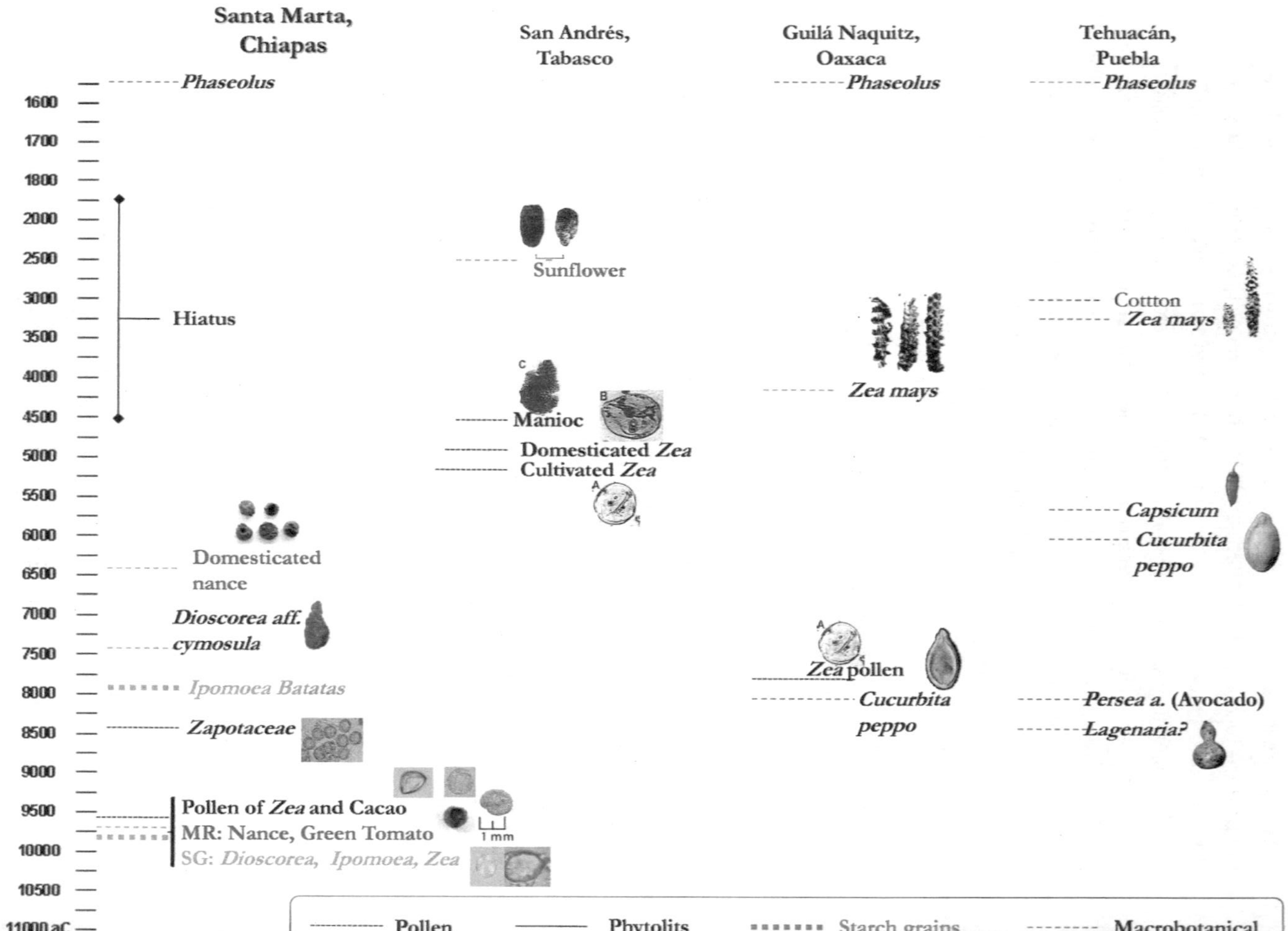


Figure 4.1. Chronology of some Mesoamerican

sort of bean (*Phaseolus* sp.), *Zea*, sweet potato (*Ipomoea batatas*), and chili (*Capsicum* sp.). Chili peppers have stimulating effects on the nervous system, while damiana is widely used as an aphrodisiac in traditional Mexican herbalism (Sandoval 1982) (Figure 4.2). Cacao is one of the major domesticated plants for the preparation of stimulating beverages in Mesoamerica (Coe and Coe 1996), and it is quite possible that even before its full domestication, the pulp rather than the seed was used for fermented beverages (McNeil 2006).

As previously noted by Chisholm and Blake (2006:166), *Zea* pollen may be closely related to the cultivation of teosinte or primitive maize for its sugar-rich cane in the preparation of chicha-like fermented beverages (see also Smalley and Blake 2003). Microfossils of *Zea* (both pollen and starch grains) indicate its use since the end of the Pleistocene. In addition, the relative lack of plants in Mesoamerica with stimulating properties (compared to South America) is a good reason for its early consumption. However, there are no reports of native teosinte in the region, and the possibility of its introduction as an exogenous species cannot be excluded.

## Agricultural Revolution and Tribal Revolution

Gordon Childe had already suggested the importance of agriculture in the development of Eastern civilizations in what he had called a true Neolithic Revolution (Childe 1954). The expansion of societies beyond the limits of the domestic unit as a production-consumption unit and the creation of closed mating networks (tribal societies) are an immediate precedent to stratified societies. First, I must explain better what is meant by "tribal society."

Compared to a hunter-gatherer community, whose social formation is fundamentally characterized by a mode of production without territorial appropriation (Bate 1986; Service 1979), the essential feature of a tribal society is appropriation (Bate 1998), resulting from an increasing investment of labor in the cultivated land or herds (if any) or from full sedentism and demographic growth. On the other hand, the tribal societies' mode of reproduction is characterized by closed mating networks (closed *connubium*) (Williams 1974); that is, couples are sought within the tribal community by means of a complex segmentary system that defines the kinship rules and situates individuals in a genealogical scheme that governs reproduction (Bate and Terrazas 2002). This difference is fundamental to understanding the rapid expansion of agricultural tribal societies. While the mode

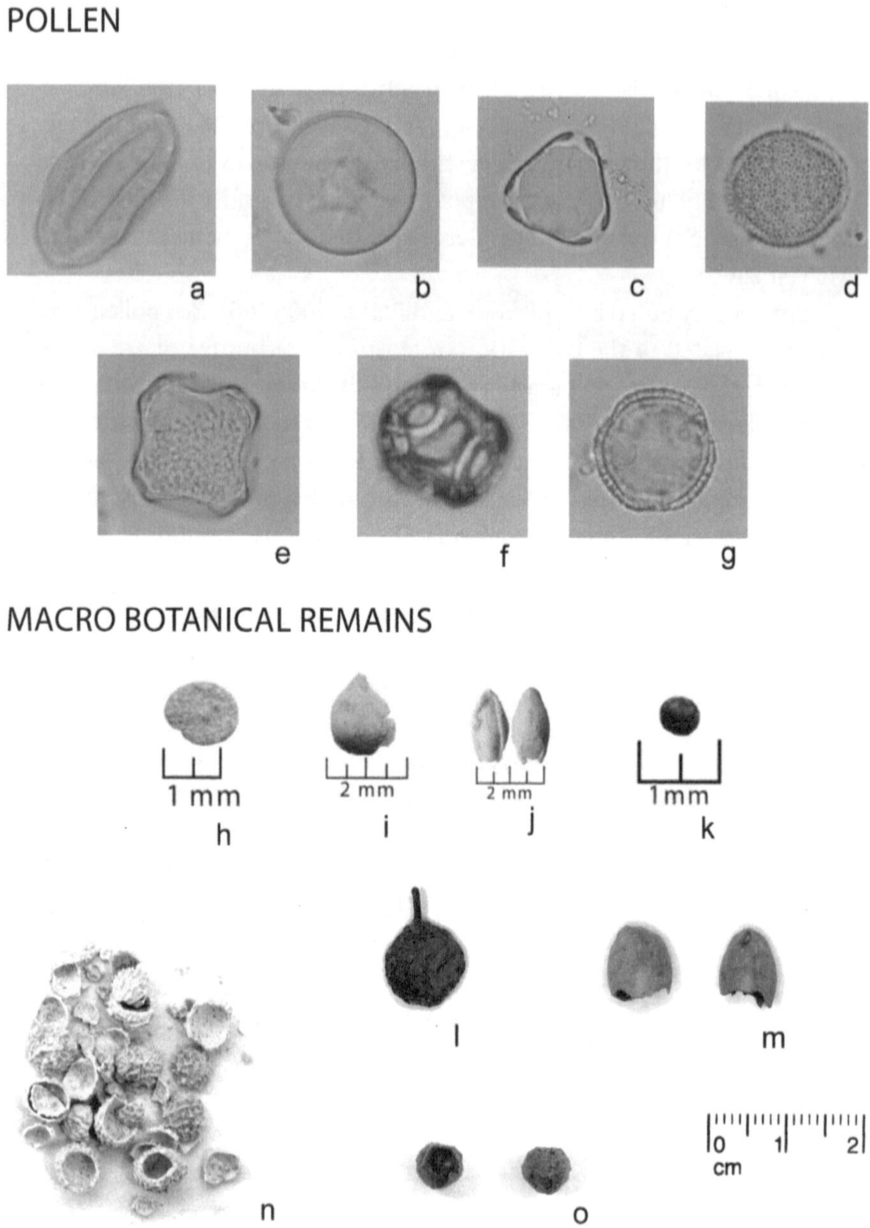


Figure 4.2. Some macro- and microbotanical remains from Late Pleistocene–Early Holocene levels of Santa Marta rockshelter: a) Arecaceae; b) Cupressaceae-Taxodiaceae; c) *Pimenta dioica*; d) Sterculiaceae; e) *Psidium* sp.; f) *Tabernaemontana* sp.; g) *Theobroma cacao*; h) *Physalis* sp.; i) *Fimbristylis* sp.; j) *Panicum* sp.; k) *Chenopodium* sp.; l) *Ficus* sp.; m) Sapotaceae; n) *Celtis* sp.; o) *Byrsonima crassifolia*.

of production of pretribal hunter communities prevents the overexploitation of natural resources by constant migration and birth control, tribal societies have no limits to their demographic processes, which produce a constant segmentation of communities and increasing competition for resources (Parkinson 2002). Consequently, tribal societies expand in a depredating manner at the expense of nontribal societies, either assimilating them or expelling them to other regions (Sahlins 1961).

Archaeological data have revealed that Mesoamerican societies did not precisely follow the Old World's Neolithic Revolution pattern. They rather followed a slow development path with a mosaic of adaptations that produced diverse local or regional trajectories (Rosenswig 2015) during the so-called Archaic period. This period, however, shows different rates of change in particular phases of the Holocene, which I would like to mention.

At the beginning of the Holocene (ca. 10,000–8000 BCE), a great variety of hunter communities thrived in the changing environment that resulted from the end of the last glacial period. Regions like Tamaulipas (MacNeish 1958) and Tehuacan (MacNeish 1961, 1967, 1972) display a predominantly gatherer pattern with low demographic density. In other regions such as the Basin of Mexico (Acosta 2009), there are still remains of megafauna hunting activities well into the Holocene. In contrast, regions like Oaxaca, Chiapas, and Panama show an increasing use of plants and grinding stones, which probably set the ground for the first domestications in Mesoamerica (Acosta 2008, 2010; Flannery 1986, 1999; Piperno 2011). Particularly in Chiapas' Santa Marta cave, a lower mobility pattern is documented by the abundance and diversity of resources as well as by the exclusive use of local raw materials. There is, however, no evidence of a more complex social organization than the hunter community.

This pattern continues well into the middle of the Holocene, when a more complex pattern of sedentary hunter-gatherers occupied the Basin of Mexico (Figure 4.3). At the beginning of the Playa phase (ca. 6000 BCE), different groups settled on the marshy environment around the lake in sites like Zohapilco (Niederberger 1976, 1979, 1987), San Vicente Chicoloapan (Romano 1963), and San Gregorio Atlapulco (McClung and Acosta 2015), where they supplemented their subsistence needs with the collection and early cultivation of wild plants. The abundance of lacustrine resources throughout the year—and the great number of archaeological remains, such as large fire pits of up to 5 m in diameter—suggests the presence of the first sedentary communities in Mesoamerica.

Such subsistence remains also suggest that these communities in the

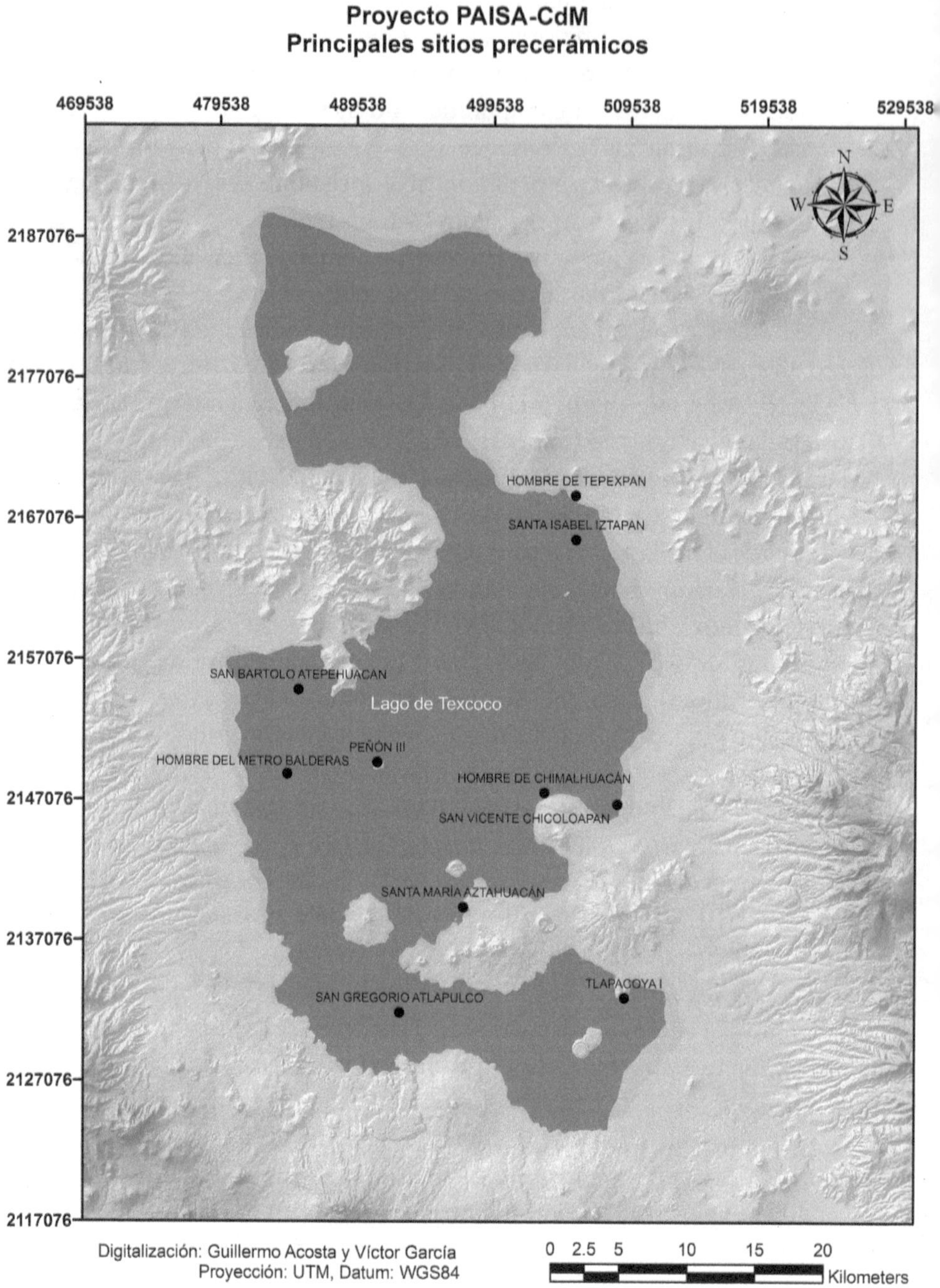


Figure 4.3. Preceramic sites in the Basin of Mexico.

Basin of Mexico exceeded the limits of pretribal hunter-gatherer groups. In San Gregorio, for instance, this period has been located in two areas of 49 $m^2$ and 240 $m^2$, respectively, indicating a dense occupation along an islet located in the middle of Lake Xochimilco. According to different authors (Testart 1982; Woodburn 1982), sedentism related to highly productive environments is often associated with processes of social complexity.

Dating of Zohapilco (7040±115 uncal. BP) and San Gregorio (7370±110 uncal. BP) for Playa phase I (ca. 6400–6000 BCE) also suggests the hunting and fishing of lacustrine fauna, mostly aquatic birds such as ducks and herons, but also white fish (*Chirostoma* sp.), axolotl (*Ambystoma* sp.), and turtle (*Kinosternon* sp.). Microfossils from grinding stones also indicate the presence of cyperaceous rhizome phytoliths, and starch grains of achira (*Canna indica*), sweet potato (*Ipomoea batatas*), and chili (*Capsicum*), as well as starches of unidentified grasses. It should be noted, however, that despite the difficulty in identifying plants located in San Gregorio Atlapulco as belonging to a domesticated variety, their cultivation should be considered a part of the long-term process of domestication. Piperno (2011:463) has pointed out that processes and periods of *predomesticated* and *nondomesticated cultivations* have received less attention in New World archaeology than in other regions.

During the so-called Zohapilco phase, there is an increase in the use of artifacts made with obsidian flakes and in the production of domesticated plants like chili (*Capsicum annuum*), squash (*Cucurbita* sp.), and chayote (*Sechium edule*). There is also an increase in the size of *Zea* pollen. Niederberger situates this period between 3000 and 2200 BC, but the "Zohapilcan" features may also be observed in San Gregorio Atlapulco as far back as 4500 BCE (Acosta 2015). These features include obsidian remains, subsistence based on lacustrine resources, and the presence of *Zea* pollen, but without clearly domesticated plants. *Zea* pollen does not exceed 90 microns, and starch grains of chili and bean cannot be definitively assigned to domesticated species. This may be due to the fact that the "Zohapilcan" occupation in San Gregorio corresponds to a transitional period to fully agricultural societies (Figures 4.4 and 4.5).

## The Basin of Mexico: An Atypical Model

The pattern of subsistence and social organization in the Basin of Mexico, with an early sedentism but a late adoption of domesticated plants, contrasts with the data from other regions, such as the semidesert areas

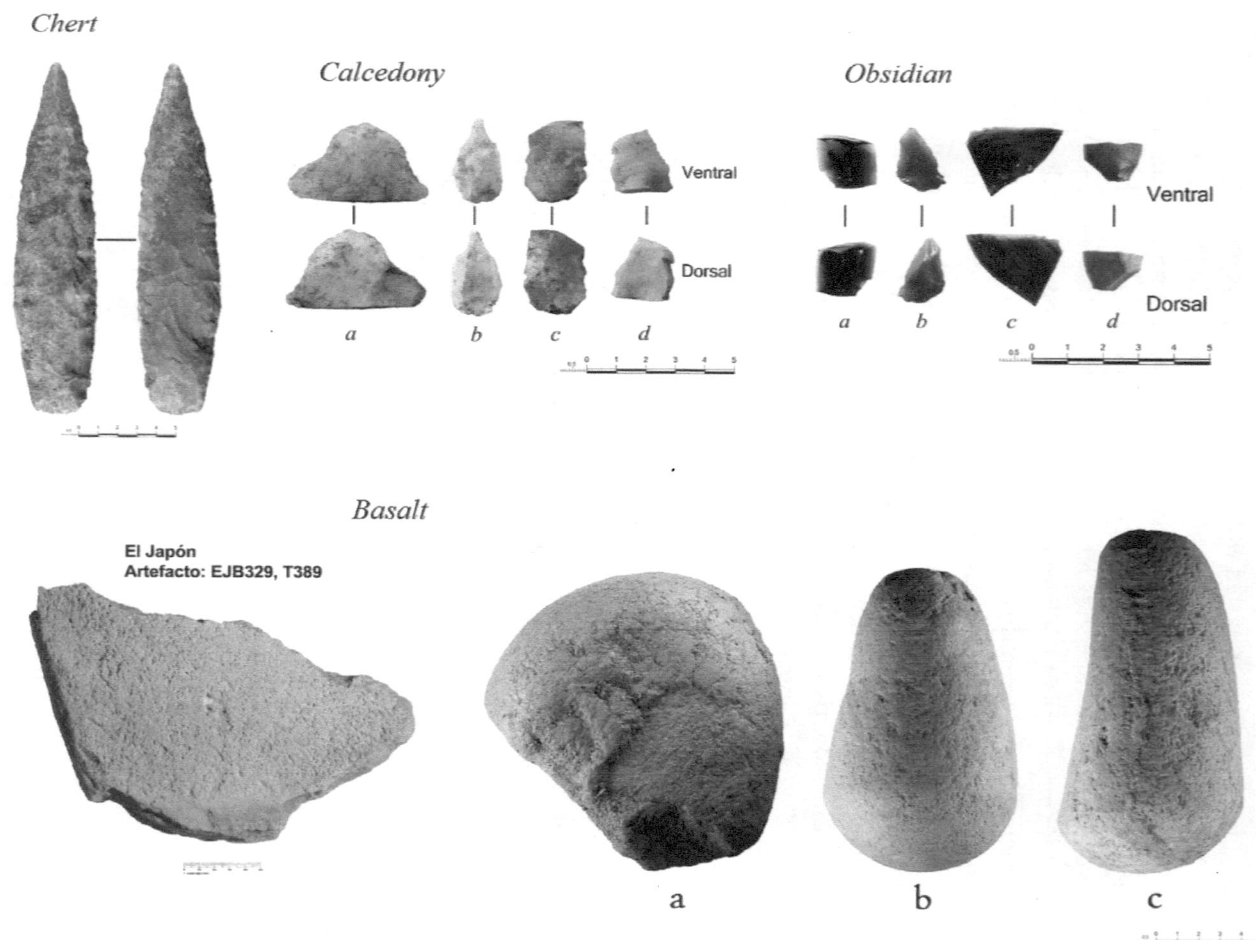


Figure 4.4. San Gregorio archaeological lithics. *Upper*: chipped stone; *lower*: ground stone.

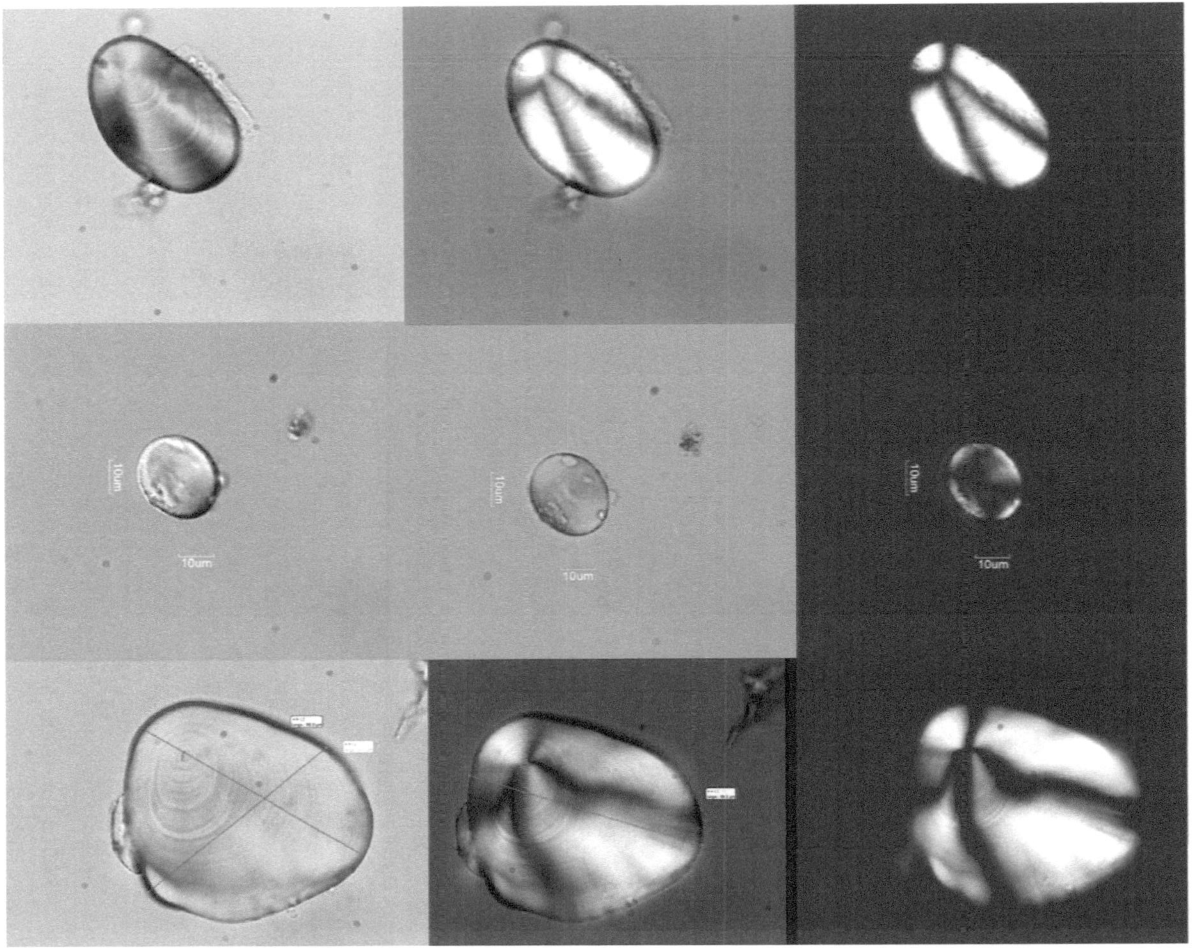


Figure 4.5. San Gregorio Atlapulco, Playa phase starch grains: *Dioscorea* sp. (*upper*), family Bean (*middle*), and Canna Indica (*lower*).

of Oaxaca and Tehuacan, or the tropical lowlands of Mesoamerica. Niederberger has proposed two models of development for the Mesoamerican highlands during the Archaic period. One is the Tehuacan Model for the semi-arid regions of Puebla, Tamaulipas, and Oaxaca, closely related to high productivity periods, which imply the aggregation of large communities (macrobands) dedicated to the extensive cultivation of cereals and other plants during the rainy seasons, and their dispersal into minor groups (microbands) dedicated to hunting and gathering in separate ecologic niches during the dry seasons. These communities displayed some agricultural practices as early as the sixth millennium BC with plants like maize, chili, avocado, and squash, but not a sedentary way of life until three thousand years later (Niederberger 1979).

In contrast, the model for the lacustrine communities in the Basin of Mexico suggests a sedentary and territorial occupation already by the sixth millennium BC. According to Niederberger (1977, 1979), this model is related to a highly productive environment, and evidence of early agricultural activities involving plants like *Zea* (tesosinte), *Amaranthus*, and *Physalis* (tomato) during Playa phase 1 (6000–5500 BCE), and an intensification of such activities during Playa phase 2 (5500–4500 BCE), but also a subsistence largely based on the collection of wild lacustrine products. It is only at Tlapacoya's Zohapilco phase (3500–2200 BCE) when a significant increase in the use of domesticated plants and lithic artifacts (grinding stones and tools) related to food processing can be observed (Niederberger 1979:139–141). Probably the early occupation of San Gregorio (4500–4000 BCE) represents a transitional period to these preceramic agricultural societies.

Recent paleoecological studies suggest a third model for the tropical lowlands in regions like the Gulf Coast (Pope et al. 2001), the basin of the Balsas River (Ranere 2009), and Soconusco (Kennett et al. 2010; Neff et al. 2006). Here we have maize pollen and increased carbon levels recovered from flotation that imply disturbance of the tropical forest. These microbotanical patterns suggest the practice of an extensive clearing and burning agriculture between the sixth and fifth millennia BC. This evidence has been frequently related to droughts and natural fires (Rosenswig 2015), but Piperno et al. (2007) have also found evidence of *Zea* pollen, carbon, and forest disturbance with frequent fires and forest clearing beginning at levels dating to ca. 5000 BCE in the Balsas River. Piperno et al. (2007:11876) propose that such disturbance, together with the presence of carbon, could not be the result of drought, because it occurred in a humid environment indicated by the rising levels of Lake Ixtacyola.

In the Maya area of northern Belize, the earliest evidence of *Zea* pollen is associated with forest clearing dated to between 2500 and 1500 BCE (Jones 1994; Pohl et al. 1996).

## Final Comments

The Archaic is a period when Middle American societies experimented with the early cultivation of wild and domesticated plants to supplement their diet, which was basically dependent on collecting strategy (Rosenswig 2015). However, agriculture, in the strict sense (societies whose subsistence is based on domesticated plants) is securely documented only after 1000 BCE. It is incorrect to say, however, that there were no changes in the subsistence and organization of the Archaic period communities in the Basin of Mexico, particularly at the end of this period (Zohapilco Phase or Late Archaic). The few Archaic period sites extensively excavated in other regions like Gheo Shih and Gudz Beckol in Oaxaca (Flannery and Spores 1984; Marcus and Flannery 2004, 2007; Winter 2014) have given the idea that the intensity and social complexity in these sites did not exceed the limits expected for a "band" society. Consequently, we need more data based on extensive excavations in domestic units, and not only paleoecological sequences.

It is accepted that domestication is a process with its roots lying deep in time, and its origins should be traced back as far as the Pleistocene–Holocene transition (Smith 2001), particularly for those societies with a deep knowledge of the tropical ecosystems for the last 12,500 years, as has been documented for the site of Santa Marta in Southern Mexico. The social needs of these communities beyond simple subsistence, such as the need for stimulating plants (*Zea*, cacao) or the use of water containers (*Cucurbita*, *Lagenaria*), could be the true reason for early cultivation.

A final issue that should be considered in the mode of production of the Archaic period societies in the Basin of Mexico is the increase of interpersonal violence due to the need for new land for the expansion and segmentation of the ruling lineages after the tribal revolution. This has been noted for other sedentary societies with limited resources, such as the Chinchorro communities on the coast of Chile (Standen et al. 2004). It is possible, however, that the Mesoamerican societies would have developed regulatory systems to reduce the conflicts among neighboring groups, such as the ritual exchange. Classical authors like Mauss (2002) and Sahlins (1972) have suggested that the exchange usually turns into peace treaties and strengthens the alliances among tribal communities. In this sense, it is worth noting the importance of obsidian, an exotic good that is consistently present at the Archaic period communities of the Basin of Mexico. Both Zohapilco (Niederberger 1976, 1979) and San Gregorio (García and Acosta 2014) show an increasing use of obsidian in relation to local raw materials (such as basalt) from Playa phase I (16 percent) to the Zohapilco phase (38 percent). This last relative percentage of obsidian is similar to levels documented from Early Formative period contexts in the Basin of Mexico (Niederberger 1976:56). The absence of artifacts with cortex in San Gregorio also suggests that obsidian was brought to the site in the form of already prepared nodules, which denies the possibility of direct access to the source (Otumba) and opens the possibility for early exchange. Recent studies on the exchange of exotic goods among sedentary communities during the Early Formative period at the site of Altica in the Basin of Mexico suggest that this process continued during the Early Ceramic period through the exchange of obsidian from Otumba for incised white-slipped ceramic from the Gulf Coast (Stoner et al. 2015).

Finally, preliminary data from San Gregorio suggest support for the model proposed by Niederberger, preceding the initial dates of the so-called Zohapilco phase by at least five centuries. Even if faunal remains suggest predominance of lacustrine resources, the wide distribution of grinding stones and related microfossils indicates the increasing importance of domestication and wild plant processing. The presence of grinding stones in San Gregorio, together with "Zohapilcan technology" (artifacts on small obsidian flakes with marginal finishing) as early as 4500 BCE, suggests two scenarios: either San Gregorio remains are from a transitional period between Playa phase II and the Zohapilco phase, or the Zohapilco phase begins at least one thousand years before the dates proposed by Niederberger four decades ago.

This and other issues about the Archaic period societies in America may be solved only by the procurement of new data from field studies that support the different interpretations on one of the largest and less-known periods of precolumbian history.

## Notes

1. For a more detailed discussion about the mode of reproduction concept, see: Bate and Terrazas 2002.

2. We refer to the term "primitive" in its etymological sense of "first" or "ancient," rather than the derogative sense used today.

3. "Practical storage is a solution to problems of activity scheduling. Social storage, by contrast, is an aspect of the rationality of resource *husbandry*. The distinction may be illustrated by comparing the implications of the commonly encountered statements that for immediate-return hunter gatherers 'the environment itself is the storehouse,' and that pastoralists 'store on the hoof.' Both statements refer to reserves in the form of living plants and animals, but there is a subtle difference in connotation" (Ingold 1983:563).

4. From here on, I will refer to the nontribal hunter social formation simply as "hunter communities" to distinguish it from the hunger-gatherers concept merely as a way of subsistence.

## References Cited


Acosta, Guillermo

1999 Procesos de trabajo determinado: La configuración de modos de trabajo en la cultura arqueológica. *Boletín de Antropología Americana* 35:17–35.

2008 *La cueva de Santa Marta y los cazadores-recolectores del Pleistoceno final–Holoceno temprano en las regiones tropicales de México*. Ph.D. thesis, UNAM, México (2 vols.).

2009 Antecedentes precerámicos de las sociedades del Formativo en el sureste de México. *THULE: Rivista Italiana di Studi Americanistici* 22/23–24/25:101–120.

2010 Late Pleistocene–Early Holocene Tropical Foragers of Chiapas, Mexico: Recent Studies. *Current Research in the Pleistocene* 27:1–4.

2015 Early Agrarian Societies in the Basin of Mexico. Paper presented at the 80th Annual Meeting of the Society for American Aechaeology, San Francisco.

Acosta, Guillermo, Felipe Bate, Patricia Pérez, Enrique Méndez, and Arturo Jiménez

2012 Arqueología marxista en Chiapas: De la agenda al programa. In *La arqueología social latinoamericana: De la teoría a la praxis*. Edited by Henry Tanta león and Miguel Aguilar, pp. 247–260. Universidad de los Andes, Bogotá.

Bate, Luis F.

1977 *Arqueología y materialismo histórico*. Ediciones de Cultura Popular, México.

1978 *Sociedad, formación económico social y cultura*. Ediciones de Cultura Popular, México.

1986 El modo de producción cazador recolector o la economía del salvajismo. *Boletín de Antropología Americana* 13:5–32.

1998 *El proceso de investigación en arqueología*. Editorial Crítica, Barcelona.

Bate, Luis, and Alejandro Terrazas

2002 Sobre el modo de reproducción en sociedad pretribales. *Revista Atlántica-Mediterránea de Prehistoria y Arqueología Social* 5:11–41.

2006 Apuntes sobre las investigaciones prehistóricas en México." In *El hombre temprano en América y sus implicaciones en el poblamiento de la cuenca de México*, edited by José Concepción Jiménez, Silvia González, José A. Pompa, and Francisco Ortiz, pp. 23–48. INAH, México.

Binford, Lewis R.

1968 *Post-Pleistocene Adaptations*. In *New Perspectives in Archeology*, edited by Susan R. Binford and Lewis R. Binford. Aldine, Chicago.

Braidwood, Robert, and Gordon Willey

1962 *Courses toward Urban Life: Archeological Considerations of Some Cultural Alternates*. Aldine, Chicago.

Childe, Vere G.

1954 *Los orígenes de la civilización*. Fondo de Cultura Económica, México.

1964 *Evolución social*. Plaza y Valdés, Universidad Nacional Autónoma de México, México.

Chisholm, Brian, and Michael Blake

2006 Diet in Prehistoric Soconusco. In *Histories of Maize: Multidisciplinary Approaches to the Prehistory, Linguistics, Biogeography, Domestication, and Evolution of Maize*, edited by Robert H. Tykot and Bruce F. Benz, pp. 161–172. Academic, New York.

Coe, Sophie, and Michael Coe

1996 *The True History of Chocolate*. Thames and Hudson, London.

Cuatrecasas, José

1964 Cacao and Its Allies: A Taxonomic Revision of the Genus *Theobroma*. *Contributions from the United States National Herbarium* 35:379–614.

Erickson, David, Bruce Smith, Andrew Clarke, Daniel Sandweiss, and Noreen Tuross

2005 An Asian Origin for a 10,000-year-old Domesticated Plant in the Americas. *Proceedings of the National Academy of Science* 102(51):18315–18320.

Flannery, Kent V.

1986 *Guilá Naquitz: Archaic Foraging and Early Agriculture in Oaxaca, Mexico*. Academic, Orlando.

1999 Los orígenes de la agricultura en Oaxaca. *Cuadernos del Sur* 14:5–14.

Flannery, Kent, and Ronald Spores

1984 Excavated Sites of the Oaxaca Preceramic. In *The Cloud People*, edited by Kent V. Flannery and Joyce Marcus, pp. 20–26. Academic, New York.

Gándara, Manuel

1990 Algunas notas sobre el análisis del conocimiento. *Boletín de Antropología Americana* 22: 5–19.

1992 El análisis teórico: Aplicaciones al estudio de la complejidad social. *Boletín de Antropología Americana* 25:93–104.

1994 Consecuencias metodológicas de la adopción de una ontología de la cultura: Una perspectiva desde la arqueología. In *Metodología y cultura*, edited by Jorge González and Jesús Galindo, pp. 24–72. CNCA, México.

García, Víctor H., and Guillermo Acosta

2014 *Intercambio de obsidiana en el Holoceno Medio en la Cuenca de México (ca. 6000–3000 a.n.e). Un análisis mediante pXRF*. Ponencia presentada en la Reunión 2014 de la Unión Geofísica Mexicana, Puerto Vallarta, México.

Ingold, Tim

1983 The Significance of Storage in Hunting Societies. *Man* (n.s.) 18(3):553–571.

Jones, John G.
1994 Pollen Evidence for Early Settlement and Agriculture in Northern Belize. *Palynology* 18:205–211.

Kennett, Douglas J.
2012 Archaic-Period Foragers and Farmers in Mesoamerica. In *Oxford Handbook of Mesoamerican Archaeology*, edited by Deborah L. Nichols and Christopher A. Pool, pp. 141–150. Oxford University Press, New York.

Kennett, Douglas, Dolores Piperno, John Jones, Hector Neff, Barbara Voorhies, Megan Walsh, and Brendan Culleton
2010 Pre-pottery Farmers on the Pacific Coast of Southern Mexico. *Journal of Archaeological Science* 37:3401–3411.

Lee, Richard
1988 Reflections on Primitive Communism. In *Hunters and Gatherers*, edited by Tim Ingold, Daniel Riches, and James Woodburn, pp. 200–216. Berg, London.

Lee, Richard, and Richard Daly (editors)
2004 *The Cambridge Encyclopedia of Hunters and Gatherers*. Cambridge University, New York.

MacNeish, Richard S.
1958 *A Preliminary Archaeological Investigation in the Sierra de Tamaulipas*. Transactions of the American Philosophical Society No. 6. Philadelphia.
1961 *First Annual Report of the Teotihuacan Archaeological-Botanical Project*. Robert S. Peabody Foundation for Archaeology, Andover.
1967 A Summary of the Subsistence. In *The Prehistory of the Tehuacan Valley: 1. Environment and Subsistence*, edited by Douglas S. Byers, pp. 290–309. University of Texas Press, Austin.
1972 The Evolution of Community Patterns in the Tehuacán Valley of México and Speculations about the Cultural Processes. In *Man, Settlement and Urbanism*, edited by Peter Ucko, pp. 67–93. Gerald Duckworth, London.

MacNeish, Richard S., and Antoinette Nelken Terner
1983 The Preceramic of Mesoamerica. *Journal of Field Archaeology* 10(1):71–84.

MacNeish, Richard S., Melvin Fowler, Ángel García Cook, Frederick Peterson, Antoinette Nelken Terner, and James A. Neely
1972 *The Prehistory of the Tehuacan Valley: 5. Excavations and Reconnaissance*. University of Texas Press, Austin.

MacNeish, Richard S., and Frederick Peterson
1962 *The Santa Marta Rock Shelter, Ocozocoautla, Chiapas, México*. Papers No. 14, New World Archaeological Foundation, Brigham Young University, Provo, Utah.

Marcus, Joyce, and Kent Flannery
2004 The Coevolution of Ritual and Society: New $^{14}$C Dates from Ancient Mexico. *Proceedings of the National Academy of Sciences* 101:18257–18261.
2007 El fechamiento por radiocarbono de edificios públicos y de rasgos rituales en el Antiguo Valle de Oaxaca. Informe entregado a la FAMSI, Foundation for the Advancement of Mesoamerican Studies.

Marx, Karl
1981 *Obras escogidas*. Editorial Progreso, Moscow.
Mauss, Marcel
2002 *The Gift: The Form and Reason for Exchange in Archaic Societies*. Routledge, London.
McClung, Emily, and Guillermo Acosta
2015 Una ocupación del periodo de agricultura temprana en Xochimilco (ca. 4200–4000 a.n.e.) *Anales de Antropología* 49(2):299–315.
McNeil, Cameron (editor)
2006 *Chocolate in Mesoamerica: A Cultural History of Cacao*. University Press of Florida, Gainesville.
Morgan, Lewis
1981 *La sociedad primitiva*. Colofón, México.
Motamayor, Juan, Ange-Marie Risterucci, Pedro Lopez, Carlos Ortiz, Andrés Moreno, and Claire Lanaud
2002 Cacao Domestication I: The Origin of the Cacao Cultivated by the Mayas. *Heredity* 89:380–386.
Neff, Hector, Barbara Pearsall, John Jones, Barbara Arroyo, and Dorothy Freidel
2006 Climate Change and Population History in the Pacific Lowlands of Southern Mesoamerica. *Quaternary Research* 65:390–400.
Niederberger, Christine
1976 *Zohapilco: Cinco milenios de ocupación humana en un sitio lacustre de la Cuenca de México*. INAH, Colección Científica, México.
1979 Early Sedentary Economy in the Basin of Mexico. *Science* 203:131–142.
1987 *Paleopaysages et archéologie préurbaine du Bassin de Mexico (Mexique)*. Centre d'Etudes Mexicaines et Centraméricaines, México.
Parkinson, William A.
2002 Introduction: Archaeology and Tribal Societies. In *The Archaeology of Tribal Societies*, edited by William A. Parkinson, pp. 13–33, Archaeological Series 15, International Monographs in Prehistory, Ann Arbor.
Piperno, Dolores
2011 The Origins of Plant Cultivation and Domestication in the New World Tropics: Patterns, Process, and New Developments. In *The Beginnings of Agriculture: New Data, New Ideas*, edited by D. Price and O. Bar-Yosef. Current Anthropology. Volume 52, No. S4, 453–470.
Piperno, Dolores, Jorge Enrique Moreno, José Iriarte, Irene Holst, Matthew Lachniet, John Jones, Anthony Ranere, and Ronald Castanzo
2007 Late Pleistocene and Holocene Environmental History of the Iguala Valley, Central Balsas Watershed of Mexico. *Proceedings of the National Academy of Sciences of the United States of America* 104:11874–11881.
Pohl, Mary, John G. Jones, John S. Jacob, Dolores R. Piperno, Susan D. deFrance, David L. Lentz, John A. Gifford, Marie E. Danforth, and J. Kathryn Josserand
1996 Early Agriculture in the Maya Lowlands. *Latin American Antiquity* 7:355–372.
Pope, Kevin O., Mary E. D. Pohl, John G. Jones, David L. Lentz, Christopher Von Nagy, Francisco J. Vega, and Irvy R. Quitmyer

2001 Origin and Environmental Setting of Ancient Agriculture in the Lowlands of Mesoamerica. *Science* 292:1370–1373.

Ranere, Anthony, Dolores Piperno, Irene Holst, Ruth Dickau, and José Iriarte

2009 The Cultural and Chronological Context of Early Holocene Maize and Squash Domestication in the Central Balsas River Valley, Mexico. *Proceedings of the National Academy of Sciences* 106:5014–5018.

Romano, Arturo

1963 Breve informe de los hallazgos de San Vicente Chicoloapan, México. *Anales del Instituto Nacional de Antropología e Historia* 15:245–249.

Rosenswig, Robert M.

2006 Sedentism and Food Production in Early Complex Societies of the Soconusco, Mexico. *World Archaeology* 38:329–354.

2015 A Mosaic of Adaptation: The Archaeological Record for Mesoamerica's Archaic Period. *Journal of Archaeological Research* 23(2):115–162.

Sahlins, Marshall

1961 The Segmentary Lineage: An Organization of Predatory Expansion. *American Anthropologist* 63:322–345.

1965 On the Sociology of Primitive Exchange. In *The Relevance of Models in Social Anthropology*, edited by Michael Banton, pp. 139–236. Tavistock, London.

1972 *Las sociedades tribales*. Editorial Labor, Barcelona.

Sandoval, Gustavo

1982 *La damiana (*Turnera diffusa, *Willd.): Una revisión bibliográfica y experiencias en su aprovechamiento e inducción al cultivo*. Ph.D. thesis, Universidad Autónoma de Chapingo, México.

Sanoja, Mario

1983 *Siete temas de debate en la arqueología social*. Cuadernos de Antropología 6. Universidad de Costa Rica, San José.

Service, Elman

1962 *Primitive Social Organization*. Random House, New York.

1966 *The Hunters*. Prentice-Hall, Englewood Cliffs.

Smalley, John, and Michael Blake

2003 Sweet Beginnings: Stalk Sugar and the Domestication of Maize. *Current Anthropology* 44:675–703.

Smith, Bruce D.

1997 The Initial Domestication of the *Cucurbita pepo* in the Americas 10,000 Years Ago. *Science* 273:865–996.

2001 Low-Level Food Production. *Journal of Archaeological Research* 9:1–43.

2005 Reassessing Coxcatlan Cave and the Early History of Domesticated Plants in Mesoamerica. *Proceedings of the National Academy of Sciences of the United States of America* 102:9438–9445.

Standen, Vivien, Calogero Santoro, and Bernardo Arriaza

2004 Síntesis y propuestas para el periodo arcaico en el extreme norte de Chile. *Chungara* 36:201–212.

Stoner, Wesley, Deborah L. Nichols, Bridget A. Alex, and Destiny L. Crider

2015 The Emergence of Early–Middle Formative Exchange Patterns in Mesoamerica: A View from Altica in the Teotihuacan Valley. *Journal of Anthropological Archaeology* 39:19–35.

Testart, Alain
1982 The Significance of Food Storage among Hunter-Gatherers: Residence Patterns, Population Densities and Social Inequalities. *Current Anthropology* 23:523–537.

Tito, Raul Y., Samuel L. Belknap, Kristin D. Sobolik, Robert C. Ingraham, Lauren M. Cleeland, and Cecil M. Lewis, Jr.
2011 Brief Communication: DNA from Early Holocene American Dog. *American Journal of Physical Anthropology* 145:653–657.

van Asch, Barbara, Ai-bing Zhang, Mattias C. R. Oskarsson, Cornelya F. C. Klütsch, António Amorim, and Peter Savolainen
2013 Pre-Columbian Origins of Native American Dog Breeds, with Only Limited Replacement by European Dogs, Confirmed by mtDNA Analysis. *Proceedings of the Royal Society B: Biological Sciences* 280.

Vargas, Iraida
1985 Modo de vida: Categoría de las mediaciones entre formación social y cultura. *Boletín de Antropología Americana* 12:5–16.
1987 La formación económico-social tribal. *Boletín de Antropología Americana* 15:45–52.
1989 Teorías sobre el cacicazgo como modo de vida: El caso del Caribe. *Boletín de Antropología Americana* 20:12–35.
1990 *Arqueología, ciencia y sociedad*. Abre Brecha, Caracas.

Vargas, Iraida, and Mario Sanoja
1999 Archaeology as a Social Science: Its Expression in Latin America. In *Archaeology in Latin America*, edited by Gustavo Politis and Benjamín Alberti, 59–75. Routledge, London.

Veloz, Marcio
1984 Arqueología de la vida cotidiana. *Boletín de Antropología Americana* 10:5–21.

Veloz, Marcio, and Bernardo Vega
1987 Modos de vida cazadores-recolectores en el Caribe. *Boletín de Antropología Americana* 15:3–12.

Williams, B. J.
1974 A Model of Band Society. *American Antiquity* 39(4):12–24.

Winter, Marcus
2014 La prehistoria en Oaxaca: Avances recientes. In *Perspectivas de los estudios de la prehistoria en México: Homenaje a la trayectoria de Joaquín García Bárcena*, edited by Eduardo Corona and Joaquín Arroyo, pp. 123–142. INAH, México.

Woodburn, James
1982 Egalitarian Societies. *Man* (n.s.) 17:431–451.

# 5

# Production and Consumption

## Theory, Methodology, and Lithic Analysis

MYRIAN ÁLVAREZ AND IVAN BRIZ GODINO

The role of production in the economic organization of a given society has been recognized by many theoretical frameworks. Materialist approaches assume that every act of human existence is linked to social processes of production and, consequently, engendered in an economic dynamic. For that reason, the analytical category "mode of production" has been considered, from the "classical" writings of Marx and Engels onward, the cornerstone of Marxist theory and, consequently, of the Marxist archaeology.

However, for a long time attention drawn by production inquiry has frequently left aside the dialectical conception of historical materialism. Despite classical texts (Marx 1939, 1859, among others), a great number of innovative and interesting archaeological researches have not taken into deep consideration the role of consumption—in economic activities or in production processes. In contrast, from the initial works of Marxism, production and consumption were considered indissoluble elements of the productive process, and their interaction the first principle of economic activity: a dialectical union between two opposites. If the most basic element of economy is the dynamic interrelation between production and consumption mediated by human labor, the analytical equivalences to recover this active relation must incorporate both dimensions of the economic activity.

From the Marxist perspective, consumption entails the utilization of use-values at the productive or individual level within a given society. *Use-value* refers to the utility of goods or the specific way in which things meet human demands, and its materialization is achieved when the object is used or introduced in a productive process. Accordingly, mode of consumption is the analytical category addressed to identify how this use-value materialization is organized, under specific historical conditions, by its reintroduction in the process of production (Marx in *Das Kapital*, 1867). This reintroduction implies basically the transference of the labor investment contained in the product, into the new product or activity mediated by human work. Nevertheless, the use-value of a new product is also related with the activities in which it is embedded.

In the last two decades, the studies on consumption have recovered a renewable impetus mainly grounded on proposals of Bourdieu (1984), Miller (1987), Douglas and Isherwood (1990), and Appadurai (1986), among others. This trend gave rise to the archaeology of consumption generally associated under the framework of agency theory (Dobres and Robb 2000). The works of Michael Dietler (1998) addressing the ancient Mediterranean world, as well as the research of Paul Mullins (2011) about the archaeology of contemporary society, provide good examples of this movement, showing the great potential of this field of knowledge. But these analyses have mainly focused on trade patterns, colonial encounters, mass consumption, or food habits (Dietler 1998; Mullins 2011; Panich 2014; Silliman and Witt 2010, among others).

The common approaches tackling lithic technology, as well as hunter-gatherer research, have remained practically outside of this debate. While the mainstream of lithic technology research has expended a lot of effort attempting to identify variations in production processes, manufacture techniques, and tool morphologies, it has devoted relatively little attention to tool consumption, defined as the process of becoming a tool. Nevertheless, as Wobst (2000) cleverly argued, lithic artifacts are linked to peoples' intentions to change something; they are the evidence of human action trying to intervene in history. Consequently, an accurate understanding of production processes cannot be separated from the consumption dynamic.

Use-wear analysis, pioneered by the Soviet researcher Sergei A. Semenov (1957, 1964) and improved by a vast group of archaeologists, is the more important independent method to discover the tasks in which stone tools were used. Although his proposal was focused on labor processes, he established the basis of a method to undertake consumption studies in lithic and bone artifacts. Over recent years residue analysis has significantly grown (Barnard and Eerkens 2007; Haslam et al. 2009). However, despite the efforts made in use-wear and residue investigation, their analytical techniques have not been included in broad research programs to study temporal variations in production/consumption or in technological changes within hunter-gatherer societies (for example, Haslam has pointed out that residues analysis has been applied to small samples to solve particular problems).

Thus, the aim of this chapter is to propose a conceptual and methodological framework addressed to production-consumption interplay in order to highlight the complex nature of the technological sphere. From our standpoint, this duality not only holds the clues to attaining a full understanding of the economic organization of a given society but is also crucial to exploring important issues of social life such as technological innovations, identity, conflicts, symbolic agency, and social changes. The chapter unfolds in two parts. In the first section we discuss the concept of consumption and relate it to lithic technology. In the second part we provide an example to illustrate this approach.

## Disentangling Consumption: Theoretical Framework

With the exponential growth of social sciences during the twentieth century, the pioneering ideas set out in *Grundrisse* (Marx 1939) have been enhanced by studies carried out in capitalist as well as in noncapitalist contexts; thus, the concept of consumption was broadened from different theoretical approaches. From our point of view, three major axes form the basis of our proposal.

First, while consumption is a practice that can be undertaken by individuals or communities, it occurs within cultural and economic relationships: it is socially mediated (Briz 2002; Wurst and McGuire 1999).

Secondly, the object of consumption is the effective use-value materialized under specific social conditions. Therefore, the utility of goods is not restricted to the labor invested in their production, or to their exchange value; it also arises from the practice or activity in which an object is consumed, going beyond its intrinsic economic yield and including the symbolic aspects embedded in material culture (García Canclini 1981). Thus, consumption provides a fruitful arena where economic capital turns into symbolic capital (Bourdieu 1990).

Third, although production and consumption are inextricably linked, there is not a straightforward relationship between production-values and use-values; consumption is not simply a mirror of production but includes specific social relations that entail human access to particular objects as well as the interactions between individuals and goods in the act of consumption. At the same time, the utilization of goods and resources requires specific skills and knowledge, different from those applied in the production process (Ingold 1997).

This analytical division between the concepts of mode of production and mode of consumption opens the possibility to explore the interactions, the internal contradiction in the economic process, and the rhythms of change in both spheres, achieving more accurate explanations of social life and providing insights into social continuities as well as into creativity and human innovation. However, they cannot be isolated, since every productive activity engenders use-values for consumption and at the same time involves consumption of social labor and resources. Simultaneously, every act of consumption implies the effective materialization of use-values due to its inclusion in a productive activity: production of new use-values, production of human life, and production of social conditions. Every consumption is intended for the addition of use-value to production (including the production of the workforce) (Ruiz and Briz 1998). Human labor is socially and historically constructed through social relations of production and consumption. Both relationships (production and consumption) are different aspects of the same phenomenon: the material specificity of social construction of the work.

The mode of consumption is the analytical tool for recognizing social access to production results and the social activities to transform these products in values of use. Consumption, like production, is a social dynamic wherein the individual activity is shaped by the social relations of consumption. The essential element of the mode of consumption is the social processes of consumption: the type of interaction between the object of consumption and the subject of consumption (a final product incorporated into a production process as tool).

In the case of lithic technology research, raw material procurement and manufacture techniques have been acknowledged as the most influential aspects for making inferences about social life: many explanatory models in technological change are based on formal and quantitative variations of material culture. Accordingly, it is necessary to readdress the focus on production/consumption dynamics, which implies exploring dialectically how artifacts were made and how they were used as a result of single spatial-temporal praxis.

To accomplish this goal, we propose an approach based on three analytical steps. The first step is to unveil the production processes using a morpho-technical analysis aimed at understanding the sequence of production practices that led to the manufacture of a tool and are recorded in its morphological traits, from raw material provisioning to the activities related to tool rejuvenation. Labor investment in production, measured by identifying the number of tasks needed for making a tool, is an important analytical point of this proposal.

The second step consists of the study of the context of use of lithic artifacts. It is important to note here that a simple description of how a tool was used or what kinds of materials were transformed is insufficient to deal with the complex nature of consumption. Therefore, the analysis of the context of use implies identifying:

a) the activities performed by the artifacts: it includes the recognition of working materials and kinematics;
b) their spatial and temporal dimension: it means assessing whether the tools were used in daily or special activities, in common or restricted spaces; and
c) the knowledge and skills related to their use.

This concept goes beyond the term *function*, which often implies the more superficial target of a tool (e.g., to cut, to scrape, etc.), leading to an atomized view of human artifacts (Sigaut 1994). The context of use implies disentangling the network of relations in which these tools are interwoven; it has paramount importance to understanding the artifact designs and technological decisions.

Use-wear and residue analysis is the starting point for recognizing used edges and to determine the material worked and the mode of action of each tool; but their results have to be linked with contextual information. For example, the context of use of a scraper used in hide working recovered in a campsite is entirely different from another scraper also used in hide working recovered in a burial as part of grave goods.

The third step of our proposal refers to the relation of the design of a given tool to its context of use. From our point of view, this relationship provides material content to the labor process as well as to the production and consumption dynamic, allowing us to reveal the links between the different aspects of the economic cycle and to reveal the social relations embedded in these practices.

The research on form/function relationship is not new in archaeological inquiry, but the attempts dealing with this question had a scant level of success. The main obstacle of these approaches consists of trying to define correlations between predetermined types of artifacts (burins, scrapers, side scrapers), defined according to the typological schemes, with singular or specific functions (for example, the work of Heidi Knecht [1988], exploring the existence of patterns in form/function relationships in the case of burins). In other words, a common assumption that underlies these perspectives is the existence of a single function for each tool type (Briz 2004).

The present proposal attempts to deconstruct the way followed by classic typologies or other methodological proposals focusing primarily on the labor processes in which stone tools were employed to explore, in a second instance, which are the elements of design associated with a particular task. The aim is to move away from the underlying idealism and assumptions of the typological reasoning. Our point of reference is the end product; consequently, the use-wear data are used to structure the analysis. The first step is to discriminate different labor processes taking into account the kinematic and the worked material; and the second step consists of quantifying the morpho-technical variables using different statistical tests.

This approach offers the opportunity to recognize the socioeconomic organization of human groups. On several occasions, and especially in the case of hunter-gatherer groups, human societies are identified by specific material items, under a typological perspective. Concepts like "Clovis Culture" do not really allow a comprehensive economic analysis of this society and, at the same time, hamper a comparative analysis between sites or assemblages. The old and famous discussion between Binford and Bordes about the Mousterian is a perfect example of this problem (Binford 1988). The analytical identification of lithic assemblages from a production–consumption point of view affords a more accurate comprehension of lithic variability providing an independent dimension to morphological diversity (Briz 2002, 2004).

To illustrate this approach, we discuss an example of hunter-gatherers and fishing societies who inhabited Isla Grande de Tierra del Fuego, South America. We will focus on changes in consumption processes analyzing lithic knapping technology. We will attempt to show that lithic technology provides new insights to study production–consumption processes, essentially of those resources which do not preserve in the archaeological record, affording a more comprehensive picture of hunter-gatherer organization.

To accomplish these goals we study different lithic assemblages, retrieved in shell midden sites, dated from 6400 BP to the period of contact with Western populations in the nineteenth century (for more detailed information, see Orquera and Piana 1999; Orquera et al. 2011). Nevertheless, due to the samples sizes, we concentrate specifically on early and late occupations that span 6400–4200 BP and 2200 BP–nineteenthth-century contact period, respectively.

## A Southern Example: Production and Consumption Strategies in the Fuegian Channels

Isla Grande de Tierra del Fuego, located in the southernmost part of South America, constitutes the highest latitude landmass in the Southern Hemisphere populated by hunter-gatherer groups during the Early Holocene. Over 7,000 years, societies who established on the coast of the Beagle Channel (an inland passage that separates Tierra del Fuego from the southern islands of the Fuegian archipelago) developed a long-lasting social organization based on hunting, fishing, and gathering strategies as well as on the development of nautical technology (Orquera and Piana 1999; Orquera et al. 2011).

Technology comprises lithic and bone tools used for processing and capture resources. Stone tools include projectile points as well as retouched and natural flakes, while bone technology mainly encompasses various types of harpoon points, wedges, awls, chisels, and beads; some of these artifacts were decorated (Fiore 2011). The study of the zooarchaeological record shows that subsistence relied on pinnipeds, guanacos (*Lama glama guanicoe*), seabirds, fishes, mussels, and occasional cetaceans (Orquera and Piana 1999; Orquera et al. 2011; Tivoli and Zangrando 2011).

This maritime economy exhibits continuity along the sequence; however, noteworthy changes were identified in the consumption of faunal resources. During the early occupations, mammals such as pinnipeds and guanacos were predominantly exploited by Beagle Channel hunter-fisher-gatherers (Orquera and Piana 1999; Tivoli and Zangrando 2011; Zangrando et al. 2010). In contrast, during the Late Holocene, the relative importance of offshore fishes and birds significantly increases in the archaeological record, showing the expansion in ranges of maritime mobility (Tivoli and Zangrando 2011).

Bone technology also experienced changes along the sequence; its relative importance decreased, and chisels made on pinniped bones and stemmed wedges are absent in the archaeological record of late occupations. At the same time, in early occupations a larger number of types of artifacts were chosen for decoration, with a much broader range of decorative designs than in the following periods; design variability as well as the types of decorated artifacts was reduced drastically in later times (Fiore 2011).

For the purpose of this chapter, lithic assemblages retrieved from shell middens and dated in different time-frames were selected (Map 5.1). The early studied assemblages correspond to layers Upper F, E, and D of Túnel I site (Beta 3270: 6200 BP + 100; Beta 21969: 6470 BP + 110) and basal shell middens of Imiwaia I (AC 1397: 5872 BP + 147) (Orquera and Piana 1999). The late assemblages comprise Ajej I (AC 1584; 1400 BP + 90; Piana et al. 2008), Mischiuen I (AC 1623: 1060 BP +, 85; Piana et al. 2001), Shamakush I (AC 1292: 1020 BP + 100; Orquera and Piana 1999), and Túnel VII (AC 871 100 BP + 45) (Orquera and Piana 1999). Microwear traces were observed under a light-reflecting metallographic microscope Olympus BHSM at a magnification ranging from 100x to 500x. Use-wear analysis of these were carried out by M. Alvarez, except in the case of Túnel VII, analyzed by I. Clemente (1997). The unit of analysis has been the edges with diagnostic use-wear data, and the sample comprises 433 edges for early occupations and 435 for late occupations.

## Results

The great majority of lithics from the Beagle Channel sites were made of metamorphized rocks of acidic composition, among which rhyolites and fine-grained tuffs were identified. These rocks belong to the Lemaire Formation (Jurassic), which emerges along the Fuegian Andes. They account for more than 80 percent of the materials used to make instruments (Álvarez 2009). In quite low frequencies, schists, basalts, and shales were also exploited. The procurement of these materials must have been made in general in secondary deposits along the Beagle Channel, where they were transported by glacial and river flows (Álvarez 2003; Terradas 1997).

During the entire human occupation of this region, lithic processing tools show a low diversity and little standardization. Selected blanks, obtained by direct percussion using a hard hammer, include flakes of various shapes and medium sizes (maximum length of 4–8 cm). These blanks were used directly or mainly modified by unifacial trimming using hard and soft hammers: the most visible differences are in the degree to which the blanks have been retouched, in the length of the retouched edge, and in the edge angles.

These technical procedures account for morphologic variability of unifacial tools from approximately 6400 BP to the contact period. Bipolar technique was also applied to quartz cobbles, after 2600 BP, but in reduced frequencies. The labor investment in unifacial tool production was not considerable, so the production value of these assemblages was relatively low.

In contrast, bifacial technique, although it can be traced back to early occupations, significantly increases around 4000 BP, closely related to points manufacture (Álvarez 2007). However, bifacial processing tools exhibit a rare frequency in all studied archaeological sites.

* * *

In relation to consumption strategies, the same worked materials and motions were identified throughout the sequence: activities such as bone, wood, and hide working were developed from early times to the contact period (Figure 5.1). The Shannon-Weaver index (which measures diversity) shows similar values from both time frames: 1.36 for early occupations, and 1.46 for late occupations. Nevertheless, the distribution of frequencies between both periods is notably different: the chi square test confirms a significant difference between both distributions ($x^2 = 148.527$; $df = 4$; >.05). While consumption of hide and wood increases in late occupations, bone working and, in general, hard materials transformation diminish. It is important to remark that hide working could be underrepresented in early times due to problems of preservation; a good part of tools with wear traces identified as soft material could have been used to process hide. However, these artifacts do not show all the diagnostic features of hide working.

At the same time, if motions are also considered, it is clear that the relative importance of practices changes between both periods under study (Figure 5.2). The chi square test to assess whether both distributions are independent allows us to reject the null hypothesis: $x^2 = 250.724$; $df = 9$; >.05. For example, bone working with longitudinal motion exhibits a high

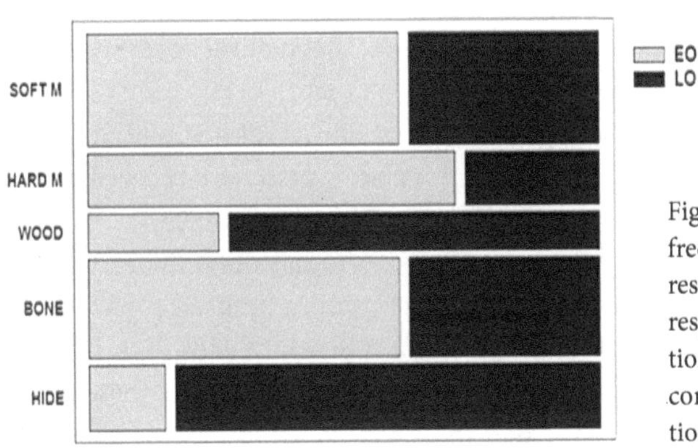


Figure 5.1. Relative frequencies of exploited resources: grey bars correspond to early occupations (EO); black bars correspond to late occupations (LO); M: material.

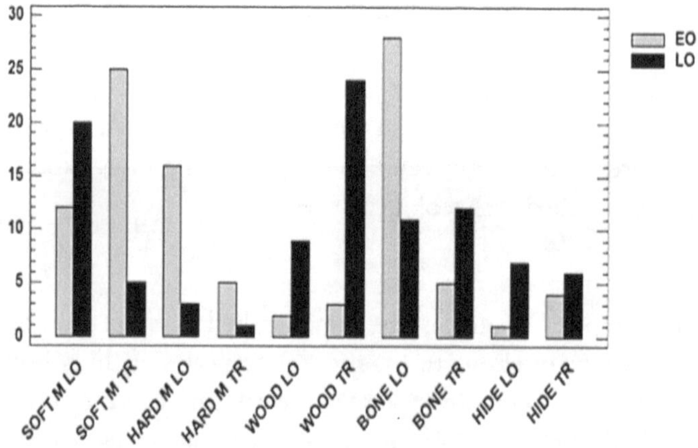


Figure 5.2. Relative frequencies of actions. TR: transverse motions; LO: longitudinal motions. Grey bars correspond to early occupations (EO); black bars correspond to late occupations (LO).

frequency during early occupations and then decreases in later times. In contrast, the ratio of bone working, with transverse motions, increases in the recent period; wood and hide working with transverse as well as longitudinal motions exhibits the same trend. In all these production activities, long and short retouched edges and unmodified flakes were used. Only bifacial tools show functional integrity: all of them were used in bone cutting.

Following our analytical line, we group the edges according to different work processes in order to unveil the design variables related to them. For the purpose of this chapter and with the aim of providing a general picture of the method, we select some variables to explore the production–consumption relationship: a) labor investment in edge modification; b) edge length, and c) edge angle.

In the first instance, we explore whether unmodified or retouched edges were related to specific tasks: one would expect that natural flakes would be chosen for longitudinal motions. In the case of early occupations (Figure 5.3), the results confirm the hypothesis ($x^2 = 58.723$; $df = 1$; >005), but in recent times (Figure 5.4) natural and retouched edges were indistinctively used for cutting and scraping activities ($x^2 = .575$; $df = 1$; >0.05).

Regarding material hardness, the data contradict our initial expectations, which proposed that retouched edges would be used for working hard materials, since they are more resistant to fracture. However, in early occupations (Figure 5.5), while natural edges were predominantly selected to process hard materials, retouched tools were used to process hard and

Figure 5.3. Relative frequencies of natural (nat) and retouched (ret) edges used in transverse (TR) and longitudinal (LO) motions in early occupations.

Figure 5.4. Relative frequencies of natural (nat) and retouched (ret) edges used in transverse (TR) and longitudinal (LO) motions in late occupations.

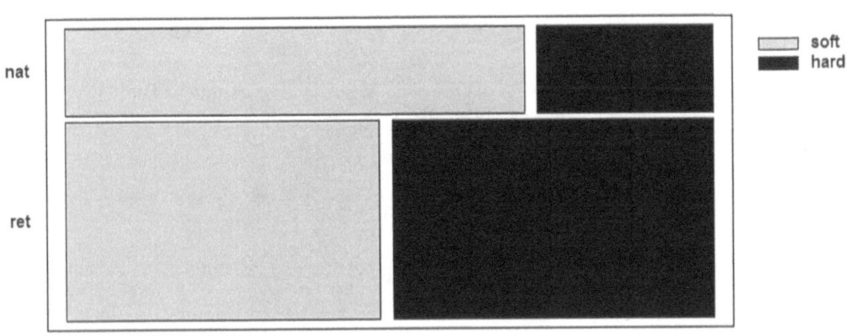


Figure 5.5. Relative frequencies of natural (nat) and retouched (ret) edges used to process soft and hard materials in early occupations.

Table 5.1. Results of the multiple range test in relation to edge length in artifacts of early occupations

| Materials and Motions | Homogeneous Groups | | | Significant Statistical Difference | Difference | ± Limits |
|---|---|---|---|---|---|---|
| Hide TR | X | | | Soft LO–Hide TR | 20,5667 | 10,3779 |
| Soft TR | | X | | Soft TR–wood TR | -12,2967 | 10,0195 |
| Bone LO | | X | | Soft TR–hide TR | 18,3588 | 9,59715 |
| Soft LO | | X | X | Hard LO–hide TR | 23,198 | 10,1883 |
| Hide LO | X | X | X | Hard TR–hide TR | 27,3632 | 12,3712 |
| Hard LO | | X | X | Bone LO–wood TR | -11,1627 | 10,0299 |
| Bone TR | | X | X | Bone LO–hide TR | 19,4929 | 9,60802 |
| Hard TR | | X | X | Bone TR–hide TR | 26,1 | 11,8067 |
| Wood LO | | X | X | Wood LO–hide TR | 29,3727 | 14,4958 |
| Wood TR | | X | | Wood TR–hide TR | 30,6556 | 12,5462 |

*Note*: TR: transverse motions; LO: longitudinal motions. X columns indicate that there are not statistical differences between the means.

soft materials ($x^2 = 19.140$; $df = 1$; >.05). The same trend was observed (Figure 5.6) in late occupations ($x^2 = 14.699$; $df = 1$; >.05).

In the cases of edge length and edge angle, we performed the multiple range test in order to compare the means values of each assemblage. This test provides significance levels for the difference between any pair of means. The result of the test comprises subsets of means, and each subset implies that they are not significantly different from one another.

For early occupations, three homogeneous groups were identified (Table 5.1). The X columns in Table 5.1 indicate that there are not statistical differences between the means. The general trend consisted of selecting larger

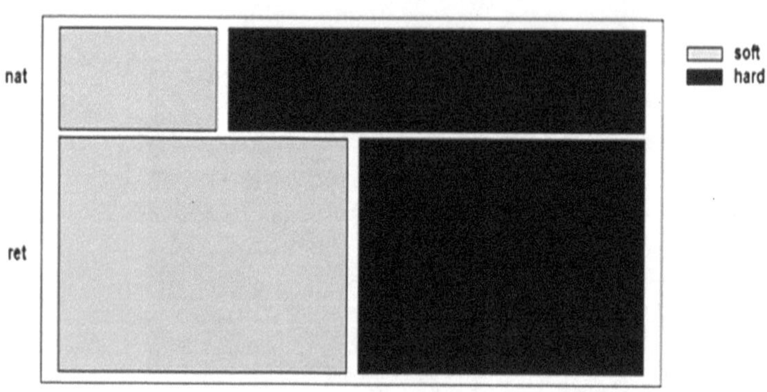


Figure 5.6. Relative frequencies of natural (nat) and retouched (ret) edges used to process soft and hard materials in late occupations.

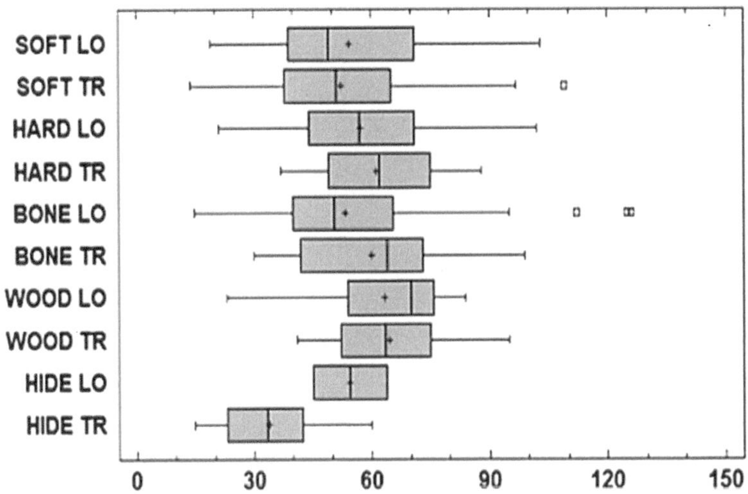


Figure 5.7. Box and whisker plots of edge length in artifacts of early occupations. TR: transverse motions; LO: longitudinal motions.

edges for longitudinal actions; however, there is a considerable overlapping between categories, except for transverse motions, where hide working displays significant differences from bone and wood working.

If we observe edge angles, two contrasting homogeneous groups are identified (Tables 5.2 and 5.3; Figure 5.8): one group formed by the artifacts

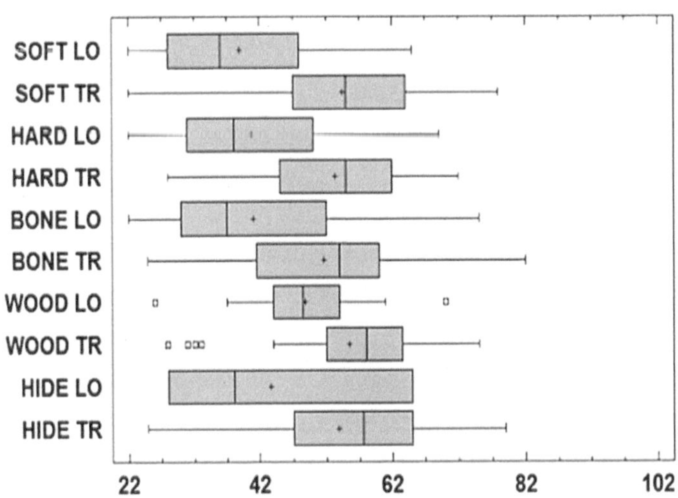


Figure 5.8. Box and whisker plots of edge angle in artifacts of early occupations. TR: transverse motions; LO: longitudinal motions.

Table 5.2. Results of the multiple range test in relation to edge angle in artifacts of early occupations

| Materials and Actions | Homogeneous Groups | |
|---|---|---|
| Soft LO | X | |
| Hard LO | X | |
| Bone LO | X | |
| Hide LO | X | X |
| Wood LO | | X |
| Bone TR | | X |
| Hard TR | | X |
| Hide TR | | X |
| Soft TR | | X |
| Wood TR | | X |

*Note*: TR: transverse motions; LO: longitudinal motions. X columns indicate that there are not statistical differences between the means.

Table 5.3. Significant statistical difference of the multiple range test in relation to edge angle in artifacts of early occupations

| Significant Statistical Difference | Difference | ± Limits |
|---|---|---|
| Soft LO–soft TR | -15,5802 | 4,13093 |
| Soft LO–hard TR | -14,4938 | 6,40495 |
| Soft LO–bone TR | -12,7633 | 5,8839 |
| Soft LO–wood LO | -9,87046 | 7,62223 |
| Soft LO–wood TR | -16,4776 | 5,8839 |
| Soft LO–hide TR | -14,9029 | 6,40495 |
| Soft TR–hard LO | 13,8046 | 4,22787 |
| Soft TR–bone LO | 13,5382 | 3,39722 |
| Hard LO–hard TR | -12,7182 | 6,4679 |
| Hard LO–bone TR | -10,9877 | 5,95236 |
| Hard LO–wood LO | -8,09481 | 7,6752 |
| Hard LO–wood TR | -14,7019 | 5,95236 |
| Hard LO–hide TR | -13,1273 | 6,4679 |
| Hard TR–bone LO | 12,4518 | 5,95818 |
| Bone LO–bone TR | -10,7213 | 5,39415 |
| Bone LO–wood LO | -7,82845 | 7,25086 |
| Bone LO–wood TR | -14,4356 | 5,39415 |
| Bone LO–hide TR | -12,8609 | 5,95818 |

*Note*: TR: transverse motions; LO: longitudinal motions.

Table 5.4. Results of the multiple range test in relation to edge length in artifacts of late occupations

| Materials and Actions | Homogeneous Groups | |
|---|---|---|
| Wood TR | X | |
| Hide TR | X | |
| Soft TR | X | |
| Hard TR | X | X |
| Hard LO | X | X |
| Bone LO | X | X |
| Bone TR | X | X |
| Wood LO | X | X |
| Soft LO | | X |

*Note*: TR: transverse motions; LO: longitudinal motions. X columns indicate that there are not statistical differences between the means.

that performed longitudinal actions, with lower values of edge angles, and a second group formed by artifacts that developed transverse actions with higher values in relation to the first one. But it is interesting to note two outcomes: a) there is not a statistical difference in the case of longitudinal hide working in regard to transverse motions; and b) in the case of longitudinal wood working, more abrupt angles were selected.

In the case of late occupations, longer edges were selected for longitudinal actions, mainly in soft materials working (Tables 5.4 and 5.5; Figure 5.9); in contrast, side transversal actions on wood, hide, and soft materials were developed with shorter edges. The analysis of edge angle shows more variability with four homogeneous groups, which indicates lower values associated with longitudinal actions and values around >50° related to transverse motions (Figure 5.10; Tables 5.6 and 5.7).

Table 5.5. Significant statistical difference of the multiple range test in relation to edge length in artifacts of late occupations

| Significant Statistical Difference | Difference | ± Limits |
|---|---|---|
| Soft LO–soft TR | 15,5 | 14,686 |
| Soft LO–bone TR | 9,8125 | 14,5542 |
| Soft LO–wood TR | 16,5667 | 14,686 |
| Soft LO–hide TR | 16,3462 | 15,0053 |

*Note*: TR: transverse motions; LO: longitudinal motions.

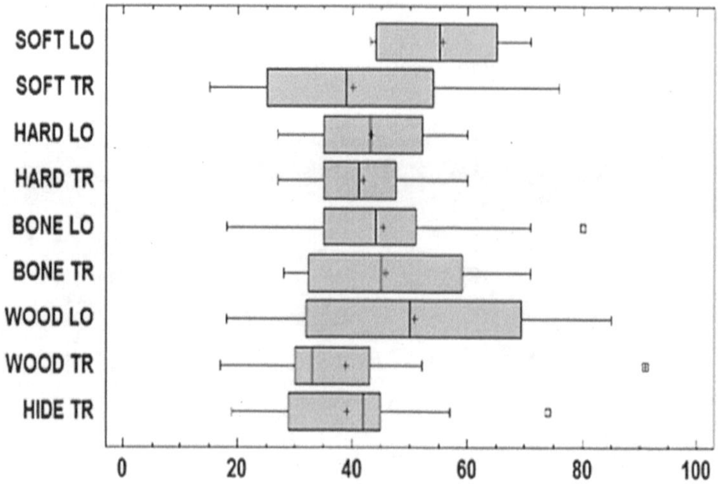


Figure 5.9. Box and whisker plots of edge length in artifacts of late occupations. TR: transverse motions; LO: longitudinal motions.

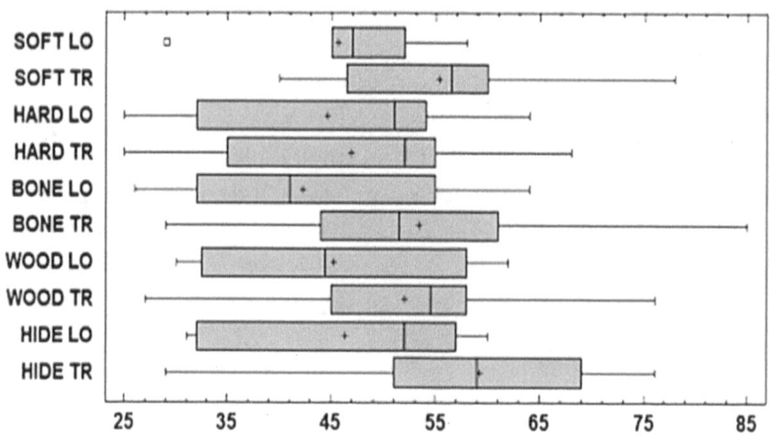


Figure 5.10. Box and whisker plots of edge angle in artifacts of late occupations. TR: transverse motions; LO: longitudinal motions.

Table 5.6. Results of the multiple range test in relation to edge angle in artifacts of late occupations

| Materials and Actions | Homogeneous Groups | | | |
|---|---|---|---|---|
| Bone LO | X | | | |
| Hard LO | X | X | | |
| Wood LO | X | X | X | X |
| Soft LO | X | X | X | |
| Hide LO | X | X | X | |
| Hard TR | X | X | | |
| Wood TR | | X | X | X |
| Bone TR | | X | X | X |
| Soft TR | | | X | X |
| Hide TR | | | | X |

*Note*: TR: transverse motions; LO: longitudinal motions. X columns indicate that there are not statistical differences between the means.

Table 5.7. Significant statistical difference of the multiple range test in relation to edge angle in artifacts of late occupations

| Significant Statistical Difference | Difference | ± Limits |
|---|---|---|
| Soft LO–soft TR | -9,68333 | 10,1994 |
| Soft LO–hide TR | -13,6111 | 10,3738 |
| Soft TR–hard LO | 10,7346 | 9,05279 |
| Soft TR–hard TR | 8,44524 | 7,93925 |
| Soft TR–bone LO | 13,0891 | 7,76904 |
| Hard LO–hide TR | -14,6624 | 9,24879 |
| Hard TR–hide TR | -12,373 | 8,16204 |
| Bone LO–bone TR | -11,1028 | 7,5778 |
| Bone LO–wood TR | -9,77759 | 7,27377 |
| Bone LO–hide TR | -17,0169 | 7,99657 |
| Hide LO–hide TR | -12,8778 | 12,8456 |

*Note*: TR: transverse motions; LO: longitudinal motions.

## Discussion

The diachronic study of production/consumption practices related to lithic technology between hunter-fisher and gatherer societies from Beagle Channel sheds light on the strategies developed by these populations in different moments of human occupation of the region.

During early and recent times, the production process related to lithic knapping technology was oriented toward the manufacture of tools with low production values, since the labor invested in reduction techniques was reduced. Examination of the production sequences showed that blanks with diverse morphologies were chosen to manufacture processing tools; the retouch resembles the form of the flake, and the differences between these artifacts lies in edge lengths and edge angles. The use-wear analysis also indicates that an important frequency of natural edges was directly used without further modifications.

These processing tools were consumed for domestic activities with the aim to transform several resources with different kinematics. Consequently, hunter-gatherer and fishing societies consumed large quantities of tools with low production costs because the same tool morphology could fulfill a wide variety of tasks. Through lithic technology, these societies achieved a high productivity level, since lithic blanks could be easily used with minor changes in edge morphology, allowing a more effective use of time. This production–consumption strategy was observed along the entire sequence of human occupation of the Beagle Channel region.

However, changes in consumption activities were also noted between early and late occupations. When comparing the resources exploited as well as actions in both time frames, there is a clear difference in the frequency of some activities. In general terms, the more striking disparities are observed in wood working, which increases in late times, and bone cutting, which relatively diminishes at the same moment. In previous works we proposed that the increment of wood working in recent times is probably related to shaft manufacture for weapon technology (Alvarez 2003).

Regarding changes related to labor investments and performance characteristics of lithic tools, we observe during early times a more specific use of natural edges related to longitudinal motions; in this case the main activities were bone and soft material cutting; contrastingly, the use of unretouched edges for transverse motions was infrequent. This practice changed in late occupations, since natural edges were employed in more varied activities that included longitudinal and transverse motions. This consumption change involved a diversification in their context of use as well as an increase of blank return rate to the extent that natural edges are less costly or require less labor investment.

A similar trend was identified with edge angles. During the first period under study, lower values of edge angles were used for longitudinal actions, and higher values for transversal motions. In late occupations more variability was detected, indicating a more flexible use of edges, though this general trend continued. In the case of edge length, the data show a considerable overlapping between actions, with slight preference for shorter edges for transverse motion, since they allow a better force application.

In sum, the results presented here suggest innovations in the production–consumption dynamic during the late occupations of the Beagle Channel region. These changes would have been part of a broader socioeconomic process that also led to transformations in subsistence strategies, land use, and bone technology. It is important to remark about several aspects here.

First, these changes do not exhibit a direct diachronic or causal correlation; the timing of these transformations did not coeval between the different spheres of production/consumption. Second, probably these modifications were gradual and took place over several hundred, or thousand, years of experimentation and practice. Although the rates of change accelerated between 2000 BP or 1500 BP and the moment of contact with Western populations, continuous transformations were, nevertheless, apparent over the entire period of occupation.

Third, these changes involved mainly quantitative variations. Throughout the historical trajectory of coastal occupations, changes in frequencies of resource exploitation were detected; in previous pages we referred to the increase of birds and fish procurement around 1500 BP. Likewise, lithic technology followed a similar trend: modifications in the relative importance of production–consumption activities as well as in labor investment were observed during late occupations. Simultaneously, decoration in portable art also experienced changes, reflected in the number of decoration techniques, the number of artifact types selected for decoration, and the motif repertoire (Fiore 2011).

Nevertheless, this fact does not imply minor or insignificant changes; on the contrary, all these changes had to involved innovations, a reorganization of practices (for example, time scheduling), and reorganization of labor to the extent that the resources exploited and the activities implied had their own dynamic (for example, temporal and spatial availability). According to the present evidence, these changes probably were closely tied to an increase in population density in the Fuegian archipelago during late occupations (Scheinsohn 1997; Zangrando 2009).

## Concluding Remarks

During recent years, the exponential improvement in archaeology of consumption has provided valuable theoretical and methodological tools for high-resolution and accurate explanations of the human past. Our present challenge is to include them in broad research programs related to lithic technology and hunter-gatherer archaeology intended to study social innovations. In order to accomplish this general goal, we propose a methodological approach to the study of production–consumption interplay, taking into account the relationship between morpho-technical and use-wear data.

Based on this approach to analyzing lithic strategies in Beagle Channel societies, a new picture of technological innovations emerges. Most of these innovations consisted of readjustments between production and consumption practices and implied changes in the frequency of resource exploitation and new strategies of taking advantage of tool morphology to increase their utility. It is important to note here that without the analysis of the context of use of stone tools, these differences would be interpreted as merely morphological variability, hampering a full comprehension of technological practices.

Probably, most of the changes presented here were geared to a better organization of time and labor and were closely linked to a process of intense innovations that included different spheres of social organization. Even though the results presented here are preliminary, they highlight the potential of this analytical line to explore subtle changes in design or morphologies, to tackle the problem of production and consumption interaction in lithic technology, and finally to understand the causal factors that gave rise to technological change.

## Acknowledgments

We are grateful to the editors of this volume for the opportunity to participate in this book. We also thank the anonymous reviewer for helpful comments. The site Túnel VII was excavated and analyzed by these projects: Contrastación Arqueológica de la Imagen Etnográfica de los Canoeros Magallánico-fueguinos de la Costa Norte del Canal Beagle (Spanish government) and Marine Resources at the Beagle Channel Prior to the Industrial Exploitation: An Archaeological Evaluation (European Union), coordinated by the Consejo Superior de Investigaciones Científicas (CSIC) of Spain. The sites Túnel I, Imiwaia I, Ajej I, Mischiuen I, and Shamakush I were excavated and analyzed in the frame of the different projects of the Proyecto Arqueológico Canal Beagle-PACB of the Centro Austral de Investigaciones Científicas of the Consejo Nacional de Investigaciones Científicas y Técnicas (CONICET) of Argentina.

## References Cited

Álvarez, Myrian

2003 Organización tecnológica en el Canal Beagle: El caso de Túnel I (Tierra del Fuego, Argentina). Doctoral thesis, Universidad de Buenos Aires, Buenos Aires.

2007 Procesos de producción y uso de instrumentos bifaciales entre los grupos canoeros del Canal Beagle. In *Arqueología de Fuego-Patagonia: Levantando piedras, desenterrando huesos . . . y develando arcanos*, edited by Flavio Morello, 247-255 CEQUA, Chile.

2009 Diversidad tecnológica en el extremo sur de Patagonia: Tendencias y continuidades en el diseño y uso demateriales líticos. In *Perspectivas actuales en arqueología argentina*, edited by Ramiro Barberena, Karen Borrazzo, and Luis Alberto Borrero, 243–267. CONICET.

Appadurai, Arjun

1986 Introduction: Commodities and the Politics of Value. In *The Social Life of Things: Commodities in Cultural Perspective*, edited by Arjun Appadurai, pp. 3–63. Cambridge University Press, Cambridge

Barnard, Hans, and Jelmer Eerkens

2007 *Theory and Practice of Archaeological Residue Analysis*. Bar International Series 1650. British Archaeological Reports , Oxford.

Bourdieu, Pierre

1984 *Distinction: A Social Critique of the Judgement of Taste*. Routledge, London.

1990 *The Logic of Practice*. Stanford University Press, Stanford.

Binford, Lewis

1998 *In Pursuit of the Past: Decoding the Archaeological Record*. Thames and Hudson, London.

Briz, Ivan

2002 Producción y consumo. In *Análisis funcional: Su aplicación al estudio de sociedades prehistóricas*, edited by Ignacio Clemente, Roberto Risch, and Juan Gibaja, pp. 43–51. Oxford: BAR International Series 1073. British Archaeological Reports, Oxford.

2004 Dinámiques econòmiques de producció-consum en el registre lític caçador-recollector de l'extrem Sud Americà: La societat Yàmana. Tesi doctoral. Servei de Publicacions de la Universitat Autònoma de Barcelona, Barcelona.

Clemente, Ignacio

1997 *Los instrumentos líticos de Túnel VII: Una aproximación etnoarqueológica*. Treball d'etnoarqueologia 2. Universitat Autònoma de Barcelona, Barcelona.

Dietler, Michael
1998 Consumption, Agency, and Cultural Entanglement: Theoretical Implications of a Mediterranean Colonial Encounter. In *Studies in Culture Contact: Interaction, Culture Change and Archaeology*, edited by John Cusick, pp. 288–315. Southern Illinois University Press, Carbondale.

Dobres, Marcia-Ann, and John Robb
2000 *Agency in Archaeology*. Routledge, London.

Douglas, Mary, and Baron Isherwood
1996 *The World of Goods: Toward an Anthropology of Consumption*. Routledge, London.

Fiore, Danae
2011 Art in Time: Diachronic Rates of Change in the Decoration of Bone Artefacts from the Beagle Channel Region (Tierra del Fuego, Southern South America). *Journal of Anthropological Archaeology* 30:484–501.

García Canclini, Néstor
1981 *Cultura y sociedad: Una introducción*. Cuadernos de Divulgación e Información para Maestros Bilingües. Dirección General de Educación Indígena. Mexico.

Haslam, Michael, Gail Robertson, Alison Crowther, Sue Nugent, and Luke Kirkwood (editors)
2009 Archaeological Science under a Microscope: Studies in residues and ancient DNA analysis in Honour of Thomas H. Loy. *Terra Australis* 30.

Ingold, Timothy
1997 Eight Themes in the Anthropology of Technology. *Social Analysis* 41:106–138.

Knecht, Heidi
1988 *Upper Palaeolithic Burins: Type, Form and Function*. BAR International Series 434. British Archaeological Reports, Oxford.

Marx, Karl
1939 *Grundrisse der Kritik der politischen Ökonomie*. Marx-Engels Institute, Moscow.
1859 *Zur Kritik der politischen Ökonomie*. Franz Dunder, Berlin.
1867 *Das Kapital, Kritik der politischen Ökonomie*. Otto Meissner, Hamburg.

Miller, Daniel
1987 *Material Culture and Mass Consumption*. Basil Blackwell, New York.

Mullins, Paul
2011 The Archaeology of Consumption. *Annual Review of Anthropology* 40:133–144.

Orquera, Luis, Dominique Legoupil, and Ernesto Piana
2011 Littoral Adaptation at the Southern End of South America. *Quaternary International* 239:61–69.

Orquera, Luis, and Ernesto Piana
1999 *Arqueología de la región del Canal del Beagle (Tierra del Fuego, República Argentina)*. Sociedad Argentina de Antropología, Buenos Aires.

Panich, Lee
2014 Native American Consumption of Shell and Glass Beads at Mission Santa Clara de Asís. *American Antiquity* 79:730–748.

Piana, Ernesto, Martín Vázquez, and Myrian Álvarez
2008 Nuevos resultados del estudio del sitio Ajej I: Un aporte a la variabilidad de estrategias de los canoeros fueguinos. *Runa* 29:87–100.

Piana, Ernesto, Martín Vázquez, and Nadia Rúa
2004 Mischiwen I: Primeros resultados de una excavación de rescate en la costa norte del Canal Beagle. In *Contra viento y marea: Arqueología de Patagonia*, edited by María Civalero, Pablo Fernández, and Gabriela Guráieb, 815–832. INAPL, Buenos Aires.

Ruiz del Olmo, Guillermina, and Ivan Briz
1998 Re-pensando la Re-producción. *Boletín de Antropología Americana* 33:79–90.

Scheinsohn, Vivian
1997 Explotación de materias primas óseas en la Isla Grande de Tierra del Fuego. Doctoral thesis. Universidad de Buenos Aires, Buenos Aires.

Semenov, Sergei
1957 Pervobitnaya technika. *Materialii i Issledovaniya po Arkheologii SSRR* 54.
1964 *Prehistoric Technology: An Experimental Study of the Oldest Tools and Artefacts from Traces of Manufacture and Wear*. Cory, Adams and Mackay, London.

Sigaut, François
1994 Technology. In *Companion Encyclopedia of Anthropology. Humanity, Culture and Social Life*, edited by Timothy Ingold, pp. 420–459. Routledge, London.

Silliman, Stephen, and Thomas Witt
2010 The Complexities of Consumption: Eastern Pequot Cultural Economics in 18th-Century New England. *Historical Archaeology* 44:46–68.

Terradas, Xavier
1997 Lithic Raw Material Procurement Strategies of the Yamana People (Tierra del Fuego, Argentina). In *Man and Flint. Proceedings of the VIIth International Flint Symposium, Warszawa–Ostrowiec Świętokrzyski, September 1995*, edited by Romuald Schild and Zofia Sulgostowska, pp. 123–126. Polish Academy of Sciences, Warsaw.

Tivoli, Angélica, and A. Francisco Zangrando
2011 Subsistence Variations and Landscape Use among Maritime Hunter-Gatherers: A Zooarchaeological Analysis from the Beagle Channel (Tierra del Fuego, Argentina). *Journal of Archaeological Science* 38:1148–1156.

Wobst, Martin
2000 Agency in (Spite of) Material Culture. In *Agency in Archaeology*, edited by Marcia-Ann Dobres and John Robb, pp. 40–50. Routledge, London.

Wurst, Lou Ann, and Randall McGuire
1999 Immaculate Consumption: A Critique of the "Shop till You Drop" School of Human Behavior. *International Journal of Historical Archaeology* 3(3):191–199.

Zangrando, A. Francisco
2009 Historia evolutiva y subsistencia de cazadores recolectores marítimos de Tierra del Fuego. Colección Tesis Doctorales, SAA, Buenos Aires.
Zangrando, A. Francisco, Luis Orquera, and Ernesto Piana
2010 Diversificación e intensificación de recursos animales en la secuencia arqueológica del Canal Beagle (Tierra del Fuego, Argentina). In *Zooarqueología a principios del Siglo XXI: Aspectos teóricos, metodológicos y casos de estudio*, edited by María Gutiérrez, Mariana De Nigris, Pablo Fernández, Miguel Giardina, Adolfo Gil, Andrés Izeta, Gustavo Neme, and Hugo Yacobaccio, 359–370. Ediciones del Espinillo, Buenos Aires.

# 6

# Kin-Mode Contradictions, Crises, and Transformations in the Archaic Lower Mississippi Valley

BRADLEY E. ENSOR

Like all modes of production, kin-ordered modes should contain contradictions within their social relations of production that lead to crises and transformations. However, the contradictions leading to crises are determined by specific kinship and marriage strategies. The effort to identify kinship relations in Marxist prehistoric archaeology is important when considering that tributary modes are relatively recent, characterizing only a small percentage of human existence in only some world regions. Marxist perspectives on prehistory should therefore be concerned with how kinship structured social relations of production, and how those relationships led to social changes over time.

This chapter takes a Marxist anthropological perspective on kinship and marriage *as* social relations of production. The ways that kinship variably structures the ownership of the means of production and how marriage systems structure surplus production are outlined. A model for contradictions and crises specific to "Crow/Omaha" kinship and marriage is described (Ensor 2003a, 2013:209–224), which is argued to explain the development and subsequent dissolution of large-scale mound building and craft exchange among Archaic foragers of the Lower Mississippi Valley (LMV), which are the earliest, and among the most enigmatic, examples of "social complexity" in North American prehistory.

## Contradictions, Crises, and Transformations

Emphasized in this chapter is Marx's premise that a given mode of production contains within its social relations of production contradictions leading to crises and ultimately transformation to a new mode of production.

This premise has been viewed as evolutionism, particularly during the reign of neoevolutionist ethnology and processualist archaeology. Classical Marxism certainly exhibits nineteenth-century evolutionism, expressed most prominently in Engels (1972). Historical perspectives of more recent post-processualist-related trends, in contrast, suggest that change is the result of historically contingent individual or collective agency, not an evolutionary trajectory of a "system." However, Marx (1964) provided an alternative perspective that would falsify the evolutionary/historical dichotomy. For Marx, every mode has its systemic trajectory caused by contradictions in its social relations of production (SRP) that channel human agency toward crises. In describing how noncapitalist modes transformed from one to another, he entertained alternative transformations as possible, and specific historical circumstances and human agency also explained the eventual outcomes. This is neither evolution nor historical but both, providing an alternative to neoevolutionist or hyper-agency perspectives. Moreover, because the contradictions leading to crises and eventual transformations are located within the SRP, this perspective lends itself to contemporary archaeological theories on change emphasizing endogenous social dynamics rather than exogenous forces.

## Kinship as SRP

Classical Marxism provides little clear guidance for understanding SRP in non-class-based societies (i.e., primitive communism) (see Rosenswig and Cunningham, chapter 1). In summarizing Marx's and Engels' knowledge, Hobsbawm states that "it was (at all events in the period when the Formen were drafted) thin on pre-history, on primitive communal societies and on precolumbian America, and virtually non-existent on Africa" (Marx 1964:26). The lacuna was left for anthropologists to fill, and the relationship between SRP and kinship was far better understood by the 1980s. This is reflected in Wolf's (1982) influential replacement of primitive communism with kin-ordered. "Put simply, through kinship social labor is 'locked up,' or 'embedded,' in particular relations between people" (Wolf 1982:91). Or, as Modjeska (1982:51) states, "to pursue the relations of production to their heart only to find structures of kinship is by now predictable."

SRP are the basis for defining modes: the ownership or control over the means of production (tools, natural resources, and lands) and the ways that labor is organized. The varied strategies by which kin groups are formed and reproduced are essential to understanding how SRP are organized in kinship modes. Unilineal descent groups are corporate groups in which members collectively own or control resources (estates), have collective obligations toward those resources, have collective obligations to one another, and share what Sahlins (2013) terms "mutuality of being": what one kin group member experiences is what all in the group experience. Gender is manipulated as a means for determining exclusive membership through either matrilineal or patrilineal descent. All other kin are excluded from membership, as they belong to their own exclusive matrilineal or patrilineal descent groups. Descent groups may be small, at the scale of the extended unilineal family, or larger, at the scales of lineages and clans. In Crow/Omaha social organization, there is segmentary structure whereby multiple unilineal families having a common unilineal ancestor form lineages (matrilineages or patrilineages), and multiple lineages having a common unilineal ancestor (known, unknown, or fictitious) form matriclans or patriclans. Typically, unilineal families own collective resources; lineages own additional collective resources or hold liens on property to assign to adult living members. At the largest scale, clans may or may not own additional resources; however, all members share mutual obligations of assistance to one another and sponsor ceremonial affairs for the group, or for the wider society. Unilineal descent groups are socially reproduced through exogamy (endogamy would dissolve the unilineal principles of membership) and unilocality (matrilocality or patrilocality), which keeps together the gender through whom descent and ownership are passed to children—the future members. In this way the children belonging to the group remain together at the estates of the group. Through unilocality, one gender is displaced from their descent groups' location to reproduce their spouses' groups. The descent groups are ideologically reproduced through ancestor veneration: those who granted all successive generations of members collective resources and obligations.

Cognatic resource-holding groups either base membership on ambilineal descent or use a flexible bilateral strategy. With ambilineal descent either line of descent can be the basis for negotiated but exclusive membership in a resource-holding group (e.g., Fox 1967). Other kin are excluded. With bilateral descent, in contrast, only household-scale corporate groups are formed. Household membership, and hence access to means of production, is negotiated through any genealogical and affinal relationships. Rather than being collectively subsumed under larger kin groups, the numerous households are interconnected through nonexclusive networks of members' bilateral relationships and marriages. Individuals and their households may flexibly use those numerous relationships for access to resources and additional support.

## Marriage as SRP

Attention to marriage systems is critical to explaining contradictions, crises, and transformations. Lévi-Strauss (1965, 1969) centralized marital alliances in kinship research, which has been significantly elaborated upon in functionalist literature (e.g., Fox 1967) and in political economic literature (e.g., Ensor 2003a, 2013:209–225; Rosman and Rubel 1971). There are three general categories of marital alliance systems: "elementary," "complex," and "Crow/Omaha." These marriage systems variably condition the need for competition through ceremony and surplus production and contain contradictions leading to crises.

Some marriage systems minimize competition among kin groups. As stated, unilineal groups must be exogamous for social reproduction. With elementary alliances, unilineal descent groups "exchange" members in a prescribed and reciprocal manner (Fox 1967; Lévi-Strauss 1969). In the "restricted" form, two exogamous unilineal groups exchange men or women across generations. In the "generalized" form, an exogamous group "gives" sons or daughters to a specified second group, which "gives" sons or daughters to a specified third group, and so forth. Although involving "indirect exchanges," the exogamous groups are linked together through the prescribed marriages, forming a reciprocal chain of alliances, reflected in the cosmological order, that ensures reciprocal access to all group's territories in times of need (e.g., Godelier 1984). Because the system is based on reciprocity, there is no intergroup competition to attract spouses, thus limiting the need for surplus production, while preventing intergroup status.

Other marriage systems compel competition among kin groups. The complex marriage system is associated with bilateral descent and the absence of descent groups. Marriage rules are *individual-based* taboos against marrying close biological relatives, not group-based rules (Fox 1967; Lévi-Strauss 1969). Marriages are potentially distributed widely around the society, unless there are preferences for localized endogamy. The implications are that each household group must compete with others to attract marriages. Unlike with elementary systems, spouses are not guaranteed. The households, as collectives, and any possible leaderships within them compete for prestige or rank through ceremony and feasting, which is also the context for marital alliances. Such competition requires surplus production, and the more successful household groups gain prestige or rank, and thus more marriage alliances. The competition required is a contradiction leading to social inequality in the distribution of marital alliances, along with potential ranking.

Among the three general marriage systems, the Crow/Omaha system requires the greatest investment in competition among kin groups. Crow/Omaha marriage has group-based proscriptions but no group-based prescriptions. Both Crow (with matrilineal descent groups) and Omaha (with patrilineal descent groups) have a primary rule for clan exogamy. In Crow societies there is usually an additional prohibition against members of one's father's clan, and often a third rule against members of the mother's father's clan (Fox 1967:224–227; Lévi-Strauss 1965). In the Omaha marriage system, there are additional prohibitions against members of one's mother's clan, and often one's father's mother's clan. In the absence of higher-order clans, the same marriage prohibitions may apply to lineages.

The Crow/Omaha marriage system structures intergroup competition and material exchanges (Rosman and Rubel 1971). Marriages often involve enormous payments by the groups (Fox 1967:232; Lévi-Strauss 1965; Rosman and Rubel 1971). Unlike elementary exchanges, the lack of prescribed marriage pools provides no guarantee of marriages and therefore creates competition among clans to attract spouses. Groups compete for prestige and marital alliances during practically all forms of ceremonies. Each household's ability to attract spouses in a Crow/Omaha marriage system is dependent upon the prestige of its clan, which is based on the group's, and its leadership's ability to successfully sponsor ceremonies and produce a substantial surplus in crafts and foods to give away. If the clan does not successfully compete for marriages, its prestige and survival are jeopardized.

## Crow/Omaha Crises Leading to Transformations

A common demographic trend resulting from competition among descent groups in a Crow/Omaha marriage system, which would not occur under the reciprocal (non-competitive) elementary system, is for some clans to grow larger as other clans decrease in population. Within the social context of Crow/Omaha kinship and marriage rules, people take action to ensure their group's survival and population growth, thus stimulating surplus production and ceremonial competition to actively attract marriages. A large population not only benefits the exogamous group as a collective but also benefits ceremonial leaders seeking to heighten their own status. Therefore, the leadership and the non-leaders of each clan utilize their labor and resources in an effort to attract more spouses than other clans. The successful clans attract more marriages than the less successful clans: the former increase in population at the expense of the latter. Once larger in population, the successful clans have a greater competitive edge in terms of labor, resources, and numbers of ceremonial leaders in addition to having a larger marriage pool with which to continue attracting spouses and initiating more families. Competitive disproportionate growth has been empirically documented among the nineteenth-century Omaha (Ensor 2003a) during a period when 96 to 100 percent of marriages adhered to the marriage rules (Ensor 2003b).

Such competitive disproportionate growth among clans should lead to crises. A "crisis in exogamy" can occur when the larger clans can no longer find enough potential spouses in the smaller clans. When considering that the rules for clan exogamy reproduce social organization, ceremonial organization, cosmology, and competitive surplus production for prestige, *a crisis in exogamy is a crisis in social reproduction* (Ensor 2003a, 2013:217–223). In other words, if the successful clans cannot maintain exogamy, then the social organization, reasons for ceremonial elaboration, and all of the social relationships based on these are threatened. Simultaneously, disproportionate growth may lead to crises in subsistence resources for the larger successful groups (e.g., Friedman 1984). Although disproportionate growth could also be expected among households competing in a complex marriage system, those groups are not necessarily reproduced through exogamy and thus would not experience the same crises.

Such crises may lead to different agency-guided transformations (Ensor 2003a; 2013:217–223). One solution is for the larger clans to fission into smaller clans, welcomed by junior leaders to form their own descent groups, which is possible if new resources are available. Although the larger clans would fission and establish newer smaller settlements, the Crow/Omaha SRP would continue, and the cycle of disproportionate growth would repeat again. Another solution is to relax the rules of exogamy, resulting in a complex marriage system that would dissolve unilineal social organization and reduce the scale of competitive surplus production. Alternatively, the descent groups could shift to an elementary, reciprocal marriage system requiring no competition.

In summary, the specific kinship strategies determine the SRP in a kin-ordered mode: how people gain membership to corporate resource-owning groups, and how those properties are collectively owned, inherited, and perpetuated. Socially reproducing the groups requires specific postmarital residence strategies to keep together those through whom membership and property flow to children: the future of the group. Ancestor veneration reproduces the groups through ideological means. Contradictions can be seen in the control over junior members' labor (although this is only temporary as juniors become elders) but particularly in the collective valuation of and control over women to reproduce memberships. The marriage systems are another aspect of SRP that contain contradictions. Elementary marriage systems may be more stable through reciprocal noncompetitive strategies. Households competing in a complex marriage system through ceremony and surplus production may lead to disproportionate growth and ranking. However, Crow/Omaha marriage systems require competition among large descent groups to attract marriages for more numerous members through far greater collective investments in ceremony and surplus production, leading to disproportionate demographic growth and, inevitably, crises in exogamy and/or resource carrying capacities, resulting in potential transformations.

## Archaeological Kinship Analysis

Because kinship changes, direct historical analogy with ethnohistoric or ethnographic characterizations is inappropriate for interpreting kinship practices long into prehistory. Linguistic semantic approaches to prehistoric kinship rely on kin terminology from historic or ethnographic societies and must make numerous methodological and theoretical assumptions to interpret ancient terminology, followed by structural functionalist assumptions to translate those into social behaviors. In contrast, archaeology and bioarchaeology have access to data that date to the prehistoric periods in question. Whereas bioarchaeological interpretive frameworks are still developing, archaeological approaches have made significant advances recently. Unlike the 1960s attempts at ceramic sociology (e.g., Deetz 1965; Hill 1966; Longacre 1964), the more recent approaches build upon research on how living spaces reflect social organization and ideology of relatedness. Middle-range factual correspondence (as opposed to merely logical coherence) between dwelling sizes and configurations have held up to cross-cultural testing, leading to plausible direct inferences on prehistoric residential groups, descent groups, and bilateral descent. These enable archaeological analyses of kinship strategies at multiple scales of organization, just as ethnographers separately analyze residence and descent. Furthermore, the framework enables archaeologists to observe variation (rather than assuming normative models typical of direct historical analogy and linguistic semantic approaches) and changes from phase to phase (rather than assuming theory-guided models of change). Archaeological kinship analysis also enables the observation of kinship practices and patterns not widely understood, described, or approachable by ethnology (e.g., Ensor 2013:97–99, 249–305).

The spatial layouts of settlements are known to reproduce both social organization and related cosmology (e.g., Keegan 2009; Knight 1998; Lewis and Stout 1998; Means 2007). Chang (1958) used HRAF-coded entries on community patterns and descent among 53 societies around the world to compare the settlement configurations of those with unilineal descent groups and bilateral descent. He found that 100 percent of the settlements for unilineal descent groups were formally planned with houses surrounding public plazas and/or ceremonial features. In contrast, settlements for bilateral societies were associated with homesteads, unplanned villages, and segmented villages, but not with planned villages (Chang 1958). Building on that early study, Ensor (2003a, 2003c) used lengthier descriptions of kinship to evaluate that included discussions on historic change and variation and the associated settlement layouts among 62 North American cultures. Comparisons were made between the settlement layouts among societies with exogamous unilineal descent groups having Crow/Omaha marriage systems and those with bilateral descent having complex marriage systems. All societies with matrilineal or patrilineal exogamous groups had formally planned settlements. Among societies with bilateral descent and complex marriage systems, settlements were unplanned: households were widely dispersed in a "ranchería" settlement pattern or aggregated into villages with informal arrangements. Therefore, exogamous unilineal descent groups can be recognized by formal layouts: habitations surrounding plazas and/or ceremonial structures. Although not distinguishing between matrilineal and patrilineal descent groups, Ember's (1973) method for identifying postmarital residence using dwelling sizes, confirmed by Divale (1977) and elaborated upon by Ensor using dwelling configurations (2003a, 2003c, 2013), can identify matrilineal versus patrilineal descent groups: they are matrilineal if accompanied by matrilocal residential groups, and patrilineal if combined with patrilocal residential groups. Where community patterns for bilateral descent are found, any form of residential groups (matrilocal, patrilocal, bilocal, etc.) are possible (see Ensor [2013] for discussion of these methods).

The explanation for the differences between settlements for unilineal descent groups and bilateral descent is that the former are corporate groups collectively sponsoring public ceremonies, dances, and feasts, which are the means by which they compete for prestige/rank and marital alliances. In addition to serving the practical purposes of hosting the competitive events, the formal layouts express the descent group's corporate identity. In contrast, settlements for communities having bilateral descent and a complex marriage system do not have village-scale collective ceremonial investments: each household group competes with others, and there is no need for settlement-wide collective ceremonial investments and formal planning. The complex marriage system structures interhousehold competitive agency, which differs from the corporate agency associated with Crow/Omaha systems.

In addition to testing for cross-cultural patterns in settlement layouts, Ensor's study (2003c:58–79) also identified cross-cultural patterns in regional settlement hierarchies associated with Crow/Omaha marriage systems. The descent group settlements with more numerous ceremonial responsibilities had larger populations, and those with fewer had small populations, which conforms to the model for disproportionate demographic growth. In contrast, none of the bilateral societies were associated with these material manifestations of ranking (Ensor 2003c:58–79). The same phenomenon should be visible through archaeological material culture: where unilineal descent group community patterns can be inferred, larger settlements can be predicted to have more ceremonial infrastructure than smaller settlements, and, with diachronic data, disproportionate growth should be observed. Diachronic disproportionate growth among descent groups competing through ceremony was also demonstrated among the prehistoric Hohokam (Ensor 2013:293–295).

Because competitive marriage systems also require feasting and vast quantities of gifts that accompany the ceremonial competition (Fox 1967:232; Lévi-Strauss 1965; Rosman and Rubel 1971), archaeological evidence for surplus food (e.g., communal food preparation, large cooking features, large storage features) and craft production of symbolic ornaments and ritual items exchanged widely should also be associated with community patterns reflecting Crow/Omaha and complex marriage systems. In contrast, unilineal descent group community patterns without much surplus production reflect noncompetitive, reciprocal alliances (elementary systems). Among the prehistoric Hohokam, craft production accelerated in an era of competing descent groups but was less intensive among household groups when bilateral descent was more common (Ensor 2013:293–295).

## The Archaic to the Tchefuncte Period in the LMV

Archaeological sites of the Early and initial Middle Archaic periods in the broader Southeast typically consist of camps for small groups (bands) and larger seasonal base camps (Bense 1994:69–72, 82). The base camps exhibit repeated use or intensive use for few episodes where food processing for feasting is evident (Bense 1994:69–71, 82). Within the LMV, the Middle and Late Archaic periods witnessed increasing mound building, production and exchange of symbolic artifacts, feasting, and plaza orientations. By the Tchefuncte period this large-scale settlement and mound building disappeared, accompanied by reductions in settlement sizes, long-distance trade, and surplus production for exchange.

### Middle Archaic (4000–2000 BCE)

The earliest mound building in North America occurred at around 3000 BCE during the Middle Archaic period in the LMV. Although the chronological data available on Middle Archaic sites are too limited to identify which sites were contemporaneous, a general picture is emerging whereby it is reasonably safe to conclude a range in settlement size and formality at any one time. There are two classes of community patterns among the Middle Archaic period sites: large formal sites with circular, elliptical, or semicircular midden ridges and mounds surrounding large plazas, and smaller semiformal sites with one to a few mounds near or adjacent to middens (Figure 6.1). The large formal mound sites (those having circular, elliptical, or semicircular midden ridges and mounds surrounding plazas) include Frenchman's Bend, Watson Brake, Caney Mounds, and Stelly Mounds (Gibson 1994; Jones 1983:121–124; Russo and Fogleman 1994; Saunders and Allen 1995:9–10; Saunders et al. 1994, 1997, 2005) (Figure 6.2a–c). These large formal settlements were occupied for most of the year and were in areas with the largest populations (Saunders 1994:133). There were more numerous semiformal sites (with one or more Middle Archaic mounds near or adjacent to Middle Archaic middens), which include the more firmly dated Lower Jackson Mound, Monte Sano, LSU, Hornsby, Banana Bayou, and Hedgepeth Mounds sites (Saunders 1994; Saunders et al. 1994, 1997, 2005). Mound excavations at some sites have demonstrated a

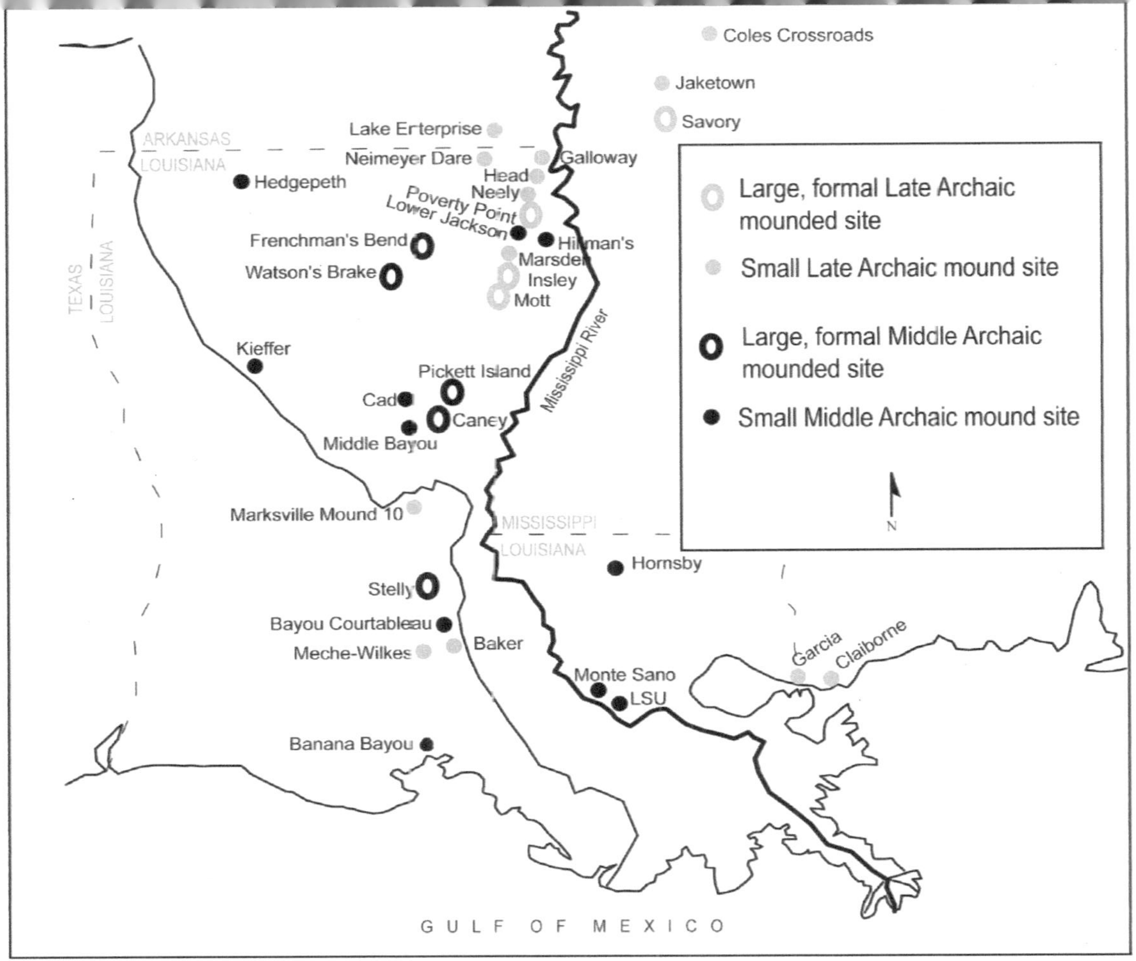


Figure 6.1. Archaic mound sites in the LMV.

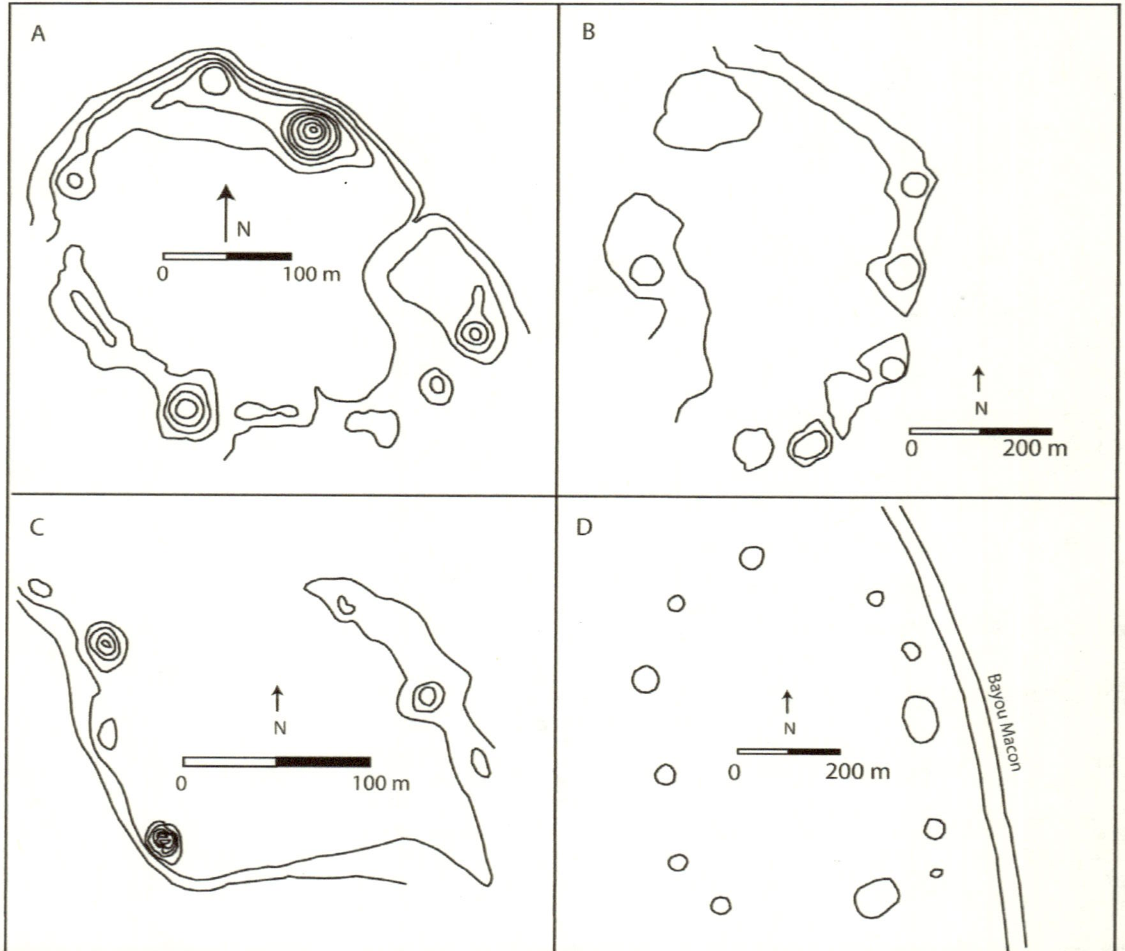


Figure 6.2. Sample of large, formal Archaic mound sites in the LMV. A) Watson's Break (redrawn from Saunders et al. 1997:Figure 1); B) Caney Mounds (redrawn from Gibson 1991:Figure 3); C) Frenchman's Bend (redrawn from Saunders et al. 1994:Figure 3); and D) the Insley site (redrawn from

shared pattern in mound construction over hearths, structures, and possible crematory features (Saunders 1994:133).

In addition to mound building was an intensification of surplus craft and food production. The large formal sites typically have several categories of nonutilitarian artifacts: beads, bannerstones, polished celts, and plummets, often from long-distance sources, in addition to lapidary tools and abraders for utilitarian and nonutilitarian craft manufacturing (Gibson 1994; Saunders 1994; Saunders et al. 1994). Assemblages also include fired clay blocks. Excavations in the middens surrounding the plazas yielded light to abundant quantities of fire-cracked rocks, indicating frequent or intensive cooking activities.

### Late Archaic and Poverty Point (2000–500 BCE)

By Late Archaic times, there are clearer indications of settlement size differences among formally planned mound-plaza settlements and smaller plaza settlements with few to no mounds (Gibson 1973, 1998; Kidder 1991; Webb 1982:13) (Figure 6.1). Despite the lack of secure dates for many of the individual mounds at Late Archaic sites, the overall picture appears to be a continuation of both large formal mound-plaza settlements and smaller formal and semiformal mound and non-mound settlements. The major differences with the Middle Archaic are the intensification in ornament production and trade and the appearance toward the end of the period of the largest village (Poverty Point) (Gibson 1994; Saunders and Allen 1995:18).

The majority of Late Archaic period mound sites are small, less formal, and have one or a few mounds. Collections at these sites include a similar range in artifacts, but in smaller quantities. The symbolic artifacts and nonlocal stone materials suggest that settlements of this size category participated in the same regional system of ceremony and exchanges but less intensively. The small mound sites that have been more firmly affiliated with the Late Archaic include the Claiborne, Lake Enterprise, Meche-Wilkes sites, and Mound 10 at Marksville (Bruseth 1980, 1991; Gibson 1994; Jackson and Jeter 1994; Webb 1970a, 1982). The Coles Crossroads, Neimeyer Dare, and Garcia sites are possible Late Archaic mound sites (Gibson 1994; Webb 1982). In addition to these sites are numerous possible, yet unconfirmed, Middle or Late Archaic mound sites (e.g., Gibson 1994; Saunders 1994) and those with a proposed Amite River phase (Gagliano and Saucier 1963).

Several large sites had formal community patterns. The Savory, Mott, Jaketown, and Insley Mounds sites (Gibson 1994; Griffing 1985; Kidder

1991; Webb 1970a, 1970b, 1982) (probable Late Archaic sites) had multiple mounds and middens forming elliptical and U-shaped community patterns surrounding extensive plazas. Insley (Figure 6.2d) is more safely affiliated with the Late Archaic (Gibson 1998) but may have been founded in the Middle Archaic.

The immense Poverty Point site represents formal community patterns to an extreme, having six parallel ridges, separated by aisles forming 36 ridge segments. The ridge segments form a semicircle around a plaza. Adjacent to the ridges and in the plaza are four mounds. Motley Mound is located to the north. Postholes, hearths, earth ovens, caches, and pits have been found on and off the ridges (Exnicios and Woodiel 1986; Gibson 1994:175; Haag 1986), indicating domestic activities. The numerous symbolic artifacts and nonlocal stone at the site suggest frequent material exchanges. Nonrandom spatial patterns in artifacts have been observed, suggesting that spatial areas were more associated with certain artifact styles even though the same artifacts can be found among other areas (Altschul 1986; Exnicios and Woodiel 1986; Gibson 1970, 1973, 1994; Haag 1986; Webb 1970b). By far the largest site in the LMV Archaic, Poverty Point gradually grew in situ over time (Gibson 1998, 2002).

There are numerous non-mound Late Archaic sites in the region surrounding Poverty Point (Gibson 1998). The Terral Lewis site may be representative, consisting of a midden similar to sites with one or few mounds. Collections yielded Poverty Point objects, steatite vessel fragments, nonlocal stone materials, and plummets found downslope from the midden (Gregory et al. 1970). The Teoc Creek site has a semicircular-shaped midden surrounding a plaza (Webb 1982:10). Similarly, the Slate site has a horseshoe-shaped artifact distribution (Lehmann 1981:41).

### Tchefuncte (500 BCE–CE 300)

The beginning of the Tchefuncte period marks the end of that early, long era of large mound sites and intensive craft production and exchange. Tchefuncte period sites are comparatively small and are widely dispersed along river levees and other areas adjacent to wetlands throughout the LMV. Both earthen and shell middens have been identified. Unlike the Middle and Late Archaic formal settlements, the Tchefuncte period middens do not encircle plazas. Low domed earthen mounds are occasionally found with middens, but there has been little investigation into their chronological associations (Neuman 1984:134). Domestic structures were found at the Lafayette and Little Oak Island sites (Ford and Quimby 1945:21; Gibson 1974:76), and

Shenkel (1981) concludes that the latter was intensely occupied, whereas the shell midden at the Morton site may have been seasonally occupied (Byrd 1976). Although the Tchefuncte period is the earliest with pottery, many of the cultural traits from the Middle and Late Archaic periods continued: Poverty Point clay objects, pipes, ornaments, plummets, bannerstones, stone vessels, abraders, faunal bone implements, and lapidary tools (Ford and Quimby 1945:29–51; Neuman 1984:127). The Tchefuncte site had two large, low *rangia cuteata* middens with 58 burials, pottery, clay pipes, Poverty Point clay objects, and utilitarian and nonutilitarian bone crafts (Lewis 1995:33). Lewis (1995:40–60) interpreted a range of ritual activities at the site in addition to the mortuary ceremonies. Burials were common in middens (Ford and Quimby 1945:25–27).

## Discussion and Conclusion

The thesis of this chapter is that like other modes of production, kin modes characterizing most of human prehistory also contain contradictions in their SRP. Focusing on Crow/Omaha kinship and marriage, unilineal descent is the relationship principle for corporate group membership and access to means of production, reproduced through exogamy and unilocal postmarital residence. Unlike noncompetitive elementary marriage systems, Crow/Omaha marriage creates competition for descent group prestige to attract spouses and ensure the success and perpetuation of the group, compelling collective intensification in ceremonial investments and surplus production. However, the marriage system results in the ethnohistorically demonstrated disproportionate demographic growth among the successful and less successful competing groups (the contradiction), hypothesized to eventually cause crises in exogamy and/or in resource carrying capacities for the larger, more successful groups. The outcomes entertained could include fissioning of the large groups and cyclical long-term repetition of disproportionate growth; shifting to a noncompetitive, reciprocal elementary marriage system; or relaxing exogamy, resulting in a complex marriage system and the consequential dissolution of unilineal descent groups. In the latter case, there would be a transformation to smaller corporate groups with bilateral descent competing less intensively in ceremony, feasting, and surplus craft production/exchange.

The cross-cultural tests of community patterns overwhelmingly support archaeological middle-range inferences on descent groups versus bilateral descent. Settlements for unilineal descent groups were always formally planned (with habitation surrounding plazas and/or ceremonial structures), whereas bilateral descent was nearly always associated with scattered *ranchería* settlement patterns or unplanned nucleated settlements. Unilineal descent groups having competitive Crow/Omaha marriage systems are most visible in mound building, plazas, surplus cooking for feasts, and craft production/exchange, which would be lacking among descent groups with noncompetitive, reciprocal elementary marriage systems. Similar surplus production, but at lesser intensity, is expected for competitive complex marriage systems associated with smaller corporate groups emphasizing bilateral descent networks.

The information available on the Archaic period of the LMV is less than ideal for testing the hypothesis on crises in Crow/Omaha SRP. Unlike with prior applications in the U.S. Southeast, Caribbean, and U.S. Southwest (Ensor 2003a, 2003c, 2013), evidence for contemporaneity, more specific chronological placements, and sequences for Archaic and Tchefuncte period LMV sites and their growth are limited. Additionally, without broad, horizontal excavation data, the specific kinds of residential groups at these sites, and hence matrilineal versus patrilineal descent groups, cannot be interpreted.

Nevertheless, some inferences on kinship and marriage can be made, which at least allow for inductive explanations on the development of the Archaic phenomena and the changes at the outset of the Tchefuncte period. Although current information does not enable specific interpretations on which form of unilineal descent groups were created, the formal plaza-focused layouts of many Archaic mound sites, which extends to the smaller non-mound sites in the Late Archaic, strongly suggest unilineal descent group organization that appeared continuously or periodically, throughout the LMV or in different localized areas, for approximately 2,500 years. The predicted co-occurrence of formally planned settlements (reflecting unilineal descent group organization) with intensified ceremony, feasting, and surplus craft production/exchange (indicating competitive marriage alliances) at those sites and increasingly through the Late Archaic suggest Crow/Omaha-like SRP. Issues of dating aside, the fact that formal settlements display potentially increasing hierarchies in sizes and numbers of mounds (including non-mounded sites also with formal layouts)—all of which participated in the same competitive feasting and surplus craft production/exchange—is expected for disproportionate demographic growth among the competing descent groups. Periodic crises in exogamy or foraging resources for the larger successfully competing descent groups may have led to eventual abandonments (partial or whole) of many of the larger sites and the establishment and growth into disproportionately sized sites after fissioning. It may be no coincidence that these trends disappeared after Poverty Point became the largest settlement ever witnessed in the region. If representing a settlement for the largest, most successfully competing exogamous descent group, then the surrounding regional populations would not be able to provide enough spouses, leading to crises in exogamy compelling regional expansion in marital alliances and surplus production through foraging. Difficult to imagine is how such dramatic disproportionate growth was sustained for several centuries. Crises in exogamy and very likely crises in foraging resources should ultimately have compelled transformative solutions.

The long era of competitive Crow/Omaha kinship and marriage appears to have ended at the beginning of the Tchefuncte period, which indicates what solutions to those crises were negotiated. The small size of the Tchefuncte period sites suggest settlements for extended households only. The middens do not surround plazas. The dispersed, informal settlements composed of small groups, and the continued albeit reduced craft production and exchange, reflect the cross-cultural pattern for bilateral descent and a competitive complex marriage system. The social transformation, therefore, can be interpreted as the consequences of relaxing the rules of exogamy, leading to new kin- and marriage-based SRP.

## References Cited

Altschul, Jeffrey H.

1986 A View from the Outside: A New Look at Areas Adjoining the Poverty Point Site. *Louisiana Archaeology* 13:101–112.

Bense, Judith A.

1994 *Archaeology of the Southeastern United States: Paleoindian to World War I.* Academic, San Diego.

Bruseth, James E.

1980 Intrasite Structure at the Claiborne Site. *Louisiana Archaeology* 6:283–318.

1991 Poverty Point Development as Seen at the Cedarland and Claiborne Sites, Southern Mississippi. In *The Poverty Point Culture: Local Manifestations, Subsistence Practices, and Trade Networks*, edited by Kathleen M. Byrd, pp. 7–25. Geoscience Publications, Baton Rouge.

Byrd, Kathleen M.

1976 Tchefuncte Subsistence: Information Obtained from the Excavation of the Morton Shell Mound, Iberia Parish, Louisiana. *Southeastern Archaeological Conference Bulletin* 19:70–75.

Chang, Kwang-Chih
1958 Study of the Neolithic Social Grouping: Examples from the New World. *American Anthropologist* 60:298–334.

Deetz, James
1965 *The Dynamics of Stylistic Change in Arikara Ceramics*. Illinois Studies in Anthropology No. 4. University of Illinois Press, Champaign.

Divale, William T.
1977 Living Floors and Marital Residence: A Replication. *Behavior Science Research* 12:109–115.

Ember, Melvin
1973 An Archaeological Indicator of Matrilocal versus Patrilocal Residence. *American Antiquity* 38:177–182.

Engels, Frederick
1972 *The Origin of the Family, Private Property, and the State*. Pathfinder Press, New York.

Ensor, Bradley E.
2003a Disproportionate Clan Growth in Crow–Omaha Societies: A Kinship-Demographic Model for Explaining Settlement Hierarchies and Fissioning in the Prehistoric U.S. Southeast. *North American Archaeologist* 23:309–337.
2003b Kinship and Marriage among the Omaha, 1886–1902. *Ethnology* 42:1–14.
2003c *Crow–Omaha Marital Alliances and Social Transformations: Archaeological Case Studies on the Taíno, Hohokam, and Archaic Lower Mississippi Valley*. Unpublished Ph.D. dissertation, University of Florida, Gainesville.
2013 *The Archaeology of Kinship: Advancing Interpretation and Contributions to Theory*. University of Arizona Press, Tucson.

Exnicios, Joan, and Deborah Woodiel
1986 Poverty Point Excavations, 1980–1982. *Louisiana Archaeology* 13:73–93.

Ford, James A., and G. I. Quimby
1945 *The Tchefuncte Culture, an Early Occupation of the Lower Mississippi Valley*. Memoirs of the Society for American Archaeology No. 2. Society for American Archaeology and Louisiana State University Press, Menasha.

Fox, Robin
1967 *Kinship and Marriage: An Anthropological Perspective*. Cambridge University Press, Cambridge.

Friedman, Jonathan
1984 Tribes, States, and Transformations. In *Marxist Analyses and Social Anthropology*, edited by Maurice Bloch, pp. 161–202. Malaby, London.

Gagliano, Sherwood M., and Roger T. Saucier
1963 Poverty Point Sites in Southeastern Louisiana. *American Antiquity* 28:320–327.

Gibson, Jon L.
1970 Intersite Variability at Poverty Point: Some Preliminary Considerations on Lapidary. *Southeastern Archaeological Conference Bulletin* 12:13–20.
1973 *Social Systems at Poverty Point*. University Microfilms, Ann Arbor.
1974 The Tchefuncte Culture in the Bayou Vermillion Basin, South Central Louisi-

ana: A Developmental Case Study. *Bulletin of the Texas Archaeological Society* 45:67–95.

1994 Before Their Time? Early Mounds in the Lower Mississippi Valley. *Southeastern Archaeology* 13:162–181.

1998 Elements and Organization of Poverty Point Political Economy: High Water Fish, Exotic Rocks, and Sacred Earth. *Research in Economic Anthropology* 19:291–340.

2002 *Behold the Wonderful Work of Their Hands: Poverty Point History and Sociality.* Paper presented at the 2002 Southeastern Archaeology Conference, Biloxi, Mississippi.

Godelier, Maurice

1984 Modes of Production, Kinship, and Demographic Structures. In *Marxist Analyses and Social Anthropology*, edited by Maurice Bloch, pp. 3–27. Malaby, London.

Gregory, Hiram F., Jr., Lester C. Davis, Jr., and Donald G. Hunter

1970 The Terral Lewis Site: A Poverty Point Complex in East-Central Louisiana. *Southeastern Archaeological Conference Bulletin* 12:35–46.

Griffing, David L.

1985 Surface Surveys of the Insley Site, Franklin Parish, Louisiana. *Louisiana Archaeology* 12:219–240.

Haag, William G.

1986 Excavations at the Poverty Point Site: 1972–1975. *Louisiana Archaeology* 13:1–36.

Hill, James N.

1966 A Prehistoric Community in Eastern Arizona. *Southwestern Journal of Anthropology* 22:9–30.

Jackson, H. Edwin, and Marvin D. Jeter

1994 Preceramic Earthworks in Arkansas: A Report on the Poverty Point Period Lake Enterprise Mound (3AS379). *Southeastern Archaeology* 153–162.

Jones, Reca B.

1983 Archaeological Investigations in the Ouachita River Valley, Bayou Bartholomew to Riverton, Louisiana. *Louisiana Archaeology* 10:103–169.

Keegan, William F.

2009 Central Plaza Burials in Saladoid Puerto Rico: An Alternative Perspective. *Latin American Antiquity* 20:375–385.

Kidder, Tristram R.

1991 New Directions in Poverty Point Settlement Archaeology: An Example from Northeast Louisiana. *Geoscience and Man* 19:27–53.

Knight, Vernon J., Jr.

1998 Moundville as a Diagrammatic Ceremonial Center. In *Archaeology of the Moundville Chiefdom*, edited by Vernon J. Knight, Jr., and Vincas P. Steponaitis, pp. 44–62. Smithsonian Institution Press, Washington.

Lehmann, Geoffrey R.

1981 The Slate Site, a Poverty Point Lapidary Industry in the Southern Yazoo Basin, Mississippi. *Louisiana Archaeology* 8:37–56.

Lévi-Strauss, Claude
1965 The Future of Kinship Studies. *Proceedings of the Royal Anthropological Institute of Great Britain and Ireland* 1965:13–22.
1969 *The Elementary Structures of Kinship*. Beacon, Boston.
Lewis, Barbara A.
1995 Tchefuncte Use of Animal Bone with Inferences for Tchefuncte Culture, Ritual, and Animal Cosmologies. *Louisiana Archaeology* 22:31–69.
Lewis, Barry R., and Charles Stout (editors)
1998 *Mississippian Towns and Sacred Spaces: Searching for an Architectural Grammar*. University of Alabama Press, Tuscaloosa.
Longacre, William A.
1964 Archaeology as Anthropology: A Case Study. *Science* 144:1454–1455.
Marx, Karl
1964 Pre-capitalist Economic Formations. International, New York.
Means, Bernard K.
2007 *Circular Villages of the Monongahela Tradition*. University of Alabama Press, Tuscaloosa.
Modjeska, Nicholas.
1982 Production and Inequality: Perspectives from Central New Guinea. In *Inequality in New Guinea Highland Societies*, edited by Andrew Strathern, pp. 50–108. Cambridge University Press, Cambridge.
Neuman, Robert W.
1984 *An Introduction to Louisiana Archaeology*. Louisiana State University Press, Baton Rouge.
Rosman, Abraham, and Paula G. Rubel
1971 *Feasting with Mine Enemy: Rank and Exchange among Northwest Coast Societies*. Columbia University Press, New York.
Russo, Michael, and James Fogleman
1994 Stelly Mounds (16SL1): An Archaic Mound Complex. *Louisiana Archaeology* 21:127–158.
Sahlins, Marshall
2013 What Kinship Is—And Is Not. University of Chicago Press, Chicago.
Saunders, Joe W., and Thurman Allen
1994 Hedgepeth Mounds, an Archaic Mound Complex in North-Central Louisiana. *American Antiquity* 59:471–489.
1995 The Archaic Period. *Louisiana Archaeology* 22:1–30.
Saunders, Joe W., Thurman Allen, and Roger T. Saucier
1994 Four Archaic? Mound Complexes in Northeast Louisiana. *Southeastern Archaeology* 13:134–153.
Saunders, Joe W., Rolfe D. Mandel, C. Garth Sampson, Charles M. Allen, E. Thurman Allen, Daniel A. Bush, James K. Feathers, Kristen J. Gremillion, C. T. Hallmark, H. Edwin Jackson, Jay K. Johnson, Reca Jones, Roger T. Saucier, Gary L. Stringer, and Malcolm F. Vidrine
2005 Watson Brake, A Middle Archaic Mound Complex in Northeast Louisiana. *American Antiquity* 70:631–668.

Saunders, Joe W., Rolfe D. Mandel, Roger T. Saucier, E. Thurman Allen, C. T. Hallmark, Jay K. Johnson, H. Edwin Jackson, Charles M. Allen, Gary L. Stringer, Douglas S. Frink, James K. Feathers, Stephen Williams, Kristen J. Gremillion, Malcolm F. Vidrine, and Reca Jones

1997 A Mound Complex in Louisiana at 5400–5000 Years before the Present. *Science* 277:1796–1799.

Saunders, Rebecca

1994 The Case for Archaic Period Mounds in Southeastern Louisiana. *Southeastern Archaeology* 13:118–134.

Shenkel, J. Richard

1981 Pontchartrain Tchefuncte Site Differentiation. *Louisiana Archaeology* 8:21–35.

Webb, Clarence H.

1970a Settlement Patterns in the Poverty Point Cultural Complex. *Southeastern Archaeological Conference Bulletin* 12:3–12.

1970b Intrasite Distribution of Artifacts at the Poverty Point Site, with Special Reference to Women's and Men's Activities. *Southeastern Archaeological Conference Bulletin* 12:21–34.

1982 *The Poverty Point Culture*, 2nd rev. ed. Geoscience and Man 17. Louisiana State University, Baton Rouge.

Wolf, Eric R.

1982 *Europe and the People without History*. University of California Press, Berkeley.

# 2

# PRE-STATE AGRICULTURALISTS

# 7

# The Tributary Mode of Production and Justifying Ideologies

## Evaluating the Wolf-Trigger Hypothesis

ROBERT M. ROSENSWIG

Long-standing tension within anthropology contrasts particularistic examination of individual case studies with generalizing research that makes cross-cultural comparisons. Particular histories matter if one is to fully understand the intricacies of the human condition. Local traditions and ideological principles provide both inspiration for and constraints upon the long-term patterns of cultural change studied by archaeologists. At the same time, identifying cross-cultural regularities is a primary strength of comparative anthropological study. The tension between research focused on particular historical trajectories and general comparative studies resulted in many archaeologists talking past each other during the "theory wars" of the 1980s and 1990s (Trigger 2006:529–548). Such scalar disagreement corresponds to the parallel divergence over whether the material or the ideational realm assumes a causative role in understanding cultural change (Lull and Mico 2011:148). In the Marxist tradition, the material-ideational dichotomy is often portrayed in terms of the architectural metaphor of a base and a superstructure. However, a basic tenet of historical materialism is that base and superstructure (as well as the economic and ideological/political realms more generally) are dialectically linked.[1] Patterson (2003:151–152) argues that "the German words translated as 'foundation' and 'superstructure' were apparently also slang terms used by German-speaking railroad workers in the mid-nineteenth century to refer to 'railroad tracks' and 'rolling stock.' If this was the case, then there was an alternative, more dynamic metaphor to the static one implied in the allusion to buildings" (see also Haldon 1993:41–46). Linking base and superstructure is the mode of production that describes the social and political organization that allows for the extraction and deployment of surplus, which is the subject of this volume (Rosenswig and Cunningham, chapter 1). The mode of production describes a dynamic and dialectical relationship, and, extending Patterson's analogy, would be the train wheels allowing boxcars to move along the track.

Ideological principles may be the result of particular local traditions as well as structures that are found cross-culturally. If local ideological traditions alone account for political and religious beliefs, then similarities in beliefs between peoples would occur only through diffusion or migration (as culture historians long ago assumed). Under such conditions, a distance-decay model would predict the distribution of ideas (organizational principles, etc.) radiating out from one (or various) ideological core zone(s). Conversely, if an ideological/political principle is documented repeatedly in unrelated areas of the world, then some sort of structural organization must be causing the convergence. Processualists generally assume organizational and ideological convergence to be ecologically determined (e.g., Binford 2001). For those influenced by the Marxist tradition, it is the mode of production where explanation should be sought to explain cross-cultural regularities. If similar ideological and/or political principles consistently occur among societies with a similar mode of production, then some aspect of political economic organization should be sought to explain the convergence. However, there is no reason that we need to make assumptions based on theoretical commitment alone. Instead, these ideas can be empirically evaluated. In this way Marxist-inspired archaeological research can provide new and unanticipated insights (e.g., McGuire and Saitta 1996) rather than support for preconceived assumptions.

## A Tributary Mode of Production and the Wolf-Trigger Hypothesis

Most of the prehistoric, complex societies studied by archaeologists have political economies organized with a tributary mode of production. In this I follow Wolf's (1982:75–100, 400–404; 2001:342–52) definition of capitalist, tributary, and kin-ordered modes of production. A tributary mode of production defines a political economy where surplus is extracted by political means. This is in contrast to a kin-ordered mode that relies on kin relations, and a capitalist mode where surplus is extracted by economic means (Rosenswig 2012:7–10; Rosenswig and Cunningham, chapter 1). In all cases surplus is defined as material goods resulting from labor beyond that needed to sustain the individual and his or her dependents.

The tributary mode defines the political economy of class-based societies that some archaeologists would call complex chiefdoms, as well as archaic states (Hirth 1996:220; Kristiansen 1991:17–18, 1998; Muller 1997:34–35). But rather than focus on typology, it is the relationship between the political and economic realms as well as local and regional power that gives the mode of production concept its dynamism (see Bate 1998:83–94; Chapman 2003:95–99; Gailey and Patterson 1988). To observe that a society operates in a manner consistent with a tributary mode of production tells us little by itself. Instead, it is far more enlightening to explore how a tributary political economy mobilizes and distributes surplus.

Eric Wolf proposed that in societies with a tributary mode of production, the economic organization would be justified by projecting earthly tribute extraction into the cosmic realm. In this he follows Gramsci's writing on hegemony where "political power could be gained through the construction of a predominant consensus" (Wolf 1999:44). That is, a society's commonsense practices and beliefs are established in such a way as to naturalize what are in fact politically charged principles that justify inequalities. For medieval European states, the justifying ideology was based upon a king's God-given right to rule. In modern nation-states, the justifying ideology of a president's or prime minister's right to rule is called democracy. In both cases this is taken as an unquestioned (unquestionable?) fact and is why (most) people willingly paid/pay taxes to underwrite a political system that did/does not represent their economic self-interests. Likewise, Wolf expects local hegemonies to make tribute payments a matter of moral responsibility by providing a religious rational. He proposed:

> The ideological model that parallels the tributary mode is typically a hierarchical representation of the cosmos in which the dominant supernatural order, working through the superior holders of power, encompasses and subjects humanity to itself. At the same time, the model displaces the real relation between power-wielding surplus takers and dominated producers to the ideological relations between superior deity and inferior "subject" (see Feuchtwang 1975). The problem of public power is thus transformed into a problem of private morality, and the subject is invited to win merit by maintaining order through the regulation of its own conduct. (Wolf 2001:348)

Wolf's assertion provides a clear hypothesis that cross-culturally documented organization of the political economy (in this case a tributary mode of production) constrains the structure of ideology. The alternative hypothesis is that beliefs about the structure of the cosmos are based on specific local traditions.

Bruce Trigger (2003) found support for Wolf's proposal among seven unrelated ancient civilizations. He documented a range of economic structures, but "cross-cultural regularities underlay the specific idiosyncratic religious beliefs of early civilizations . . . [that] . . . the universe nourished and sustained humanity but also that, if humans in turn did not nourish these deities with sacrifices, the deities would die and the universe lapse into chaos" (Trigger 2006:493). Trigger (2006:493) further concluded that "the beliefs that evolved independently multiple times in early civilizations were probably metaphorical projections of tributary relations that existed on the human plane into the cosmic realm" (see also Trigger 2008:63). The structure of elite appropriation of surplus production was reflected in a hierarchical cosmic realm. Trigger also notes the inverse: that societies with a kin-ordered mode of production envision the cosmos in terms of kin relations. As an example, "the Cree of northern Quebec regard human as only one among many forms of personhood that make up the cosmos and believe that good relations between hunters and animal spirits, usually expressed in terms of kinship, causes animals to sacrifice their lives to feed humans" (Trigger 2003:491). Trigger arrives at the same conclusion based on his sample of seven ancient states as did Wolf (1982) from his study of ethnographic and historic data.

Trigger and Wolf thus both present their observation that the economic relations underlying the tributary mode of production are reflected in the cosmos. I refer to this as the Wolf-Trigger Hypothesis, derived from each scholar's lifetime of anthropological research influenced by classical Marxist theory.[2] In the remainder of this chapter, I evaluate the Wolf-Trigger Hypothesis with ethnographic data from the Human Relations Areas Files' online database, eHRAF World Cultures (hereafter eHRAF). The eHRAF database (accessible at ehrafworldcultures.yale.edu/) is used to identify a representative sample of cultures and evaluate whether a society's cosmological structure is a reflection of its earthly tributary relations. The analysis that follows also evaluates the converse, that is, whether in societies that mobilize surplus through kin relations, this relationship is also reflected in the cosmic realm. Marx's *Ethnological Notes* (1974 [1880–1882]) and Engels' *Origins of the Family, Private Property and the State* (1972 [1891]) are examples of cross-cultural studies that were based on the newly emerging ethnographic record in the second part of the nineteenth century. I find it reasonable to propose that systematic cross-cultural research (such as that facilitated by eHRAF) is precisely the sort of empirical ethnographic study that Marx and Engels would have been interested in if they had had access to such resources (and see Anderson 2010:197–236; Gailey 2006).

## Material and Methods

The search for cross-cultural ethnographic patterns is a long-established method from which archaeologists infer prehistoric behavior and belief. This was an important part of what Binford (1962), rather idiosyncratically, called middle range theory (see Raab and Goodyear 1984; M. Smith 2011:168–170). Trigger (2006:508–519) broadens the range of linking arguments and refers to them as middle-ranging theory (also including ethnographic, experimental, and direct historical analogies). Cross-cultural patterns are referred to as "behavioral correlation" by Trigger (2006:509) that "depends on establishing, on the basis of ethnographic evidence, a cross-cultural correlation between two forms of behavioral or between a behavior and a belief." As defined in the previous section, the Wolf-Trigger Hypothesis is just such a proposed correlation between the organization of surplus extraction and forms of political/religious belief. The rationale for which the HRAF culture and subject classification systems were established is precisely to explore such cross-cultural patterns and establish an empirically based middle-ranging theory (Ember and Ember 1995; Peregrine 2001). The eHRAF database provides a research context within which ethnographic data can be queried in a reproducible manner and cross-cultural patterns can be sought.[3]

During the winter of 2014, when this study was undertaken, eHRAF provided ethnographic data on 280 societies from around the globe (the number has subsequently increased). The advantage of the eHRAF database is that hundreds of ethnographies are indexed on a paragraph-by-paragraph basis so that information can be efficiently and systematically searched. The cross-cultural approach undertaken here follows well-known studies such as that by Carr (1995), who used the HRAF system to follow up on Binford's (1971) and others' proposals about mortuary remains. Similarly, Feinman and Neitzel (1984) used cross-cultural analysis and concluded that redistribution was not actually a common feature of chiefdoms as Peebles and Kus (1977) (among others) had proposed. Cross-cultural studies are still regularly employed by archaeologists (e.g., Peregrine 2001; B. Smith 2011), and I will not review the literature further.

There are limitations to ethnographically based, cross-cultural studies.

For one thing, as Wobst (1978) is often cited for pointing out, what has been recorded by ethnographers is only a small part of all the cultures that have ever existed and all the forms of political and economic organization or ideological principles that have existed in the history of humankind. Another limitation is that virtually all ethnography is from the twentieth century and recorded in the context of European colonization and administration of conquered peoples. However, despite the limitations, the twentieth-century ethnographies are the only record we have. Therefore, just as with the archaeological record, which provides an incomplete and distorted material reflection of past behavior, it is more productive to account for (and control) biases than to despair at the limits they impose. The study that follows employs the incomplete and biased ethnographic record to evaluate the relationship between forms of surplus extraction and the nature of the cosmos in tributary and kin-ordered societies.

### Tribute

The following account represents my first attempt to use the eHRAF database and presents sufficient detail for the study to be replicated. I began by searching eHRAF for tribute in the "Browse Subjects" tab. This gave three results: 1) Tribute (peace term); 2) Tribute (praise); and 3) Tribute (public income). The third of these is what I was looking for and corresponds to the Outline of Cultural Materials (OCM) code 651 (Taxation and public income), described as follows:

> Sources of public income (e.g., gifts and bribes, tribute, registration and license fees, ground rents, profits from public enterprises, fines, confiscations, tolls, taxes); types of taxes (e.g., taxes in kind, labor levies, poll taxes, property taxes, stamp taxes, excise taxes, customs duties, income taxes, inheritance taxes); importance of and revenue from each type; differentiation by administrative level; principles of taxation; tax law; mode of fixing and collecting taxes; specialized personnel (e.g., tax collectors, tax consultants); tax exemptions; etc.

The search for this code, from the 280 societies in the HRAF database as of winter 2014, resulted in 8,582 paragraphs in 1,166 documents from 219 cultures. I further limited this sample using the Probability Sample Files (PSF), a stratified random sample of cultures distributed across 60 subregions of the world. The PSF sample consists of preindustrial societies that meet certain quality controls such as the ethnographers spending at least one year in the field (Naroll 1976). The result of my PSF sample of the

219 cultures resulted in a subsample of 52 cultural groups (Appendix 7.1). These 52 cultures include 331 documents (between 1 and 23 per culture), with 2,226 relevant paragraphs (between 1 and 267 per culture). I further limited the 52 cultures to the 37 with subsistence practices classified as intensive agricultural (n = 14), horticultural (n = 16) and hunter-gatherers (n = 7). Omitted from consideration were societies classified as pastoralist (n = 6) and "Other Subsistence Combinations" (n = 9). These 15 societies were omitted in order to generate clearer differences in the degree of intensification between subsistence practices. The resulting database of 37 societies is comparable in size to the 31 societies used by Carr (1995:126) to investigate ideological structures of burial practices.

My first goal was to determine whether the study was feasible (i.e., if eHRAF contained the type of information I needed) and to refine my coding variables. I began by reviewing only those societies with intensive agriculture. Being unfamiliar with eHRAF, I was not sure what tribute among hunter-gatherers would be referring to, and, if this might be simply taxation by colonial governments. The decision to begin by exploring societies with intensive agriculture was further made, as I thought that peoples with more intensive subsistence practices would have the most information on tribute and, so, the most productive way to begin coding the range of tribute patterns. The decision to begin with intensive agriculturalists was also based on the ease with which sample results, after an eHRAF "Advanced Search," can be limited by their subsistence types. By reading through each paragraph that eHRAF identified, I developed and then coded the three variables listed in Table 7.1 to characterize types of tribute.

For cultures with a small number of documents and paragraphs, it helped to also search for the keyword *tribute* in eHRAF's "Advance Search" function. So, for example, with the Ifugao of the Philippine highlands the search of OCM 651 (Taxation and public income) resulted in only one document, with each entry detailing *corvée* labor conscripted by colonial authorities in the mid-twentieth century for road building. However, a keyword search for *tribute* made it clear that there had in fact been no precolonial tribute among the Ifugao. This was the case for most hunter-gatherer societies. References to the word *tribute* among cultures that paid no tribute (in the extractive sense) were usually in relation to reciprocal gift-giving practices that had nothing to do with colonial rule or indigenous organization of the political economy. A common example is tobacco given as tribute in order to pass through a neighboring group's territory. This was the case for both the Ona of South America and the Ojibwa of subarctic North America.

Table 7.1. Coding variables to document tribute

| | |
|---|---|
| 1) Type of tribute | |
| 0 | unable to determine |
| 1 | crops/food/salt/craft objects |
| 2 | labor (military service, public works projects) |
| 3 | money |
| 4 | none |
| 2) Right of collecting tribute/taxes/fees: | |
| 0 | unable to determine |
| 1 | secular political office in nation-state |
| 2 | traditional chieftain/elite class with coercive power |
| 3 | traditional headman without coercive power |
| 4 | colonial official of a nation-state |
| 5 | none |
| 6 | conquering group in pre-European era but no rights internal to the culture |
| 3) Transference of rights to collect tribute | |
| 0 | unable to determine |
| 1 | position inherited |
| 2 | official appointed in theory but inheritance in practice |
| 3 | official appointed by higher power such as an indigenous king |
| 4 | individual elected by local community or appointed due to personal attributes |
| 5 | official appointed by colonial power |
| 6 | none |

Similarly, among the Blackfoot of the North American plateau, tobacco was offered before entering a body of water as tribute to water spirits, in order to be allowed to pass through their domain. The lack of any mention to tribute in political economic contexts allowed me to conclude that I was accurately documenting a lack of tribute and not just a lack of evidence.

## Cosmology

Two eHRAF OCM categories were used to ascertain how the cosmology of each culture related (or did not) to tribute relations. The first category explored was "General character of religion" (771), defined by eHRAF's OCM subject classification system as:

> Conception of what constitutes religion; differentiation of the sacred and the profane; distinctions drawn between religion and superstition; relation of religion to the unknown and the unpredictable; relative prominence of magical and anthropomorphic elements; evidence of the expression of projective mechanisms in religious beliefs; primary orientation of the religious system (e.g., ancestor worship, nature worship, totemism, ritualism, mysticism, redemptive religion); social and individual role of religion (e.g., services and disservices); incidence of faith, indifference, and skepticism; existence of non-supernatural ideologies supported with a faith akin to that in religion (e.g., ethical systems, political philosophies); etc.

The second category was Cosmology (772), defined in the OCM as: "Conception of the universe; cosmological systems (e.g., heavens and hells); universal categories (e.g., dualism of nature); etc." The search of these two categories resulted in a total 6,758 paragraphs in 615 documents for the 52 cultures.[4] For each of the 37 cultures that form the basis of this study, the search began with *Cosmology*, and frequently this produced all the information needed. If not, I proceeded with "General characteristics of religion." The variables listed in Table 7.2 were coded to characterize the nature of the cosmos relative to tribute when it existed and to characterize the organizing principles of the cosmos when it did not.

## Results

Of the sample of 37 cultures examined from eHRAF, 23 collected tribute (Table 7.3, Appendix 7.1). The subsistence economy of each cultural group did not always correspond to the presence or absence of tribute relations. For example, the Tlingit were hunter-gatherers who paid tribute, whereas two intensive agricultural groups (the southeast Asian Ifugao and North American Hopi) did not. However, these would appear to be the exceptions that emphasize a general pattern, as 85.7 percent of intensive agriculturalists in the sample paid tribute, and 83.3 percent of hunter-gatherers did not (see Table 7.3, Figure 7.1). Horticulturalists were more evenly split, with nine cultures (56.3 percent) with tribute and seven without (43.8 percent). A general pattern emphasized by this study is that more-intensive subsistence practices correspond to an increased likelihood of tributary relations. This is not surprising, as more intensive resources production corresponds with a greater surplus available to be appropriated. Intensification is by

Table 7.2. Variables used to characterize the cosmology of each culture

| | |
|---|---|
| **1) Source of order** | |
| 0 | unable to determine |
| 1 | divine hierarchy controls chaos of evil spirits and devils |
| 2 | royalty mediating between the dead and the living realms (including mediating relations with dead ancestors) |
| 3 | biological/organic analogy for well-being of the universe |
| 4 | principal of symmetry or balance in the universe |
| 5 | order per se is moot, as spirits inhabiting most living things (i.e., animism) or are based in local geographic features such as villages, rivers, mountains, etc. |
| 6 | chief's physical well-being (wealth) affects the health of the lands he controls and/or peoples who pay him tribute |
| **2) Cosmic organization parallels that on earth** | |
| 0 | unable to determine |
| 1 | yes, hierarchical |
| 2 | yes, non-hierarchical |
| 3 | no, earth hierarchical but cosmos non-hierarchical |
| 4 | no, earth non-hierarchical but cosmos hierarchical |
| **3) Direct analogy made between celestial god(s) and earthly political rulers or celestial order embodied by ruler** | |
| 0 | unable to determine |
| 1 | yes |
| 2 | no |
| 3 | yes, but spirits of indigenous peoples are viewed as good, and spirits of European colonials viewed as bad (e.g., Tzeltal) |
| **4) Political leaders well versed in religious books and/or religious traditions** | |
| 0 | unable to determine |
| 1 | yes |
| 2 | no, and society is literate |
| 3 | no, and society is nonliterate |
| **5) Major religious tradition introduced by colonial forces** | |
| 0 | unable to determine |
| 1 | Christian |
| 2 | Muslim |
| 3 | Confucian |
| 4 | Buddhist |
| 5 | Taoist |
| 6 | Hindu |
| 7 | Other |

Table 7.3. Subsistence practices in relation to tribute

| | With Tribute | | Without Tribute | |
|---|---|---|---|---|
| Subsistence | Count | % | Count | % |
| Hunter-gatherer (n = 6) | 1 | 16.7 | 5 | 83.3 |
| Horticultural (n = 16) | 9 | 56.3 | 7 | 43.8 |
| Intensive agriculture (n = 14) | 12 | 85.7 | 2 | 14.3 |

definition greater labor input resulting in increased production output. As ethnographic data are largely static, it is not possible to determine whether intensification of food production *caused* political hierarchy or if, inversely, political hierarchy caused increased resource production. These data simply show a correspondence.

The Tlingit case (of a hunter-gatherer group with tribute) highlights that it is not subsistence practices per se but the ability to produce surplus that increases the likelihood that tribute will be collected. Tlingit chiefs collected tribute for the use of fishing sites and hunting areas that they controlled access to. These same chiefs also controlled the labor of slaves and multiple wives and acquired wealth with which to host potlatches.[5] Such

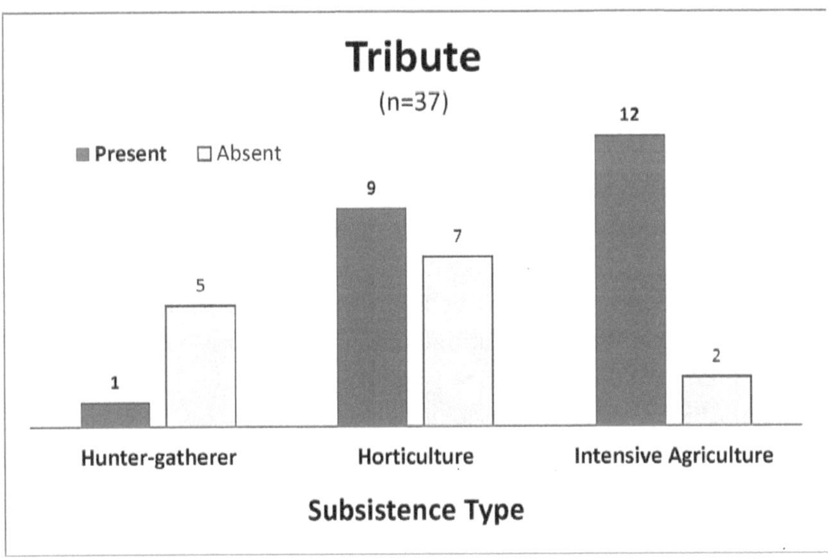


Figure 7.1. Tribute by subsistence practices among 37 cultures from PSF sample.

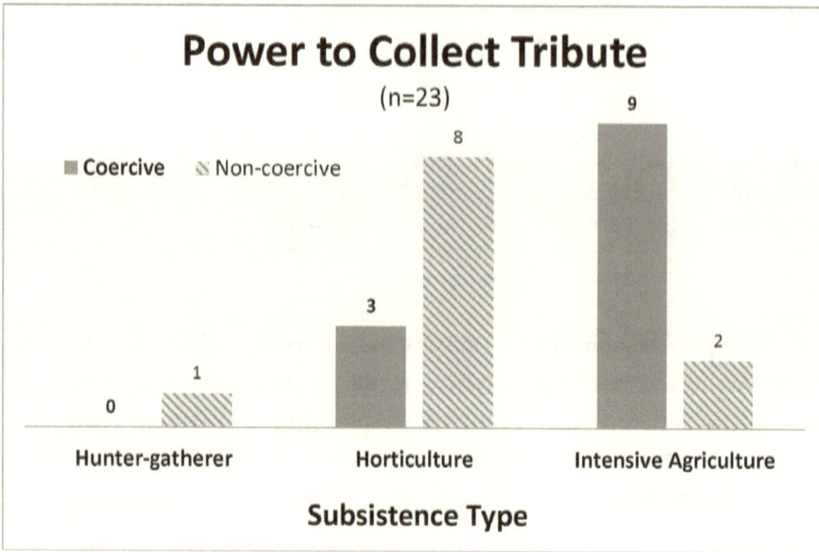


Figure 7.2. Right to collect tribute among 23 cultures in PSF sample with tribute.

earthly tribute relations were mirrored in the cosmic realm. The Tlingit believed that in the land above the sky (*Kiwa'a*), the playful activities of the dead are visible on earth as the Northern Lights. In this happy land there is also a chief who lives in a finely decorated house (DeLaguna 1972:795b). The Tlingit were thus an exception that proved the rule, because the wealth and prestige differences among the Tlingit on earth were also part of how they envisioned the celestial realm, providing a cosmic parallel to naturalize the elevated status and fine houses of earthy chiefs.

Earthly tribute was reflected in the cosmos. In 12 of the 23 societies in the subsample with evidence of tribute, rulers had coercive power to punish people for nonpayment (Figure 7.2). Of these 12 societies with coercive power, nine (six agriculturalists and three horticulturalists) made a direct connection between tribute-extracting rulers and a cosmos where rulers mediated between the supernatural and earthly realms. Only three cultures did not have this connection (Azande, Korea, Taiwan Hokkien), and among the Shluh of North Africa, the ethnographic account did not allow me to tell. For the Shluh, it was perhaps the influence of Islam that infused an egalitarian cosmic ethos into an otherwise hierarchical social order. Similarly, the Azande of southern Sudan and the Congo had chiefs who were paid tribute, and in precolonial times possessed coercive power and

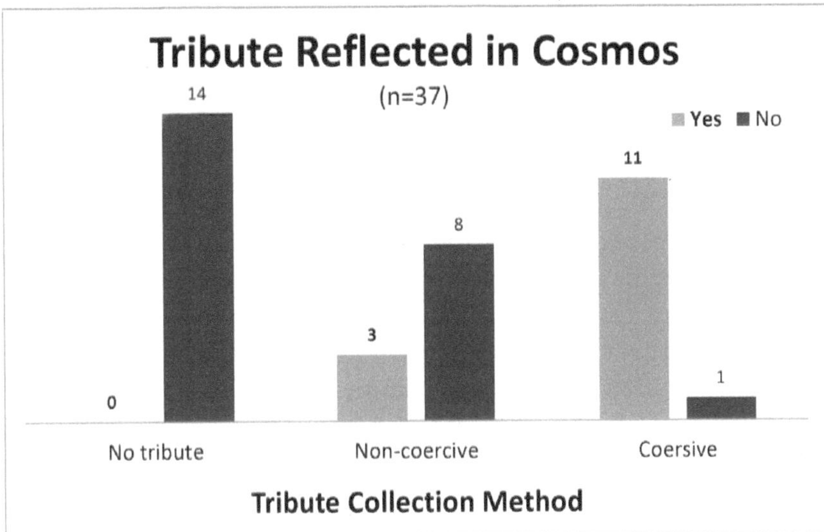


Figure 7.3. Tribute reflected in cosmology of 37 cultures from PSF sample.

could kill subjects for failure to pay tribute. However, in the cosmic realm, Mboli is the supreme force that embodies all living things in a nonhierarchical manner. Again, this cosmic egalitarianism could be due to deep-rooted Muslim syncretism.

The Wolf/Trigger Hypothesis was confirmed by how tribute was (or was not) reflected in the cosmos among the 37 culture samples from eHRAF (Figure 7.3). Of the 14 cultures without tribute, none had tribute incorporated into their cosmologies. Further, only the Azande (of the 12 cultures where tribute was extracted under coercive conditions) did not have tribute reflected in the cosmic realm. In contrast, all 11 other cultures with coercive tribute extraction did link earthly tribute payments to cosmic order. And of the eleven, eight cultures from the sample made direct and explicit links between rulers collecting tribute in the earthly realm and gods being paid tribute in the cosmic realm (Amhara, Ganda, Akan, Korea, Taiwan Hokkien, Sinhalese, and Central Thai). Neither finding is particularly surprising. However, only three of the 12 cultures with noncoercive tribute relations (Tlingit, Trobriands, and Kogi) had tribute reflected in their cosmologies, whereas nine cultures did not. It thus appears that the degree of coercive power possessed by a tribute-extracting elite has a clear impact on the likelihood that a supporting hegemony is in place. Wolf's and Trigger's observations, that cosmological justifying ideologies support earthly tribute collection, are consistent with my randomly selected sample of ethnographic cultures from around the world.

## Discussion

One of the values of grounding proposals derived from social theory in actual ethnographic data is to confront and explore exceptions to otherwise general patterns. Among the Trobriands, tribute payments to their chief are not really a matter of private morality (as Wolf proposed), and the cosmos was not arranged in a hierarchical manner to mirror the tribute paid to chiefs. However, failure to pay tribute throughout one's life was considered dangerous to one's health:

> . . . a man may be attacked because his gardens are too good. He can then be accused of emulating his betters, of not giving a fair proportion of his crops to the chief and to his relatives by marriage, and thus of acting disloyally and pandering to his own vanity and greed. This criticism is also not without its point, and when it comes to death, which is always attributed to sorcery, many a man is believed to have died because of his good gardens. Among the wabu, the marks which are found on the corpse at the exhumation which takes place soon after the first burial and which reveal the cause of death, there are not a few which are believed to mean that death was due to an excessive ambition or success in gardening. Taro-shaped tumours or an inordinate craving for this vegetable shortly before death signify that the deceased had too splendid taro-gardens or did not pay sufficient tribute of this commodity to the chief. (Malinowski 1965:175)

Therefore, while the cosmological realm does not reflect the political economy directly, there are serious supernatural repercussions for not complying with the tribute obligations. A similar belief was reported among the Kogi of northwestern South America, where earthly coercion was not necessary for the local Mamas (priests) to collect monthly tribute payments in food, because failure to pay was believed to bring sickness. Therefore, while not as simple as Wolf proposed, the end result was similar, as supernatural forces legitimized the indigenous political economy. As is often the case, exceptions to the rules are more illuminating in understanding why and how these rules function.

An insightful observation that emerges from this study is that recent colonial tax/tribute extraction was not reflected in the local ideology of any of the cultures from the eHRAF sample I explored. Instead, it was only indigenous traditions of tribute payment that were sanctioned cosmologically. This is true for all cases of recent colonial taxation by European powers. It is also true for cases where tribute was paid to non-European foreign colonizers. For example, the Iban of Sarawak in eastern Malaysia paid tribute to the sultan of Brunei through local hereditary representatives prior to direct contact with Europeans. During the fifteeth through eighteenth centuries, the sultan collected a door tax from each family, which was paid in rice. The Iban had an egalitarian ideology reflected in their conception of the cosmos. Further, local legends frequently tell of famous Iban warriors who successfully defied the sultan's tax collectors. Europeans were therefore not the first colonial power to demand tribute, and when the British arrived they simply took over the sultan's demands for regular rice payments. However, neither of these foreign tribute demands was supported by Iban conceptions of the cosmos, nor was either foreign power's tribute demands seen as legitimate. Similarly, the Tiv of Nigeria had no indigenous tribute tradition, and this is reflected by a nonhierarchical view of the cosmos. However, the Tiv did pay taxes to the colonial powers and grew beniseed as a cash crop solely to pay their taxes. The historical moment of twentieth-century ethnography captures a time when foreign powers were extracting tribute in a manner deemed illegitimate by most local peoples. If tribute collection had continued for a longer time, it is possible that beliefs could have been incorporated into local traditions, and so, eventually be seen as legitimate. However, the Iban case, with three centuries of Sarawak tribute demands, suggests that this might take a very long time.

## Conclusions

The Wolf-Trigger Hypothesis is supported by this study of 37 cultures randomly selected using eHRAF. My investigation confirms what Wolf (1982, 2001) "knew" based on his career as a comparative ethnographer and what Trigger (2003, 2008) documented among the seven ancient literate states he examined. That is, societies with a tributary mode of production generally understand the cosmic realm in a manner that reflects surplus extraction on the earthly plane. This is remarkable when we consider that ethnographic and historical records were created as European colonial powers were extracting tribute (what they tried to legitimize by calling taxes) that supplanted and appropriated traditional economic relations. The relationship between rulers and ruled is dependent on the legitimacy of the former and the compliance of the latter.

The cosmologically sanctioned right to collect tribute, and parallel hierarchies in the cosmic and earthly realms, should not necessarily be understood as simple false consciousness. Instead, economic relations of surplus extraction were negotiated in cosmic terms. Trigger (2003:490) notes that in the seven early civilizations he examined, "rulers and deities depended for their survival and well-being on the labour of farmers no less that farmers depended for an ordered, habitable, and fruitful universe on the upper classes and the gods. The three groups were linked by a pragmatic interdependence." This means that failure to pay taxes was a matter of moral responsibility (Wolf 2001:348), but also that unreasonable tribute/taxation was equally seen as a moral violation. Commoners could not criticize rulers in political terms but instead in terms of moral and religious wrongdoing. Such recourse to negotiable taxation rates thus formed a "religious constitution" of sorts (Trigger 2003:490–494).

I will not provide a detailed treatment of whether this makes commoners dupes and the victims of false consciousness. Briefly, my feeling is that many ancient commoners were dupes (but others were not) similar to the twenty-first-century citizens of nation-states who uncritically accept what their governments and media outlets tell them, while others do not. Are modern people dupes if they believe that the secular justifying ideology of political democracy and equality under the law justifies current economic inequalities in the United States and other wealthy countries? (I would answer yes). Furthermore, why is the egalitarian ethos of the cosmos espoused by the Judeo-Christian-Islamic tradition (i.e., that everyone goes to a heaven, where souls are all equal) so at odds with the unprecedented hierarchical earthly reality? Ever-increasing concentrations of wealth in a tiny elite class are a matter of morality and should be criticized as immoral in both secular and religious terms.

As is often the case, anthropological inquiry is enlightening for the cultures we study as well as for the insights provided into our own society. Modern "dupes" of political propaganda who consistently vote against their own economic/class interests are evidently part of a long-standing pattern of false consciousness that stretches into prehistory. While frustrating to modern political activists advocating change, this observation focuses analysis to those factors of ideology that result in individuals "buying in" to the political economy that exploits them. Marxist-inspired scholarship can thus inquire as to why and how this would be so. Future cross-cultural research could productively investigate the factors that contribute to exploited groups within society that buy in to exploitive relations versus factors that resist such relations (e.g., Scott 2008). For prehistoric societies where wealth discrepancies are documented, this study suggests that it is reasonable to assume local political/religious/jural institutions (aka superstructure) would have supported and justified the economic organization of these societies. The local detail (and specific forms of support) may vary from culture to culture, but the *function* of justifying ideologies will be broadly similar. That is, either political/religious/jural institutions support the economic organization of a society or else change will eventually occur. And how could it be otherwise? A political system deemed unjust can persist only with tremendous expense of colonization and military administration.

## Appendix 7.1

See page 168.

## Acknowledgments

Thanks are extended to Christiane Cunnar and the staff at HRAF for reading an earlier version of this paper and making sure I cited this important resource in the correct manner.

## Notes

1. I would further argue that the balance between the strengths of the causal arrow depends on whether one is interested in ultimate or proximate causality (Rosenswig 2012, 2015; and see Robb 2013). Proximate causality must be explained by the immediate, particular, and historically situated conditions. However, larger processes (be they environmental, adaptive, or organization of the political economy) account for cross-cultural regularities and ultimate causes. See Carr's (1995:115) discussion of ultimate/proximate causality in terms of Binford's (1971) cross-cultural approach to mortuary studies.

2. Hirth (1996:225–226) presents a similar proposal from a non-Marxist political economy perspective.

3. It is more common for archaeologists to employ ethnographic data to provide examples of the type of behavior they infer from archaeological remains. Such particularistic

use of ethnographic evidence is not as powerful a form of middle-ranging theory, because generalizable principles cannot be established. I am not arguing that the nonsystematic use of ethnographic information is without value, and, like most archaeologists, I have engaged in it (e.g., Rosenswig 2000, 2007).

4. I originally included an additional three OCMs: Mythology (773), Spirits and gods (776), and Theological systems (779). However, together the five categories generated 36,767 paragraphs in 859 documents for the 52 cultures. This seemed excessive, so the search parameters were reduced. Further, I originally attempted to combine Cosmology (772) with Chief executive (643) to try to get at the cosmological nature of rulers, but this did not produce the results I had hoped for.

5. This emphasizes the fact that exploring a society's political economic organization (generally) and mode of production (specifically) can provide more insight than comparing them simply in terms of their subsistence practices.

## References Cited

Anderson, Kevin B.

2010 *Marx at the Margins: On Nationalism, Ethnicity and Non-Western Societies.* University of Chicago Press, Chicago.

Bate, Luis Filipe

1998 *El proceso de investigación en arqueología.* Crítica, Barcelona.

Binford, Lawrence R.

1962 Archaeology as Anthropology. *American Antiquity* 28:217–225.

1971 Mortuary Practices: Their Study and Their Potential. In *Approaches to the Social Dimensions of Mortuary Practices,* edited by James A. Brown, pp. 6–29. Memoirs 25. Society for American Archaeology, Washington, D.C.

2001 *Constructing Frames of Reference: An Analytical Method For Archaeological Theory Building Using Hunter-Gatherer and Environmental Data Sets.* University of California Press, Berkeley.

Carr, Christopher

1995 Mortuary Practices: Their Social, Philosophical-Religious, Circumstantial, and Physical Determinants. *Journal of Archaeological Method and Theory* 2:105–199.

Chapman, Robert

2003 *Archaeologies of Complexity.* Routledge, London.

DeLaguna, Frederica

1972 *Under Mount Saint Elias: The History and Culture of the Yakutat Tlingit.* 3 vols. Smithsonian Contributions to Anthropology 7. Smithsonian Institution Press, Washington, D.C.

Ember, Melvin, and Carol R. Ember

1995 Worldwide Cross-Cultural Studies and Their Relevance for Archaeology. *Journal of Archaeological Research* 3:87–111.

Engels, Frederick

1972 [1891] *The Origins of the Family, Private Property and the State.* Pathfinder, New York.

Feinman, Gary, and Jill Neitzel
1984 Too Many Types: An Overview of Sedentary Prestate Societies in the Americas. *Advances in Archaeological Method and Theory* 7:39–102.
Feuchtwang, Stephan
1975 Investigating Religion. In *Marxist Analyses and Social Anthropology*, edited by Maurice Bloch, pp. 61–82. London, Malaby Press.
Gailey, Christine W.
2006 Community, State and Questions of Social Evolution in Karl Marx's *Ethnological Notebooks*. In *The Politics of Egalitarianism: Theory and Practice*, edited by Jacqueline Solway, pp. 31–52. Berghahn, New York.
Gailey, Christine W., and Thomas C. Patterson
1988 State Formation and Uneven Development. In *State and Society: The Emergence and Development Of Social Hierarchy and Political Centralization*, edited by John Gledhill, Barbara Bender, and Mogens Trolle Larsen, pp. 77–90. Unwin Hyman, London.
Haldon, John F.
1993 *The State and the Tributary Mode of Production*. Verso, London.
Hirth, Kenneth G.
1996 Political Economy and Archaeology: Perspectives on Exchange and Production. *Journal of Archaeological Research* 4:203–239.
Kristiansen, Kristian
1991 Chiefdoms, States and Systems of Social Evolution. In *Chiefdoms: Power, Economy and Ideology*, edited by Timothy Earle, pp. 16–43. Cambridge University Press, Cambridge.
1998 *Europe before History*. Cambridge University Press, Cambridge.
Lull, Vicente ,and Rafael Mico
2011 *Archaeology of the Origins of the State*. Oxford University Press, Oxford.
Malinowski, Bronislaw
1965 *Coral Gardens and Their Magic: Soil-Tilling and Agricultural Rites in the Trobriand Islands*. Vol. 1. Indiana University Press, Bloomington.
Marx, Karl
1974 [1880–1882] *The Ethnological Notebooks of Karl Marx (Studies of Morgan, Phear, Maine, Lubbock)*. Translated and edited by Lawrence Krader. Van Gorcum, Netherlands.
McGuire, Randall H., and Dean J. Saitta
1996 Although They Have Petty Captains, They Obey Them Badly: The Dialectics of Prehispanic Western Pueblo Social Organization. *American Antiquity* 61:197–216.
Muller, Jon
1997 *Mississippian Political Economy*. Plenum, New York.
Naroll, Raoul
1967 The Proposed HRAF Probability Sample. *Behavior Science Notes* 2:70–80.
Patterson, Thomas C.
2003 *Marx's Ghost: Conversations with Archaeologists*. Berg, Oxford.

Peebles, Christopher S., and Susan M. Kus

1977 Some Archaeological Correlates of Ranked Societies. *American Antiquity* 42:421–448.

Peregrine, Peter N.

2001 Cross-Cultural Comparative Approaches in Archaeology. *Annual Review of Anthropology* 30:1–18.

Raab, L. Mark, and Albert C. Goodyear

1984 Middle-Range Theory in Archaeology: A critical Review of Origins and Applications. *American Antiquity* 49: 255–268.

Robb, John

2013 Material Culture, Landscapes of Action, and Emergent Causation: A New Model for the Origins of the European Neolithic. *Current Anthropology* 54:657–683.

Rosenswig, Robert M.

2000 Some Political Processes of Ranked Societies. *Journal of Anthropological Archaeology* 19:413–460.

2007 Beyond Identifying Elites: Feasting as a Means to Understand Early Middle Formative Society on the Pacific Coast of Mexico. *Journal of Anthropological Archaeology* 26:1–27.

2012 Materialism, Mode of Production and a Millennium of Change in Southern Mexico. *Journal of Archaeological Method and Theory* 19:1–48.

2015 A Mosaic of Adaptation: The Archaeological Record for Mesoamerica's Archaic Period. *Journal of Archaeological Research* 23:115–162.

Scott, James C.

2008 *Weapons of the Weak: Everyday Forms of Peasant Resistance.* Yale University Press, New Haven.

Smith, Bruce D.

2011 General Patterns of Niche Construction and the Management of "Wild" Plant and Animal Resources by Small-Scale Pre-industrial Societies. *Philosophical Transactions of the Royal Society* 366:836–848.

Smith, Michael E.

2011 Empirical Urban Theory for Archaeologists. *Journal of Archaeological Method and Theory* 18:167–192.

Trigger, Bruce G.

2003 *Understanding Ancient Civilizations: A Comparative Study.* Cambridge University Press, Cambridge.

2006 *History of Archaeological Thought.* 2nd ed. Cambridge University Press, Cambridge.

2008 Early Cities: Craft Workers, Kings, and Controlling the Supernatural. In *The Ancient City: New Perspectives on Urbanism in the Old and New World*, edited by Joyce Marcus and Jeremy A. Sabloff, pp. 53–66. SAR Press, Santa Fe.

Wobst, H. Martin

1978 The Archaeo-Ethnology of Hunter-Gatherers or the Tyranny of the Ethnographic Record in Archaeology. *American Antiquity* 43:303–309.

Wolf, Eric
1982 *Europe and the People without History*. University of California Press, Berkeley.
1999 *Envisioning Power: Ideologies of Dominance and Crisis*. University of California Press, Berkeley.
2001 The Mills of Inequality: A Marxian Approach. In *Pathways of Power: Building an Anthropology of the Modern World*, by Eric Wolf, pp. 335–352. University of California Press, Berkeley.

Appendix 7.1

| | | Basic eHRAF Data | | | | Tribute Documents | |
|---|---|---|---|---|---|---|---|
| Country | Subregion | Culture Name | OWC | Subsistence Type | Samples | Documents | Paragraphs |
| Africa | Central Africa | Azande | FO07 | Horticulturalists | PSF | 8 | 111 |
| Africa | Central Africa | Mbuti | FO04 | Hunter-gatherers | PSF | 1 | 3 |
| Africa | Eastern Africa | Amhara | MP05 | Intensive Agriculturalists | PSF | 7 | 93 |
| Africa | Eastern Africa | Ganda | FK07 | Intensive Agriculturalists | PSF, SRS | 19 | 148 |
| Africa | Eastern Africa | Maasai | FL12 | Pastoralists | PSF | 2 | 7 |
| Africa | Eastern Africa | Somali | MO04 | Pastoralists | PSF | 6 | 24 |
| Africa | Northern Africa | Libyan Bedouin | MT09 | Pastoralists | PSF | 7 | 30 |
| Africa | Northern Africa | Shluh | MW11 | Intensive Agriculturalists | PSF | 4 | 28 |
| Africa | Southern Africa | Bemba | FQ05 | Horticulturalists | PSF | 4 | 38 |
| Africa | Southern Africa | Lozi | FQ09 | Other Subsistence Combinations | PSF | 8 | 90 |
| Africa | Western Africa | Akan | FE12 | Horticulturalists | PSF | 18 | 242 |
| Africa | Western Africa | Dogon | FA16 | Intensive Agriculturalists | PSF | 6 | 11 |
| Africa | Western Africa | Hausa | MS12 | Other Subsistence Combinations | PSF | 12 | 267 |
| Africa | Western Africa | Kanuri | MS14 | Intensive Agriculturalists | PSF | 6 | 59 |
| Africa | Western Africa | Tiv | FF57 | Horticulturalists | PSF | 7 | 31 |
| Africa | Western Africa | Wolof | MS30 | Horticulturalists | PSF | 16 | 92 |
| Asia | East Asia | Korea | AA01 | Intensive Agriculturalists | PSF | 23 | 146 |
| Asia | East Asia | Taiwan Hokkien | AD05 | Intensive Agriculturalists | PSF | 20 | 69 |

| | Tribute Data | | Cosmos Documents | | Cosmology Data | | | | | |
|---|---|---|---|---|---|---|---|---|---|---|
| | | | Documents | Paragraphs | | | | | | |
| e | Right | Transferring | | | Order | Parallel | Analogy | Well-versed | Colonial Religion | Done |
| 2 | 2 | 0 | 8 | 108 | 5 | 3 | 2 | 3 | 1 | 1 |
| | 5 | 6 | 5 | 53 | 5 | 2 | 2 | 3 | 7 | 1 |
| | 1 | 2 | 11 | 60 | 1 | 1 | 1 | 1 | 1 | 1 |
| 2 | 1 | 1 | 10 | 80 | 2 | 1 | 1 | 1 | 1 | 1 |
| | | | 8 | 17 | | | | | | |
| | | | 18 | 78 | | | | | | |
| | | | 4 | 16 | | | | | | |
| _3 | 2 | 2 | 4 | 27 | 0 | 1 | 0 | 0 | 2 | 1 |
| 2 | 2 | 1 | 5 | 250 | 6 | 0 | 1 | 3 | 0 | 1 |
| | | | 3 | 3 | | | | | | |
| 2 | 2 | 1 | 20 | 123 | 2 | 1 | 1 | 0 | 1 | 1 |
| | 4 | 5 | 24 | 683 | 3 | 2 | 2 | 3 | 2 | 1 |
| | | | 11 | 241 | | | | | | |
| | 2 | 1 | 4 | 12 | 1 | 1 | 2 | 1 | 2 | 1 |
| | 5 | 6 | 12 | 170 | 4 | 2 | 2 | 3 | 1 | 1 |
| 2 | 3 | 1 | 14 | 53 | 5 | 3 | 2 | 0 | 2 | 1 |
| 3 | 2 | 1 | 32 | 318 | 4 | 1 | 1 | 1 | 3_4 | 1 |
| 3 | 1 | 3 | 30 | 489 | 4 | 1 | 1 | 0 | 4_5 | 1 |

(*continued*)

Appendix 7.1—*Continued*

| Basic eHRAF Data | | | | | | Tribute Documents | |
|---|---|---|---|---|---|---|---|
| Country | Subregion | Culture Name | OWC | Subsistence Type | Samples | Documents | Paragrap |
| Asia | North Asia | Chukchee | RY02 | Pastoralists | PSF | 1 | 3 |
| Asia | North Asia | Yakut | RV02 | Other Sub-sistence Combinations | PSF | 7 | 49 |
| Asia | South Asia | Garo | AR05 | Horticulturalists | PSF | 5 | 8 |
| Asia | South Asia | Khasi | AR07 | Other Sub-sistence Combinations | PSF | 9 | 36 |
| Asia | South Asia | Santal | AW42 | Intensive Agriculturalists | PSF | 3 | 13 |
| Asia | South Asia | Sinhalese | AX04 | Intensive Agriculturalists | PSF | 3 | 24 |
| Asia | Southeast Asia | Central Thai | AO07 | Intensive Agriculturalists | PSF | 12 | 34 |
| Asia | Southeast Asia | Eastern Toraja | OG11 | Horticulturalists | PSF | 5 | 14 |
| Asia | Southeast Asia | Iban | OC06 | Horticulturalists | PSF | 9 | 53 |
| Asia | Southeast Asia | Ifugao | OA19 | Intensive Agriculturalists | PSF | 1 | 10 |
| Europe | British Isles | Highland Scots | ES10 | Other Sub-sistence Combinations | PSF | 7 | 25 |
| Europe | Scandinavia | Saami | EP04 | Pastoralists | PSF | 14 | 155 |
| Europe | Southeastern Europe | Serbs | EF06 | Intensive Agriculturalists | PSF | 9 | 51 |
| M America | Central America | Kuna | SB05 | Horticulturalists | PSF | 6 | 44 |
| M America | Maya Area | Tzeltal | NV09 | Horticulturalists | PSF | 5 | 8 |
| M America | Northern Mexico | Tarahu-mara | NU33 | Agro-pastoralists | PSF | 3 | 3 |
| N America | Arctic and Subarctic | Ojibwa | NG06 | Hunter-gatherers | PSF | 2 | 6 |
| N America | Eastern Woodlands | Iroquois | NM09 | Horticulturalists | PSF | 10 | 21 |

| Tribute Data | | | Cosmos Documents | | Cosmology Data | | | | | |
|---|---|---|---|---|---|---|---|---|---|---|
| | | | Documents | Paragraphs | | | | | | |
| pe | Right | Transferring | | | Order | Parallel | Analogy | Well-versed | Colonial Religion | Done |
| | | | 4 | 99 | | | | | | |
| | | | 11 | 46 | | | | | | |
| 4 | 5 | 6 | 12 | 43 | 5 | 2 | 2 | 2 | 1 | 1 |
| | | | 11 | 74 | | | | | | |
| _2 | 3 | 0 | 7 | 57 | 4 | 2 | 2 | 3 | 0 | 1 |
| _3 | 2 | 3 | 6 | 131 | 1 | 1 | 1 | 0 | 4_6 | 1 |
| _2 | 2 | 2 | 19 | 365 | 1 | 1 | 1 | 0 | 4 | 1 |
| _2 | 6 | 5 | 5 | 87 | 3 | 2 | 2 | 3 | 2 | 1 |
| 1 | 6 | 5 | 19 | 124 | 5 | 2 | 2 | 3 | 2 | 1 |
| 4 | 5 | 6 | 19 | 125 | 5 | 2 | 2 | 3 | 7 | 1 |
| | | | 13 | 163 | | | | | | |
| | | | 15 | 67 | | | | | | |
| 3 | 1 | 5 | 9 | 59 | 1 | 3 | 2 | 3 | 1 | 1 |
| 4 | 5 | 6 | 16 | 107 | 1 | 3 | 2 | 3 | 1 | 1 |
| 4 | 1 | 4 | 3 | 20 | 5 | 3 | 3 | 2 | 1 | 1 |
| | | | 7 | 57 | | | | | | |
| 4 | 5 | 6 | 26 | 217 | 5 | 2 | 2 | 3 | 1 | 1 |
| 4 | 5 | 6 | 28 | 530 | 4 | 2 | 2 | 3 | 1 | 1 |

(*continued*)

Appendix 7.1—*Continued*

| | | Basic eHRAF Data | | | | Tribute Documents | |
|---|---|---|---|---|---|---|---|
| Country | Subregion | Culture Name | OWC | Subsistence Type | Samples | Documents | Paragraph |
| N America | Northwest Coast and California | Tlingit | NA12 | Hunter-gatherers | PSF | 1 | 5 |
| N America | Plains and Plateau | Blackfoot | NF06 | Hunter-gatherers | PSF | 3 | 8 |
| N America | Plains and Plateau | Klamath | NR10 | Hunter-gatherers | PSF | 3 | 10 |
| N America | Southwest and Basin | Hopi | NT09 | Intensive Agriculturalists | PSF | 5 | 9 |
| Oceania | Melanesia | Trobriands | OL06 | Horticulturalists | PSF | 4 | 13 |
| Oceania | Micronesia | Chuuk | OR19 | Other Subsistence Combinations | PSF | 7 | 37 |
| Oceania | Polynesia | Lau Fijians | OQ06 | Other Subsistence Combinations | PSF | 4 | 12 |
| Oceania | Polynesia | Tikopia | OT11 | Horticulturalists | PSF | 4 | 6 |
| S America | Amazon and Orinoco | Saramaka | SR15 | Other Subsistence Combinations | PSF | 1 | 1 |
| S America | Amazon and Orinoco | Yanoama | SQ18 | Horticulturalists | PSF | 1 | 1 |
| S America | Central Andes | Aymara | SF05 | Horticulturalists | PSF | 4 | 42 |
| S America | Eastern South America | Bahia Brazilians | SO11 | Intensive Agriculturalists | PSF | 3 | 20 |
| S America | Eastern South America | Guaraní | SM04 | Other Subsistence Combinations | PSF | 2 | 7 |
| S America | Northwestern South America | Kogi | SC07 | Horticulturalists | PSF | 2 | 6 |
| S America | Southern South America | Mataco | SI07 | Primarily Hunter-gatherers | PSF | 1 | 2 |
| S America | Southern South America | Ona | SH04 | Hunter-gatherers | PSF | 1 | 1 |

| Tribute Data | | | Cosmos Documents | | Cosmology Data | | | | | |
|---|---|---|---|---|---|---|---|---|---|---|
| | | | Documents | Paragraphs | | | | | | |
| Type | Right | Transferring | | | Order | Parallel | Analogy | Well-versed | Colonial Religion | Done |
| 1 | 3 | 1 | 14 | 102 | 5 | 1 | 2 | 3 | 1 | 1 |
| 4 | 5 | 6 | 16 | 78 | 5 | 2 | 2 | 3 | 1 | 1 |
| 4 | 5 | 6 | 4 | 18 | 5 | 0 | | 3 | 1 | 1 |
| 4 | 5 | 6 | 38 | 241 | 5 | 2 | 2 | 0 | 7 | 1 |
| 1 | 3 | 1 | 11 | 12 | 6 | 3 | 2 | 3 | 1 | 1 |
| | | | 8 | 73 | | | | | | |
| | | | 4 | 18 | | | | | | |
| 1 | 3 | 1 | 14 | 392 | 4 | 3 | 2 | 3 | 1 | 1 |
| | | | 6 | 17 | | | | | | |
| 1_2 | 3 | 4 | 4 | 18 | 5 | 2 | 2 | 3 | 1 | 1 |
| 1_2 | 2_6 | 1 | 9 | 71 | 5 | 3 | 2 | 3 | 1 | 1 |
| | | | 5 | 27 | | | | | 1 | 1 |
| | | | 7 | 147 | | | | | | |
| 1_2 | 3 | 4 | 11 | 215 | 5_3 | 2 | 2 | | | 1 |
| 4 | 5 | 6 | 5 | 52 | 4 | 2 | 2 | 3 | 1 | 1 |
| 4 | 5 | 6 | 6 | 125 | 4 | 2 | 2 | 3 | 7 | 1 |

# 8

## The Ritual Mode of Production in the Casas Grandes Social Field

JERIMY J. CUNNINGHAM

The history of archaeology is often described as a succession of theoretical paradigms. Antiquarianism becomes classic evolutionism, which prompts a cultural historical backlash, then a return to evolutionism in American processual archaeology, whose scientism prompted a post-processual rejoinder (e.g., Johnson 1999). Viewed broadly, these transitions reflect deep time oscillations between materialist and idealist cultural ontologies and their associated epistemic positions (Trigger 1998, 2003a). Yet there is also a sense—especially for the most recent of these oscillations—that the story has been too clean. It overlooks the work of the moderate majority: those scholars who found little convincing in the excesses of the processualist–post-processualist debate and instead embraced an eclectic array of theoretical principles retrospectively identified as "processualism-plus" (Hegmon 2003) and/or Social Archaeology (Meskell and Preucel 2004). At the same time, "big man"-focused histories also overlook important theoretical contributions made by individuals who did the nuts and bolts of archaeology's daily labor (Berggren and Hodder 2003; Conkey 2007). In the wake of such reevaluations, archaeologists have recently opted for terminological experimentation in an attempt to define new theoretical spaces where the older binaries can be transcended (e.g., Fowles 2013; Hodder 2012).

Given this abbreviated history, it would seem counterintuitive to argue for the viability of a "mode of production" approach that cannot but smell musty against the neologisms permeating the discipline. The concept of a mode of production was given its most famous definition in the mid-nineteenth century and has been remade several times on both overtly Marxian (Althusser 2005 [1965]; Childe 1951; Friedman 1974, 1989; McGuire 1992; Patterson 2003; Wessman 1981; Wolf 1982) and more general terms (Sahlins

1972; Polanyi 1957). Any call to revisit a concept such as mode of production faces two immediate reactions. For some, the birth of the mode of production concept in Marxist theory makes it a nonstarter. As the demise of the Soviet Union seemingly demonstrates, the socialist utopia Marxism anticipated led instead to totalitarianism and eventual collapse, hinting that Marxist concepts are critically flawed (after Kolakowski 1978a:1ff). For others, a call to "revisit" mode of production analysis implies erroneously that Marxist theory was abandoned in the social sciences (following Wolf 1982:20; and Saitta 2005:27–8). Even the New Archaeology, considered by some to be an outgrowth of American postwar capitalist ideology (Hodder 1985:20f; Trigger 2006; Patterson 1986, 1999), originated from a neoevolutionary approach that was itself based in a reading of historical materialism stripped of its political implications (e.g., White 1959). Subsequent critics, aware of such connections and opposed to the New Archaeology's environmental determinism, might reasonably suspect that mode of production approaches are inevitably doomed to a similar reductive economics, captured succinctly perhaps by Engels' often-repeated phrase that "the determining factor in history is, in the last resort, the production and reproduction of immediate life" (Engels 1972 [1884]:25–6). It is no wonder that Bruce Trigger's (1993:186) now 20-year-old survey of Marxism in western archaeology concluded that it had lost all meaning and instead deserved a "decent burial."

However, there are several reasons why a more explicit engagement with Marxist theory might be helpful to archaeology at this particular time in its history. Reading Marx inoculated many archaeologists against the naïve reductionisms that occurred in both processual and post-processual archaeology, because Marx argued that society had to be understood as a dialectically interrelated whole. Trigger's internment of Marxism in archaeology might then be read as a challenge to neo-Marxists at the time who focused their analysis exclusively on power and meaning. Citing Gordon Childe (1949, 1956), Trigger (1993:178–9) reminded us that while people adapt to the world only through their culturally inherited ideas about it, those ideas cannot be radically divorced from reality if societies continue to survive. Like Jean-Paul Sartre (1963), Maurice Block (1983), and Randy McGuire (1992, 1993), Trigger (1993, 1998, 2003a) proposed that we find inspiration in Marxism's dialectical understanding of society and use careful historical analysis to give flesh and blood to its theoretical bones. In this expression, Marxian concepts such as mode of production anticipate the various border crossings typical of recent theoretical oeuvres in the discipline. The

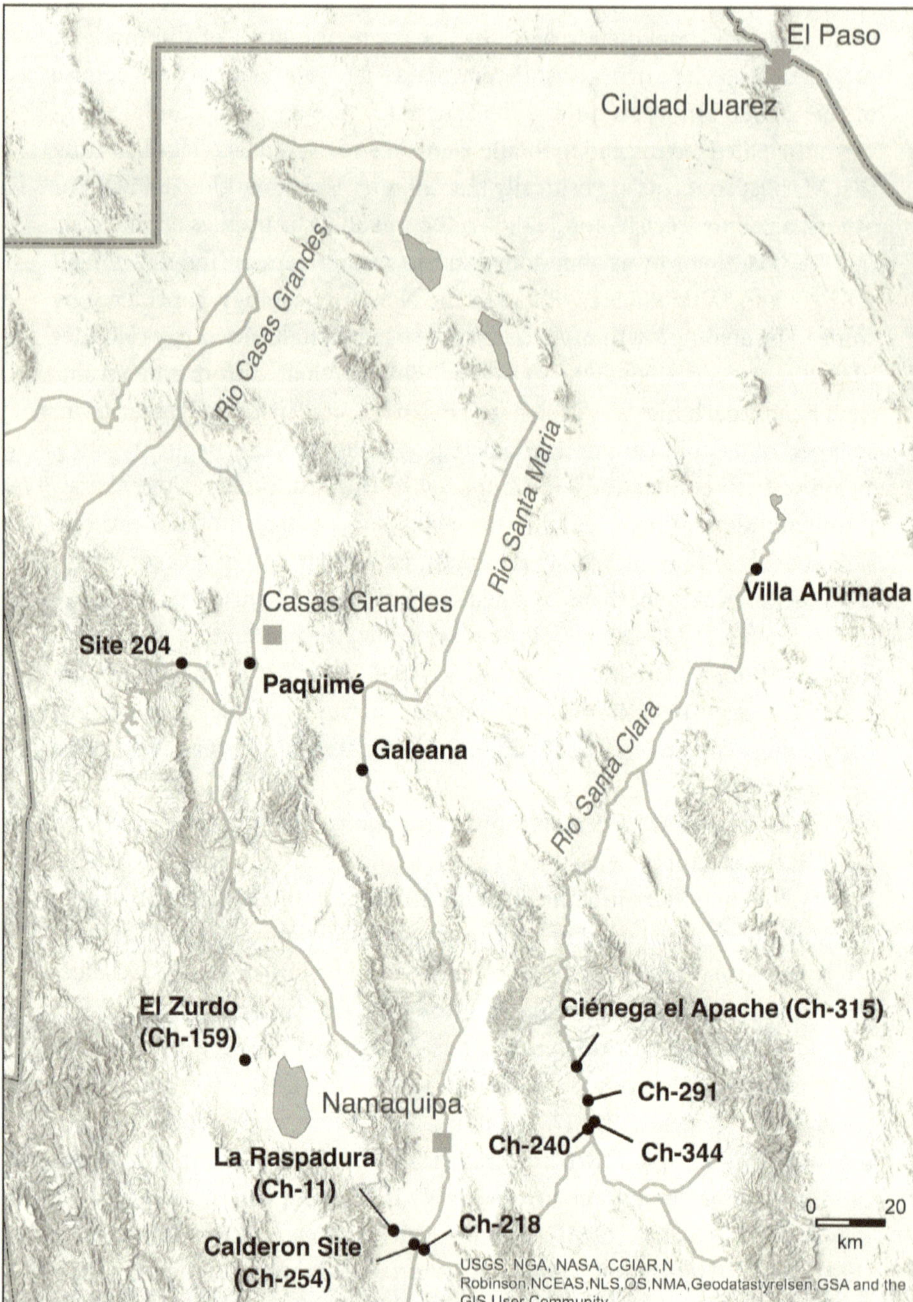


Figure 8.1. Map of sites in Casas Grandes region.

reason to reconsider mode of production at this time in archaeology's history is that it too inscribes a theoretical space with the potential to produce a new and more robust form of theory pluralism in the discipline.

In what follows I develop a historical materialist interpretation of the emergence of complexity in the Casas Grandes region of Chihuahua, Mexico. I argue that a mode of production approach focused on labor and how it is transformed shows how ritual activities and changes in agricultural and craft production were dialectically intertwined. I begin by describing my approach to modes of production and then develop an analysis of how the appropriation of surplus labor changed between the tenth and fifteenth centuries in Northern Mexico when a "domestic mode of production" began to develop elements of a "ritual mode" (Spielmann 2002) that found its most sophisticated expression at the site of Paquimé.

## Conceptual Terrain

In his massive three-volume analysis of Marxist thought, Leszek Kolakowski (1978a:408–416) notes that, taken as a whole, Marx combined the Romantic critique of modernity and Enlightenment rationalist science with a Promethean motif emphasizing humanity's ability to create a better world through labor. In many ways, Marx's historical materialism cannot be separated from a particular phase in European intellectual history, in this case, in a rejection of the Kantian and Hegelian idealisms that dominated in the early nineteenth century. Hegel thought that humanity's essence was a spiritual consciousness and that history was the result of processes that first objectified that consciousness in a contingent world and then reabsorbed that externalized consciousness through a process of sublation. History was a series of steps toward self-awareness, which would end with the emergence of freedom created by the human spirit's understanding of itself. Marx replied to Hegelianism in kind by also asking how objectification and sublation might result in a species-wide movement toward self-awareness. However, he set Hegel "right side up" by arguing that humanity's nature was not to be found in a spiritual essence but lay in human activities in the natural world. Human nature was directed at free and creative labor, and the process of objectifying oneself through productive acts would result in people coming to know both the natural world and themselves as they sublated that experience (see Kolakowski 1978a:132–138; cf. Miller 2005). Structural changes in the way creative labor was organized and the types of understandings people achieved from them would result in different "modes of production," which would lead to a future in which people would know themselves and define a system of production that allowed them to produce freely.

Despite a relatively clear context for the emergence of Marx's materialist conception of history, his specific writings have enough ambiguities to allow divergent interpretations and contrasting schools of Marxist thought (Kolakowski 1978c; McGuire 1992). Abridged definitions of key concepts, such as those found in the preface to *A Contribution to the Critique of Political Economy* or the frequently read *Communist Manifesto* have not reined in discordant interpretations. For example, the most widely quoted definition of mode of production appears in the preface:

> In the social production of their life, men enter into definite relations of production which correspond to a definite stage of development of their material productive forces. The sum total of these relations of production constitutes the economic structure of society, the real foundation, on which rises a legal and political superstructure and to which correspond definite forms of social consciousness. The mode of production of material life conditions the social, political, and intellectual life process in general. It is not consciousness of men that determines their being but, on the contrary, their social being that determines their consciousness. At a certain stage of their development, the material productive forces of society come into conflict with the existing relations of production. . . . Then begins an epoch of social revolution. With the change of the economic foundations the entire immense superstructure is more or less rapidly transformed. . . . In broad outlines Asiatic, ancient, feudal, and modern bourgeois modes of production can be designated as progressive epochs in the economic formation of society. (Marx 1977a [1859]:389–90)

One of the most substantive conflicts in twentieth-century Marxism focused on the extent to which this definition meant that economic factors alone caused modal change (Kolakowski 1978a:158–159, 1978c). Interpretations varied depending on whether one stressed Marx's early and more overtly Hegelian-inspired writings or the later economic analyses of the "mature" Marx (Althusser 2005 [1965]). Engels' "in the last resort" statement quoted above (1972 [1884]:25; also Engels 1978a [1890]:760) could be contrasted with other passages where he suggests the reciprocal independence of the superstructure (ibid: 764) or noted the possibility for unexpected "zigzags" in historical materialism (1978b [1894]: 768). Marxism's core writing thus inspired both vulgar materialist (e.g., Harris 1968) and idealist (e.g., Gramsci 1992) readings, with French structural Marxists such as Louis Althusser (Althusser 2005 [1965]; Althusser and Balibar 2009 [1968]) going so far as to conclude that "overdetermination" caused the forces of production, relations of production, and superstructure to be independent of one another and manifest their own unique temporalities. Practical attempts at mode of production analyses were equally conflicted. The "mode of production debates" diverged over the issue of how capitalism and semifeudal sharecroppers were articulated in postcolonial India (Thorner 1982a–c for a review).

One of the substantial questions for archaeologists interested in using a mode of production analysis is thus sorting through such alternatives. I follow others (e.g., Kolakowski 1978a:177–181) in stressing continuities in Marx's thought and see the analysis of social labor as the core of mode of production approaches. Engels (1978a [1890]:762) lamented that his and Marx's polemic against Hegelian idealism was frequently misread as a form of reductionism not consistent with their dialectical perspective. The first complete definition of a materialist conception of history, for example, appears in *The German Ideology* and was introduced as a reply to Hegelianism. It stresses that a materialist approach to history necessarily begins with an interest in humans as biological rather than spiritual entities, and thus the polemic builds by assessing the means of subsistence, which in turn requires people to work together socially to transform nature for their interests, leading to a division of labor, the creation of distinct interests associated with those divisions and a series of developments in the way that labor is organized (Marx 1977b:160ff). The components of a mode of production summarized in the preface thus derive from this initial concern with creative labor and how human praxis creates production systems that are vulnerable to transformation.

Not surprisingly, this particular emphasis on social labor has attracted anthropologists interested in modes of production (e.g., Wolf 1982; also Donham 1999; Saitta 1994). Anthropologists study societies that do not fit neatly into the various modes Marx and Engels identified for European history (see Anderson 2010). A focus on social labor allows modes of production to be less an exercise in typology than an analysis of how sets of relations create potentials for structural transformations. Concepts such as forces of production, relations of production, or superstructure gain precision only during the dialectics of analyses in which concrete historical realities are understood through theoretical abstraction (McGuire 1992,

1993; see Harvey 2010; Ollman 2003). Eric Wolf's celebrated *Europe and the People without History* used modes of production to foreground the strategic relationships that emerge in production (Wolf 1982:76). He introduced capitalist, tributary, and kin modes to assess these relations, but his subsequent study emphasized real histories and the way that social labor was deployed during European expansion. Other anthropologists have used similar approaches to identify domestic (Meillassoux 1981), petty commodity (Binford and Cook 1991), and African (Coquery-Vidrovitch 1969) modes. I follow these approaches to explore how social labor in Casas Grandes changed during the Viejo and Medio periods.

## Paquimé and the Casas Grandes Region

The site of Paquimé on the Rio Casas Grandes in northwest Chihuahua, Mexico, is conventionally understood as a major political and ritual center that fluoresced in the mid-fourteenth century and then produced a wider Casas Grandes Region defined by stylistic and adaptive continuities (Minnis and Whalen, eds. 2015; Whalen and Minnis 2001a, 2009). Prior to Paquimé's emergence, the Viejo period conforms to a wider Mogollon pattern that includes small to moderate-sized pithouse villages, some with larger community houses, and red on brown pottery. Viejo sites appear perhaps as early as AD 600 and participate in regional exchange systems that bring shell, turquoise, and Mimbres pottery into the region. At around AD 1200, the Viejo period transitions to the Medio period, marked by the appearance of pueblo communities and polychrome pottery. By the middle of the Medio period, larger sites develop an "architecture of power" (Whalen and Minnis 2001b) that includes platform mounds, ball courts, and thick-walled multistory domestic structures. The site of Paquimé grows to cover one square kilometer and has 1,100 rooms and perhaps 2,500 people as well as up to four ball courts, effigy mounds, elite burials, and three million pieces of shell. The site's inhabitants produced ground stone metates and Ramos polychrome pottery, and raised macaws (Whalen et al. 2010). Ramos polychromes begin to carry vivid motifs focused on horned serpents and other liminal creatures considered to reflect the emergence of a new religious ideology associated with elites (VanPool and VanPool 2007; Rakita 2009). By AD 1450 construction at the site ends and goes into rapid decline (Phillips and Gamboa 2015), although the degree to which the region is abandoned is currently unknown (Whalen and Pitezel 2015:122ff).

Archaeologists hold a loose consensus that Paquimé's elites combined irrigation agriculture, interregional exchange, and new belief systems about water to produce a "complex" political entity in the fourteenth century. The evidence for elites at Paquimé is found both indirectly in "architecture of power" and possible sacrifices, as well as directly in burial tomb "44–13," in which high-status burials of older and more well-nourished individuals were associated with turkey sacrifices and hand drums and several disarticulated internments that likely reflect offerings to ancestors (Offenbecker et al. 2014; Rakita 2009). However, if elevated status is obvious, the origin and nature of this elite power is actively debated (VanPool and VanPool 2015:89). Two general models exist for the appearance of elites, one that stresses external stimulus, and a second that emphasizes local sociocultural evolution. Charles Di Peso and Eduardo Contreras' excavations at Paquimé and nearby sites in the 1960s remains the single largest project conducted in the region, defining key phases of the chronology and laying the groundwork for many subsequent studies based on reanalysis of their excavation materials. Di Peso (1974) argued that Paquimé was an outpost that emerges as Toltec *pochteca*-like traders arrived in search of peyote and turquoise. Viejo period populations were reorganized into a hydraulic society by *pochteca* elites who used both trade and up to four ritual complexes to produce a Medio period polity that was administered from Paquimé. While reassessments of the dendrochronology showed that Di Peso's dates for the site were 150 years too early and out of synch with Toltec ethnohistory (Dean and Ravesloot 1993; Lekson 1984), others have continued to tie Paquimé's emergence to Mesoamerica, especially a diffusion of ideas from West Mexico along trade networks (Kelley 2000; Mathiowetz 2011; Riley 2005). Steve Lekson (1999) similarly attributes Paquimé's emergence to foreign elites but suggests they originated at Chaco Canyon and arrived in the Casas Grandes Valley to reorganize sparse Viejo populations and migrants from the Mimbres region into a new political center.

Researchers actively working in Chihuahua have stressed continuities in the sequence from the Viejo period onward to argue instead that local evolutionary processes caused Paquimé's emergence (Whalen and Minnis 2003). In the thirteenth century, populations throughout the Southwest aggregated in basins where irrigation agriculture made it possible to survive erratic rainfall patterns (Fish, Fish, and Gumerman 1994; see Cordell and McBrinn 2012:251ff). Researchers in Chihuahua have argued that the Casas Grandes Valley is an example of this wider pattern (Van Pool and Van Pool 2003). Michael Whalen and Paul Minnis' (e.g., 2001a, 2009) surveys and excavations around Paquimé show that the site grew to become a primate center as a result of peer-polity dynamics that started in the early fourteenth century. Based on their analyses of "architecture of power" (Whalen and Minnis 2001b), they argue that Paquimé's was a small chiefdom that developed direct political control over an inner core zone 15km around Paquimé and influenced a wider region ranging up to about 80 km (see Whalen and Pitezel 2015 for a recent summary). Rulers at Paquimé have been interpreted as shamanic leaders (VanPool 2003), elders of high-ranking lineages associated with powerful ancestors (Rakita 2009; Ravesloot 1994), or (followed a more "Southwestern pattern") as sodality or cult leaders focused on the distinct architectural elements that ring the site (after Nelson 2004:294).

Recent findings are also suggesting that regional complexity was less a derivative of Paquimé's florescence than a product of social changes occurring widely in the early Medio Period. Based on excavations of a midden at Site 204, Whalen and Minnis (2012) argue that Ramos polychrome pottery with vivid iconography appeared from a local antecedent called White Paste Babícora in the mid-fourteenth century. Ramos iconography marks the emergence of a new religious ideology associated with elite status, which means that these changes at Paquimé occurred some 150 years after Medio period lifeways appeared. Moreover, Jane Kelley's excavations in the southern uplands show that the shift from Viejo to Medio period occurred at around AD 1200 in the Upper Santa Maria and Santa Clara drainages (Kelley et al. 2012; Stewart et al. 2005). Hence, rather than Paquimé florescing and producing a wider Medio period hinterland, it appears that Medio period culture was in place as a regional entity by around AD 1200, and it is out of this shared "social field" (after Kohl 2008; Cunningham 2009, 2011, n.d.) that Paquimé's complexity develops in the late Medio period. Sites such as Galeana have oversized architectural walls (VanPool et al. 2005), and my own field program in the Santa Clara Valley recently identified and mapped an I-shaped ball court at Ciénega el Apache, some 130 km from Paquimé (Cunningham 2014). The existence of such "architectures of power" well outside of the core area around Paquimé identified by Whalen and Minnis suggests that the emergence of new systems of authority in the late Medio period may have been a regional phenomenon. Rather than the cause of regional "complexity," Paquimé may simply have been its most spectacular example.

The key question at this point in Casas Grandes archaeology is how to understand such regional transformations. Archaeologists committed to neoevolutionary typologies often think of Paquimé's emergence as a shift from "tribes" to "chiefdoms." Yet such terminologies hide more than they reveal, because the appearance of institutionalized authority rarely clusters with other social variables (Ames 2007; McGuire 2011a). It would also be too extreme to see Paquimé as reflecting the emergence of a new "tributary" mode of production out of a "kin" mode (following Wolf 1982). Instead of a structural transformation, late Medio period complexities seem to reflect subtle changes in the way surplus labor was deployed and extracted within the kin or domestic mode (see McGuire 1989: 48). Original approaches to the study of domestic modes of production considered households to be relatively autonomous production cells (e.g., Meillassoux 1981). Since then anthropologists have stressed the slipperiness of households as a concept (e.g., Guyer 1981; Yanagisako 1979) and shown their heterogeneity as production and consumption spaces that incorporate people who are imbricated by different systems of labor, value, obligation, and exchange (e.g., Douglas and Gonlin 2012; Hendon 1996; Joyce and Gillespie 2000). Donald Donham (1999) has developed perhaps the most extensive revision of the domestic mode in his analysis of the Maale kingdom in East Africa. Drawing on the work of G. A. Cohen (1978), Donham (1999:58ff) redefines key mode of production terminology to focus attention on how social labor is deployed and circulated between domestic units and wider social and economic structures. The forces of production are redefined as "productive powers" and include all the resources people use during labor to produce. This definition includes tools and raw materials but reemphasizes the way that human skill, knowledge, and even social organization become resources during production. The relations of production likewise gain new treatment as "productive inequalities" (Donham 1999:62). Because many of the societies anthropologists study usually have collective ownership over the means of production, conventional Marxist approaches that emphasize exploitation as a function of ownership over key "productive powers" obscure the source of contradiction in the domestic mode. A focus on productive inequalities shows how divisions of labor in households and communities allow some individuals to live systematically off the surplus production of others. Finally, superstructure becomes "reproductive schemata" to emphasize its role in "naturalizing" productive inequalities, adjudicating social conflicts, and mobilizing coercive force. While Meillassoux (1981) saw the primary contradictions in domestic production to be between elders and juniors in autonomous household production units,

Donham emphasizes the interdependence of households and the way surplus flows of both labor and goods change during the life cycle of a house, resulting in different contradictions at each stage (Donham 1999:42, 86f).

In what follows I use Donham's approach to productive powers, productive inequalities, and reproductive schemata to look at the flows of surplus labor in Viejo and early Medio period communities and then seek to trace how these may have been redirected in the late Medio period, when a new form of "complexity" appears.

## The Domestic Mode of Production

Viejo period productive powers were focused intensively on maize horticulture, supplemented by beans and squash and the collecting of wild plants. Maize in the north appears early and as part of a broad-spectrum foraging strategy associated with terraced hills such as Cerro Juañequenia (Hard and Roney 1998). Most agriculture from the Viejo period onward likely relied primarily on dryland farming (Kelley and Searcy 2015:26). Carbon isotopes in the south show that by AD 1000 up to 80 percent of the diet was based on C4 plants (Webster and Katzenberg 2008). A recent summary of paleobotanical remains from central Chihuahua likewise shows a dependency on maize, beans, and squash, as well as regular use of piñon and juniper fruits and nuts (Adams n.d.). Hence, corn-based agriculture seems to have been a dominant component of the subsistence system from the Viejo onward.

Farmers living in the Casas Grandes Valley in the Medio period used two types of farming systems, lowland river valley farming and upland terraced fields (Minnis and Whalen 2015). Corn, beans, squash, gourds, cotton, and chili are found on Medio sites in the region (Whalen and Minnis 2009:Table 7.1), with lowland sites growing maize, beans, and cotton, and upland fields agave and maize. Paquimé is estimated to have had perhaps 2,000 ha of river-bottom farmland within 5 km of the site (Minnis and Whalen 2015:47). While irrigation canals in the lowlands seem to be a distinctive component of late Medio agriculture associated with Paquimé's emergence (Doolittle 1993), their use at earlier time periods remains unknown. Agave from upland fields also becomes the focus of feasting at Paquimé but may have been used widely in the region. In addition to cultigens, wild plants included cacti such as prickly pear, agave, and yucca. Acorns, piñon nuts, juniper berries, and goosefoot, pigweed, and purslane would have moved into cleared fields and were harvested (Minnis and Whalen 2015:51). Small circular and horseshoe-shaped structures are known in upland locations and may reflect temporary camps or hunting blinds for jackrabbits, antelope, wild turkey, or waterfowl.

Corn-based horticulture was probably organized through kin structures. Known Viejo communities show a two-level site hierarchy that includes both small, scattered pithouse communities and larger sites ranging up to 15,000 $m^2$ (Kelley and Searcy 2015:33). Small sites in particular suggest that extended families organized their labor to work nearby agricultural plots, with larger communities being aggregates of similarly sized production units. Small, isolated room blocks are also the most frequently encountered Medio sites in the Santa Clara Valley, with larger multifamily sites appearing in areas where the otherwise narrow floodplain widens to provide more farmland. In the north, full coverage surveys also show that over half of Medio period sites in the Casas Grandes Valley have fewer than 10 rooms and perhaps had 20 people (Whalen and Pitezel 2015:112f), suggesting a similar pattern of household production. Upland terraced farming plots near Paquimé are also small (.8 ha) and have been interpreted as land for extended families or perhaps modest lineages (Minnis et al. 2006:711; also Schmidt and Gerald 1988). Thus, agricultural production systems for maize horticulture seem to have been similar during the Viejo and Medio periods, including when irrigation-based river-valley farming appears in the Casas Grandes Valley in the late Medio period. Throughout the entire sequence, Casas Grandes thus conforms to orthodox definitions of a kin or domestic mode of production: land is a productive power, and agricultural production is focused on the use of human labor organized through households and aided by simple hand tools (Donham 1999; Meillassoux 1981).

A core assumption of domestic modes of production is that its main contradictions relate to a family's primacy in a region and divisions of labor within households based on age and gender (Donham 1999; McGuire 1989:47–48). Elder males are assumed to control a family's agricultural surpluses. In Viejo sites, crops were generally stored in exterior storage pits near pithouses. At Ch-218 in the Santa Maria Valley, a small circular structure adjacent to a pithouse has been interpreted as a granary (Kelley et al. 2012). The association of storage features with specific pithouses suggests that individual households controlled agricultural surpluses, while the presence of storage features outside the household might also mean that members of extended families living in other structures had access to it. A persistent settlement pattern in which some houses have overly large storage facilities and others have none could indicate that lineage elders oversaw agricultural surpluses, but to date too few Viejo settlements have been fully investigated.

Constructions of gender are also central to any understanding of the domestic mode. Based on Ramos polychrome iconography, Christine and Todd VanPool (2006) have suggested that gender complementarity defined late Medio ritual activities in which men and women were both considered essential to success. A late Viejo household excavated in the Santa Clara in 2010 and 2012 hints that gender complementarity also defined Viejo period gender roles. Excavations uncovered a round pithouse and a square storage room that was burned and left an intact floor deposit (Figure 8.2). Six radiocarbon dates on annuals in the square structure are in the late eleventh century (Kelley et al. 2012:100), which suggests the house burned early in the Viejo to Medio period transition. The structure contained storage pots holding maize and beans, a foamlike substance consisting of mesquite and prickly pear phytoliths (McNamee 2013), beehive-shaped storage bins with carbonized corn, and a milling station with a mano and metate. In addition, the structure contained a ceramic production area with a pot of raw clay, a stone mortar, a pot with interior pigment stains, two sherd scrapers, and cobble furniture. Taken together, the structure seems to reflect the emergence of a new interior space defined by a distinctly female gendered taskscape during the shift to pueblo architecture. Storage features dominate this new structure, but they were not large enough to hold even a modest harvest for a small family. Instead, larger vessels may have been dedicated to the long-term storage of seed corn and beans. Holes were abraded into some of the storage vessels, perhaps to prevent rot and/or combustion. The association of women's gendered spaces with stored seed for both corn and beans suggests that even if elder men controlled surpluses, women may have remained stewards of fertility and renewal within a domestic political economy.

The presence of a resident potter also shows that women maintained webs of interdependence that extended beyond their community (Mobley-Tanaka 2007). Mata and Achonda red on brown pottery types were identified in the house, as well as a Mata polychrome base that had been reworked into a scoop. Petrographic analysis of the vessels suggests that a variety of paste and temper categories are represented, and extensive systems of exchange and/or gifting may have connected not just craft workers to their clients but also craft workers to one another. Other types of Viejo craftwork are less well known, but seem similarly to be characterized by varying intensities of household production dispersed throughout the

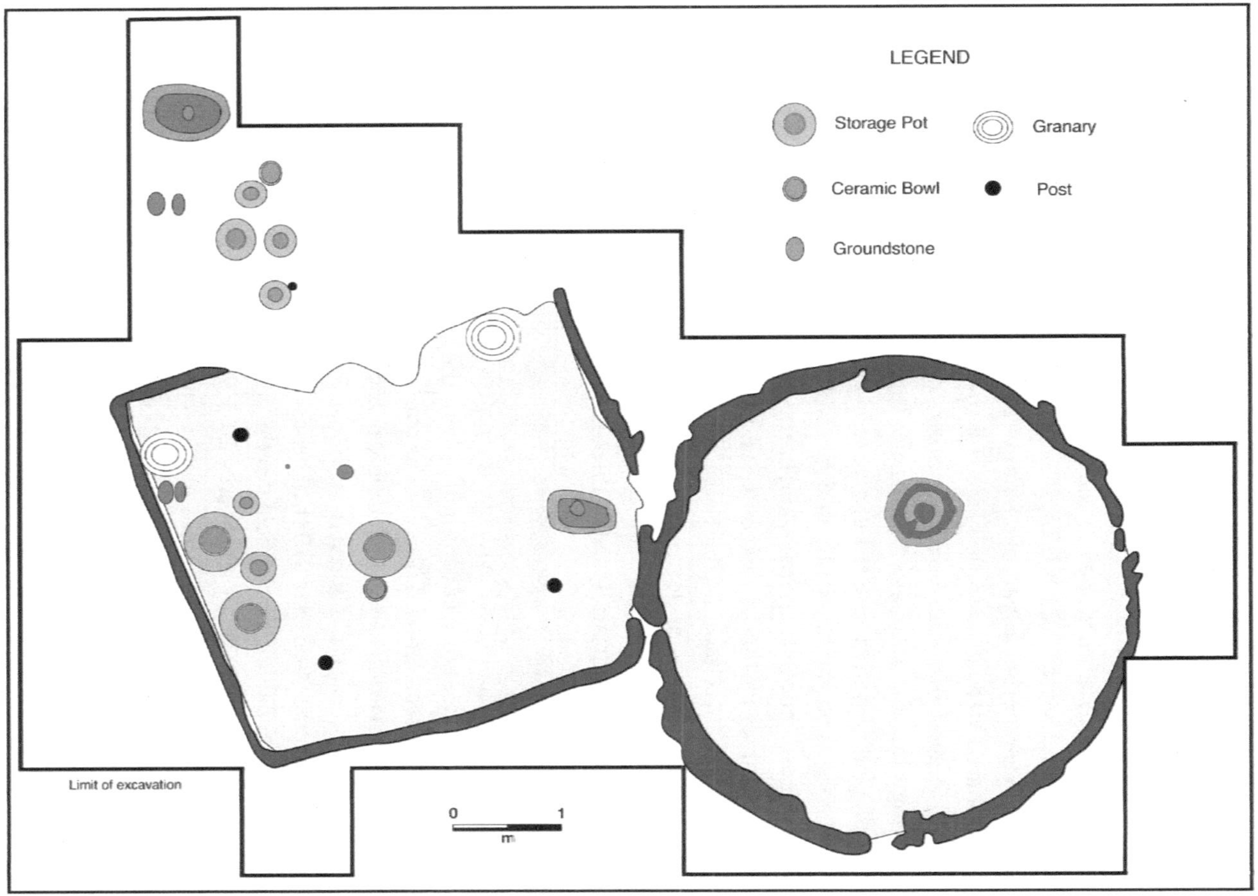


Figure 8.2. Ch-240 house from the upper Santa Clara Valley.

region wherever people accessed clays for ceramic production, vesicular basalts for ground stone, and a variety of cherts and rhyolites for chipped stone (after Costin 1991).

Given the importance of ritual transformations in current models of Paquimé's florescence, our limited understanding of Viejo period reproductive schemas remains a substantial challenge to any interpretation. Jane Kelley and Michael Searcy's recent review of the Viejo period argues that "religious rites and developing ritual power were tied to water, growth, and renewal, probably with a visible leader who may have had personal leadership ability that functioned in the face of a great many leveling devices" (Kelley and Searcy 2015:35). These interpretations rely on a broad reading of the Viejo period as part of a Southwestern pattern with deep time roots and shared ideological tropes. Jane Hill and Kelley Hays-Gilpin (1999; Hill 1992) suggest that Uto-Aztecan speakers diffused a "Flower World" cosmology into the Southwest during the spread of agriculture. The spread of this belief system resulted in a general emphasis on a layered universe and a focus on water, fertility, and renewal. West Mexican influences later introduced chocolate, macaws, and horned serpent imagery into Hohokom communities by the tenth century and then into the rest of the Greater Southwest (McGuire 2011b:38–39). Phillips and colleagues (2006) see two specific pulses of horned serpent ideology into the Southwest from Mesoamerica, one at AD 1000 and a second at AD 1300. Hence, a common ideological substrate exists throughout the region from perhaps the middle Viejo period onward, into which secondary diffusions of ideas are incorporated.

Direct archaeological evidence for reproductive schemata in the Viejo is sparse but does hint at continuities with the later and better-known Medio period (see below). Lithic "venus star" eccentrics have been found in the south at various sites, including Ch-240 (Kelley et al. 2012). The most stunning find is a child burial from House 5 at the Calderon site (Ch-254). The burial possessed over 940 shell beads, a large shell pendant, and a quadrupedal medallion that anticipates the Mound of the Cross at Paquimé (Kelley et al. 2012; Kelley and Searcy 2015:36). While the medallion shows that key iconographic elements were present in the region before Paquimé's florescence (Figure 8.3), the concentration of shell in the burial could reflect a desire to mobilize the materiality of sacred goods in a way similar to Paquimé's later shell caches (Whalen 2013), although whether the child was a subadult sacrifice similar to those proposed for Paquimé is uncertain. A double burial at the El Zurdo site (Ch-159) in the Bustillos basin was

Figure 8.3. Pendant from an infant burial at House 5 at Ch-254.

covered with a slab (Kelley 2009), which may have allowed recurrent access to the dead, hinting that the ties seen between elite power and ancestors had Viejo roots.

Altogether, the domestic mode of production found in the Casas Grandes sequence seems to have been focused on maize horticulture that was carried out by extended family households in which gender complementarity counterbalanced productive inequalities based on age. These productive inequalities were likely naturalized through the fetishization of ancestral power and a sense that high-ranking individuals had some control over the flow of water. At different stages of a household's life cycle, productive inequalities may have shifted between men and women and elders and juniors, producing both potentials for low-level exploitation and the conflicting interests that mode of production analysis often emphasizes as key to social change.

Outside the household, larger community structures have been identified at Ch-254 in the Santa Maria Valley, and the Convento and Reyes sites in the Casas Grandes Valley (Di Peso 1974; Kelley et al. 2012; Kelley and Searcy 2015:24). Community houses likely functioned as administrative and ritual space through which labor was organized at a community level, perhaps allowing individuals with systemic access to those spaces to redefine "social logics" in ways that could institutionalize authority at the expense of those excluded from those spaces (following Flannery and Marcus 2012). Leaders associated with community houses may have organized reciprocal flows of labor between families for house construction or terrace building and administered communal labor. Community houses like the one at Convento, for example, could have allowed community leaders to mobilize work on shared agricultural infrastructure, including any irrigation canals that might have predated Paquimé's emergence. Community houses likely also provided a milieu where ritual leaders organized labor for activities aimed at ensuring the flow of water for community renewal.

## The Ritual Mode of Production at Paquimé

The primary productive inequalities in Casas Grandes prior to Paquimé's emergence thus likely fell along lines of gender, age, and community leadership. Yet, even when some individuals had privileged access to the products of surplus production, the contradictions of the kin mode remained embedded in a dialectic of communalism and inequality (after McGuire and Saitta 1996). Saitta (1994:205) argues that, in communal societies where there is shared ownership over the means of production, surpluses may be appropriated by community and ritual leaders without exploitation occurring as long as those surpluses remain accessible as "communal social entitlements" (Saitta 1997:9). A community may decide to augment production and allocate a portion of that surplus to ranked individuals, who organize and distribute these communal social entitlements. Because community and ritual leaders organize the activities that maintain the production system, they act as a "subsumed class" (after Resnick and Wolff 1981, 1987) whose consumption of surpluses is compensative rather than exploitative (Saitta 1994:207; also McGuire and Saitta 1996:202).

Shifts in inequality in the Casas Grandes region were likely seeded by contradictions between local farmers and the subsumed leadership in community houses, as well as between subsumed leaders in neighboring communities. The overall trajectory of change may then have related to the ways community leadership and associated "social logics" were redefined in the direction of increasingly exploitive relations, leading eventually to Paquimé's centralized authority. Shifts in the real status of elites, however, may be incredibly subtle, because even in unambiguous examples of exploitation, elite privilege is justified by the logics of a "subsumed class." For example, Donham's (1999) analysis shows that the Maale kingdom relied on a nested structure of exploitation anchored in reproductive schemata that fetishize fertility. Fertility originates with kings but is then passed sequentially to regional chiefs, lineage heads, and men in households. The flow of fertility justifies a return flow of the products that result from that fertility, so that kings can call upon surplus labor or tribute from regional chiefs, chiefs from lineages, lineage heads from stem families, and men from women. The nested nature of both the ideology and the exploitation it supports produces stability, because inequalities at one level cannot be challenged without simultaneously undermining the basis of privilege at another. The fertility distributed by Maale elites makes them appear as an essential component of the production process. Similarly, Bruce Trigger's (2003b:670–672) comparative study of early civilizations shows that elites are usually defined as carrying out essential roles as intermediaries between society and supernaturals. Elites assemble and use a portion of agricultural production to nourish deities and themselves, and the deities in turn provide the fertility essential to perpetuating human communities (also Rosenwig, chapter 7). Thus, exploitive states such as the Maale and those early civilizations studied by Trigger tend to conceptualize elites as providing an essential service. The emergence of elite status may then depend in part on the ability of would-be elites to frame new inequalities as an extension of the communal roles they played previously as a subsumed class.

The key question in Casas Grandes is thus how ritual leaders may have subtly redefined existing Viejo period reproductive schemata focused on communal social entitlements in a domestic mode to increase their social power. Scholars working on Casas Grandes have identified a series of religious changes that correlate with Paquimé's emergence (VanPool and VanPool 2015 for a summary). These reflect a noticeable reworking or "quickening" (Riley 2005) of religious principles that were already present in the region into a new configuration. Christine VanPool's (2003; VanPool and VanPool 2007:chapter 2; Phillips et al. 2006) detailed analysis of Ramos polychrome iconography suggests that existing Flower World cosmologies were refocused to a concern with the flow of water between the watery spiritual underworld, the middle world of human existence, and the sky world. While the importance of water and rainmaking in Medio period rituals has been noted by most Casas Grandes scholars (VanPool and VanPool 2015:96), VanPool argues further that a unique "shamanic" elite emerged at Paquimé and acted as rainmakers who interceded with horned serpents to ensure the flow of water from the underworld. Shamans depicted on Ramos iconography may have used hallucinogenic substances to travel into the underworld to communicate with horned serpents that inhabited liminal spaces between the worlds, such as streams, lakes, and springs. Paquimé's architecture provided an infrastructure for ritual interactions between shamans and horned serpents, including platform mounds, plazas, ball courts, and large roasting ovens. The canal that brought water from Ojo Vareleño (see below) to a reservoir adjacent to the Mound of Offerings may have allowed horned serpents to visit the site to view ritual rainmaking performances. Elites may also have appealed to supernaturals in private rituals at locations such as the Walk-in Well (VanPool and VanPool 2007:31) and through turkey and macaw sacrifices (Rakita 2009).

Katherine Spielmann (2002) has suggested that economic intensification in the Southwest frequently occurs for ritual purposes, creating what she calls a "ritual mode of production." Rather than a distinct mode, however, the ritual mode is best understood as an intensification of production in the domestic mode that creates new potentials for exploitation. Community leaders throughout the Casas Grandes region may have competed with one another similar to Whalen and Minnis' (2001a, 2009) peer-polity model. However, like Maale kings, Paquimé's "shamans" may have been particularly successful at transcending the limits normally placed on the accumulation of power by subsumed classes by reworking reproductive schemata to make their appeals to horned serpents appear increasingly essential to the production process. The key part of this transformation may have been the dialectic between new religious beliefs and the expansion of irrigation agriculture.

In central Chihuahua, Adams (in press) notes that botanical remains show that dry farming in the Viejo period was more successful than in the Medio period, perhaps underscoring why irrigation farming become so important in the Casas Grandes Valley in the Medio period. Doolittle (1993) identified two canal systems in the Casas Grandes Valley lowlands. The first consists of agricultural canals that drew off the Rio Casas Grandes to water local fields. Their extent has largely been obscured by recent agriculture, but Doolittle's review proposes that canals started at least 5 km south of Paquimé and extended some distance to the north. The coordination of the maintenance of these canals from Paquimé might have associated the site's ritual elites with successful harvests. However, the second canal system overtly makes this connection. It drew from the Ojo Vareleño spring on Cerro del Ojo and brought water to a reservoir in Paquimé and then out of the site through drainage canals that pass through the pueblo and emptied into agricultural canals below the site. While this canal contributed a modest amount of water to agricultural production (Doolittle 1993:139), it affirmed Paquimé as—quite literally—the intermediary between horned serpents at the springs and successful irrigation. In kin-based production systems where a distinct class does not own productive powers, one of the few avenues for the institutionalized appropriation of surpluses by elites may depend on their ability to define a quality that they control or embody—in this case, their ability to intercede with horned serpents to ensure the flow of water—as a productive power.

The new importance of elites seems to have resulted in changes to specific types of agricultural and craft production related to ritual activities. In addition to the small family-oriented fields found in the uplands around Paquimé, Minnis and colleagues (2006) identified six large fields that were greater than 10 ha in size. They suggest that these may have been worked by labor drawn from local farmers for communal feasts, elite subsistence, or likely both. Recent agriculture has obscured any evidence of similar large fields in the irrigated lowlands, but indirect evidence comes from a cache of uniform Type 1A metates at Paquimé (see below) that suggests that corn grinding and maize or maize beer consumption were part of ritual feasting (VanPool and Leonard 2002; VanPool and VanPool 2006). Large ovens, such as Unit 9 at Paquimé, could prepare over 3,000 kg of agave (Whalen and Pitezel 2015:53; Minnis and Whalen 2005), and alcoholic beverage preparation may have been a focus at Site 204. Paquimé also shows special procurement of animals, including macaws, turkeys, bear, and waterbirds. Food animals were likely rabbits and medium-sized mammals, but larger mammals such as bison tend to be associated with ceremonial centers and either elite or ritual consumption (Rakita and Cruz 2015:52–53). Hence, the most fundamental changes in late Medio period subsistence associated with religious transformations seem to have been irrigation agriculture and an expansion of products for ritual feasting.

In contrast to Di Peso's view that Paquimé was the center for ceramic, shell, and copper production, recent analyses suggest the site was primarily a location where both local and exotic goods were consumed (Rakita and Cruz 2015; also Minnis 1988). Ramos polychrome pottery was made in several locations in the Casas Grandes region (following Woosley and Olinger 1993; Bishop et al. 1998), likely by people who were part-time craft producers (Sprehn 2003). Metates fall into two general forms, a "Type 1B" that is irregular and widely distributed, and a more standardized "Type 1A" associated with architectures of power, including 10 stored in a single room at Paquimé (VanPool and Leonard 2002; also Rakita and Cruz 2015:66). The differences between these two forms seem to reflect different amounts of labor invested in their production. Rather than produced in Paquimé's workshops, turquoise (Maxwell and Cruz 2008), copper (Vargas 1995, 2001), and shell all seem to have been made elsewhere and then consumed at the site (Rakita and Cruz 2015:74). Michael Whalen (2013; cf. Bradley 1999) has recently suggested that shell was primarily an ideological device whose materiality was hoarded at Paquimé to underscore the sacred nature of the site. Type 1A metates and Ramos polychromes required additional surplus labor for their production, perhaps through special commissions to particularly skilled artisans (see Sprehn 2003:239–240). Overall, late Medio period craft production was still organized around households (Rakita and Cruz 2015:81) but seems to have require expanded work to make items for use at Paquimé.

The domestic mode of production found in the Viejo and early Medio periods thus remained intact into the late Medio period but saw surplus labor increasingly centralized for feasting activities and the production of objects that contributed directly to ritual life. The more difficult question is the extent that this shift to "complexity" actually changed exploitation. In Marx's economics, exploitation is measured by assessing the amount that people work beyond what is necessary in a given social context for their maintenance and reproduction (Kolakowski 1978a:279). Changes in the working day are thus an indicator of relative exploitation (e.g., Marx 1990 [1867]: 340ff)). However, because surplus production may be directed at communal ends (Saitta 1994), studies of exploitation must also asses the degree to which surplus value is no longer under the control of the community that produces it (Kolakowski 1978a:333). Both of these variables are difficult to measure in the archaeological record and are almost impossible to trace with any precision given our current knowledge of Casas Grandes archaeology. However, a few questions seem particularly suitable for future work.

What sets the late Medio period apart does not seem to be the introduction of surplus labor flows beyond the household, but instead the ability of elites at Paquimé to increasingly capture existing surplus labor flows from a wider region. Community houses in Viejo sites are the product of communal labor and were also the context where agricultural tasks and ritual activities were organized. Ritual leaders associated with Viejo period community houses were likely checked by leveling mechanisms that ensured surpluses were focused toward local communal social entitlements. A similar pattern may have defined Medio period communities at the apex of two level site hierarchies, such La Raspadura and Galeana in the Santa Maria drainage and Ciénega El Apache in the Santa Clara. In contrast, the expansion of irrigation agriculture seems to have resulted in higher population densities in Paquimé's immediate hinterland, allowing more people to contribute to the pool of surplus labor that the site received. The almost total lack of ritual architecture at sites in Paquimé's "core zone" suggests that the site's elites had centralized control over the distribution of surplus for most community-level ritual observances. The concentration of high-value goods such as macaws, turquoise, and shell at Paquimé also suggests that it acquired most of these materials as they entered a larger Casas Grandes region. Paquimé is perhaps unique, then, for having a small number of individuals who seem to control ritual activities and associated flows of surplus labor from a comparatively dense population. The ability of elites to define themselves as intermediaries with horned serpents and thus become a productive power in their own right may have been the key to this centralization.

Articulations between kin-based production and wider systems of exploitation are usually a function of time, specifically the proportion of labor directed to the domestic mode versus that siphoned off by ritual or tributary relations. The interpretations people give for changes in the flow of surplus labor are important, because historical materialism suggests that the frictions that cause social transformations appear when people become conscious of their inability to produce freely within a mode of production. Given these insights, the expansion of agriculture and craft goods for feasting and ritual might have been allowed because such changes did not significantly transform the proportion of surplus labor each person contributed to ritual activities compared to preceding periods. Indeed, as irrigation agriculture expanded and required more collaborative work for subsistence, proportional increases in surplus production for ritual activities might not have been extraordinary. Additionally, if communities that provided surplus labor to Paquimé continued to receive a portion of that production through feasting and access to ritual performances and ball games, then increases in labor demands may have been understood as an expansion of communal social entitlements and not exploitation by emerging elites. So while differences in rank increased, that may not have resulted in the complete transformation of subsumed class relations and overt exploitation. Indeed, the status of Paquimé's elites seems to have been defined primarily by their performative activities.

It is important to note that the ability of Paquimé's elites to redefine themselves as essential to regional fecundity through performance was likely aided by the materiality of the site itself. Like polychromes and agave fields, Paquimé's impressive ritual architecture was produced by surplus labor. Initially the site may have been a place where horned serpents and humans could assemble near springs while negotiating community renewal. The expansion of the site's domestic and ritual architecture in the Medio period likely required regular contributions of surplus labor, and these acts would have allowed for the subjectivities of both leaders and non-elites to be reconstituted as the site grew. As Marx's concept of commodity fetishism highlights, over time people may no longer recognize the things they produce as such. Instead, the ritual architecture and associated ritual schedule may have caused Paquimé to seem autonomous of the labor objectified in its production. In effect, the site may have transitioned from being a tool that people purposefully used to a fetish that seemingly demanded ongoing contributions of labor by local farmers, potters, hunters, and ritual leaders. Such transformations may have been particularly effective in the Casas Grandes Valley, because farmers who invest in agricultural infrastructures such as irrigation canals are less likely to "vote with their feet" as inequality appears (Trigger 2003b:662, 676f), giving Paquimé's elites both a spectacular stage on which to affirm their essential connection to agricultural productivity and an audience to watch their performances of power (after Mills 2007).

## Conclusion

Paquimé is thus an example of how the kin mode may develop wider systems of inequality without transitioning to a tributary mode. A "ritual mode of production" increases surplus production for ritual activities and generates greater ranked separations but does so firmly within an ideological framework defined by communal social entitlements. The key dynamic at Paquimé in particular, and perhaps in a ritual mode of production more generally, is a function of the tensions that occur over the flow of social labor. As people direct surplus value into rituals that promise to ensure rainfall and fertility, they remove labor from their own domestic activities. In times of subsistence stress, ritual requirements increase as elites—acting as a productive power—try to stimulate regional fertility by siphoning more surplus labor from the domestic mode, which may undermine the kin-based subsistence activities that ensure reproduction. Persistent failures to produce fecundity challenge elite status as a productive power and create the seeds of crisis. However, where Di Peso saw Paquimé end in a violent abandonment, recent analyses show that a local population may have continued to live and bury their dead at Paquimé long after construction ceased at AD 1450 (Casserino 2009). This pattern might be expected from the ritual mode, because its primary contradiction is not tied to ownership over productive powers, which requires in capitalism a revolutionary transformation, but over the definition of elites *as* a productive power. Hence, the collapse of the ritual mode is not revolutionary but occurs as praxis produces a new social consciousness, which exposes the ideological basis of elite power and leads people to redirect their surplus labor back into the village-focused communal social entitlements of the domestic mode.

## References Cited


Adams, Karen R.

in press  Ancient Plant Use in West-Central Chihuahua. In *Not Far from Casas Grandes: The Archaeology of West-Central Chihuahua*. University of Utah, Salt Lake City.

Ames, Kenneth M.

2007  The Archaeology of Rank. In *Handbook of Archaeological Theories*, edited by R. Alexander Bentley, Herbert D. G. Maschner, and Christopher Chippendale, pp. 487–513. AltaMira, Lanham, Maryland.

Anderson, Kevin B.

2010  *Marx at the Margins: On Nationalism, Ethnicity, and Non-Western Societies*. University of Chicago Press, Chicago.

Althusser, Louis

2005  [1965] *For Marx*. Translated by Ben Brewster. Verso, London.

Althusser, Louis, and Etienne Balibar

2009  [1968]. *Reading* Capital. Translated by Ben Brewster. Verso, London.

Berggren, Åsa, and Ian Hodder

2003  Social Practice, Method, and Some Problems of Field Archaeology. *American Antiquity* 68(3):421–434.

Binford, Leigh, and Scott Cook

1991  Petty Production in Third World Capitalism Today. In *Marxist Approaches in Economic Anthropology*. Monographs in Economic Anthropology No. 9, edited by Alice Littlefield and Hill Gates. University Press of America, Lanham, Maryland.

Block, Maurice

1983  *Marxism and Anthropology: The History of a Relationship*. Oxford University Press, New York.

Bradley, Ronna J.

1999  Shell Exchange within the Southwest: The Casas Grandes Interaction Sphere. In *Greater Mesoamerica: The Archaeology of West and Northwest Mexico*, edited by Michael S. Foster and Shirley Gorenstein, pp. 221–240. University of Utah Press, Salt Lake City.

Burd Larkin, Karin, Jane H. Kelley, and Mitchel J. Hendrickson
2004 Ceramics as Temporal and Spatial Indicators in Chihuahua Cultures. In *Surveying the Archaeology of Northwest Mexico*, edited by Gillian E. Newell and Emiliano Gallaga, pp. 177–204. University of Utah Press, Salt Lake City.

Casserino, Christopher Michael
2009 Bioarchaeology of Violence and Site Abandonment at Casas Grandes, Chihuahua, Mexico. Unpublished Ph.D. dissertation, University of Oregon, Eugene.

Childe, V. Gordon
1949 *Social Worlds of Knowledge*. Oxford University Press, London.
1951 *Social Evolution*. Collins Fontana Library, London.
1956 *Society and Knowledge: The Growth of Human Traditions*. Harper, New York.

Cohen, G. A.
1978 *Karl Marx's Theory of History: A Defence*. Clarendon Press, Oxford.

Conkey, Margaret W.
2007 Questioning Theory: Is There a Gender of Theory in Archaeology? *Journal of Archaeological Method and Theory* 14:285–310.

Coquery-Vidrovitch, Catherine
1969 Recherches sur un mode de production africain. *La Pensée* 144:61–78.

Cordell, Linda S., and Maxine E. McBrinn
2012 *Archaeology of the Southwest*. 3rd ed. Left Coast Press, Walnut Creek, California.

Costin, Cathy Lynne
1991 Craft Specialization: Issues in Defining, Documenting and Explaining the Organization of Production. *Archaeological Method and Theory* 3:1–56.

Cunningham, Jerimy J.
2009 Water and Ritual Power in the Casas Grandes "Regional System." Paper presented at the Theoretical Archaeology Group, Durham, UK. December 2009.
2011 Casas Grandes as Social Field. Paper presented at the Chacmool Conference, Calgary. November 2011.
2014 Proyecto Arqueológico Santa Clara, Informe de la Temorada 2012. Informe técnico presentado al Consejo de Arqueología, Instituto Nacional de Antropología e Historia, México.
n.d. Casas Grandes as a Social Field. Manuscript on file in the Department of Anthropology, University of Lethbridge.

Dean, Jeffrey S., and John C. Ravesloot
1993 The Chronology of Cultural Interaction in the Gran Chichimeca. In *Culture and Contact: Charles Di Peso's Gran Chichimeca*, edited by Anne I. Woosley and John C. Ravesloot, pp. 83–104. Dragoon: An Amerind Foundation Publication; University of New Mexico Press, Albuquerque.

Di Peso, Charles C.
1974 *Casas Grandes: A Fallen Trading Center of the Gran Chichimeca*. Volumes 1–3. Amerind Foundation, Dragoon; Northland Press, Flagstaff.

Donham, Donald. L.
1981 Beyond the Domestic Mode of Production. *Man* (n. s.) 16:515–541.

1999 *History, Power, Ideology: Central Issues in Marxism and Anthropology.* University of California Press, Berkeley.

Doolittle, William E.

1993 Canal Irrigation at Casas Grandes: A Technological and Developmental Assessment of Its Origins. In *Culture and Contact: Charles C. Di Peso's Gran Chichimeca*, edited by Anne I. Woosley and John C. Ravesloot, pp. 133–152. Bulletin of the History of Archaeology Vol. 4, No. 2, pp.23–28. University of New Mexico Press, Albuquerque.

Douglas, John E., and A. C. MacWilliams

2015 Society and Polity in the Wider Casas Grandes Region. In *Ancient Paquimé and the Casas Grandes World*, edited by Paul Minnis and Michael E. Whalen, pp. 126–147. Amerind Studies in Anthropology, University of Arizona Press, Tucson.

Douglas, John E., and Nancy Gonlin (editors)

2012 *Ancient Households of the Americas: Conceptualizing what Households Do.* University Press of Colorado, Boulder.

Engels, Frederick

1972 [1884] *The Origin of the Family, Private Property, and the State.* Pathfinder, New York.

1978a [1890] Letter to Joseph Block. In *The Marx–Engels Reader*, 2nd ed., edited by Robert C. Tucker, pp. 760–765. W. W. Norton, New York.

1978b [1894] Letter to H. Starkenburg. In *The Marx–Engels Reader*. 2nd ed., edited by Robert C. Tucker, pp. 767–768. W. W. Norton, New York.

Fish, Paul R., Suzanne K. Fish, and George J. Gumerman

1994 Toward an Explanation for Southwestern Abandonments. In *Themes in Southwestern Prehistory*, edited by George J. Gumerman, pp. 135–165. School of American Research, Santa Fe.

Flannery, Kent, and Joyce Marcus

2012 *The Creation of Inequality: How Our Prehistoric Ancestories Set the Stage for Monarchy, Slavery, and Empire.* Harvard University Press, Cambridge.

Fowles, Severin M.

2013 *An Archaeology of Doings: Secularism and the Study of Pueblo Religion.* School for Advanced Research Press, Santa Fe.

Friedman, Jonathan

1974 Marxism, Structuralism, and Vulgar Marxism. *Man* (n.s.) 9:444–469.

1989 *System, Structure, and Contradiction: The Evolution of Asiatic Social Formations*, 2nd ed. AltaMira, Walnut Creek, California.

2002 Modernity and Other Traditions. In *Critically Modern: Alternatives, Alterities, Anthropologies*, edited by Bruce M. Knauft, pp. 287–313. Indiana University Press, Bloomington.

Guyer, Jane I.

1981 Household and Community in African Studies. *African Studies Review* 24(2/3):87–137.

Gramsci, Antonio

1992 *Prison Notebooks*. 3 vols. Edited by Joseph A. Buttigieg. Columbia University Press, New York.

Hard, Robert J., and John R. Roney

1998 A Massive Terraced Village Complex in Chihuahua, Mexico, 3000 Years before Present. *Science* 279:1661–1664.

Harris, Marvin

1968 *The Rise of Anthropological Theory: A History of Theories of Culture*. Thomas Y. Cromwell, New York.

Harvey, David

2010 *A Companion to Marx's* Capital. Verso, London.

Hegmon, Michelle

2003 Setting Theoretical Egos Aside: Issues and Theory in North American Archaeology. *American Antiquity* 68:213–243.

Hendon, Julia A.

1996 Archaeological Approaches to the Organization of Domestic Labor: Household Practice and Domestic Relations. *Annual Review of Anthropology* 25:45–61.

Hill, Jane H.

1992 The Flower World of Old Uto-Aztecan. *Journal of Anthropological Research* 48:117–144.

Hill, Jane H., and Kelley A. Hays-Gilpin

1999 The Flower World in Material Culture: An Iconographic Complex in the Southwest and Mesoamerica. *Journal of Anthropological Research* 55:1–37.

Hodder, Ian

1985 Postprocessual Archaeology. *Advances in Archaeological Method and Theory* 8:1–26.

2012 *Entangled: An Archaeology of the Relationships between Humans and Things*. Wiley-Blackwell, Malden, Massachusetts.

Johnson, Matthew

1999 *Archaeological Theory: An Introduction*. Blackwell, Malden, Massachusetts.

Joyce, Rosemary A., and Susan D. Gillespie (editors)

2000 *Beyond Kinship: Social and Material Reproduction in House Societies*. University of Pennsylvania Press, Philadelphia.

Kelley, J. Charles

2000 The Aztatlan Mercantile System: Mobile Traders and the Northwestward Expansion of the Mesoamerican Civilization. In *Greater Mesoamerica: The Archaeology of West and Northwest Mexico*, edited by Michael S. Foster and Shirley Gorenstein, pp. 137–154. University of Utah Press, Salt Lake City.

Kelley, Jane H.

2009 *El Zurdo: A Small Prehistoric Village in West-Central Chihuahua, Mexico*. Maxwell Museum Technical Series No. 9. Maxwell Museum of Anthropology, University of New Mexico, Albuquerque.

Kelley, Jane H., Richard D. Garvin, and Jerimy J. Cunningham

2012 *Proyecto Arqueológico Chihuahua: Informe de la Temporada de 2010*. Informe al Consejo de Arqueología. Instituto Nacional de Antropología e Historia, México, D.F.

Kelley, Jane H., A. C. MacWilliams, Joe D. Stewart, Karen R. Adams, Jerimy J. Cunningham, Richard E. Garvin, J. M. Maillol, Paula J. Reimer, and Danny Zborover

2012 The View from the Edge: The Proyecto Arqueológico Chihuahua (PAC) 1990 to 2010: An Overview. *Canadian Journal of Archaeology* 36:82–107.

Kelley, Jane H., and Michael T. Searcy

2015 Beginnings: The Viejo Period. In *Ancient Paquimé and the Casas Grandes World*, edited by Paul Minnis and Michael E. Whalen, pp. 17–40. Amerind Studies in Anthropology, University of Arizona Press, Tucson.

Knauft, Bruce M. (editor)

2002 *Critically Modern: Alternatives, Alterities, Anthropologies.* Indiana University Press, Bloomington.

Kohl, Philip L.

2008 Shared Social Fields: Evolutionary Convergence in Prehistory and Contemporary Practice. *American Anthropologist* 110:495–506.

Kolakowski, Leszek

1978a *Main Currents of Marxism: Its Rise, Growth and Dissolution, 1: The Founders.* Translated by P. S. Falla. Clarendon Press, Oxford.

1978b *Main Currents of Marxism: Its Rise, Growth, and Dissolution, 2: The Golden Age.* Translated by P. S. Falla. Clarendon Press, Oxford.

1978c *Main Currents of Marxism: Its Origins, Growth and Dissolution, 3: The Breakdown.* Translated by P. S. Falla. Clarendon Press, Oxford.

Lekson, Stephen H.

1984 Dating Casas Grandes. *Kiva* 50:55–60.

1999 *The Chaco Meridian: Centers of Political Power in the Ancient Southwest.* AltaMira Press, Walnut Creek, California.

Marx, Karl

1973 *Grundrisse.* Translated by Martin Nicolaus. Penguin, London.

1977a [1859] Preface to *A Critique of Political Economy.* In *Karl Marx: Selected* Writings, edited by David. McLellan, pp. 388–92. Oxford University Press, New York.

1977b [1964] *The German Ideology.* In *Karl Marx: Selected* Writings, edited by David. McLellan, pp. 159–191. Oxford University Press, New York.

1990 [1867] *Capital: A Critique of Political Economy.* Vol. 1. Translated by Ben Fowkes. Penguin, London.

Maxwell, Timothy D., and Rafael Cruz Antillón

2008 The Production and Exchange of Turquoise in the Casas Grandes Region: A View from the East. Paper presented at the 73rd Annual Meeting of the Society for American Archaeology, Vancouver.

Mathiowetz, Michael D.

2011 The Diurnal Path of the Sun: Ideology and Interregional Interaction in Ancient Northwest Mesoamerica and the American Southwest. Unpublished Ph.D. dissertation, University of California, Riverside.

McGuire, Randall H.
1989 The Greater Southwest as a Periphery of Mesoamerica. In *Centre and Periphery: Comparative Studies in Archaeology*, edited by Timothy C. Champion, pp. 40–63. Unwin Hyman, London.
1992 *A Marxist Archaeology.* Academic Press, San Diego.
1993 Archaeology and Marxism. *Archaeological Method and Theory* 5:101–157.
2008 *Archaeology as Political Action.* University of California Press, Berkeley.
2011a Rethinking Social Power and Inequality in the Aboriginal Southwest/Northwest. In *Movement, Connectivity and Landscape Change in the Ancient Southwest*, edited by Margaret C. Nelson and Colleen Strawhacker, pp. 57–72 University Press of Colorado, Boulder.
2011b Pueblo Religion and the Mesoamerican Connection. In *Religious Transformation in the Late Pre-Hispanic Pueblo World*, edited by Donna M. Glowacki and Scott Van Keuren, pp. 23–49. University of Arizona, Tucson.

McGuire, Randall H., and Dean J. Saitta
1996 Although They Have Petty Captains, They Obey Them Badly: The Dialectics of Prehispanic Western Pueblo Social Organization. *American Antiquity* 61:197–216.

McNamee, Calla
2013 A Phytolith Analysis of Viejo Period Ceramic Vessel Sediments from House 2, Ch-240. Report on file with the Department of Anthropology, University of Lethbridge.

Meillassoux, Claude
1981 *Maidens, Meal and Money: Capitalism and the Domestic Economy.* Cambridge, Cambridge University Press.

Meskell, Lynn, and Robert W. Preucel
2004 *A Companion to Social Archaeology.* Blackwell, Malden.

Miller, Daniel
2005 Materiality: An Introduction. In *Materiality*, edited by Daniel Miller, pp. 1–50. Duke University Press, Durham, NC.

Mills, Barbara
2007 Performing the Feast: Visual Display and Suprahousehold Commensalism in the Puebloan Southwest. *American Antiquity* 72:210–239.

Minnis, Paul E.
1988 Four Examples of Specialized Production at Casas Grandes, Northwestern Chihuahua. *Kiva* 53(2):181–193.

Minnis, Paul E., and Michael E. Whalen (editors)
2015 *Ancient Paquimé and the Casas Grandes World.* Amerind Studies in Anthropology. University of Arizona Press, Tucson.

Minnis, Paul E., and Michael E. Whalen
2005 At the Other End of the Puebloan World: Feasting at Casas Grandes, Chihuahua, Mexico. In *Engaged Anthropology: Research Essays on North American Archaeology, Ethnobotany, and Museology*, edited by Michelle Hegmon and B. Sunday Eiselt, pp. 114–128. Museum of Anthropology, University of Michigan, Ann Arbor.

2015 Ecology and the Food Economy. In *Ancient Paquimé and the Casas Grandes World*, edited by Paul E. Minnis and Michael E. Whalen, pp. 41–57. Amerind Studies in Anthropology. University of Arizona Press, Tucson.

Minnis, Paul E., Michael E. Whalen, and R. Emerson Howell
2006 Fields of Power: Upland Farming in the Prehispanic Casas Grandes Polity, Chihuahua, Mexico. *American Antiquity* 71:707–722.

Mobley-Tanaka, Jeannette L.
2007 Households, Communities, and the Social Reorganization of the Pueblo III World. In *Engendering Households in the Prehistoric Southwest*, edited by Barbara J. Roth, pp. 34–49. University of Arizona Press, Tucson.

Nelson, Ben A.
2004 Current and Future Directions in Northwest Mexican Archaeology. In *Surveying the Archaeology of Northwest Mexico*, edited by Gillian E. Newell and Emiliano Gallaga, pp. 289–296. University of Utah Press, Salt Lake City.

Offenbecker, Adrianne, Kyle D. Waller, Jane H. Kelley, and M. Anne Katzenberg
2014 Mortuary Variability at Paquimé and Its Implications for Sociocultural Differentiation. Paper presented at the Society for American Archaeology Meetings, Austin, Texas. April.

Ollman, Bertell
2003 *Dance of the Dialectic: Steps in Marx's Method*. University of Illinois Press, Urbana.

Patterson, Thomas C.
1986 The Last Sixty Years: Toward a Social History of Americanist Archaeology in the United States. *American Anthropologist* 88(1):7–26.
1999 The Political Economy of Archaeology in the United States. *Annual Review of Anthropology* 28:155–74.
2003 *Marx's Ghost: Conversations with Archaeologists*. Berg, New York.

Phillips, David A., Jr., and Eduardo Gamboa
2015 The End of Paquimé and the Casas Grandes Culture. In *Ancient Paquimé and the Casas Grandes World*, edited by Paul E. Minnis and Michael E. Whalen, pp. 148–171. Amerind Studies in Anthropology. University of Arizona Press, Tucson.

Phillips, David A., Jr., Christine S. VanPool, and Todd L. VanPool
2006 The Horned Serpent Tradition in the North American Southwest. In *Religion in the Prehispanic Southwest*, edited by Christine S. VanPool, Todd L. VanPool, and David A. Phillips, Jr., pp. 17–29. AltaMira Press, Lanham, Maryland.

Polanyi, Karl
1957 The Economy as Instituted Process. In *Trade and Market in the Early Empires: Economies in History and Theory*, edited by Karl Polanyi, Conrad M. Arensbert, and Harry W. Pearson, pp. 243–270. Free Press, New York.

Rakita, Gordon F. M.
2009 *Ancestors and Elites: Emergent Complexity and Ritual Practices in the Casas Grandes Polity*. AltaMira, Walnut Creek, California.

Rakita, Gordon F. M., and Rafael Cruz
2015 Organization of Production at Paquimé. In *Ancient Paquimé and the Casas Grandes World*, edited by Paul E. Minnis and Michael E. Whalen, pp. 58–82. Amerind Studies in Anthropology. University of Arizona Press, Tucson.

Resnick, Stephen, and Ricard D. Wolff
1981 Classes in Marxian Theory. *Review of Radical Political Economics* 13:1–18.
1987 *Knowledge and Class*. University of Chicago, Chicago.

Riley, Carroll
2005 *Becoming Aztlan, Mesoamerican Influence in the Greater Southwest, 1200–1500*. University of Utah Press, Salt Lake City.

Sahlins, Marshall
1972 *Stone Age Economics*. Aldine de Gruyter, New York.

Saitta, Dean
1994 Agency, Class, and Archaeological Interpretation. *Journal of Anthropological Archaeology* 13:201–227.
1997 Power, Labor, and the Dynamics of Change in Chacoan Political Economy. *American Antiquity* 62:7–26.
2005 Dialoguing with the Ghost of Marx: Mode of Production in Archaeological Theory. *Critique of Anthropology* 25:27–35.

Sartre, Jean-Paul
1963 *Search for a Method*. Translated by Hazel E. Barnes. Vintage Books, New York.

Schmidt, Robert H., Jr., and Rex E. Gerald
1988 The Distribution of Conservation-Type Water-Control Systems in the Northern Sierra Madre Occidental. *Kiva* 53:165–179.

Spielmann, Katherine A.
2002 Feasting, Craft Specialization, and the Ritual Mode of Production in Small-Scale Societies. *American Anthropologist* 104:195–207.

Sprehn, Maria S.
2003 Social Complexity and the Specialist Potters of Casas Grandes in Northern Mexico. Unpublished Ph.D. dissertation, University of New Mexico, Albuquerque.

Stewart, Joe D., Jane H. Kelley, A. C. MacWilliams, and Paula J. Reimer
2005 The Viejo Period of Chihuahua Culture in Northwestern Mexico. *Latin American Antiquity* 16:169–192.

Thorner, Alice
1982a Semi-feudalism or Capitalism? Contemporary Debate on Classes and Modes of Production in India, Part 1. *Economic and Political Weekly* 17:1961–1968.
1982b Semi-feudalism or Capitalism? Contemporary Debate on Classes and Modes of Production in India, Part 2. *Economic and Political Weekly* 17:1993–1999.
1982c Semi-Feudalism or Capitalism? Contemporary Debate on Classes and Modes of Production in India, Part 3. *Economic and Political Weekly* 17:2061–2066.

Trigger, Bruce G.
1993 Marxism in Contemporary Western Archaeology. *Archaeological Method and Theory* 5:159–200.

1998 Archaeology and Epistemology: Dialoguing across the Darwinian Chasm. *American Journal of Archaeology* 102:1–34.

2003a Archaeological Theory: The Big Picture. Department of Anthropology, Brigham Young University, Provo, Utah.

2003b *Understanding Early Civilizations.* Cambridge University Press, New York.

2006 *A History of Archaeological Thought.* 2nd ed. Cambridge University Press, New York.

VanPool, Christine

2003 The Shaman-Priests of the Casas Grandes Region, Chihuahua, Mexico. *American Antiquity* 68:696–717.

VanPool, Christine S., and Todd L. VanPool

2006 Gender in Middle Range Societies: A Case Study in Casas Grandes Iconography. *American Antiquity* 71:53–75.

2007 *Signs of the Casas Grandes Shamans.* University of Utah Press, Salt Lake City.

2015 Religion and Cosmology in the Casas Grandes World. In *Ancient Paquimé and the Casas Grandes World*, edited by Paul E. Minnis and Michael E. Whalen, pp. 83–102. Amerind Studies in Anthropology. University of Arizona Press, Tucson.

VanPool, Todd L., and Christine S. VanPool

2003 Agency and Evolution: The Role of Unintended Consequences of Action. In *Essential Tensions in Archaeological Method and Theory*, edited by Todd L. VanPool and Christine S. VanPool, pp. 89–113. University of Utah Press, Salt Lake City.

VanPool, Todd L., Christine S. VanPool, and Robert D. Leonard

2005 Casas Grandes Core and Periphery. In *Archaeology between the Borders: Papers from the 11th Biennial Jornada Mogollon Conference*, edited by Marc Thompson, Jason Jurgena, and Lora Jackson, pp. 25–35.

VanPool, Todd L., and Robert D. Leonard

2002 Specialized Ground Stone Production in the Casas Grandes Region of Northern Chihuahua, Mexico. *American Antiquity* 67:710–730.

Vargas, Victoria D.

1995 *Copper Bell Trade Patterns in the Pre-Hispanic U.S. Southwest and Northwest Mexico.* Arizona State Museum Archaeological Series 187. University of Arizona, Tucson.

2001 Mesoamerican Copper Bells in the Pre-Hispanic Southwestern United States and Northwestern Mexico. In *The Road to Aztlan: Art from a Mythic Homeland*, edited by Virginia M. Fields and Victor Zamundio-Taylor, pp. 196–211. Los Angeles County Museum of Art, Los Angeles.

Webster, Monica, and M. Annie Katzenberg

2008 Dietary Reconstruction and Human Adaptation in West Central Chihuahua. In *Celebrating Jane Holden Kelley and Her Work*, edited by Meade Kemrer, pp. 71–102. New Mexico Archaeological Council Special Publication No. 5. New Mexico Archaeological Council, Albuquerque.

Wessman, James W.

1981 *Anthropology and Marxism.* Schenkman, Cambridge.

Whalen, Michael E.

2013 Wealth, Status, Ritual, and Marin Shell at Casas Grandes, Chihuahua, Mexico. *American Antiquity* 78:624–639.

Whalen, Michael E., and Paul E. Minnis

1996 Ball Courts and Political Centralization in the Casas Grandes Region. *American Antiquity* 61:732–746.

2001a *Casas Grandes and Its Hinterland: Prehistoric Regional Organization in Northwest Mexico.* University of Arizona Press, Tucson.

2001b Architecture and Authority in the Casas Grandes Area, Chihuahua, Mexico. *American Antiquity* 66:651–688.

2003 The Local and the Distant in the Origin of Casas Grandes, Chihuahua, Mexico. *American Antiquity* 68:314–332.

2009 *The Neighbors of Casas Grandes: Medio Period Communities of Northwestern Chihuahua: Excavating Medio Period Communities of Northwest Chihuahua, Mexico.* University of Arizona Press, Tucson.

2012 Ceramics and Polity in the Casas Grandes Area, Chihuahua, Mexico. *American Antiquity* 77:403–423.

Whalen, Michael E., and Todd Pitezel

2015 Settlement Patterns of the Casas Grandes Area. In *Ancient Paquimé and the Casas Grandes World*, edited by Paul E. Minnis and Michael E. Whalen, pp. 103–125. Amerind Studies in Anthropology. University of Arizona Press, Tucson.

Whalen, Michael E., A. C. MacWilliams, and Todd Pitezel

2010 Reconsidering the Size and Structure of Casas Grandes, Chihuahua, Mexico. *American Antiquity* 75:527–550.

White, Leslie

1959 *The Evolution of Culture.* McGraw-Hill, New York.

Williams, Raymond

1983 *Keywords: A Vocabulary of Culture and Society.* Rev. ed. Oxford University Press, New York.

Wolf, Eric

1982 *Europe and the People without History.* University of California Press, Los Angeles.

1990 Distinguished Lecture: Facing Power—Old Insights, New Questions. *American Anthropologist* 93:586–596.

Yanagisako, Sylvia Junko

1979 Family and Household: The Analysis of Domestic Groups. *Annual Review of Anthropology* 8:161–205.

# 9

## Bronze Economy and Mode of Production

### The Role of Comparative Advantages in Temperate Europe during the Bronze Age

JOHAN LING, PER CORNELL, AND KRISTIAN KRISTIANSEN

> Modes of production are manifest in social formations—i.e., societies and cultures in the process of becoming and dissolving.
>
> (Marx 1953)

In the beginning of the second millennium BC we have evidence of extensive trade in metals, and on mobility in persons and things in temperate Europe (Kristiansen 1998). Also, we see the rapid emergence of boundaries as manifested in the regional appearance of distinctive patterns of metalwork, housing, and burial rites (Figure 9.1), features that altogether broadly can be associated with certain modes of productions.

To understand the nature of European Bronze Age societies in terms of interaction, trade, and boundaries, we must acknowledge both the specific social conditions of material life and the larger economic framework on which they depended (Marx 1973:63; Kristiansen 1998; Ling and Rowlands 2013). In our definition a bronze economy is constituted by particular workings in a larger social formation with certain common interests (e.g., metal-using societies). An important condition for such an economy is the general development of new technologies for transport by land and sea, which enabled the expansion of international exchange and trade. The boundaries of such a social formation are fuzzy and defined by the geographical scale of interdependence rather than by cultural boundaries. Social and economic reproduction depends on the intricate interactions of multiple communities. Particularities in the socioeconomic and cultural setting, on the other hand, play an important part in defining local and regional polities and ethnicities, and in the formation of institutional power (Kristiansen 2014).

Figure 9.1. Map showing the European Bronze Age metal boundaries/cultures and a schematic overview of the comparative advantages of the different regions in Bronze Age Europe.

We thus envisage a bronze economy as a general praxis and structure pertaining to specific historical processes, in this case temperate Europe between 1500 and 1100 BC. This praxis and structure reproduced the ideologies in which bronze played an important role on many levels.

To explore the specific historical conditions of Bronze Age temperate Europe, we apply a simplified version of David Ricardo's concept of "comparative advantage" to the Bronze Age, which, put simply, implies that every region in Europe was able to enter the Bronze Age metal trade by providing goods that they controlled but others needed or valued, such as amber from the Baltic, tin from Cornwall, salt and silver from the Carpathians, wool from Hungary and the Po Delta, etc. (Figure 9.1). Thus, the Nordic region would more or less stop consuming amber with the beginning of the Bronze Age, because it was more profitable to use it in exchange for copper and tin. Consumption moved in this way to regions where amber was in the highest demand: Wessex, south Germany, and especially the Aegean and the Near East. It illuminates how mechanisms of value differences worked as an economic mechanism of growth and wealth accumulation. Thus, the universal need for copper and tin stimulated the development of new needs and values in other fields, which in turn supported an economic division of labor in Europe. It granted some regions specific economic opportunities, at times unexpectedly, but in the long term it stimulated a large number of regions to specialize in providing products that other regions craved, which over time would also include warriors, slaves, and horses. Furthermore, Marx's concept of fetishism could be useful when considering "the wealth exchange" in the Bronze Age of valuable materials such as metal and amber and the hidden and illusory social labor behind these materials. Finally, we employ the theoretical concept of a Germanic mode of production/decentralized political economy (Kristiansen and Earle 2015) for northern Europe during the period 1500–1100 BC. We shall briefly present its history and will address its potential and limitations in discussing the political economy of decentralized polities.

## Political Forms, Socioeconomic Process, and Large-Scale Interaction in Bronze Age Europe

There are evident rampant differences across Europe during the Bronze Age. These differences concern availability of certain raw materials and particularities of location but are also related to socioeconomic process, political forms, and cultural elements. We would argue that these differences are not secondary or a merely anecdotal detail to the broader historical process. Rather, these differences are crucial for any understanding of wider and larger historical process.

The differences play a major role in social interaction and exercise a strong effect over the general historical development. Thus, we must, step by step, integrate knowledge of such particularities in order to understand larger and more general socioeconomic processes and political forms.

Knowledge of the particularities of the political forms in different regions is still limited. On one hand, there is a lack of systematic empirical studies, and at present we lack substantial data for several areas. On the other hand, our theories and concepts of the political are still clumsy and limited, and future work must refine the theoretical base. Much archaeology is still heavily marked by Weber's sociology, in which political authority is the key point in society, and characterized by "ideal type" concepts. It is easy to see in the archaeological evidence that there are areas in Europe where the political form is relatively evident and easy to detect, and the available data seem to indicate a centralized political form, at times resembling the famous chiefdom model (cf., e.g., Earle 1997; Service 1975). As is well known, to Service the chief was largely a positive and benign person , while the chief in Earle's model is exploitative. In both models the notion of extracting tribute is crucial. Particularly in Service's model, but also to some extent in Earle's, redistribution is the focus and helps to reinforce the position of the chief. But in several areas of Bronze Age Europe, indicators for a strong centralized chiefdom are weak. Earle has insisted on this point and the decentralized polities in Scandinavia, in which redistribution is close to nonexistent. Still, there is indirect information pointing to the importance of certain kinds of political relations, but our understanding of these political forms is still extremely limited.

In the classic anthropological study on African political forms (Fortes and Evans-Pritchard 1940), a major inspiration for Service, examples with evident chiefs or kings are contrasted to others in which the political form is more segmentary and diffuse (Radcliffe-Brown 1940; cf. Gluckman 1940; Oberg 1940; Wagner 1940). However, even in the anthropological examples in this book, the variability goes far beyond such a simple division (cf. Aijmer 1979, 2015). Further, much focus has been on the political leadership and juridical functions, and less on other aspects of advanced political forms, such as their varied institutions, their character and distribution. In more advanced state-like societies, the institutional form and its distribution are at least as important as the form of leadership itself.

Concerning socioeconomic forms, we also lack more elaborate archaeological discussion. While Weber highlighted the notion of political authority, Marx is famous for addressing the political only indirectly in *Capital*, while hinting at some ideas on the political in smaller studies. To Marx, mode of production describes particular processes of the socioeconomic, not the political. Marx is explicit in arguing that several modes may exist simultaneously in one particular "society." For the sixteenth century he discusses the *feudal mode,* a *mercantilistic mode,* a mode of *semi-independent artisans,* and *relatively autonomous peasants* as a fourth mode. The Bronze Age of Europe probably also consisted of several modes, some simultaneously existing in the same area or region with strong articulations to each other (cf. the theoretical discussion in Amin [1973]) However, we still lack attempts at clarifying in more detail possible modes from Bronze Age Europe.

Yet an important point in Marx's *Capital* is that a mode of production is a process, a trend to develop in a certain way. This is established through particular interrelations between a large set of factors (cf. Bois 1976; Kliman [2012] for efforts at empirical applications). In archaeology, there have been a very limited number of systematic attempts at such studies. Kristiansen (1978, 1984) intended to apply a similar thinking to the Bronze Age of Jutland, inspired by Friedman's anthropological analysis of the Kachin case (1979; cf. Leach 1954). One of the parameters of Kristiansen's argument was that an overexploitation of the landscape led to the establishment of moorland, which led to a social collapse. This example is intriguing and could be productively developed. Recent historical studies on the enclosure movement in England during the sixteenth century indicate an interesting possibility. The landowner's intention in this case was to transform arable land to a pastoral landscape for wool production, which thus implies a partially conscious creation of moorlands. It is not impossible to envision similar processes in the Bronze Age, at another scale, and we hope future studies may prove or disprove such an idea. The mode of production is to Marx no absolute process, there is no certain determined end to the process, and several other factors may affect the development of a particular mode. Concerning the sixteenth century, Marx again introduces another interesting notion that there were also other actors, who did *not* form modes of production—notably the *merchants*—but still had profound effects on development.

But there is yet another important level of analysis, concerning the interactions and relations between people, modes, political forms, and other factors. Thus, given the intensity of certain kinds of interaction in Bronze Age Europe, this is an important dimension, which in itself produces certain patterns or processes, while also producing particularities in certain areas. It is here that the notion of comparative advantage may play a crucial role in our understanding (Figure 9.1). To address this point, several important issues must also be addressed. One of these is the relation between mode of production and political form. Precisely from the notion that they constitute two different phenomena, an interesting and productive dynamic discussion can be established. Amin, and also Bidet, has interestingly discussed this point, and, despite a somewhat structural discussion, particularly in Bidet, they are interesting inspirations. Another important point relates to the question of interaction itself. In traditional social theory (e.g., *diffusionism* or *kulturkreislehre*, still affecting our discussions), there was *only* a possibility of bringing knowledge or objects from culture A to culture B, and no discussion on the possibility of an encounter and interaction that as such established effects on both parties. There is a need for a more refined and complex discussion here (cf. Cornell 2015).

## Scandinavian Bronze Age, the Concept of the Germanic Mode of Production and Beyond

Engels and Marx produced some interesting texts on precapitalist socio-economic settings. Engels' classic study on kinship, property, and the state (2001 [1884]) remains a very interesting contribution. One of the problems in Engels' work, inspired by Morgan (1870), is the fixation on kinship as a definition of prehistoric society. While kinship is a major factor, there are also other socio-economic factors and institutions operating in any social setting (cf., e.g., Godelier 2004; Godelier et al. 1998; Lowie 1937; Schneider 1984). Marx has only hinted at questions on prehistoric socioeconomic settings. In *Grundrisse*, (1857–1858 [1953]), he discussed the "Germanic mode of production" (cf., e.g., Cornell 1993; Tilley 1996). In Bronze Age research several scholars have used this concept (Earle 1997; Friedman and Rowland 1978; Gilman 1995; Kristiansen 1998).

Marx's discussion of the Germanic mode in *Grundrisse* must be understood in its context. One major problem is that he constructs two parallel models, which largely mirror each other. The Germanic mode is characterized by individual independent households, which engage with each other in a decentralized political form, while the Asiatic mode is characterized by collectively organized villages, which are subordinated to a totalitarian state power (cf. Cornell 1993; Zizek 2012:597). In line with general theories in Europe during Marx's time, Asia was characterized by totalitarianism in prehistory and early history, while Europe was characterized by independent entrepreneurs. In order to develop another discussion on the Germanic mode, it is important to look at it as a more general model, one which should not be understood in relation to a supposed Asiatic Mode.

In the Germanic mode, the political economy is clearly decentralized and related largely in autonomous households. Gilman (1995 cf. Cornell 1993). Cornell and Fahlander 2002b:123–126) summarized the Germanic mode of Production in a short and coherent way.

1. The autonomy of households in their production (every individual household contains an entire economy, forming an independent center of production (Marx 1964:79)
2. The coalition of households into tribal assemblies
3. The development of hereditary leadership from the military and judicial activities of the assembly

What is probably of greatest interest in the Germanic mode model is that it focuses on the role of relatively small and relatively autonomous social units and their interaction. The Scandinavian longhouse tradition (cf. Artursson 2009) may possibly be related to such a model. The maritime economy in the same areas had strong connections to agricultural production but the maritime sphere possesses certain socioeconomic traits that cannot be reduced to agricultural production (cf. below). Regarding the conceptual frames for describing different economic steps like Wolf's kin/tributary/capitalist modes (see Rosenswig and Cunningham, chapter 1), we find them a bit too general, and hard to apply to the situation in Bronze Age Scandinavia. Kristiansen has in previous studies used the concept "proto tributary" for Bronze Age Scandinavia. There were certainly tributary elements connected to stratified Bronze Age society in Scandinavia, but this concept is not sufficient to describe the intricacy of the social economy (Amin 1973; Wolf 1982).

What must be stressed is the social inequality of the social settings in the southern half of Scandinavia during the Bronze Age. There are differences between social units (longhouse extended households), probably also social differences within them, and notable differences between geographical areas.

Still, our knowledge of the agricultural practices in Scandinavian Bronze Age contexts and their change is limited. There are indications of a certain focus on domestic animals, at least in certain areas, and there are even discussions in the bibliography of a "pastoral economy." There are notable differences in the field of agriculture and husbandry across time and space in the southern half of Scandinavia in the Bronze Age, and we need more in-depth studies on this (cf., e.g., Hjörungdal's [2013] discussion on gender in this context, and Oma's suggestions on animal–human relationships in the Iron Age). There is also a need for more intense studies on textile production (cf. Bergerbrant 2007), house building, boat production (sadly little is known in terms of direct empirical evidence), ceramics, rock picking, and several other fields of productive activity. The role of the metal can be addressed only within this general framework, still little known.

Elsewhere, Ling and Cornell (2010) have suggested the existence of varied contemporaneous spheres in Scandinavian Bronze Age societies, even within a given area. In future work it would be inspiring to go back to Bohannan's general idea of social spheres, with different logics and different principles of exchange (Bohannan and Bohannan 1968). It could well be that the differences between such spheres are crucial. Concerning the Bronze Age, there seem to be at least two spheres, one related to the inland, with agriculture and husbandry, and one to the sea and the coastal rocks, a more maritime sphere focusing on seaborne transport, trade, and raids (Figures 9.2 and 9.3). Rock art has a strong maritime dimension in this area (and in several other areas with an abundance of rock art in the southern half of Scandinavia)—by no means the only dimension of the rock art, but an important one (Figures 9.2 and 9.3).

Finally, the abundance of metal in Bronze Age Scandinavia is certainly remarkable and constitutes an important aspect of this social and economic setting. The raw material was imported (Figure 9.4), while the production of items largely took place in Scandinavia and represents yet another important productive activity with particular characteristics. The way the raw material reached Scandinavia is a crucial question and must be related to a large set of various means of exchange, ranging from the symbolic gift exchange over barter to exchange based on value equivalents.

There are important practical uses of bronze objects, in agriculture for example. There is also an evident use of bronze in weapons and related paraphernalia, and Kristiansen (1998) has demonstrated through use-wear analysis that they have been in active use. Other objects were used in dressing in various ways. But these objects must also have been prestigious. One of the strong indicators of this is their high frequency in certain burials, which seem to be related to the elite. Depositing bronze objects in burials also has another implication, however. It is a means of trying to put the objects out of circulation, out of exchange, by trade or otherwise. This, in a way, is a question of inalienability, as discussed by Weiner (1992) and Godelier (1996). It is noteworthy that the highest frequency of bronze in

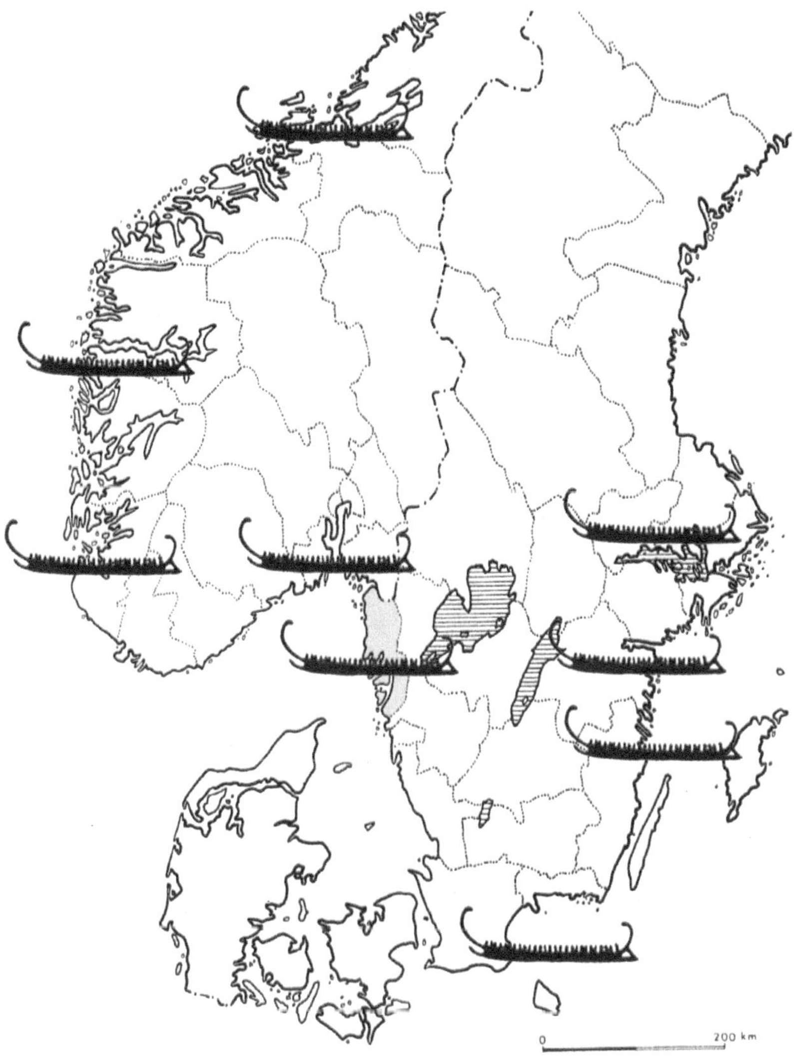


Figure 9.2. Map showing the major Bronze Age rock art areas in Scandinavia.

burials in Scandinavia seems to be related to areas with a strong agricultural/pastoral economy.

The fixation on bronze is in itself highly interesting. The Bronze Economy in the Bronze Age must be conceived largely in terms of fetishism and reification. While differing dramatically from the fetishism of capitalism discussed by Marx, the Bronze economy evidently has ideological symbolic

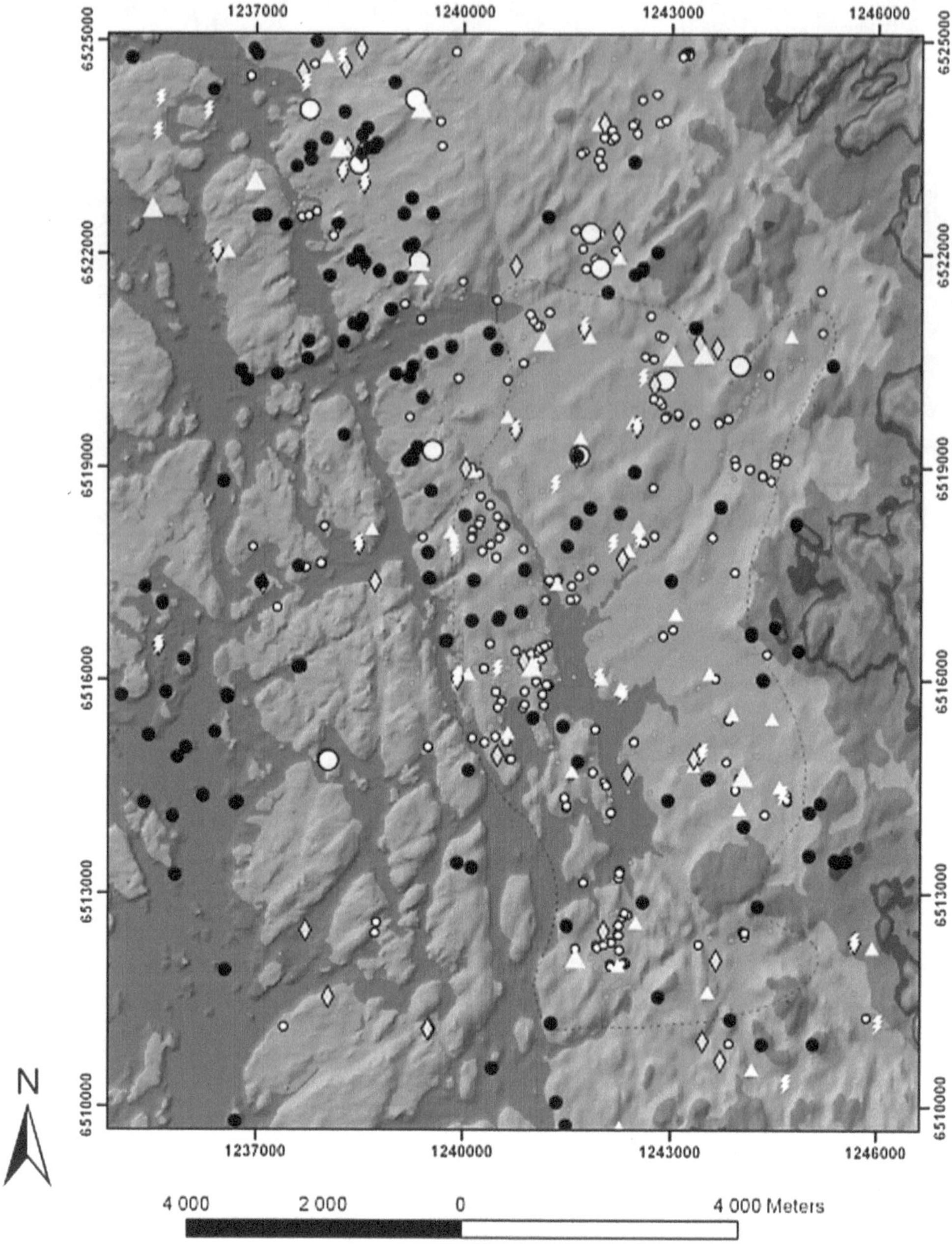


Figure 9.3. The decentralized Bronze Age society in the coastal region of Tanum, western Sweden, illustrated by different Bronze Age remains and showing a shoreline about 15 m higher than at present: red dots = rock art sites; white dots = cup mark sites; black dots = cairns; large buff triangles = settlement finds (carbon dates, ceramics, or other features) dated to the Bronze Age; small buff triangles = indicative settlement sites from the Bronze Age; yellow dots = bronze items; blue diamonds = flint daggers; white flashes = flint sickles.

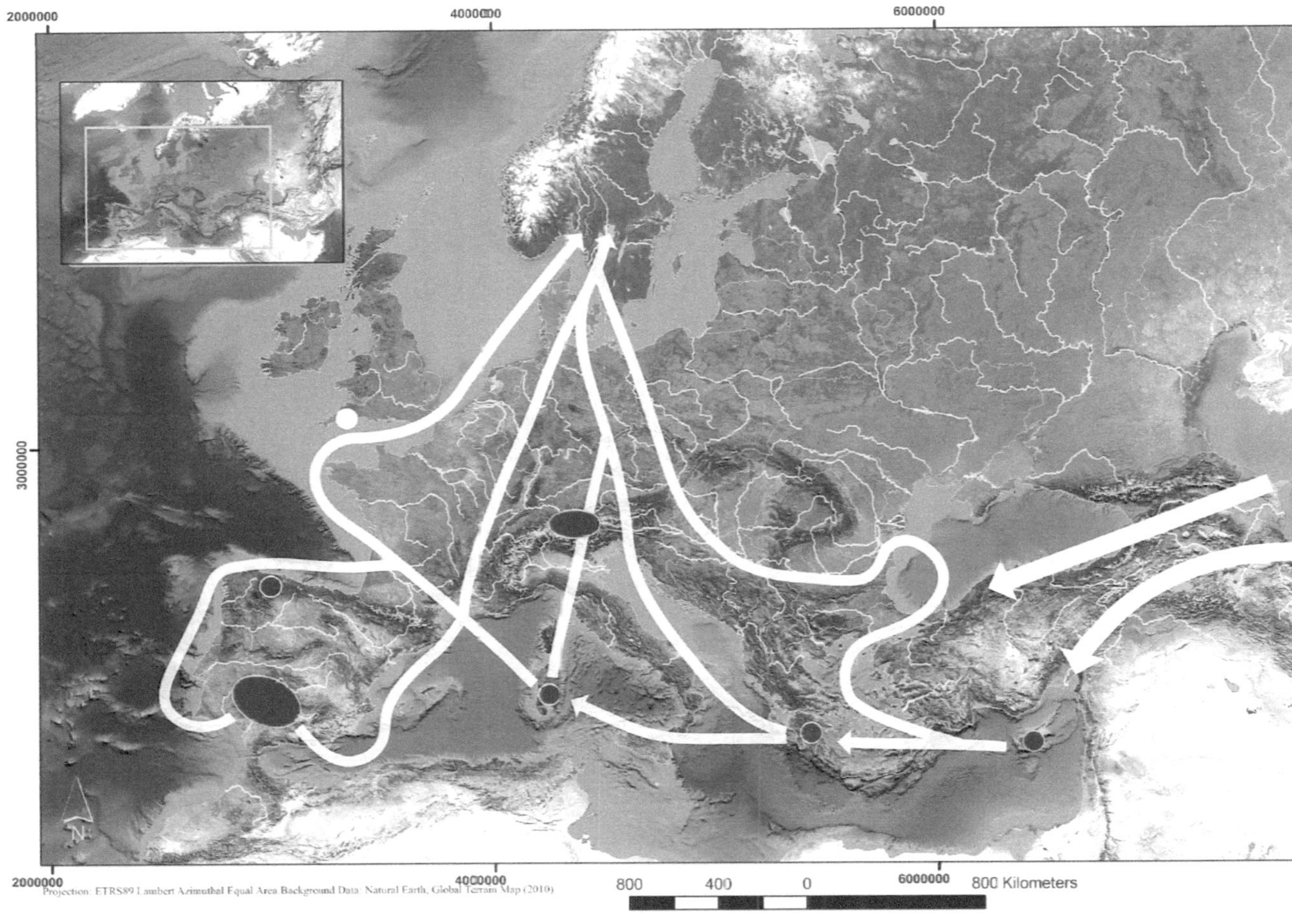


Figure 9.4. Model that indicates directional flows of European copper and tin routes supplying Scandinavia during the Bronze Age. Areas marked in black denote copper-bearing regions, matching metal signatures in Scandinavian bronze artifacts (after Ling et al. 2014). The tin-bearing region in Cornwall is marked with white, while the white arrows signify an eastern influx of tin.

dimensions similar to the fetishism of capitalism, as discussed by Marx (cf. Zizek 2006:308–317; Thomson 1955). Further, the Bronze Age rock art in Scandinavia has strong unhomely dimensions (cf. Cornell 2007), which may possibly be linked to a fetishized economy.

To summarize, our knowledge of Bronze Age society in Scandinavia is still very limited. We see a large variability, but also several common denominators. There are important differences between areas, which could be described as regions if these are looked upon as temporary and historical constructions. There were also varied social spheres. Among these, the longhouse unit, a kind of extended household, played a central role. There seem also to have been sociopolitical entities, but not of a centralized type. The metal, with the raw material coming in from abroad, probably creates a special sphere, or a series of spheres, of crucial importance.

## Comparative Advantage

How, then, can we look at the ways the raw material for bronze production entered Scandinavia? To better understand how northern Europe became integrated into a Bronze Age economy during the second millennium BC, we employ the concept of "comparative advantage." The rule of comparative advantage, as defined by Ricardo (1817) implies the rationality of specializing in production of something to enter exchange rather than trying to be self-sufficient. The simple situation would be an advanced economy taking advantage of a weaker socio-economic setting, by means of economic exploitation. Advantage may, however, emerge in other ways and not necessarily be rationally understood by the actors from the beginning. Amin (1973) has discussed how, in certain conditions, a negative asset (e.g., uneven economic development) can be transformed over time to a possibility. The advantage may be related to differences in environment, resources, skill, know-how, social power, and social organization and transmitted into a special labor and knowledge in order to create a surplus (Rowlands and Ling 2013). The Ricardian model depends on a universal theory of labor as a commodity for the extraction of accumulated wealth through unequal exchange. A pure idea of commodity value would not apply in precapitalist contexts (and many would argue not in modern capitalism either), so we have to imagine entirely different modal logics, in which a large set of factors intervened, including status, age, and gender (Figure 9.1). Unequal exchange was probably embedded in varying socioeconomic settings through which the value of labor was filtered and transformed.

Comparative advantage relates to modes of production in at least two different ways. It produces vertical relations within societies and, at times, between areas or regions.

## The Emergence of Social Stratification and the New Political Economy

The shift from the Neolithic to the Bronze Age was a profound structural transformation based on a changing political economy (Earle and Kristiansen 2010). This change involved various aspects of the social, economic, and political setting, which did not necessarily take place at the same time. Large-scale exchange, in metals and other wealth, by formal trade and other means across Europe developed in the Bronze Age. One crucial parameter in this context is that the new metal technology for tin-bronze required copper and tin, two metals smelted from ores that typically derived from different regions, often quite distant from each other (O'Brien 2014; Pare 2000). Tin-bronze was used for producing various objects, including weapons, tools, and jewelry, and their flows selectively or dramatically transformed or changed local social institutions. In locations removed from long-distance trade, group ownership of agro-pastoral resources would have continued largely unchanged from Neolithic patterns. However, in certain areas articulated to metal exchange and trade, investment in ownership of ships and metal goods helped to define elite status, marked by displays seen in burials and hoards.

In simple terms, the Bronze Age witnessed an emergence of social stratification based on control over maritime technology, long-distance exchange and trade and flows of products. As competitive advantages of open ocean trade increased, a strong advantage would come to those with better boats, able to navigate successfully under unpredictable conditions, able to carry larger cargoes, and able to hold more specialized mariners and warriors to protect cargoes. As the size and complexity of boats increased during the Bronze Age, the ability to fund their construction and distant voyaging would have provided a new bottleneck based on ship ownership. This would have favored what we may call the "trading economies" of Scandinavia and perhaps elsewhere. Such socioeconomic regions formed networks that extended across distances, intertwined by competition and cooperation.

In short, one of the major differences between the Neolithic and the Bronze Age was that certain parts of the elite invested in the maritime forces of production and long-distance trade. This investment led to an

Figure 9.5. Bronze Age rock art panel from Tanum, western Sweden, displaying typical features of Bronze Age maritime warriorhood. Ink tracing. Photo by G. Milstreu, Tanums Hällristningsmuseum Underslös, SHFA.

Figure 9.6. Social positions and social inequality in Bronze Age rock art ship from Bohuslän (after Ling 2008).

expansion of certain households and thereby to a more pronounced social inequality.

The spatial distribution of large and independent households, with affluent grave goods, in the landscape in southern Scandinavia keys the decentralized political economy (Earle 2002; Kristiansen 1998; cf. Holst et al. 2013). [ . . . ] stylistic regions are approximately 500–1,000 km$^2$, 20–40 km across, normally with one or a few central places. [ . . . ] Within this region, local settlement units (individual chiefdoms) are defined by clusters of barrows typically only a few kilometers across (Kristiansen 1991:27).

Social inequality may be reflected in the uneven distribution of goods in burials. Population estimates and dating of nonexcavated burials are tricky, but it has been suggested that only a limited number, about 10–15 percent, of the population was buried with several elaborative metals and in monumental constructions (Holst et al. 2013). Social inequality is also to be very pronounced in Scandinavian Bronze Age rock art (Figures 9.5 and 9.6). The clearest examples depict enlarged warriors together with numerous smaller anonymous "collective" oarsmen. This representation indicates strongly that certain individuals in society controlled the ships and thereby the maritime trade (Ling 2008:202ff; Figure 9.6). The location of the Scandinavian rock art and burial cairns keys the decentralized societal organization of the costal societies in Scandinavia in the Bronze Age (Figure 9.3). In other regions barrows and metal hoards seems to have had a similar key function (Kristiansen 1998).

## Exchange and Comparative Advantage in the Bronze Age of Northern Europe

Traded commodities in BA Europe included copper, tin, gold, silver, amber, wool, hides, textiles, furs, salt, shells, ivory, glass, and jet, each giving uneven comparative advantages to different regions (Figure 9.1). The Alpine region could have focused on copper and salt, and the Carpathians on precious metals, copper, and wool. In Western Europe, the British Isles could have specialized in supplying tin, copper, and perhaps also gold; Spain, copper, and silver, and maybe also tin; Sardinia, copper and silver. For the Nordic area, one of the relevant products of interest in other regions was the Baltic amber, furs, and hides, all products which may have constituted important components of a Nordic comparative advantage. In fact, the Baltic amber constitutes the most concrete evidence of a Scandinavian product traded southward for copper. This is indicated by the findings of Baltic amber roughly in the same ore-bearing districts that show consistency with isotopes for Scandinavian artifacts (Ling et al. 2014).

For instance, the amber in Jutland, the Danish isles, and Scania was evidently systematically collected during the Bronze Age (Earle and Kristiansen 2010; Goldhahn 2013). From being abundant in graves from the Neolithic, it almost disappears from the Scandinavian burial scene during the Bronze Age, and at the same time amber becomes a common feature in prestige contexts in Europe, not least in the Mediterranean world.

Scandinavia's dependence on metals in the Bronze Age triggered the need to enter wider metal networks. Earle and Kristiansen have stressed that the development of boat technology and maritime skills was of major importance for the rise of regional polities in Scandinavia during the Bronze Age, not least with regard to the new role of exchange and trade (Earle and Kristiansen 2010:226–230).

On basis of the control of the metal trade, a mutual dependence was established between two spheres of production, the agro-pastoral (already established during the Neolithic) and the "new" maritime sphere of production, but perhaps also including or articulating to other spheres. We thus suggest the possibility of the existence of at least two socioeconomic spheres, the agricultural/pastoral sphere and a maritime sphere. It is not too farfetched to envision the emergence of two distinct modes of production, which articulated to each other.

The interaction between highly varied regions in terms of environment, production, skills, and socioeconomic and political settings was key, since it slowly created a rationality of specializing in production. For instance, many of the coastal areas with rock art had access to timber, a feature that was scarce and lacking in the deforested agro-pastoral regions. The coastal areas also benefited from the knowledge of the sea and transportation on water (Figures 9.2 and 9.3). The so-called agricultural accumulation areas manifest barrows and large bronze hoards (Holst et al. 2013), and these regions were also the ones that deposited the most metal, that is, ended their exchange cycle. The coastal regions foremost in Sweden and Norway were deeply involved in building, crewing ships, and creating and maintaining maritime institutions, manifested by rock art, cairns, and ship-shaped graves (Ling 2008). This maritime sphere was more fragile, due to the instability of the sources of exchange, that is amber, metals, and other products (Ling 2008).

## The Nordic Maritime Comparative Advantage

The palpable maritime sphere corresponds to a kind of ideology that became one of the cornerstones of the Nordic Bronze Age, grounded in a maritime reality with an emphasis on building and crewing ships for maritime activities, including trading, raiding, and warfare (Figure 9.4). In terms of maritime position the, southern zone in Scandinavia had a very strategic location and could have controlled the flow of traffic from both the North Sea and the Baltic. The Danish isles held a favorable position in terms of metal supply coming through the riverine routes of the Oder and Vistula and overland routes from Central Europe. Moreover, all metal imported from the west had to pass Jutland. According to recent analyses, a large percentage of the analyzed EBA metal in Sweden derived from western sources in Europe (Ling et al. 2014:Figure 4) at this time (i.e., the British Isles and the western Mediterranean). After the large expansion of metallurgy in the Nordic zone from ca. 1600 BC, most of the copper in the artifacts analyzed from there seem to have been channeled through a western "maritime route" following old Beaker networks bringing copper from the Western Mediterranean and the British Isles (Ling et al. 2014:Figure 4). Thus, the rise of power in northern Jutland during this period makes perfectly good sense. Scandinavia's success in the "global" metal networks in the Bronze Age could broadly be explained by its particular regional particularities, the special socioeconomic and political forms, and notably in the capacity to organize long-distance sea ventures. The products "exported" included, as mentioned above, amber, furs, and hides.

The interactive ties in the Bronze Age between Scandinavia, Central Europe, and the Atlantic Europe/western Mediterranean world are remarkable (cf. Harding 1984; Murillo-Barosso and Martinón-Torres 2012; Rowlands and Ling 2013). However, due to alterations in mining activity and the seasonal collection of amber, the maritime western network was probably very fragile. The direct interaction between these remote regions was probably not so frequent, and this western network did not influence Scandinavia in terms of metal forms, burial rites, and housing. These spheres' social practices and forms were instead inspired by the more intense and stable "terrestrial" networks that were established with central Europe already in the Neolithic. This relation to varied socioeconomic settings, affecting different spheres, is highly interesting in theoretical terms (cf. Cornell and Fahlander 2002a). The trade with the Central European networks had a broader repertoire of both staple products and high-value items, including finished metal objects, raw metals, textiles, and amber, as well as cattle and agrarian products (cf. Bergerbrant 2007; Earle and Kristiansen 2010). The stability of the terrestrial networks was sustained by closer and more intense political interaction as well as marriage alliances, which in turn led to strong similarities in metal forms and burial rites. In short, Scandinavia practiced two types of exchange with the "foreign" world (cf. Rowlands and Ling 2013)—exchange of stable goods and wealth exchange with the "terrestrial networks" in Central Europe—and a maritime system based on other products (metal, amber, etc.) between Scandinavia and the Atlantic networks.

## Conclusion

To be able to understand what is specific to the socioeconomics of the Scandinavian Bronze Age, we must know the specific social conditions and relations of material life. At the moment there is an increasing amount of empirical evidence available that allows us to speculate on modes of production for this particular historical phase. The amount of excavated habitational sites and graves has increased considerably over the last decades. Moreover, new scientific methods, as C14, C13, strontium, oxygen isotopes, lead isotopes and aDNA has improved our knowledge of diet, mobility, and interaction. However, there are still some notable gaps in our knowledge that must be recognized.

In any case, adopting Marx's social perspective accordingly underscores that the mode of production is of greatest importance in the creation of economies, ideologies, and boundaries. It is important to stress that mode of production corresponds to particular historical processes, rather than a fixed general structure. It is very important to recognize that Marx considered a mode of production as process rather than afixed model and that mode of production only exists in time.

In terms of the Germanic mode of production, it must be stressed that it is insufficient to describe the complexity of Scandinavian Bronze Age economy and society. One of the major problems is that it is focused on terrestrial production and does not recognize the importance of the maritime sphere. Both the agrarian and maritime spheres were important elements in the Scandinavian political economy of the Bronze Age. In fact, one of the major differences between the Neolith and the Bronze Age was the investments in the maritime forces of production during the Bronze Age. The Bronze Age economy demanded maritime enterprises for long-distance barter and trade. To understand the nature of Bronze Age interaction and trade, the concept of comparative advantage is highly relevant and could help to highlight the intricate interactions between socioeconomic regions in the Bronze Age. Unequal exchange was probably embedded in varying socioeconomic settings through which the value of labor was filtered and transformed. Thus, comparative advantage relates to modes of production in at least two different ways. It produces vertical relations within societies and, at times, between areas or regions. Again, when we start comparing transregional interaction, we must not forget the palpable character of the reality of mundane social life. Life at the farmstead or the maritime livelihood creates very different experiences and actions. In this context we may recall Marx's famous description of the social organization of the steam-powered factory, or of the mercantile processes of the sixteenth century.

## References Cited

Aijmer, Göran
1979 Reconciling Power with Authority: An Aspect of Statecraft in Traditional Laos. *Man* (n.s.) 14:734–749.
2015 Dominance in a Traditional State. *Anthropos* 110:43–62.

Amin, Samir
1973 *Unequal Development.* Monthly Review Press, New York.

Artursson, Magnus
2009 *Bebyggelse och samhällsstruktur: Södra och mellersta Skandinavien under senneolitikum och bronsålder 2300–500 f. Kr.* GOTARC B:49. Department of Archaeology, University of Gothenburg, Gothenburg.

Bergerbrant, Sophie
2007 *Bronze Age Identities: Costume, Conflict and Contact in Northern Europe 1600–1300 BC.* Department of Archaeology, Stockholm University, Stockholm.

Bidet, Jacques
2004 *Explication et reconstruction du* Capital. Presses Universitaires de France, Paris.

Bohannan, Paul, and Laura Bohannan
1968 *Tiv Economy.* Northwestern University Press, Evanston.
Bois, Guy
1976 *Crise du feudalisme.* Presses de la Foundation Nationale des Sciences Politiques, Paris.
Brumfiel, Elizabeth, and Timothy Earle
1987 Introduction. In *Specialization, Exchange and Complex Societies,* edited by Elizabeth Brumfiel and Timothy Earle, pp. 1–21. Cambridge University Press, Cambridge.
Cornell, Per
1993 *Early Centres and the Household.* GOTARC B:3, University of Gothenburg, Gothenburg.
2007 Unhomely Space. In *Encounters/Materialities/Confrontations: Archaeologies of Social Space and Interaction*, edited by Per Cornell and Fredrik Fahlander, pp. 100–122. Cambridge Scholars, Newcastle.
2015 Colonial Encounters, Time, and Social Innovation. In *Rethinking Colonialism: Comparative Archaeological Approaches*, edited by Craig N. Cipolla and Katherine H. Hayes, pp. 99–120. University Press of Florida, Gainesville.
Cornell, Per, and Fredrik Fahlander
2002a Microarchaeology, Materiality and Social Practice. *Current Swedish Archaeology* 10:21–38.
2002b *Social praktik och stumma monument. Introduktion till mikroarkeologi.* GOTARC C:46. Department of Archaeology, University of Gothenburg, Gothenburg.
Earle, Timothy
2002 *Bronze Age Economics: The Beginnings of Political Economies.* Westview, Cambridge, Massachusetts.
1997 *How Chiefs Come to Power: Political Economy in Prehistory.* Stanford University Press, Stanford.
1991 Property Rights and the Evolution of Chiefdoms. In *Chiefdoms: Power, Economy, and Ideology*, edited by Timothy K. Earle, pp. 71–99. Cambridge University Press, Cambridge.
Earle, Timothy K., and Kristian Kristiansen (editors)
2010 *Organizing Bronze Age Societies: The Mediterranean, Central Europe, and Scandinavia Compared.* Cambridge University Press, Cambridge.
Earle, Timothy K., Johan Ling, Claes Uhnér, Zofia Stos-Gale, and Lene Melheim
2015 The Political Economy and Metal Trade in Bronze Age Europe. *European Journal of Archaeology* 18(4):633–657.
Engels, Frederick
1973 Base and Superstructure. From letter to W. Borgius. In *Marxism and Art: Essays Classic and Contemporary*, edited by Maynard Solomon, p. 33. Vintage Books, New York.
2001 *The Origin of the Family, Private Property, and the State.* Electric Books, London.

Fortes, Meyer, and E. E. Evans-Pritchard (editors)
1940 *African Political Systems.* Oxford University Press, London.

Friedman, Jonathan
1979 *System, Structure and Contradiction in the Evolution of "Asiatic" Social Formations.* National Museum of Copenhagen, Copenhagen.

Gilman, A.
1995 Prehistoric European Chiefdoms: Rethinking "Germanic" Societies. *Foundations of Social Inequality*, edited by T. Douglas Price and Gary Feinman, pp. 235–251. Plenum, New York.

Gluckman, Max
1940 The Kingdom of the Zulu of South Africa. In *African Political Systems*, edited by Meyer Fortes and E. E. Evans-Pritchard, pp. 25–55. Oxford University Press, London.

Godelier, Maurice
1996 *L'énigme du don.* Flammarion, Paris.
2004 *Métamorphoses de la parenté.* Fayard, Paris.

Godelier, Maurice, Thomas R. Trautman, and F. E. Tjon Sie Fat
1998 *Transformations of Kinship.* Smithsonian Institution Press, Washington.

Goldhahn, Joakim
2013 *Bredarör på Kivik—en arkeologisk odyssé.* Simrishamn: Artes liberals.

Harding, A. F.
1984 *The Mycenaeans and Europe.* Academic, London.

Hjörungdal, Tove
2013 Budsene for Better or for Worse: Diffractions of the Lives of Farmer Women in the Late Bronze Age. In *Counterpoint: Essays in Archaeology and Heritage Studies in Honour of Professor Kristian Kristiansen*, edited by Sophie Bergerbrant and Serena Sabatini, pp. 159–164. BAR International Series 2508. British Archaeological Reports, Oxford.

Holst, Mads Kähler, Marianne Rasmussen, Kristian Kristiansen, and Jens-Henrik Bech
2013 Bronze Age "Herostrats": Ritual, Political, and Domestic Economies in Early Bronze Age Denmark. *Proceedings of the Prehistoric Society* 79:265–296.

Kliman, Andrew
2012 *The Failure of Capitalist Production: Underlying Causes of the Great Recession.* Pluto, London.

Kristiansen, Kristian
1978 The Consumption of Wealth in Bronze Age Denmark: A Study in the Dynamics of Economic Processes in Tribal Societies. In *New Directions in Scandinavian Archaeology*, edited by Kristian Kristiansen and Frederik Paludan-Müller, pp. 158–190. National Museum of Denmark, Copenhagen.
1984 Ideology and Material Culture: An Archaeological Perspective. In *Marxist Perspectives in Archaeology*, edited by Matthew Spriggs, pp. 72–100. Cambridge University Press, Cambridge.
1991 Chiefdoms, States, and Systems of Social Evolution. In *Chiefdoms: Power, Economy, and Ideology*, edited by Timothy K. Earle, pp. 16–43. Cambridge University Press, Cambridge.

1998 *Europe before History.* Cambridge University Press, Cambridge.

Kristiansen, Kristian, and Thomas B. Larsson

2005 *The Rise of Bronze Age Society: Travels, Transmissions and Transformations.* Cambridge University Press, Cambridge.

Kristiansen, Kristian, and Michael J. Rowlands

1998 *Social Transformations in Archaeology: Global and Local Perspectives.* Routledge, London.

Kuper, Adam

1991 *The Invention of Primitive Society: The Transformation of an Illusion.* Routledge, London.

Leach, Edmund

1954 *Political Systems of Highland Burma: A Study of Kachin Social Structure.* G Bell & Son, London.

Ling, Johan

2008 *Elevated Rock Art: Towards a Maritime Understanding of Bronze Age Rock Art in Northern Bohuslän.* Ph.d. dissertation. Göteborgs Universitet, Göteborg.

2012 War Canoes or Social Units: Human Representations in Rock Art Ships. *European Journal of Archaeology* 15(3):1–21. Sage, London.

Ling, Johan, and Per Cornell

2010 Rock Art as Secondary Agent? Society and Agency in Bronze Age Bohuslän. *Norwegian Archaeological Review* 43(1):26–43.

Ling, Johan, and Michael Rowlands

2013 Structure from the North and Content from the South. Rock Art, Metal Trade and Cosmopolitical Codes. In *Art as a Source of History—L'arte come sorgente di storia*, edited by Emmanuel Anati, pp. 187–196. XXV Valcamonica symposium 2013. Capo di Ponte (Bs) Italy. September 20 to 26. Edizione del Centro.

Ling, Johan, Zofia Stos-Gale, Lena Grandin, Kjell Billström, Eva Hjärthner-Holdar, and Per-Olaf Persson

2014 Moving Metals II: Provenancing Scandinavian Bronze Age Artefacts by Lead Isotope and Elemental Analyses. *Journal of Archaeological Science* 41:106–132.

Lowie, Robert H.

1937 *The History of Ethnological Theory.* Holt, Rinehart and Winston, New York.

Marx, Karl

1953 *Grundrisse der Kritik der politischen Ökonomie: (Rohentwurf) 1857–1858: Anhang 1850–1859.* Dietz, Berlin.

1973 The Immanence of Artistic Development, II, from *Theories of Surplus Value.* In *Marxism and Art: Essays Classic and Contemporary,* edited by Maynard Solomon, pp. 63–64. Vintage Books, New York.

Morgan, Lewis Henry

1877 *Ancient Society.* Charles M. Kerr, Chicago.

Murillo-Barroso, Marcos, and M. Martinón-Torres

2012 Amber Sources and Trade in the Prehistory of the Iberian Peninsula. *European Journal of Archaeology* 15(2):187–216.

Oberg, Kalervo

1940 The Kingdom of Ankole in Uganda. In *African Political Systems,* edited by

Meyer Fortes and E. E. Evans-Pritchard, pp. 121–162. Oxford University Press, London.

O'Brien, William

2014 *Prehistoric Copper Mining in Europe: 5500–500 BC*. Oxford University Press, Oxford.

Oma, Kristin Armstrong

2007 *Human–Animal Relationships: Mutual Becomings in Scandinavian and Sicilian Households 900–500 BC*. Oslo Archa Serie 9. University of Oslo, Oslo.

Pare, Christopher

2000 Bronze and the Bronze Age. In *Metals Make the World Go Round: Supply and Circulation of Metals in Bronze Age Europe*, edited by Christopher Pare, pp. 1–38. Oxbow Books, Oxford.

Radcliffe-Brown, A. R.

1940 Preface. In *African Political Systems*, edited by Meyer Fortes and E. E. Evans-Pritchard, pp. xi–xxiii. Oxford University Press, London.

Ricardo, David

1817 *On the Principles of Political Economy and Taxation*. J. Murray, London.

Rowlands, Michael, and Johan Ling

2013 Boundaries, Flows and Connectivities: Mobility and Stasis in the Bronze Age. In *Counterpoints: Essays in Archaeology and Heritage Studies in Honour of Professor Kristian Kristiansen*, edited by Sophie Bergerbrant and Serena Sabatini, pp. 517–531. BAR International Series 2508, British Archaeological Reports, Oxford.

Schneider, David M.

1984 *A Critique of the Study of Kinship*. University of Michigan Press, Ann Arbor.

Service, Elman R.

1975 *Origins of the State and Civilization: The Process of Cultural Evolution*. Norton, New York.

Thomson, George

1955 *The First Philosophers: Studies in Ancient Greek Society*. Lawrence and Wishart, London.

Tilley, Christopher

1996 *An Ethnography of the Neolithic: Early Prehistoric Societies in Southern Scandinavia*. Cambridge University Press, Cambridge.

Trautman, Thomas R.

1987 *Lewis Henry Morgan and the Invention of Kinship*. University of California Press, Berkeley.

Wagner, Gunter

1940 The Political Organization of the Bantu of Kavirondo. In *African Political Systems*, edited by Meyer Fortes and E. E. Evans-Pritchard, pp. 197–236. Oxford University Press, London.

Weiner, Annette B.

1992 *Inalienable Possessions: The Paradox of Keeping-While-Taking*. University of California Press, Berkeley.

Wolf, Eric R.
1982 *Europe and the People without History.* University of California Press, Berkeley.

Zizek, Slavoj
2006 *The Parallax View.* MIT Press, Cambridge.
2012 *Less than Nothing: Hegel and the Shadow of Dialectical Materialism.* Verso, London.

# 3
# ANCIENT STATES

# 10

## Social Formations Analysis

### Modes, Class, Gender, and the Multiple Contexts for Agency

BRADLEY E. ENSOR

This chapter describes and illustrates ways by which Marxist perspectives are appropriate for addressing contemporary archaeological questions of class and gender agency. Ethnographic frameworks perceived social formations as comprising multiple sets of social relations of production, providing complex portrayals of contradictions and contexts for agency. More recently, Marxist archaeological perspectives seek to explain the social contexts that guide agency (e.g., Brumfiel 1991; McGuire 1992; McGuire and Saitta 1996; Peregrine 1999; Saitta 2000), in line with Bourdieu's (1977) thesis that contexts—routine relationships situating individuals vis-à-vis one another—structure agency. Building on these efforts, and following the ethnographic perspectives on social formations, one challenge for archaeology is to identify the multiple modes and forms of production within a given social formation to avoid simplistic interpretations of only one set of social relations of production producing only one contradiction. An analytical framework (after Ensor 2000) is outlined here for interpreting multiple sets of social relations of production characterizing modes and their different forms to better identify the contradictions and the responses of actors. Case studies on the prehispanic Chontal Maya (Tabasco, Mexico) and Hohokam (central Arizona, United States) demonstrate the capacity for Marxist archaeology to better contextualize class- , gender- , and even age-based contradictions promoting agency.

### Modes and Forms of Production

A given mode of production is defined by its social relations of production (SRP): the relationships surrounding the ownership/control of the means of production, labor, and rights to the resulting products/commodities. These are the contexts that agents manipulate or change. Different modes have different SRP and hence variably structure contradictions and agency. Each mode, however, can have variation in the ways that its SRP are organized (alternate forms of a mode), which are meaningful distinctions for understanding human experience.

### Modes of Production

In addressing noncapitalist societies, Marx (1964) described communal, feudal, Asiatic, and Germanic modes and how these historically appeared or transformed. Wolf (1982), using categories as analytical concepts for broad comparative purposes, viewed "primitive communism" as a "kinship mode" after numerous ethnographers found kinship relations at the heart of SRP in non-class-based societies (e.g., Friedman 1984; Godelier 1982, 1984; Modjeska 1982:51; Peletz 1995). He also viewed "feudal" and "Asiatic" as two ends of a continuum within a "tributary mode." Although modes have been, and will likely continue to be, variably defined and labeled, Wolf's categories serve well enough for introductory orientation as long as an analysis leads to the identification of the specific expressions of SRP within the given community examined.

In a kinship mode, the SRP entail kin-group ownership of the means of production. The resources with which people survive are collectively owned by the kin group. As corporate property-holding groups, members of the kin group are both owners and laborers, and this codependence creates mutual obligations of support among members. The ways by which the SRP are organized will vary depending on the specific use of filiation, affiliation, and marriage being practiced. And, just as all things cultural change, so too do the ways by which gender is collectively manipulated for matrilineal, patrilineal, or cognatic strategies for determining group membership, rights, and mutual obligations. Some societies will have reciprocal prescriptive marriage systems and ceremonial contributions to promote egalitarianism (e.g., Godelier 1984), whereas others have competitive proscriptive marriage systems that are the basis for establishing collective group status and leadership status (e.g., Ensor, this volume, 2013a; Rosman and Rubel 1971). To ensure the success and perpetuation of the kin groups, ranked leaders or elders influence or control junior members' production and marriage, along with women's reproduction.

The SRP in a tributary mode involve social classes defined by their relationship as owners and laborers. Because resources do not produce wealth on their own, those that own need the labor of non-owners to convert the resources into wealth. In a feudal version, a class of lords (elite corporate estate-owning kin groups) own the lands, and a class of serfs is permitted to work those lands on the condition they produce a surplus for tribute to the lords. Membership in the classes is by birth and marriage. In an Asiatic version, the state's apical nobility owns all, and each class possesses lands with which to survive and produce surplus for tribute. Between these extremes, commoners might possess their own lands, on the condition they provide the required surplus for the state. In either, each stratum of nobility is entitled certain percentages of the surplus and ultimately transfer a percentage to the state. Non-food-producing craft manufacturers are essentially the same. Whether possessing their own resources and tools or using those owned by lords, they must produce a surplus in crafts in the form of tribute. The living conditions of food producers and craft manufacturers may differ, yet both are engaged in the same tributary relationship with the nobility (e.g., Marcus 1992). Additional commoner tribute is paid in the form of *corvée* labor, whether for construction, agriculture, other industries, or war. Forced production is the bond that defines the relationship between the owning and laboring classes, and a religious ideology legitimizing the roles of the nobility reproduces the SRP.

In summary, the particular ways by which production is socially organized among owning and laboring groups—the SRP—determine the mode in a Marxist analytical framework. In any version of a kinship mode, the kin groups both own the means of production and provide the labor for collective survival, perpetuation, and competition. In any version of the tributary mode, the nobility own the means of production, and commoners are forced to use those for surplus tribute in exchange for usufruct rights limited to subsistence. Different modes variably structure human contexts, conditions, contradictions, and hence agency.

## Forms of Production

Forms of production are variations of a mode of production. The term "form of production" was used by Patterson (1986:56–57) to refer to five distinct variations in "primitive communism": "egalitarian," in which adults directly share in production and obligations; "chieftainship," whereby chiefs' power over production derives from kinship relations; "lineage," in which those with higher status control descent group land and members; "Germanic," whereby SRP are atomized in the domestic unit; and "big-manship," whereby individuals gain prestige using exchange to control the production of personal followers. Smith (1986) also used the term "form of production" to distinguish different ways that petty commodity production was organized in colonial to independent Guatemala. Already described were different forms of the tributary mode.

Several "modes" commonly described in the 1970s to 1980s are merely variable forms of the kinship mode. For example, the "lineage mode" involves large descent groups that collectively own property, whereby leadership (through ranking, achieved prestige, or by elders) controls the labor, marriages, and reproduction of junior members, valuing women as reproductive agents, to enhance their status by ensuring the success and perpetuation of the descent group (e.g., Gailey and Patterson 1988). What Marx described as "Germanic" relations of production are better known by anthropologists as *peasantries*: nuclear or extended families that own small agricultural landholdings as a means of subsistence and sell whatever surplus they produce on markets. Petty commodity production (family-owned and family-operated non-food production) was sometimes viewed as a different mode of production, yet this too is merely a variably organized kinship mode.

Alternative forms of the kinship mode may therefore entail large corporate descent groups with strong elder/leader control over junior men and women at one end of the spectrum and conjugal family peasant agriculture or petty commodity production at the other extreme. Extended family cooperatives, be these smaller unilineal groups or bilateral temporary work groups, may fall in between. Although not constituting separate modes of production, the social experiences among these various forms of the kinship mode are qualitatively distinct. For example, women's collective and public group activities tend to mediate control by men, whereas tasks limited to supporting only nuclear family members are associated with greater gender inequality (Brown 1975; Draper 1975:78; Ember 1983; Remy 1975; Rubbo 1975:357; Sacks 1975).

## Social Formations: Articulating Modes and Forms

One negative stereotype of Marxist archaeology is that the interpretation of a particular mode of production, as an end in itself, leads to dull portrayals of lives that were likely far more dynamic. With neoevolutionism, there was a need to classify cultures into categories, in this case modes of production. What we learned about a given society was that it had primitive communism, or that it was tributary and had two social classes. If that is the end of interpretation, then such portrayals are indeed uninspiring when trying to understand social relations. Instead, past societies can be assumed to have multiple sets of SRP providing multiple contexts and contradictions.

Anthropologists long noted that cultural change entails reactions to expanding global capitalism's integration with and impacts on other modes of production. This thesis originated in Marxist anthropology. Early examples from structural Marxism emphasized how multiple modes of production articulate with one another within a social formation (e.g., Althusser and Balibar 1970; Friedman 1979; Laclau 1971). Tributary and capitalist modes are known to be "dominant," influencing the specific forms of the kinship mode (e.g., Foladori 1983, 1986; Kahn 1975, 1980; Smith 1984, 1986; Terray 1984; Wolf 1982). In addressing ancient state formation, Gailey and Patterson (1988) indicate that the "lineage mode" may develop at the peripheries of weak tribute-based states as a defense against state encroachment, but that strong tribute-based states are able to restructure labor, subsistence, and reproduction favoring the "Germanic mode." Meanwhile, resource-owning and laboring kin groups may occasionally employ the labor of others, which integrates a secondary set of SRP into descent-group, peasant, or petty-commodity production (e.g., Kahn 1975; Stoler 1977).

As power relations within nonstratified societies gained increasing attention in archaeology, studies found complex social dynamics in what were thought to be uniform egalitarian relations (e.g., McGuire and Saitta 1996). For example, Saitta (1997:8–10) points out that variability in labor and power relations may be subsumed in the same social formation. Essentially, these studies illustrate how ancient social formations may comprise multiple forms of a single mode. Such insights call for the investigation of variation in modes and the way these articulate within a given social formation.

Although recognizing that social formations comprise multiple modes or forms of production, groups or populations are typically equated with the modes or forms of production in these examples. In other words, people are understood to partake in only one kind of SRP. However, the equation of a population or group to one mode/form of production articulating with a mode/form of another population could be misleading. More commonly, people are involved in multiple modes/forms that create their totality of social experiences (Ensor 2000).

The history of interconnected modes enables anthropologists to observe the changes in practice and meaning to participants (e.g., Ong 1987; Roseberry 1989; Taussig 1980). Within the total web of relations that people experience, their crossings between different SRP provide them with different relationships, conflicts, and interests. Ethnographically, the felt differences between communal production, petty commodity production, marketing, and semi-proletarianization are part of a totality in which people's sets of interrelations are distinguished by them. People recognize the differences, place different values on them, and can resist them individually or collectively. Individuals may find better contexts in one form of social relations than others they engage in on a daily or seasonal basis. Although a preferred system of relations does not necessarily exist in isolation, separable from others, those relations provide an "ideal" form or quality and may even be used collectively as a means or goal for resistance against the unpreferred system of relations. The social formations perspective enables archaeologists to move beyond the dull, uninspiring labeling of a single mode of production, or a single form of production, to charting the constellation of interconnected SRP that shape contexts influencing people's reactions and possibilities for agency.

## Archaeological Analysis

Modes and forms of production must be interpreted from an analysis of SRP. Because a social formation may involve people crossing multiple modes or multiple qualitatively distinct forms of a mode, the analysis must focus on multiple activities rather than only one. Different activities may involve different modes or different forms of the same mode. The analytical framework advocated here involves three components for interpreting the SRP in each identifiable activity: 1) identifying the ownership/control of the means of production, 2) identifying those engaged in the production, and 3) identifying those who consume or benefit from the production (Ensor 2000).

The ownership/control of the means of production and those engaged in production for each activity is best interpreted from the distribution of individualized or collective tools and production-related features. As a hypothetical example, we could envision shell ornament manufacturing in a Neolithic society. The means of production would include the stone tools for cutting, engraving, piercing, and polishing, along with the raw unworked shell. If these means of production, and their debitage by-products, are located at only one dwelling within a village, then we can assume that only the members of that residential group owned or controlled the means of production and took part in the labor. In contrast, a concentration of these means of production in a public work space may suggest collective ownership of the means of production and collective public labor. If shell ornament manufacturing can be engendered, then that gender can be interpreted to have engaged in either residential group production or collective village-wide production.

Continuing with this hypothetical example, identifying those who consumed the shell ornaments is critical to interpreting social relations of production. In the first possibility, whereby one residential group owned and worked the means of production, three possible forms of production could be imagined. First, the same group might be the only one consuming the shell ornaments, as evidenced by the distribution of finished shell ornaments exclusively in the dwelling's location, in which case the form of the kinship mode was entirely residential-group-based. Second, if all residential groups consumed the resulting shell ornaments, then the form of production would entail residential-group surplus production for larger groups' consumption either to develop its own prestige or for material exchanges for other products or services. Third, if only one or few other residential groups interpreted to be of high status consumed the shell ornaments, then we could interpret a tributary mode of production whereby the one residential group produced the ornaments but only elites received and consumed them.

The second hypothetical scenario involves collective ownership and labor in a public work space. Two alternatives may be envisioned. If all residential spaces contained the finished shell ornaments, then a collective form of the kinship mode could be interpreted—large groups collectively producing and consuming the fruits of their labor. Alternatively, if only one or few other residential groups interpreted to be of high status consumed the shell ornaments, then we could interpret a tributary mode of production whereby the collective produced the ornaments for elite consumption yet were denied access to the products of their labor.

Of course, this hypothetical example illustrates only one activity. Other activities may be organized differently. It is therefore essential for archaeologists to conduct analyses of SRP on as many activities as their data enable to arrive at an understanding of the multiple sets of SRP humans experienced. Doing so turns dull generic single-mode interpretations into more dynamic images of lives, contexts, and contradictions, enabling interpretations of diverse contradictions that agents can manipulate or react against.

## Islas de Los Cerros

One case study employed this analytical framework on a state society with a tributary mode of production (Ensor 2013b; Ensor et al., n.d.). Islas de Los Cerros (ILC) comprises five sites on mangrove islands and a peninsula near the mouth of the Mecoacán Lagoon, Gulf Coast of Tabasco, Mexico (Figure 10.1). Although first occupied in the Late Formative period, the extant residential mounds and other features were all built during the Late Classic period (ca. CE 600–850) when the Chontal Maya emerged as a definable regional "culture" and linguistic group, headed by the interior capital of Comalcalco, ca. 12 km upriver from ILC. Thousands of tons of oyster shell from ILC were used to construct the brick, mortar, and plaster in monuments at Comalcalco, where coastal fauna are identified and epigraphic evidence indicates a tributary relationship. Together, these data attest to ILC's role as a resource procurement zone serving the capital's ruling dynasty (Ensor 2003, 2013b; Ensor and Tun Ayora 2011). Although Ensor et al. (n.d.) interpreted three classes at ILC, Ensor (2013b) revised this interpretation to two commoner classes and two elite classes, based on an analysis of SRP in fishing, construction, and food processing.

One elite class and one commoner class interacted directly in *corvée* tributary production for surplus fishing and construction materials manufacturing (Ensor 2013b). The South Group of Isla Chable was the location of a segment of an elite class, organized into a small patrilineage (Ensor 2013b), that oversaw collectivized fishing-related activities at an adjacent linear shoreline platform, and temper manufacturing (and possibly lime production) at an adjacent large deposit of crushed shell (Figure 10.1). Mortared/plastered architectural remains, vertebrate remains, and ground stone for maize processing were present at the residential mounds built of more stable shell and earth deposits. In contrast, the class with the largest population had less stable earthen mounds and perishable architectural materials and was widely distributed across the islands in a neolocal settlement pattern (Ensor 2013b). This class was defined by the near absence of stone tools and faunal remains (neither vertebrate nor invertebrate remains), and the lack of ground stone, yet with pottery morphologies primarily for cooking and serving stews. The highly unusual lack of basic tools and food remains at these residences, along with the neolocal settlement pattern cross-culturally associated with people who lack control over resources, suggested this class was dependent on *corvée* tributary labor using the lagoon, tools,

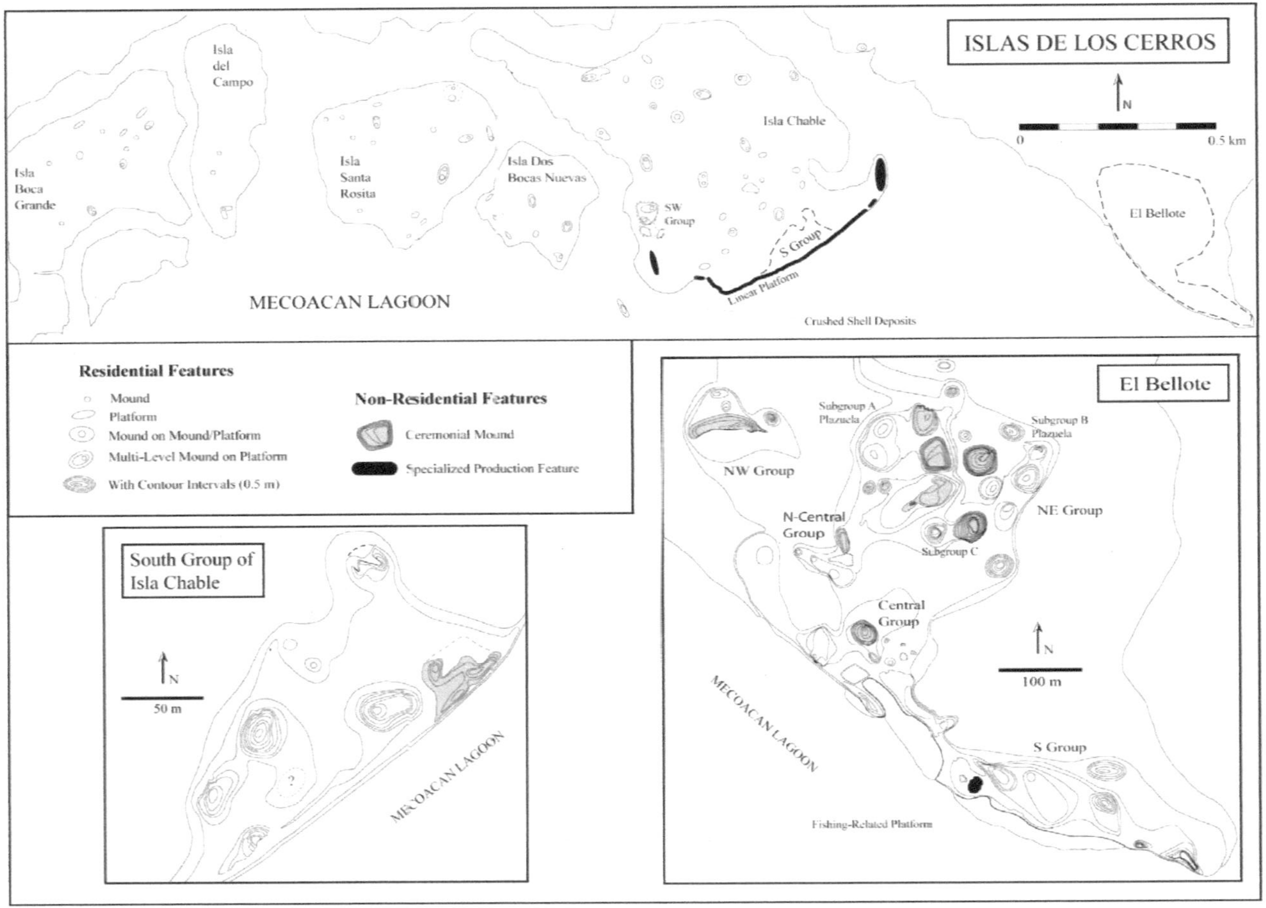


Figure 10.1. Islas de Los Cerros (compiled and redrawn from Ensor and Tun Ayora [2004:Figure 16] and Ensor et al. [2008:Figures 1 and 13]).

and features controlled by the elites. Thus, *corvée* tributary labor defined the SRP between these two classes (Ensor 2013b; Ensor et al., n.d.).

Direct historical analogy with the sixteenth century would suggest that men were involved in fishing and construction, while women were involved in food processing. The implications were that women of the neolocal resource-deprived commoners depended on men's *corvée* labor for foods initially processed elsewhere, a circumstance cross-culturally associated with extreme gender inequality. In contrast, the distribution of gendered tools among the resource-controlling elites suggested that those men oversaw the collectivized production, while elite women contributed to food processing tasks for nuclear families (an alternative interpretation is that they had domestic servants from the resource-deprived commoner class). Those domestic tasks were more numerous than their commoner counterparts and included ground stone for processing maize. As members of a lineage, these women likely had undetected collectivized tasks and potentially support from their natal elite groups, both of which could mediate gender inequality (Ensor 2013b).

Another commoner class lived in residential groups reflecting bilocal extended households and had access to their means of production: both tools and lagoon resources (Ensor 2013b). One segment was located at the Southwest Group of Isla Chable, adjacent to a smaller deposit of crushed shell for mortar/plaster manufacturing. Its architecture lacked these architectural materials, which are instead found at the two elite classes' residences and ceremonial mounds, indicating extended family tributary production for elites. Another segment was located at the South Group of El Bellote, which included a platform with an unusually high density of faunal remains, stone cutting tools, and net sinkers suggesting collectivized fishing activities by men, presumably for tributary surplus for elites. This use of commoner-owned means of production for tributary surplus is a second form of the tributary mode. These artifacts were also found at the South Group's individual nuclear-family dwellings, alongside ground stone fragments for processing maize. Therefore, the men of this group engaged both in collectivized tributary fishing labor using their own means of production and in fishing for nuclear family consumption. Women's food processing was similar to that of the resource-controlling elite class: wider in range than the class of *corvée* laborers, yet restricted to nuclear-family production (and possibly unrecognized collectivized labor for the bilocal residential groups).

The highest-ranked elite class was located in the Northeast Group and the Northwest Group of El Bellote. The Northeast Group was the largest segment, having a community pattern suggesting a patrilineage comprising two patrilocal residential groups and a third smaller subgroup, each of which had ceremonial mounds (Ensor 2013b; Ensor and Tun Ayora 2011). The differences in residential architecture and number of ceremonial mounds among the three subgroups suggest internal lineage ranking. These groups had the most abundant high-quality mortar and stucco and included brick architecture in the ceremonial mounds. As described, these materials were produced by the *corvée* labor of the resource-deprived commoners, and by one residential group of resource-owning commoners. Apart from the collective ceremonial roles, however, this class of elites had no other materials that could be associated with men's engendered tasks. In contrast, a wide range of food-processing tools were associated with nuclear-family dwellings, indicating women's production for nuclear families (alternatively by servants from the resource-deprived commoners) and potentially had undetected collectivized roles for the lineage. The men of this elite class appear to have had only two tasks: the ideological reproduction of the tributary social order through ceremony (plausibly alongside women belonging to the lineage) and the responsibility to ensure surplus tribute to Comalcalco.

The Late Classic period social formation at ILC was dominated by a tributary mode, which was organized into two forms of the tributary mode and two forms of the kinship mode. Among the resource-deprived commoners, men were engaged in collectivized tributary *corvée* labor, while women were restricted to nuclear-family production. Neither appears to have crossed into different social relations of production. This context would have promoted contradictions, first between the elite appropriators and the commoner *corvée* laborers, and second within the resource-deprived commoners' nuclear-family form of the kinship mode whereby women were dependent on men for their domestic means of production. Among the resource-owning commoners, men traversed kin-based collective production for tributary surplus and nuclear-family production. Women were involved in nuclear-family production but also could have collectivized additional labor within their bilocal kin-groups. These contexts would have promoted contradictions between elder and junior members of the corporate bilocal groups, between genders as women's labor was primarily restricted to the nuclear-family form of the kin mode and who were also valued for reproducing the group, and between the elite who appropriated surplus product and the commoner men who produced that surplus.

Among the two elite classes, men's labor was devoted to controlling tributary production. The resource-controlling elites collectively oversaw the tributary production of *corvée* laborers. The local nobility collectively oversaw tribute to Comalcalco, while also collectively manipulating the ceremonies that ideologically reproduced the tributary order, for which they demanded additional *corvée* labor for the materials and construction of their residential and ceremonial architecture. Elite women produced for their nuclear families but also may have developed collective roles for their kin groups. These contexts would have promoted contradictions: first, between the ranked patrilocal groups within their lineages; second, between genders, as women's labor was primarily restricted to the nuclear-family form of the kin mode and who were also valued/controlled for reproducing the elite groups; and third, between the two elite classes and the two commoner classes through the appropriation of surplus product. These interpretations take us far beyond traditional single-mode interpretations toward a more dynamic view of divergent social relations of production and consequential contexts for agency by class and gender.

## Pueblo Patricio

An example of a social formation comprising multiple forms of the kinship mode, along with the introduction of the analytical framework used herein, was presented in Ensor (2000) and is summarized here. The site of Pueblo Patricio (Cable and Allen 1982; Cable and Doyel 1987; Cable et al. 1982, 1983, 1984, 1985; Henderson 1995), in the original town site of Phoenix, Arizona, was used as an illustration. The six successive Hohokam components date to between CE 0 and 700, when the site was used by increasingly more sedentary farming groups (Figure 10.2). The activities analyzed included subsistence, food processing, and craft production. Direct historic analogy, mortuary data, and skeletal analyses suggested that Hohokam women were responsible for food production (with the assistance of men), gathering, food processing, and expedient tool manufacturing, whereas men were responsible for hunting and hunting-related tool manufacturing (Crown 1997; Mills 1997). Both men and women participated in craft production (Mills 1997). The kinship practices were later interpreted by Ensor (2013a).

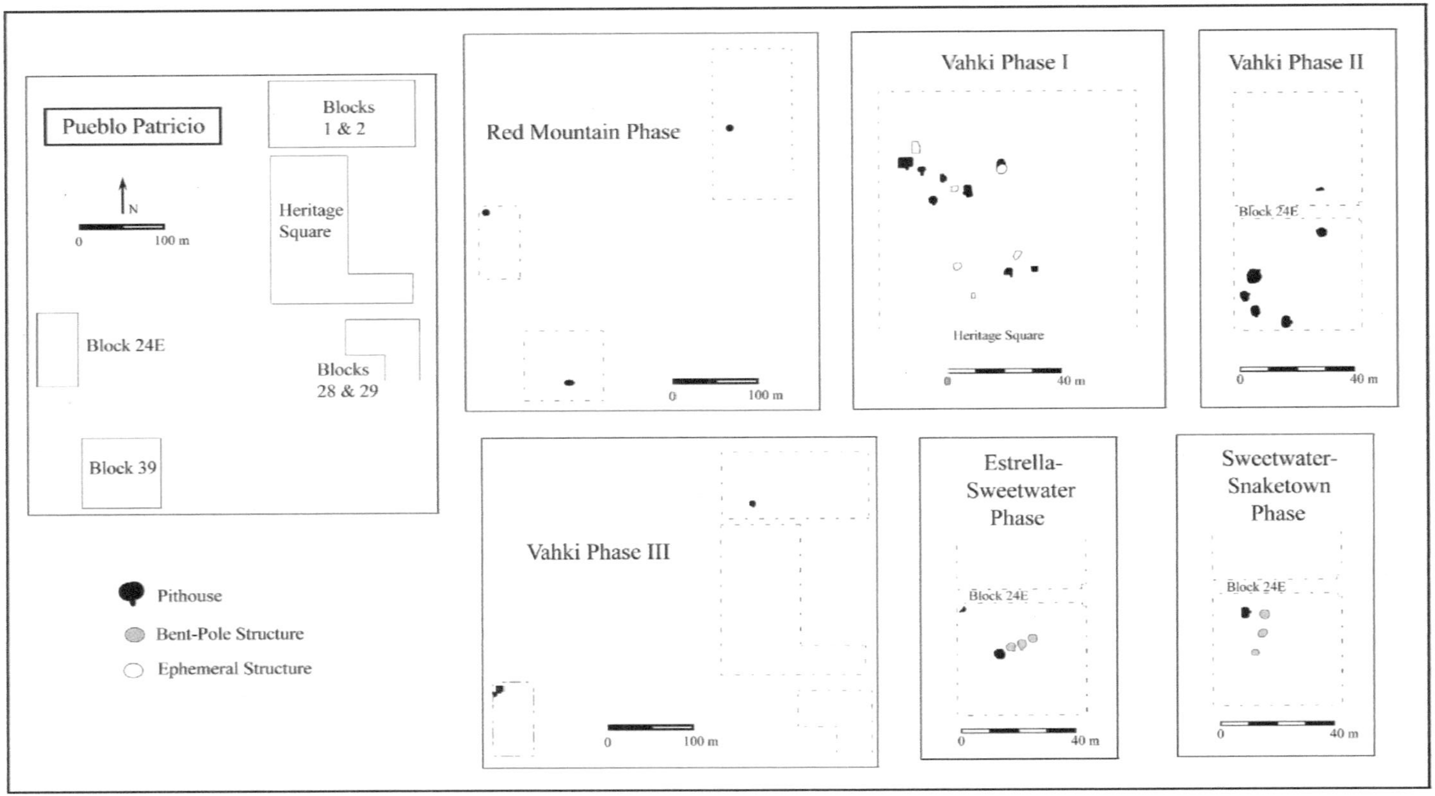


Figure 10.2. Pueblo Patricio (compiled and redrawn from Ensor 2013a:Figures 6.1–6.4).

The earliest occupations at Pueblo Patricio date to the Red Mountain phase (ca. CE 0–300). Seasonal neolocal residences were established where land was available for colonization. Men, women, and likely children all participated in agriculture for their nuclear family. Ground stone and cooking features were associated with the neolocal dwellings, suggesting women's food processing was also for the nuclear family. Crafts and tools were also produced and consumed by the nuclear families. Thus, only one form of the kinship mode could be interpreted: nuclear families owned, labored, and consumed as autonomous groups. All of the gendered social relations of production were limited to this one form of production.

There were three successive components in the subsequent Vahki phase (ca. CE 300–550). In the first, neolocal residences seasonally occupied the site at different times, and the distribution of artifacts and features illustrates a continuation of the same nuclear-family form of the kinship mode. In the second component, a bilocal residential group occupied the site. Two forms of the kinship mode were interpreted. First, men's and women's agricultural labor was collective at the scale of the extended residential group. Some women's cooking activities, using hearths in communal settings, indicate that women also labored in collectives for the extended residential group, although this was limited. Second, craft and tool production, and also most of women's food processing, was produced for and consumed by nuclear families. In the third component, there was one large dwelling supporting a bilocal residential group, and all labor and consumption could only be interpreted as communal at the scale of the extended residence. The Vahki phase components demonstrate a shift from nuclear-family relations of production to extended residential-group communal relations of production, with some women's activities shifting between the nuclear-family form and the collective form.

The next two occupations date to the transition between the Estrella and Sweetwater phases (ca. CE 550–650) and the transition between the Sweetwater–Snaketown phases (ca. CE 650–700). Each of these consisted of one bilocal residential group. Because women's activities seemed to have increased at the settlements, men may have played a greater role in the collective agricultural production for the extended residences. The distribution of craft and tool production-related artifacts indicate production by nuclear family groups, perhaps by both men and women, for their own use and symbolic exchanges with other groups. The distributions of hearths and ground stone, all associated with nuclear-family dwellings, suggested that women continued to process foods for their individual nuclear families. Men were involved in integrated collective labor for the extended residential groups but also crossed into the nuclear-family form of production for other activities. Women were likely still assisting with the integrative extended residential-group labor in farming, yet many of their activities were restricted to labor for the consumption of their nuclear families. However, in the latest occupation, hearths and a large roasting pit in a communal space suggest that women increasingly crossed into the collective extended residential-group form of production.

Because it determined residence, the dominant form of production would have been the extended residential-group form. This context would have promoted contradictions between elders and the juniors whose labor they controlled, and between genders whereby women were valued for reproducing the extended kin group. Women's labor was also primarily restricted to the nuclear-family form of production associated with greater gender inequality, presenting another gendered contradiction. However, the introduction of the collective form of food processing for the extended groups was interpreted as an active response by women to negotiate the increasing control exerted by men (Ensor 2000). In this example, the multiple forms of the kinship mode of production can be seen to have changed over time, with men's activities increasingly in the collective form, while women's activities were primarily in the nuclear-family form until they responded by creating a collective form of food processing (Ensor 2000). Nevertheless, the elder–junior contradictions may have remained, as would have the collective control over women as reproductive assets for the bilocal residential groups.

## Conclusions

This chapter argues for the need to contextualize agents within SRP, which requires archaeological analysis of the relationships by which people own productive resources, labor, and consume products/commodities. Furthermore, because single-mode interpretations oversimplify those contexts, a social formations perspective is advocated that interprets the multiple sets of SRP and the different qualitative experiences these incur. The constellation of SRP peoples engage in produces multiple contradictions and the possibilities for reactions.

The two case studies provide examples of situating people within multiple sets of SRP. Without attention to the multiple forms of production, only a vague depiction of a tributary mode with two classes and their one contradictory relationship would characterize life for men and women at ILC. Likewise, without considering multiple forms of production at Pueblo Patricio, only a vague understanding of a kinship mode would result. However, the social contexts that structure contradictions and agency appear far more complex when inferring multiple interacting modes and forms of production through analyses of SRP for multiple activities.

## References Cited

Althusser, Louis, and Etienne Balibar
1970 *Reading* Capital. Pantheon Books, New York.
Bourdieu, Pierre
1977 *Outline of a Theory of Practice*. Cambridge University Press, Cambridge.
Brown, Judith
1975 Iroquois Women: An Ethnohistoric Note. In *Toward an Anthropology of Women*, edited by Rayna R. Reiter, pp. 235–251. Monthly Review Press, New York.
Brumfiel, Elizabeth M.
1991 Weaving and Cooking: Women's Production in Aztec Mexico. In *Engendering Archaeology: Women and Prehistory*, edited by Joan M. Gero and Margaret W. Conkey, pp. 244–251. Basil Blackwell, Oxford.
Cable, John S., and W. Allen
1982 Part I: The Prehistoric Component. In *City of Phoenix, Archaeology of the Original Townsite: Blocks 1 and 2*, edited by John S. Cable, Susan L. Henry, and David E. Doyel, pp. 13–179. Publications in Archaeology No. 1. Soil Systems, Phoenix.
Cable, John S., and David E. Doyel
1987 Pioneer Period Village Structure and Settlement Pattern in the Phoenix Basin. In *The Hohokam Village: Site Structure and Organization*, edited by David E. Doyel, pp. 21–70. American Association for the Advancement of Science, Glenwood Springs.
Cable, John S., Susan L. Henry, and David E. Doyel
1982 *City of Phoenix, Archaeology of the Original Townsite: Blocks 1 and 2*. Publications in Archaeology No. 1. Soil Systems, Phoenix.
1983 *City of Phoenix, Archaeology of the Original Townsite: Block 28-North*. Publications in Archaeology No. 2. Soil Systems, Phoenix.
1984 *City of Phoenix, Archaeology of the Original Townsite: The Murphy's Addition*. Publications in Archaeology No. 3. Soil Systems, Phoenix.
Cable, John S., Karen S. Hoffman, David E. Doyel, and Frank Ritz
1985 *City of Phoenix, Archaeology of the Original Townsite: Block 24-East*. Publications in Archaeology, no. 8. Soil Systems, Phoenix.

Crown, Patricia L.
1997 *Food Processing, Preparation, and Gender in the Greater American Southwest.* Paper presented at the 62nd Annual Meeting of the Society for American Archaeology, Nashville.

Draper, Patricia
1975 !Kung Women: Contrasts in Sexual Egalitarianism in Foraging and Sedentary Contexts. In *Toward an Anthropology of Women*, edited by Rayna R. Reiter, pp. 77–109. Monthly Review Press, New York.

Ember, Carol R.
1983 The Relative Decline in Women's Contribution to Agriculture with Intensification. *American Anthropologist* 85:285–304.

Ensor, Bradley E.
2000 Social Formations, Modo de Vida, and Conflict in Archaeology. *American Antiquity* 65:15–42.
2003 Islas de Los Cerros: A Coastal Site Complex near Comalcalco, Tabasco, Mexico. *Mexicon* 25:106–111.
2013a *The Archaeology of Kinship: Advancing Interpretation and Contributions to Theory*. University of Arizona Press, Tucson.
2013b *Crafting Prehispanic Maya Kinship*. University of Alabama Press, Tuscaloosa.

Ensor, Bradley E., Concepción Herrera Escobar, and Gabriel Tun Ayora
n.d. La formación social del periodo Clásico Tardío en las Islas de Los Cerros, Tabasco: Una comparación del modo de vida entre clases sociales. In *Las memorias del VII Coloquio Pedro-Bosch-Gimpera*, edited by Guillermo Acosta Ochoa and Edith Ortiz Diaz.

Ensor, Bradley E., and Gabriel Tun Ayora
2004 *Proyecto Arqueológico Islas de Los Cerros, 2004*. Report to the Consejo de Arqueología de INAH. México, D.F.
2011 The Site of El Bellote, Tabasco, Mexico and Preliminary Observations on Late Classic Period Chontal Regional Integration. *Mexicon* 33:116–126.

Ensor, Bradley E., Gabriel Tun Ayora, and Concepción Herrera Escobar
2008 *Proyecto Arqueológico Islas de Los Cerros, 2007*. Report to the Consejo de Arqueología de INAH. México, D.F.

Foladori, Guillermo
1983 Formas de valor y formas de intercambio. *Cuadernos Antropologicos* 1:49–63.
1986 *Proletarios y campesinos*. Editorial Universidad Veracruzana, Xalapa, Mexico.

Friedman, Jonathan
1979 *System, Structure and Contradiction*. National Museum of Denmark, Copenhagen.
1984 Tribes, States, and Transformations. In *Marxist Analyses and Social Anthropology*, edited by Maurice Bloch, pp. 161–202. Malaby, London.

Gailey, Christine W., and Thomas C. Patterson
1988 State Formation and Uneven Development. In *State and Society: The Emergence of Social Hierarchy and Political Centralization*, edited by John Gledhill, Barbara Bender, and Mogens Trolle Larsen, pp. 77–90. Routledge, London.

Godelier, Maurice
1982 Social Hierarchies among the Baruya of New Guinea. In *Inequality in New Guinea Highland Societies*, edited by Andrew Strathern, pp. 3–34. Cambridge University Press, Cambridge.
1984 Modes of Production, Kinship, and Demographic Structures. In *Marxist Analyses and Social Anthropology*, edited by Maurice Bloch, pp. 3–27. Malaby, London.

Henderson, T. Kathleen
1995 *The Prehistoric Archaeology of Heritage Square*. Anthropological Papers No. 3, Pueblo Grande Museum, Phoenix.

Kahn, Joel S.
1975 Economic Scale and the Cycle of Petty Commodity Production in West Sumatra. In *Marxist Analyses and Social Anthropology*, edited by Maurice Bloch, pp. 137–158. Malaby, London.
1980 *Minangkabau Social Formations: Indonesian Peasants and the World-Economy*. Cambridge University Press, Cambridge.

Laclau, Ernesto
1971 Feudalism and Capitalism in Latin America. *New Left Review* 67:19–38.

Marcus, Joyce
1992 Royal Families, Royal Texts: Examples from the Zapotec and Maya. In *Mesoamerican Elites: An Archaeological Assessment*, edited by Diane Z. Chase and Arlen F. Chase, pp. 221–241. University of Oklahoma Press, Norman.

Marx, Karl
1964 *Pre-capitalist Economic Formations*. International, New York.

McGuire, Randall
1992 *A Marxist Archaeology*. Academic, San Diego.

McGuire, Randall H., and Dean J. Saitta
1996 Although They Have Petty Captains, They Obey Them Badly: The Dialectics of Prehispanic Western Pueblo Social Organization. *American Antiquity* 61:197–216.

Mills, Barbara J.
1997 *Gender, Labor, and Inequality: Dynamics of Craft Production in the American Southwest*. Paper presented at the 62nd Annual Meeting of the Society for American Archaeology, Nashville.

Modjeska, Nicholas
1982 Production and Inequality: Perspectives from Central New Guinea. In *Inequality in New Guinea Highland Societies*, edited by Andrew Strathern, pp. 50–108. Cambridge University Press, Cambridge.

Ong, Aihwa
1987 Spirits of Resistance and Capitalist Discipline: Factory Women in Malaysia. State University of New York Press, Albany.

Patterson, Thomas C.
1986 La creación de cultura en las formaciones sociales pre-estatales y no-estatales. *Boletín de Antropología Americana* 14:53–61.

Peletz, Michael G.
1995 Kinship Studies in Late Twentieth-Century Anthropology. *Annual Review of Anthropology* 24:343–372.

Peregrine, Peter N.
1999 Legitimation Crises in Prehistoric Worlds. In *World-Systems Theory in Practice: Leadership, Production, and Exchange*, edited by P. Nick Kardulias, pp. 37–52. Rowman & Littlefield Lanham.

Remy, Dorothy
1975 Underdevelopment and the Experience of Women: A Nigerian Case Study. In *Toward an Anthropology of Women*, edited by Rayna R. Reiter, pp. 358–371. Monthly Review Press, New York.

Roseberry, William
1989 *Anthropologies and Histories: Essays in Culture, History, and Political Economy*. Rutgers University Press, New Brunswick.

Rosman, Abraham, and Paula G. Rubel
1971 *Feasting with Mine Enemy: Rank and Exchange among Northwest Coast Societies*. Columbia University Press, New York.

Rubbo, Anna
1975 The Spread of Capitalism in Rural Colombia: Effects on Poor Women. In *Toward an Anthropology of Women*, edited by Rayna R. Reiter, pp. 333–357. Monthly Review Press, New York.

Sacks, Karen
1975 Engels Revisited: Women, the Organization of Production, and Private Property. In *Toward an Anthropology of Women*, edited by Rayna R. Reiter, pp. 211–234. Monthly Review Press, New York.

Saitta, Dean J.
1997 Power, Labor, and the Dynamics of Change in Chacoan Political Economy. *American Antiquity* 62:7–26.
2000 Theorizing the Political Economy of Southwestern Exchange. In *The Archaeology of Regional Interaction: Religion, Warfare, and Exchange across the American Southwest and Beyond*, edited by Michelle Hegmon, pp. 151–166. University Press of Colorado, Boulder.

Smith, Carol A.
1984 Local History in Global Context: Social and Economic Transitions in Western Guatemala. *Comparative Study of Society and History* 26:193–228.
1986 Reconstructing the Elements of Petty Commodity Production. *Social Analysis* 20:29–46.

Stoler, Ann
1977 Rice Harvesting in Kali Loro: A Study of Class and Labor Relations in Rural Java. *American Ethnologist* 4:678–698.

Taussig, Michael T.
1980 *The Devil and Commodity Fetishism in South America*. University of North Carolina Press, Chapel Hill.

Terray, Emmanuel
1984 Classes and Class Consciousness in the Abron Kingdom of Gyaman. In *Marxist Analyses and Social Anthropology*, edited by Maurice Bloch, pp. 85–135. Malaby, London.

Wolf, Eric R.
1982 *Europe and the People without History*. University of California Press, Berkeley.

# 11

# Re-envisioning Prehispanic Mesoamerican Economies

## Modes of Production, Fiscal Foundations of Collective Action, and Conceptual Legacies

GARY M. FEINMAN AND LINDA M. NICHOLAS

Concepts, relations, and perspectives inspired loosely from Marx's historical writings and its derivatives have long had an undergirding role in North American archaeological interpretation (McGuire 1993, 2002; Rosenswig 2012:3–7; Sherratt 1989; Smith 2009; Trigger 2003:51–52). Materialist frames, foci on production, means of transfer, labor, property, the financing of power as well as other aspects of political economy, and dialectical relations between the powerful and the powerless are all broadly applied aspects of standard archaeological interpretations, especially comparative approaches (e.g., Earle 2000; Rosenswig 2012; Spencer 1990:5). In contrast, explicit applications of Marxist terminology or strict Marxist analyses have been much less central to date.

In fact, the legacies of Marxist thought are spread so widely in contemporary archaeology that they ground seemingly contrastive perspectives, even including idiosyncratic approaches that appear to eschew both comparison and materialism (McGuire 1993; Trigger 1993). Perhaps this is not as surprising as it first seems, given the volume of analytic efforts undertaken by Marx, the number of people who have built off of his original texts, and the absence in Marx's writing of a single set of rules or a guidebook on how to proceed. When read and studied, Marxist approaches or philosophies (Trigger 1993:162), like the voluminous compendia of writings associated with belief systems, often spur different followers to reach diverse conclusions and to take alternative paths, promoting a multitude of legacies (McGuire 2002:viii).

Here we focus on shifts in the framing tenets employed to understand prehispanic economies in highland Mexico during the Classic (ca. AD 250–850) and Postclassic (AD 850–1520) periods with an emphasis on the Valley of Oaxaca, where we have directed archaeological field research at several analytical scales (Feinman and Nicholas 2012). Our aim is not principally to offer a full discussion or description of prehispanic economic practices across this wide region over more than a millennium. That would be a worthy but much more extensive enterprise. Rather, we endeavor to outline how the original framing tenets, derived from Marx's (1971) Asiatic mode of production and other related sources (Palerm and Wolf 1957; Polanyi et al. 1957; Wittfogel 1957), that have guided this research with productive results since the mid-twentieth century now require reevaluation in the face of the new and reprioritized empirical findings inspired and fomented by that framework.

We propose that these new theoretical frames, with alternate roots in central elements of historical materialist thought, now conform more closely with the amplified empirical record for late prehispanic Mesoamerica (Feinman and Nicholas 2012). More specifically, we focus on and amplify two key concepts central to materialist thought, the mode of production and broadly conceived relations of production, which include the ways in which labor and its products are marshaled to support governance and power. We see the interplay of these key material relations as more flexible and potentially changeable than traditionally defined modes that often are linked in a rather deterministic way to specific historical or geographic settings (e.g., the Asiatic mode). The proposed reframing, which decouples domestic production from self-sufficiency and direct top-down economic control, offers implications for a broader understanding of preindustrial urban economies, including their considerable spatial and temporal diversity, as well as the key dialectics and dyadic relations at the core of governance, power, and their fiscal underpinnings.

## Framing Early Studies of Prehispanic Mesoamerican Economies

Archaeological study of prehispanic Mesoamerica, particularly highland Mesoamerica, took a key conceptual turn after World War II from the more time-space focus on high culture, museum collectibles, and artifact categorization to a greater focus on social-science-related questions concerning sustenance, political power, urbanism, and dynamic historical transitions that occurred in that part of the world during the millennia before Spanish Conquest (Wolf 1994:3–4). This mid-century conceptual reframing, championed by prolific scholars including Eric Wolf (1959), Angel Palerm (Palerm and Wolf 1957), and William Sanders (Sanders 1956; Sanders and Price

1968), was undergirded by explicitly comparative, materialist approaches inspired by the writings of Marx (1971), Wittfogel (1957), Polanyi (Polanyi et al. 1957), and Childe (1950), as well as White (1949), Steward (1955), Fried (1960), and Service (1962). Both direct and more indirect, implicit intellectual threads to historical materialism and modes of production are woven through these works that endeavored to understand prehispanic Mesoamerica economies.

This mid-century recasting of interests and queries regarding the prehispanic Mesoamerican past promoted several generations of archaeological and textual research programs and projects, including highly informative field archaeological studies of urban layouts, regional settlement patterns, agricultural systems, and domestic excavations (Blanton et al. 1993; Flannery 1976; Flannery and Marcus 1983; Sanders et al. 1979; Santley and Hirth 1993; Wolf 1976). Based on the decades-long implementation of these investigations, now not only do we know orders of magnitude more about the people who inhabited this prehispanic world, but the empirical grounding for the evaluation and discussion of theoretical positions and tenets is much more ample than was the case six decades ago. In this reconsideration of the frameworks that underpinned the mid-to-late-twentieth-century research initiatives in prehispanic Mesoamerica, our aim is not to criticize those who engineered and employed these highly productive advances; rather, we endeavor to reconsider and adjust conceptual perspectives in the face of what we have learned (McGuire 2002:viii).

Early models of the prehispanic Mesoamerican economy drew heavily from the Asiatic mode of production, Polanyi's conceptions of redistributive economies, and Wittfogel's discussion of hydraulic civilizations (Isaac 1993). Those who built on these frames envisioned centralized, autocratic states, an interpretation seemingly underpinned by the labor investments in monumental construction that long had been recognized at prehispanic Mesoamerican sites (e.g., Holmes 1895). In line with theoretical divides drawn (e.g., Polanyi 1960) between the unfettered markets of capitalism and the redistributive, command economies of preindustrial times (see also Rosenswig 2012:7; Wolf 1982:75–100), production and exchange were seen as politically monitored or controlled, which afforded an economic basis for rule. In accord with Wittfogel (1957), the management of irrigation systems was reckoned to promote the centralization of political power and economic control over production and distribution (Sanders and Price 1968:178–180). In 1955 Palerm (1955:39) opined, "We view the development of irrigation in the Valley of Mexico not so much as the result of many small-scale initiatives by small groups, but as the result of large-scale enterprise, well-planned, in which an enormous number of people took part, engaged in important and prolonged public works under centralized and authoritative leadership." Later, Carrasco (2001:363) wrote in a similar vein: "Ancient Mexico had a politically integrated economy. The government controlled the basic means of production, land, and labor, and accumulated the surplus in the form of tribute." We reference Carrasco here as he formulated some of the most explicit and current perspectives on prehispanic Mesoamerican economies.

Not all scholars of this era saw the utility of Wittfogel's (1957) hydraulic frame for prehispanic Mesoamerican political economy. For example, Wolf (1959:16) observed that "the very lay of the land inhibited the growth of large-scale irrigation, and thus of the all-dominant overweening hydraulic state." Both empirical and theoretical questions concerning the presumed catalytic role of large-scale irrigation in political-economic change in ancient Mesoamerica also have been subsequently raised (e.g., Baker 1998; Kirkby 1973; Lees 1973; Offner 1981a, 1981b). As early as the 1950s and 1960s, it became evident that not only were massive canal irrigation or large water control facilities geographically restricted in Mesoamerica (e.g., there is basically no evidence of it in highland Oaxaca), but where it was found (such as the Aztec-era Basin of Mexico), its construction was very late in the prehispanic period, well after the rise of states in most regions. Prior to the Postclassic period, even in the Basin of Mexico, most empirically evidenced irrigation, such as small, temporary canals for floodwater farming, could have been built and maintained by small-scale cooperative arrangements (Doolittle 1990; Nichols and Frederick 1993; Scarborough 1991, 2006:224–235; Spencer 2000:175). Although canalization has been reported as early as 700 BC, clear associations between the state and the construction and maintenance of water systems are not apparent until the Aztec period (AD 1320–1520) (Scarborough 1991:128). Thus, given the preponderance of small-scale irrigation in Mesoamerica, it is difficult to argue that the management of irrigation prompted the political control of the economy or the rise of political complexity in Mesoamerica (Butzer 1996; Pyburn 1998; Scarborough 2006:233).

In the sixteenth-century documentary sources on the Aztec, two features of the economy stand out. The first is diverse kinds of tribute (but see Smith 2004, 2014), a matter of great economic concern to the conquering Spanish, as they wished to follow earlier practices and extract resources from the natives (e.g., Berdan and Anawalt 1992). The second is marketing and markets, whose size and activity greatly impressed many of the Spanish chroniclers, some of whom were already familiar with the Mediterranean centers of European commerce (e.g., Díaz del Castillo 2003). Integrating these documentary accounts into the models advanced by Marx, Wittfogel, and Polanyi, Carrasco (2001) generally stressed the centrality of tribute and state control of production and exchange, while underplaying the role of markets. For example, Sanders, Parsons, and Santley (1979) not only describe the Aztec economy as redistributive despite the vital role of markets but also question whether Aztec marketers had any concern with deriving profit. In general, prehispanic Mesoamerican markets have been viewed, until recently, as trafficking only in local, low-value goods, and/or as being a late prehispanic function of the Aztec empire and so not widespread in time or space.

Despite the repeatedly expressed reservations regarding the appropriateness of Wittfogel's model and the clear late prehispanic significance of markets, most archaeologists, until recently, have conceptualized or modeled ancient Mesoamerican economies as redistributive or managed and therefore in broad accord with conceptions of the Asiatic mode of production. Tribute has been stressed and seen as a central driver of the economy (cf. Kowalewski 1990:54). The prevailing presumption remains that prehispanic polities controlled production, that exchange occurred mostly through centralized redistributive or tributary networks, and that most households were largely self-sufficient food producers, pulled out from that role only by political coercion or demographic stress. In other words, a key tenet of this long-held perspective is that commoners or subalterns had little or no agency, autonomy, or economic rationality.

Based on this general model, we would expect that the prehispanic Mesoamerican economy was characterized by little nonagricultural production in domestic contexts (self-sufficiency) and especially little variation from house to house in what was produced at each settlement or across a region (basic self-sufficiency). Whatever domestic production is evidenced should be devoted to basic necessities, required by the residents themselves or to be contributed as tax/tribute. High-status households would have a managerial focus rather than be active producers themselves. Large centralized storage facilities should be present at politically important sites and in elite contexts to facilitate redistribution. Pooling or an even distribution of nonlocal goods from one house to another should be the rule, given a reliance on redistributive transfers, and market-based exchange should have relatively little economic significance (Table 11.1).

Table 11.1. Traditional expectations for prehispanic Mesoamerican economies

| | |
|---|---|
| 1. | Little nonagricultural production in domestic contexts (self-sufficiency); little variation in production from house to house in each settlement or across a region |
| 2. | Domestic production devoted to basic necessities |
| 3. | High-status households managerially focused |
| 4. | Large centralized storage facilities at politically important sites and in elite contexts as basis for redistribution |
| 5. | Pooling or even distribution of nonlocal goods among houses |
| 6. | Market-based exchange not economically significant |

In essence, our investigation requires vantages at several analytical scales, most importantly, the household. Is there evidence of basic self-sufficiency? Are there indications that most household members had access to the same exotics through pooled redistributions, or did access vary house to house? A key question is how likely it is that production and distribution were closely monitored or controlled. Furthermore, are there indications that the occupants of higher-status households were economic managers or producers? Were higher-status householders associated with large-scale storage? A second vantage is a focus on large central settlements. Do we find evidence of centralized storage? And, at the scale of macroregions, are there indications that long-distance economic distributions or transfers were politically controlled?

## Classic and Postclassic Era Mesoamerican Economies: New Empirical Perspectives

The economies of the Classic and Postclassic periods in Mesoamerica were highly diverse, spanning semiarid highlands and wetter lowlands, as well as large empires, small dynastic polities, and the hinterlands of early urban centers. For the temporal era in focus, our cumulative archaeological knowledge is not sufficient to address each of the six points outlined in Table 11.1 for all Mesoamerican regions. Nevertheless, we now know enough about later prehispanic Mesoamerica to question key elements of these points.

In a previous study (Feinman and Nicholas 2012), we addressed these points (Table 11.1) in relation to the Classic period economy of the Valley of Oaxaca. We do not repeat the full detail of that discussion here, although we refer you to the early analysis (Feinman and Nicholas 2012). Nevertheless,

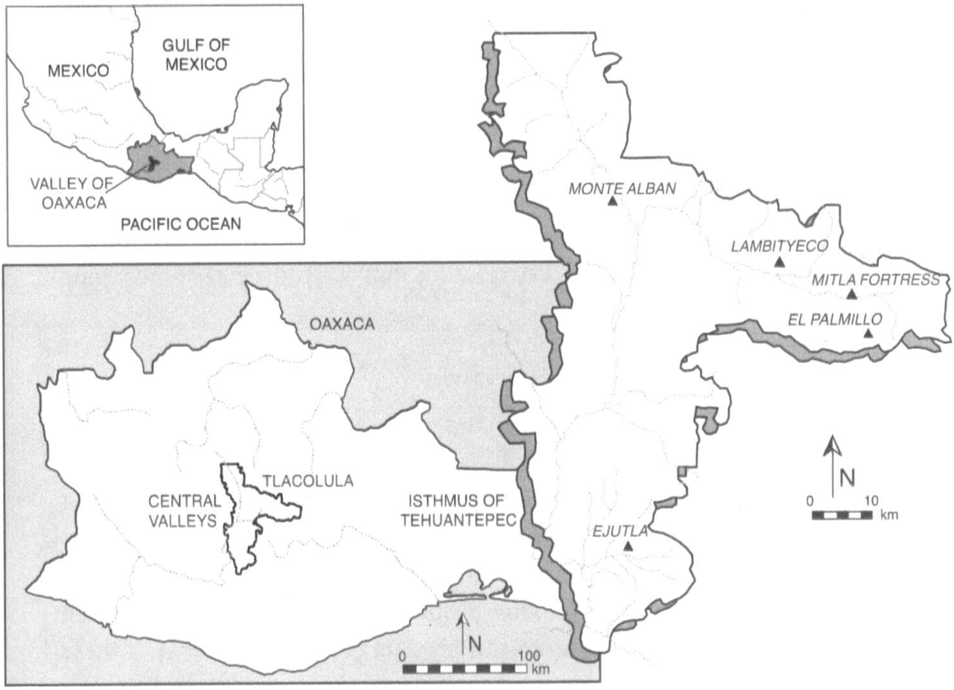


Figure 11.1. Map of Oaxaca showing places mentioned in the text.

we summarize the principal findings with the aim to build on and extrapolate from them. In a few instances we add new information from the Valley of Oaxaca that amplifies and supports the original arguments (Feinman and Nicholas 2012). At times we also extrapolate more broadly to other regions of Mesoamerica to illustrate that a number of the patterns noted for Classic period Oaxaca likely were applicable more widely across the macroregion.

The Valley of Oaxaca, Mexico, is one of the largest highland valleys in Mesoamerica. For over a millennium (500 BC–AD 850) the regional landscape was dominated by one central hilltop city, Monte Albán (Figure 11.1). The city's apogee in size and monumentality as well as the beginning of its depopulation and decline are bracketed by the Classic period (AD 250–850) (Blanton et al. 1993). We have excavated Classic-period houses at four secondary and tertiary settlements in the region (Ejutla, El Palmillo, the Mitla Fortress, and Lambityeco). Earlier, we also participated in a series of systematic regional archaeological settlement pattern projects that located and mapped the surface remnants of past occupations across the Valley of Oaxaca (Blanton 1978; Blanton et al. 1982; Feinman and Nicholas 2013; Kowalewski et al. 1989). More recently we also have collaborated with other researchers in the region to source obsidian found in archaeological contexts in the Valley of Oaxaca (Feinman et al. 2013). Those data have been integrated with a more spatially extensive and larger archive of obsidian samples that have source provenience (Golitko and Feinman 2015). Analysis of this archive yields a broad spatial and deep temporal vantage on the procurement patterns for this key resource that was transferred across long distances in Mesoamerica.

## Domestic Production and Consumption

During the Classic period, there are no clear indications for basic domestic self-sufficiency in the Valley of Oaxaca; in fact, we see the opposite: a high degree of connectivity or interdependence. We have studied a total of 13 Classic period domestic contexts at El Palmillo (8), the Mitla Fortress (3), Ejutla (1), and Lambityeco (1), and in each we have recovered evidence indicating the production of specific goods for exchange as well as the consumption of resources and products that the residents of these houses neither made nor accessed themselves (Feinman 1999a; Feinman and Nicholas 2010, 2011, 2012). This domestic-scale specialization was not likely full-time, and in various cases domestic multicrafting is evidenced (Feinman 1999a; Feinman and Nicholas 2007), but each excavated house has evidence of production for exchange. The specific economic foci varied from site to site, and even from house to house at El Palmillo, the one settlement where our sample is sufficiently large to recognize these differences (Feinman and Nicholas 2007, 2012, 2013).

In each of the four communities, much as with many villages in the Valley of Oaxaca today, householders were tied into intersettlement economic networks (Feinman and Nicholas 2012). The prime economic foci were xerophytic plant products, local chert tools, and rabbits at El Palmillo; xerophytic plant products, obsidian, and turkeys at the Mitla Fortress; pottery and salt production at Lambityeco; and shell ornaments and pottery at Ejutla. Many of the goods that were produced for exchange were utilitarian or essential (pottery, stone tools), while others (shell ornaments) were not. Most were made using locally available raw materials, but others (marine shell, obsidian) involved the acquisition of resources from long distances.

Although the sample size is small, we also found evidence of craft activities in the three El Palmillo elite residences that we excavated (Feinman and Nicholas 2012). The occupants of the palaces did not have a purely managerial role and were involved in specialized production. The high-status involvement in basic production activities also is noted for the residents of the Maya Lowlands during this same period (e.g., Aoyama 2007; Halperin and Foias 2010; Inomata 2001). Even if some of the palace production was enacted by suprafamilial "attached specialists" (*sensu* Brumfiel and Earle 1987:5), there is no evidence of larger-scale workshop contexts in the palaces, which indicates that these activities were basically enacted at a domestic scale.

The prevalence of domestic-scale production noted for the Classic period Valley of Oaxaca is a broadly recognized pattern across prehispanic Mesoamerica. In fact, given the long-held ideas regarding the political control of economic production, there is surprisingly little Mesoamerican craft manufacture associated with either workshop/factory-scale contexts (Feinman 1999a) or public buildings. The association of obsidian production with the Pyramid of the Moon at Teotihuacan is one of the few known exceptions (Carballo 2013:122). If craft production was widely dispersed, often part-time, with a high degree of interdependence between domestic producers and consuming households, then the centralized control of production would be nearly impossible to achieve, especially considering the heavy reliance on foot transportation.

Based on our sample from four Classic period sites in the Valley of Oaxaca, we also find little support for self-sufficiency when we examine access and consumption. Every household imported certain finished goods and sometimes raw materials from outside their immediate hinterland. Obsidian acquired from networks that extended outside the limits of the present state of Oaxaca (no mines are situated in Oaxaca) was present in every excavated house. Marine shell, greenstone, and other stone materials also were accessed from outside the immediate hinterlands of the sites studied. At El Palmillo, the representations of the obsidians acquired by each household were not equivalent; they did not have the same source compositions, so at the house scale there is no empirical basis to assert centralized pooling (Feinman et al. 2013). When considered from the bottom-up, there is little indication that either nonagricultural production or distribution was heavily controlled or monopolized by political authorities in the Classic period Valley of Oaxaca.

In regard to agricultural production, the determination of how it was managed at the domestic scale is challenging when dependent on archaeological data. For the sixteenth-century Aztec, for whom we can rely on textual accounts as well as archaeology, Michael Smith (2014) describes land taxes, labor drafts, and rent charged to farm on noble estates (the latter applied to only a small percentage of the population), but little indication of direct top-down control of farming. Of course, most, if not all, Central Mexican households also participated in the vibrant market system (Blanton 1996; Nichols 2013). For the Classic period Valley of Oaxaca, our vantage on farming is most accessible at a broad regional scale from which it is clear that major centers in (and sectors of) the region could not have been entirely self-sufficient, as the spatial and temporal periodicities of water access were too unpredictable (Nicholas 1989).

### Economic Distribution: The Regional Scale and Beyond

For the Classic period in the Valley of Oaxaca, obsidian provides a window to examine patterns of trade and exchange, although one class of goods certainly cannot serve as a proxy for others. Based on the large obsidian samples with known source proveniences for Classic period Oaxaca, we do not find that the observed distribution was achieved through pooling either by a central authority at Monte Albán or even by local political leaders, such as at El Palmillo (Feinman and Nicholas 2012; Feinman et al. 2013; Golitko and Feinman 2015). Rather, we note considerable degrees of variation at several scales. As noted, individual houses at El Palmillo had different source distributions as well as quantities of obsidian. In addition, the obsidian assemblages from different Classic period sites in the region are highly variable from one to another.

Based on preliminary compositional analyses of ceramic samples from Classic period sites in the Valley of Oaxaca (Faulseit et al. 2015), we also do not find any evidence for redistribution or pooling at the regional level. For the most part, each settlement appears to have produced the bulk of the pottery used by the inhabitants of that site. But the patterns also do not conform to a high degree of self-sufficiency, as every site also included a component of exotic ceramics in its assemblage. Along with Monte Albán, El Palmillo, where other craft goods were produced domestically for exchange and where we recorded few indications of ceramic production during survey or excavations (Feinman and Nicholas 2012, 2013), had the greatest quantities of imported pottery.

Large central storage facilities have not been found in Classic period Oaxaca. Given the volume of excavations at Monte Albán (Caso et al. 1967) and other sites, it seems doubtful that such facilities existed in the valley during this period. During the Late Postclassic period, at the much larger Aztec capital of Tenochtitlán, there were royal granaries (Hassig 1981), but their contents were much too meager to feed the bulk of the populace during famine episodes. Certainly, such facilities were inadequate to have served as storehouses for the large-scale centralized collection and redistribution of staple foods to significant segments of the populace. In fact, a comparison of sixteenth-century Spanish accounts of the Aztec and the Inca offers a dramatic contrast in regard to centralized food storage and large-scale transfers of edibles for these two late prehispanic empires (D'Altroy and Earle 1985). Whereas Spanish conquest of Peru would have been nearly impossible without their repeated raiding of Inca food stores, Cortés and his forces made little mention of such central storage facilities. They did write repeatedly and with considerable animation about the scale and size of Aztec era markets (e.g., Berdan 1977; Blanton 1996; Feinman and Nicholas 2010).

In the Classic period Valley of Oaxaca, the apparent absence of community-wide storage at major settlements calls into question the long-held presumption of large-scale, centralized redistribution as the main means of economic distribution. Furthermore, because so many of the largest valley settlements at that time were situated on hilltops, with high-status residences placed near the apexes of these sites, redistribution would have required many energetically demanding trips up and down steep hills to spatial settings adjacent to (and easily monitored by) the residences of rulers. Although negative evidence alone should never be conclusive, when considered in conjunction with the aforementioned artifact distributions, it is hard to see the large-scale redistribution of basic commodities as a key element of the Classic period Valley of Oaxaca economy.

Marketplace exchange is notoriously difficult to determine with archaeological data alone (Feinman and Garraty 2010; Feinman and Nicholas 2010; Minc 2006; Stark and Garraty 2010). For the sixteenth century in highland Oaxaca, the existence of marketplace exchange was recorded in textual accounts, albeit without the depth and flair of the contemporary Central Mexican records (Pohl et al. 1997; Spores 1965). These spatial differences reflect both where the Spanish traveled and the scale of prehispanic settlement at that time. Of course, no such texts exist for Classic period Oaxaca, although expanding suites of data have now been marshaled for the importance of marketplace exchange across Mesoamerica at least by the Classic period (Chase and Chase 2014; Garraty and Stark 2010; Hirth and Pillsbury 2013; Kowalewski 2012; Masson and Freidel 2012; Shaw 2012). Given the scale of sixteenth-century Central Mexican markets, it is not surprising that there must have been significant antecedents.

In the sixteenth century, Oaxaca marketplaces generally were open areas that were positioned at the edges of settlements (Pohl et al. 1997). Provocatively, earlier Classic period settlements in the region often have extensive plazas located at their peripheries and with little or no monumental construction. For example, at Monte Albán, Blanton (1978:86) suggested an open area near the base of the site as a likely setting for market activities, as it was adjacent to a major road and was surrounded by many residential terraces that had surface indicators of craft activities. Likewise, we (Feinman and Nicholas 2004:59, 123–124, 2010:95) suspect that similarly situated open plazas at El Palmillo and the Mitla Fortress also may have been marketplaces. The areas of these open plazas correspond respectively with the sizes of secondary and tertiary marketplaces in contemporary Oaxaca (Feinman and Nicholas 2010:95; Pluckhahn 2009).

To synthesize from a multiscalar perspective, the economy of the Valley of Oaxaca during the Classic period was grounded in household production (Flannery 1983:339) that entailed a high degree of domestic interdependence. This preeminent pattern (Feinman 2006; Feinman and Nicholas 2012; Kowalewski 2003a) has remained relatively persistent in the region to the present day (Beals 1970, 1975; Parsons 1936), despite the presence of some small elite estates during the Postclassic era (Flannery and Marcus 1983:277; Marcus and Flannery 1983:220) and haciendas during colonial times (Baskes 2005:192–193; Taylor 1972). Neither household self-sufficiency nor direct political control of economic production and distribution seems to have been a central element for the Classic period Valley of Oaxaca economy or the prehispanic Mesoamerican economy more generally. Nevertheless, the extent of the political role in the economy likely was not stable over time. Taxes, tribute, and other fiscal exactions clearly were present, as we know they were for the Aztec empire (Smith 2014), although the specific constitutions for funds of power also were variable. In a sense, for much of the prehispanic history of Mesoamerica, a domestic mode of production supported large and small states, even empires, with a growing body of evidence that marketplace exchanges helped bridge interdependent communities (Kowalewski 2003b). For ancient Mesoamerica, the fundamental importance and time-space prevalence of domestic production and markets force us to reconsider prehispanic economies. So, how do we proceed from here?

## Alternative Legacies: Fiscal Theories of Collective Action

In regard to later prehispanic Mesoamerican economies, a "hard-headed confrontation between theory and [empirical] reality" is in order (Trigger 1993:184). Long-standing conceptual approaches that wove together ideas drawn from Polanyi, Wittfogel, and Marx's Asiatic mode require disentangling and rethinking (Feinman and Nicholas 2012; Garraty and Stark 2010; Hirth and Pillsbury 2013; Smith 2004). The data and knowledge that we have collected raise serious conflicts and doubts regarding the core tenets of these long-standing frames, such as heavy-handed state control of economic production and distribution, a reliance on centralized redistributive transfers, basic presumptions that households were self-sufficient until forced to change, and a general diminishment of marketplace exchange. These prevailing premises that have guided our frames for several generations are no longer tenable as foundational stakes for understanding prehispanic Mesoamerican (and likely many other preindustrial) economies (e.g., Blanton and Fargher 2008).

At the same time, several more specific issues also require redress. As Smith (2014) has asserted, the oft-used referent to "tribute" in discussions of the economic revenues that underpinned preindustrial states—prehispanic Mesoamerica in particular—is problematic for several reasons. Most notably, in line with how "tribute" and "tax" are employed and distinguished in broader historical contexts, the Aztec for the most part paid taxes—"regular, routinized collections"—and not tribute—one-time, lump-sum payments, usually made under duress (Smith 2014:19; Tarschys 1988:1–7). Although some tribute or "irregularly-timed gifts" were paid in Aztec times (Smith 2014:20), most revenues came to governing authorities through steady, regular disbursements or taxes, and it is important to recognize that such payments generally were not the direct outcome of war or force. In fact, the fiscal foundations of the Aztec empire were complex and diversified, and reference to these varied exactions simply as "tribute" masks that complexity and the evident parallels to the financial regimes of other states (Smith 2014:19).

In the analytical effort "to avoid the extremes of ecological and technological determinism on the one hand and of cultural determinism on the other" (Trigger 1993:183), we also must find ways to broaden the application of agency in our models beyond those with power and economic clout (Sewell 2005). The relations of prehispanic Mesoamerican political economy were multiscalar, requiring consideration of micromotives and foundations as well as macrobehaviors and processes (e.g., Schelling 2006). In moving forward, our intent is neither an extended critique or dissection of extant texts and frames nor an assignment of labels. Rather, we aim to draw and build on the legacies of long-productive approaches, including key elements of mode of production analysis along with other theoretical frames, to outline new perspectives for conceptualizing variation and change in prehispanic Mesoamerican economies.

In his cogent discussion of modes of production analysis, Eric Wolf (1982:73–76) stresses that an essential element is neither the definition nor the number of specific historical modes, but rather an approach that recognizes the importance of human social labor and the dynamic or dialectical connections or relations between labor, production, and other spheres of human life, social fields or networks, and institutions (see also McGuire 2002:212–214). Both Marx and Wolf recognized the sociality of humankind and that "humans exist in organized pluralities" (Wolf 1982:73). To phrase it another way, they have a keen ability to cooperate (e.g., Nowak 2011), but large-scale enduring cooperation is not easy, requiring some (albeit different) means of governance (Feinman 2013). In consequence, a key dialectical link or relation is recognized to be the way that the outcomes of production and surpluses are transferred to undergird the organizations and institutions that govern human pluralities (Wolf 1982:73–100).

Past approaches to Mesoamerican economies, modeled in part on Marx's Asiatic mode of production (see also Wolf's [1982:79–88] tributary mode), have tended to assume that surplus was exacted by domination, force, military threat, and/or subterfuge, granting no agency to subaltern "others" (Blanton and Fargher 2008:5–8). But force is expensive and difficult to maintain, especially if employed over generations and centuries. Monte Albán endured as the primary urban center in the Valley of Oaxaca for more than a millennium. Teotihuacan dominated the Basin of Mexico for almost as long. More to the point, for prehispanic Mesoamerica there is little evidence for direct political control over either production or distribution. Given the transport limitations, how easy would it be for governors or principals to directly manage production if many, possibly most, households were producing for exchange? In prehispanic Mesoamerica, means of governance and rule varied across space and time (Blanton et al. 1996; Feinman 2001): does that variation relate in part to ways that governance and power were financed or to the kinds of resources and the means through which production was appropriated? If force and domination are not uniformly employed or effective, how else is surplus exacted?

### Fiscal Theories of Collective Action

Humans have a great potential to cooperate, but they are not always good at it. Shared interests do not necessarily translate into collective action, because rational individuals may not elect to act in the common interest (e.g., Hechter 1988; Olson 1965). It is in part for this reason that "men make history but they do not know which one" (Furet 1978:44; quoted in Przeworski 1985:400). At the same time, individual thoughts and actions construct institutions, but those institutions then, in turn, influence and constrain individual preferences and behaviors (Levi 1988:8; North 1991). Human cooperation is situational and contingent; to start to understand differential appropriations and diverse manifestations of governance and power, these contingencies and the institutions that constrain them must be considered and explored.

These underlying tenets, including broader applications of agency, are embodied in fiscal theories of collective action (e.g., Blanton and Fargher 2008; Levi 1988). The general approach is framed to understand the variable and dialectical relations through which principals appropriate resources and the products of labor. At the same time, this frame provides a basis to account for differentials in the manifestations of leadership and power, along continua from more collective to more autocratic, which have been widely noted in different comparative schemes, but not sufficiently explained (for examples, see Feinman 2012).

Rulers or principals endeavor to maximize their resource intake, but they cannot do just as want; they may be checked by their subjects or clients who strive to meet their own basic needs (Levi 1988:10–11). The crux of the approach views the relative degrees of ruler agency and taxpayer compliance as the outcome of a dynamic cooperative arrangement or bargaining that reflects on the kinds of resources that are produced and controlled by each (Blanton and Fargher 2008:14). In other words, the outcomes of such bargaining or "social contracts" are variable depending on the kinds of resource endowments both parties control. Embedded in this dialectic is the contingent, situational aspect of cooperation.

When rulers are less dependent on the social labor and production of taxpayers for their revenues and can rely on what have been termed external resources, they are less likely to be responsive to the needs of their local

Table 11.2. Internal and external revenues

| Internal | External |
|---|---|
| Advantages to aggregation (defense) | Valued spot resources |
| Entrenched agrarian interests | Position on trade route, coastal location |
| Expanding empire | War booty |
| | Elite estates |

populace and freer to act autocratically (Table 11.2). Alternatively, when principals rely heavily on the labor and production of their local population for their revenues (internal resources), the latter have greater bargaining power and voice, which tends to result in more collectively organized systems of governance with less concentrated power. More collective forms of governance, dependent on the appropriation of internal resources, generally are more broadly responsive, delivering more ample public goods and requiring larger bureaucratic investments to implement those initiatives and to collect the revenues to pay for them (Figure 11.2) (Blanton and Fargher 2008:254).

From this perspective, agrarian polities, heavily reliant on exactions from the local agricultural producers for their revenue basis, would (all things being equal) be expected to have relatively collective forms of governance. Governors, dependent on the local population for their funds of sustenance and power, would be apt to deliver public goods and services to encourage taxpayer compliance and to minimize subaltern resistance and out-migration, both of which undercut revenues. When rulers had access to external resources, such as personal estates, spot resources, or the direct control of trade networks, they could act less collectively, wield more power, and behave more autocratically. The expectations from this frame are at odds with more traditional ideas that have been near-truisms regarding the interpretation of preindustrial polities. Most notably, in the absence of ruler-owned estates or centrally controlled water resources, ruling authorities dependent on the appropriation of local agrarian resources from small farmers would be expected to have more collective forms of governance and not be intensely despotic with centralized control over production and exchange. At the same time, more nuanced perspectives on ancient construction and infrastructure are in order. Many kinds of monumental building, such as walls, grid plans, open plazas, and public temples, may represent, at least in part, the delivery of public goods that served the interests of more than just the powerful and were not simply indicative of

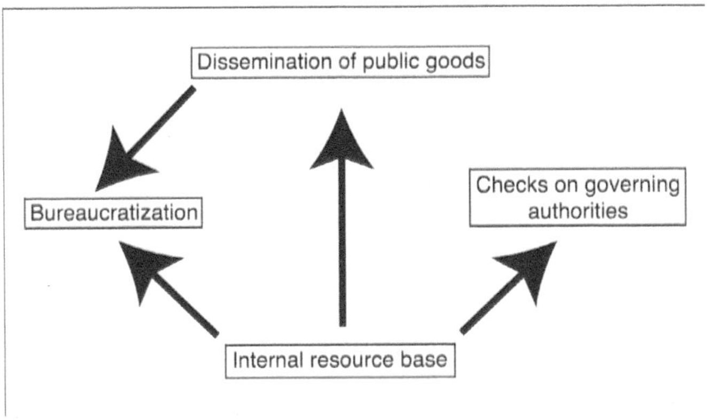


Figure 11.2. Fiscal model of collective action (adapted from Blanton and Fargher 2008:Figure 10.2).

largesse. Alternatively, elaborate palaces, tombs, and the associated wealth buried within may be more reflective of ostentatious signaling and wielding of more concentrated power. Clearly, these distinctions are just starting points, but they do open up long-held views, such as non-Western subalterns as "helpless victims rather than active agents" (Attwood 1997:147) to in-depth reassessment (see also Popkin 1979).

## Reassessing Mesoamerican Economies: Temporal Variation in Prehispanic Oaxaca

A key way to assess the utility of a conceptual lens is to apply it to evaluate data, particularly for cases where there seem to be contradictions or inexplicable findings when looked at from extant frames. Here, we briefly return to the Valley of Oaxaca during the prehispanic era to reassess aspects of the Classic period political economy as well as to draw contrasts with that of the Postclassic. Although there are important economic continuities between these periods, there also are key differences (Feinman 1999b), which we aim to explicate more fully by looking at them through a different lens.

As elaborated above, the basic economy in the Valley of Oaxaca for at least the 1,500 years prior to the incorporation of the region into the present world economy during the first half of the twentieth century generally was underpinned by domestic-scale craft and agrarian production, diverse means of socioeconomic connectivity, demographic mobility in and out of the region, and market exchange (e.g., Beals 1970, 1975; Feinman 2006; Feinman and Nicholas 2012; Kowalewski 2003a). Our aim here is not to explain these rather enduring economic underpinnings for the Valley of Oaxaca; neither do we wish to diminish the significant changes that occurred during these millennia. Rather, we suspect that certain economic practices often tend to have a better chance of working, providing sustenance in specific social, economic, and ecological contexts than alternatives. These more successful ways of life may be remembered favorably and so have a greater chance at resilience or to become reinvented traditions.

Inequalities in power and access were certainly part of the Valley of Oaxaca economy during this period, but these relations were more variable. Can we understand these differences in part by considering the modes of appropriation, relations of production, and how revenues of governance were acquired? For the Classic period, the fiscal model of collective action helps us address some of the seeming paradoxes between the architectural monumentality of Monte Albán, its resilience as the region's largest center, and the rather modest trappings of elite status found in Classic period tombs and elite residences. We strongly suspect that Monte Albán's rulers appropriated agricultural surpluses and labor to support governance. In return, such public goods as ceremonial spaces (the Main Plaza), central and neighborhood temples, defensive features, roads, and the infrastructure for marketing were built and maintained (Blanton 1978). As long proposed (Blanton et al. 1996), and in accord with a reliance on internal resources, governance was relatively collective, with few signs of aggrandizing behavior by rulers, who remained relatively faceless until late in the Classic period (Feinman and Nicholas 2013:141–156).

We hypothesize that the relatively collective governance practices at Monte Albán may have fostered resilience, as contrasted with the numerous shorter-lived Classic period centers in the Maya region, where governance and rule was more autocratic and individualized. Demographic growth and building episodes at Monte Albán coincided with the rapid expansion and/or movement of people to the foothills adjacent to this hilltop center (Blanton et al. 1993:91–94). The movement of this labor close to the city likely resulted in much greater overall agrarian production near Monte Albán, especially during high rainfall years (Nicholas 1989). We doubt that these episodes of population growth and in-migration were forced; they more probably occurred because smallholders perceived certain advantages for their domestic well-being by living close to the regional capital.

We suspect that many of the fundamental, long-standing economic underpinnings, such as small-scale production and domestic interdependence, of the Classic period economy were maintained into the Late

Postclassic period. But there also were important differences. We (and others) long have argued that marketing activities and the long-distance movement of goods (and people) increased in volume during the last centuries of the prehispanic era (Blanton and Feinman 1984; Blanton et al. 1993; Golitko and Feinman 2015; Kowalewski et al. 1983; Smith and Berdan 2003). Changes in these flows also likely had effects on how (and how much) revenues were derived by elites from the rest of the population, thereby providing a theoretical basis for understanding some of the key differences and changes between the Classic and Postclassic periods in the Valley of Oaxaca (e.g., Feinman 1999b, 2007). For example, Late Postclassic caciques in Oaxaca may have derived greater proportions of their resources through long-distance elite exchanges (through both the markets and gifting), warfare, and production on small elite estates (as opposed to the taxing of small-scale agrarian production). The larger proportions of revenue appropriated from external sources allowed Valley of Oaxaca lords to concentrate that wealth for their own households. The diminished dependence on commoner producers may help account for the much greater concentration of resources in Late Postclassic elite funerary contexts (e.g., Caso 1969; Gallegos Ruiz 1978) as compared to those of the earlier Classic period. Late Postclassic valley settlements were "palace-oriented" (Feinman 2007; Flannery and Marcus 1983:279).

During the Classic era, valley rulers may have been more dependent on local agricultural production for their revenues, and so their reliance on local commoner populations was greater. As a consequence, elite–commoner differentials in wealth were somewhat dampened or depressed during the Classic period as compared to later, a difference indicated by the less elaborate burial furniture present in the earlier period tombs. As discussed above, these earlier, more collective arrangements also were marked by much greater investments in public goods, such as plazas and temples. These findings provide a basis to understand an apparent paradox: while some Valley of Oaxaca Late Postclassic sites had elaborate palaces and tombs, investments in most domestic architecture and access to portable wealth were minimized compared to prior phases (Kowalewski and Finsten 1983:424–425).

## Synthetic Reflections

With the Valley of Oaxaca as our primary focus, we have marshaled empirical support to call into question the long-standing frame that has been employed to model prehispanic Mesoamerican economies. In lieu of high degrees of state controls over production and distribution and an "anti-market mentality" (e.g., Cook 1966; see also Feinman and Garraty 2010), the core economic underpinnings of the later ancient Mesoamerican world were domestic production, socioeconomic interdependence, markets, and the absence of beasts of burden. Marx, of course, was unaware of the much richer historical picture that we now have for prehispanic Mesoamerica, and so it is not surprising that elements of the models that he (and others) devised principally for Eurasia were not entirely on the mark.

Nevertheless, a mode of production perspective that directs focus to both the means and relations of production, including analytical attention to the fiscal foundations of governance and power, continues to offer a productive foundation for moving forward. Linking to the collective action approach, we build on that base in ways that account for the agency of subalterns and the contingency of human cooperation. The application of this conceptual lens helps clarify seeming contradictions and paradoxes regarding prehispanic Mesoamerican economies, their variation and change, while outlining issues and directions for further comparative research.

## References Cited

Aoyama, Kazuo

2007 Elite Artists and Craft Producers in Classic Maya Society: Lithic Evidence from Aguateca, Guatemala. *Latin American Antiquity* 18:3–26.

Attwood, Donald W.

1997 The Invisible Peasant. In *Economic Analysis beyond the Local System*, edited by Richard E. Blanton, Peter N. Peregrine, Deborah Winslow, and Thomas D. Hall, pp. 147–169. Monographs in Economic Anthropology No. 13, Lanham, Maryland.

Baker, Jeffrey L.

1998 The State and Wetland Agriculture in Mesoamerica. *Culture and Agriculture* 20:78–86.

Baskes, Jeremy

2005 Colonial Institutions and Cross-Cultural Trade: *Repartimiento* Credit and Indigenous Production of Cochineal in Eighteenth-Century Oaxaca. *Journal of Economic History* 65:186–210.

Beals, Ralph L.

1970 Gifting, Reciprocity, Savings, and Credit in Peasant Oaxaca. *Southwestern Journal of Anthropology* 26:231–241.

1975 *The Peasant Marketing System of Oaxaca, Mexico*. University of California Press, Berkeley.

Berdan, Frances F.
1977 Distributive Mechanisms in the Aztec Economy. In *Peasant Livelihood: Studies in Economic Anthropology and Cultural Ecology*, edited by Rhoda Halperin and James Dow, pp. 91–101. St. Martin's, New York.
Berdan, Frances F., and Patricia R. Anawalt
1992 *The Codex Mendoza*. University of California Press, Berkeley.
Blanton, Richard E.
1978 *Monte Albán: Settlement Patterns at the Ancient Zapotec Capital*. Academic, New York.
1996 The Basin of Mexico Market System and the Growth of Empire. In *Aztec Imperial Strategies*, edited by Frances F. Berdan, Richard E. Blanton, Elizabeth H. Boone, Mary G. Hodge, Michael E. Smith, and Emily Umberger, pp. 47–84. Dumbarton Oaks, Washington, D.C.
Blanton, Richard, and Lane Fargher
2008 *Collective Action in the Formation of Pre-modern States*. Springer, New York.
Blanton, Richard E., and Gary M. Feinman
1984 The Mesoamerican World System. *American Anthropologist* 86:673–682.
Blanton, Richard E., Gary M. Feinman, Stephen A. Kowalewski, and Peter N. Peregrine
1996 A Dual-Processual Theory for the Evolution of Mesoamerican Civilization. *Current Anthropology* 37:1–14.
Blanton, Richard E., Stephen A. Kowalewski, Gary M. Feinman, and Jill Appel
1982 *Monte Albán's Hinterland, Part I: The Prehispanic Settlement Patterns of the Central and Southern Parts of the Valley of Oaxaca, Mexico*. Museum of Anthropology Memoirs No. 15. University of Michigan, Ann Arbor.
Blanton, Richard E., Stephen A. Kowalewski, Gary M. Feinman, and Laura M. Finsten
1993 *Ancient Mesoamerica: A Comparison of Change in Three Regions*. 2nd ed. Cambridge University Press, Cambridge.
Brumfiel, Elizabeth, and Timothy Earle
1987 Specialization, Exchange, and Complex Societies: An Introduction. In *Specialization, Exchange, and Complex Societies*, edited by Elizabeth Brumfiel and Timothy Earle, pp. 1–9. Cambridge University Press, Cambridge.
Butzer, Karl W.
1996 Irrigation, Raised Fields and State Management: Wittfogel Redux? *Antiquity* 70:200–204.
Carballo, David M.
2013 The Social Organization of Craft Production and Interregional Exchange at Teotihuacan. In *Merchants, Markets, and Exchange in the Pre-Columbian World*, edited by Kenneth G. Hirth and Joanne Pillsbury, pp. 113–140. Dumbarton Oaks, Washington, D.C.
Carrasco, Pedro
2001 Economic Organization and Development. In *The Oxford Encyclopedia of Mesoamerican Cultures: The Civilizations of Mexico and Central America*, edited by Davíd Carrasco, pp. 363–366. Oxford University Press, Oxford.

Caso, Alfonso
1969 *El tesoro de Monte Albán*. Memorías 3. Instituto Nacional de Antropología e Historia Mexico City.
Caso, Alfonso, Ignacio Bernal, and Jorge R. Acosta
1967 *La cerámica de Monte Albán*. Memorías 8. Instituto Nacional de Antropología e Historia, Mexico City.
Chase, Diane Z., and Arlen F. Chase
2014 Ancient Maya Markets and the Economic Integration of Caracol, Belize. *Ancient Mesoamerica* 25:239–250.
Childe, V. Gordon
1950 The Urban Revolution. *Town Planning Review* 21:3–17.
Cook, Scott
1966 The Obsolete "Anti-Market" Mentality: A Critique of the Substantive Approach to Economic Anthropology. *American Anthropologist* 68:323–345.
D'Altroy, Terence N., and Timothy K. Earle
1985 Staple Finance, Wealth Finance, and Storage in the Inka Political Economy. *Current Anthropology* 26:187–197.
Díaz del Castillo, Bernal
2003 *The Discovery and Conquest of Mexico*. Translated by Alfred P. Maudsley. Da Capo Press, Cambridge.
Doolittle, William E.
1990 *Canal Irrigation in Prehistoric Mexico: The Sequence of Technological Change*. University of Texas Press, Austin.
Earle, Timothy
2000 Archaeology, Property, and Prehistory. *Annual Review of Anthropology* 29:39–60.
Faulseit, Ronald K., Gary M. Feinman, and Linda M. Nicholas
2015 Ceramic Paste Distribution and Market Exchange in the Tlacolula Valley, Oaxaca, Mexico. Paper presented at the 80th Annual Meeting of the Society for American Archaeology, San Francisco.
Feinman, Gary M.
1999a Rethinking Our Assumptions: Economic Specialization at the Household Scale in Ancient Ejutla, Oaxaca, Mexico. In *Pottery and People: A Dynamic Interaction*, edited by James M. Skibo and Gary M. Feinman, pp. 81–98. University of Utah Press, Salt Lake City.
1999b The Changing Structure of Macroregional Mesoamerica: The Classic–Postclassic Transition in the Valley of Oaxaca. In *World-Systems Theory in Practice*, edited by P. Nick Kardulias, pp. 53–62. Rowman and Littlefield, Lanham, Maryland.
2001 Mesoamerican Political Complexity: The Corporate–Network Dimension. In *From Leaders to Rulers*, edited by Jonathan Haas, pp. 151–175. Kluwer Academic/Plenum, New York.
2006 The Economic Underpinnings of Prehispanic Zapotec Civilization: Small-Scale Production, Economic Interdependence, and Market Exchange. In *Ag-*

*ricultural Strategies*, edited by Joyce Marcus and Charles Stanish, pp. 255–280. Cotsen Institute of Archaeology, University of California, Los Angeles.

2007 The Last Quarter Century of Archaeological Research in the Central Valleys of Oaxaca. *Mexicon* 29:3–15.

2012 Comparative Frames for the Diachronic Analysis of Complex Societies: Next Steps. In *The Comparative Archaeology of Complex Societies*, edited by Michael E. Smith, pp. 21–43. Cambridge University Press, Cambridge.

2013 The Emergence of Social Complexity: Why More than Population Size Matters. In *Cooperation and Collective Action: Archaeological Perspectives*, edited by David M. Carballo, pp. 35–56. University Press of Colorado, Boulder.

Feinman, Gary M., and Christopher P. Garraty

2010 Preindustrial Markets and Marketing: Archaeological Perspectives. *Annual Review of Anthropology* 39:167–191.

Feinman, Gary M., and Linda M. Nicholas

2004 *Hilltop Terrace Sites of Oaxaca, Mexico: Intensive Surface Surveys at Guirún, El Palmillo, and the Mitla Fortress*. Fieldiana Anthropology No. 37. Field Museum of Natural History, Chicago.

2007 Craft Production in Classic Period Oaxaca: Implications for Monte Albán Political Economy. In *Craft Production in Complex Societies: Multicraft and Producer Perspectives*, edited by Izumi Shimada, pp. 97–119. University of Utah Press, Salt Lake City.

2010 A Multiscalar Perspective on Market Exchange in the Classic-Period Valley of Oaxaca. In *Archaeological Approaches to Market Exchange in Ancient Societies*, edited by Christopher P. Garraty and Barbara L. Stark, pp. 85–98. University Press of Colorado, Boulder.

2011 Domestic Craft Production and Classic Period Economy of Oaxaca. In *Producción artisanal y especializada en Mesoamérica: Áreas de actividad y procesos productivos*, edited by Linda R. Manzanilla and Kenneth G. Hirth, pp. 29–58. Instituto Nacional de Antropología e Historia and Universidad Nacional Autónoma de México, Mexico City.

2012 The Late Prehispanic Economy of the Valley of Oaxaca, Mexico: Weaving Threads from Data, Theory, and Subsequent History. *Research in Economic Anthropology* 32:225–258.

2013 *Settlement Patterns of the Ejutla Valley, Oaxaca, Mexico: A Diachronic Macroscale Perspective*. Fieldiana Anthropology No. 43. Field Museum of Natural History, Chicago.

Feinman, Gary, Linda Nicholas, and Mark Golitko

2013 Exchange in the Valley of Oaxaca, Mexico: Late Classic Obsidian Procurement. *Mexicon* 35:60–68.

Flannery, Kent V.

1983 Precolumbian Farming in the Valleys of Oaxaca, Nochixtlán, Tehuacán, and Cuicatlán: A Comparative Study. In *The Cloud People: Divergent Evolution of the Zapotec and Mixtec Civilizations*, edited by Kent V. Flannery and Joyce Marcus, pp. 323–339. Academic Press, New York.

Flannery, Kent V. (editor)
1976 *The Early Mesoamerican Village*. Academic Press, New York.
Flannery, Kent V., and Joyce Marcus
1983 An Editorial Opinion on the Mixtec Impact. In *The Cloud People: Divergent Evolution of the Zapotec and Mixtec Civilizations*, edited by Kent V. Flannery and Joyce Marcus, pp. 277–279. Academic Press, New York.
Flannery, Kent V., and Joyce Marcus (editors)
1983 *The Cloud People: Divergent Evolution of the Zapotec and Mixtec Civilizations*. Academic Press, New York.
Fried, Morton H.
1960 On the Evolution of Social Stratification and the State. In *Culture and History: Essays in Honor of Paul Radin*, edited by Stanley Diamond, pp. 713–731. Columbia University Press, New York.
Furet, Francois
1978 *Penser la revolution française*. Gallimard, Paris.
Gallegos Ruiz, Roberto
1978 *El señor 9 flor en Zaachila*. Universidad Nacional Autonóma de México, Mexico City.
Garraty, Christopher P., and Barbara L. Stark (editors)
2010 *Archaeological Approaches to Market Exchange in Ancient Societies*. University Press of Colorado, Boulder.
Golitko, Mark, and Gary M. Feinman
2015 Procurement and Distribution of Pre-Hispanic Mesoamerican Obsidian 900 B.C.–A.D. 1520: A Social Network Analysis. *Journal of Archaeological Method and Theory* 22:206–247.
Halperin, Christina T., and Antonia E. Foias
2010 Pottery Politics: Late Classic Maya Palace Production at Motul de San José, Petén, Guatemala. *Journal of Anthropological Archaeology* 29:392–411.
Hassig, Ross
1981 The Famine of One Rabbit: Ecological Causes and Consequences of a Pre-Columbian Calamity. *Journal of Anthropological Research* 37:172–182.
Hechter, Michael
1988 *Principles of Group Solidarity*. University of California Press, Berkeley.
Hirth, Kenneth G., and Joanne Pillsbury (editors)
2013 *Merchants, Markets, and Exchange in the Pre-Columbian World*. Dumbarton Oaks, Washington, D.C.
Holmes, William H.
1895 *Archaeological Studies among the Ancient Cities of Mexico*. Field Columbian Museum Publication 8. Field Museum of Natural History, Chicago.
Inomata, Takeshi
2001 The Power and Ideology of Artistic Creation: Elite Craft Specialists in Classic Maya Society. *Current Anthropology* 42:321–349.
Isaac, Barry L.
1993 AMP, HH, & OD: Some Comments. In *Economic Aspects of Water Management in the Prehispanic New World*, edited by Vern L. Scarborough and Barry

L. Isaac, pp. 429–447. Research in Economic Anthropology Supp. 7. JAI Press, Greenwich, Connecticut.

Kirkby, Anne V. T.

1973 *The Use of Land and Water Resources in the Past and Present Valley of Oaxaca.* Museum of Anthropology Memoirs No. 5. University of Michigan, Ann Arbor.

Kowalewski, Stephen A.

1990 The Evolution of Complexity in the Valley of Oaxaca. *Annual Review of Anthropology* 19:39–58.

2003a Scale and Explanation of Demographic Change: 3,500 Years in the Valley of Oaxaca. *American Anthropologist* 105:313–325.

2003b What Is the Community? The Long View from Oaxaca, Mexico. *Social Evolution and History* 2:4–24.

2012 A Theory of the Ancient Mesoamerican Economy. *Research in Economic Anthropology* 32:187–234.

Kowalewski, Stephen A., Richard E. Blanton, Gary M. Feinman, and Laura Finsten

1983 Boundaries, Scale, and Internal Organization. *Journal of Anthropological Archaeology* 2:32–56.

Kowalewski, Stephen A., Gary M. Feinman, Laura Finsten, Richard E. Blanton, and Linda M. Nicholas

1989 *Monte Albán's Hinterland, Part II: Prehispanic Settlement Patterns in Tlacolula, Etla, and Ocotlán, the Valley of Oaxaca, Mexico.* Museum of Anthropology Memoirs No. 23. University of Michigan, Ann Arbor.

Kowalewski, Stephen A., and Laura Finsten

1983 The Economic Systems of Ancient Oaxaca: A Regional Perspective. *Current Anthropology* 24:413–426.

Lees, Susan H.

1973 *Sociopolitical Aspects of Canal Irrigation in the Valley of Oaxaca.* Museum of Anthropology Memoirs No. 6. University of Michigan, Ann Arbor.

Levi, Margaret

1988 *Of Rule and Revenue.* University of California Press, Berkeley.

Marcus, Joyce, and Kent V. Flannery

1983 An Introduction to the Late Postclassic. In *The Cloud People: Divergent Evolution of the Zapotec and Mixtec Civilizations*, edited by Kent V. Flannery and Joyce Marcus, pp. 217–226. Academic Press, New York.

Marx, Karl

1971 *A Contribution to the Critique of Political Economy.* Lawrence and Wishart, London.

Masson, Marilyn A., and David A. Freidel

2012 An Argument for Classic Era Maya Market Exchange. *Journal of Anthropological Archaeology* 31:455–484.

McGuire, Randall H.

1993 Archaeology and Marxism. *Archaeological Method and Theory* 5:101–157.

2002 *A Marxist Archaeology.* Percheron Press, Clinton Corners, New York.

Minc, Leah D.
2006 Monitoring Regional Market Systems in Prehistory: Models, Methods, and Metrics. *Journal of Anthropological Archaeology* 25:82–116.

Nicholas, Linda M.
1989 Land Use in Prehispanic Oaxaca. In *Monte Albán's Hinterland, Part II: Prehispanic Settlement Patterns in Tlacolula, Etla, and Ocotlán, the Valley of Oaxaca*, by Stephen A. Kowalewski, Gary M. Feinman, Laura Finsten, Richard E. Blanton, and Linda M. Nicholas, pp. 449–505. Museum of Anthropology Memoirs No. 23. University of Michigan, Ann Arbor.

Nichols, Deborah L.
2013 Merchants and Merchandise: The Archaeology of Aztec Commerce at Otumba, Mexico. In *Merchants, Markets, and Exchange in the Pre-Columbian World*, edited by Kenneth G. Hirth and Joanne Pillsbury, pp. 49–83. Dumbarton Oaks, Washington, D.C.

Nichols, Deborah L., and Charles D. Frederick
1993 Irrigation Canals and Chinampas: Recent Research in the Northern Basin of Mexico. In *Economic Aspects of Water Management in the Prehispanic New World*, edited by Vern L. Scarborough and Barry L. Isaac, pp. 123–150. Research in Economic Anthropology Supp. 7. JAI Press, Greenwich, Connecticut.

North, Douglass C.
1991 Institutions. *Journal of Economic Perspectives* 5:97–112.

Nowak, Martin A.
2011 *SuperCooperators: Altruism, Evolution, and Why We Need Each Other to Succeed.* Free Press, New York.

Offner, Jerome
1981a On the Inapplicability of "Oriental Despotism" and the "Asiatic Mode of Production" to the Aztecs of Texcoco. *American Antiquity* 46:43–61.
1981b On Carrasco's Use of "First Principles." *American Antiquity* 46:69–74.

Olson, Mancur
1965 *The Logic of Collective Action.* Harvard University Press, Cambridge.

Palerm, Angel
1955 The Irrigation Basis of Urban Civilization in Mesoamerica. In *Irrigation Civilizations: A Comparative Study*, edited by Julian H. Steward, pp. 28–42. Social Science Monographs Vol. 1. Pan American Union, Washington, D.C.

Palerm, Angel, and Eric R. Wolf
1957 Ecological Potential and Cultural Development in Mesoamerica. *Pan American Union Social Science Monograph* 3:1–37.

Parsons, Elsie C.
1936 *Mitla, Town of Souls.* University of Chicago Press, Chicago.

Pluckhahn, Thomas J.
2009 Plazas y mercados en la Mixteca Alta prehispánica. In *Bases de la complejidad social en Oaxaca*, edited by Nelly Robles García, pp. 277–293. Instituto Nacional de Antropología e Historia, Mexico City.

Pohl, John M. D., John Monaghan, and Laura R. Stiver

1997 Religion, Economy, and Factionalism in Mixtec Boundary Zones. In *Códices y documentos sobre México: Segundo simposio*, vol. 1, edited by Salvador Rueda Smithers, Constanza Vega Sosa, and Rodrigo Martínez Baracs, pp. 205–232. Instituto Nacional de Antropología e Historia, Mexico City.

Polanyi, Karl

1960 On the Comparative Treatment of Economic Institutions in Antiquity with Illustrations from Athens, Mycenae, and Alalakh. In *City Invincible*, edited by Carl H. Kraeling and Robert M. Adams, pp. 329–350. University of Chicago Press, Chicago.

Polanyi, Karl, Conrad Arensberg, and Harry Pearson (editors)

1957 *Trade and Market in the Early Empires*. Free Press, Glencoe, Illinois.

Popkin, Samuel L.

1979 *The Rational Peasant*. University of California Press, Berkeley.

Przeworski, Adam

1985 Marxism and Rational Choice. *Politics and Society* 14:379–409.

Pyburn, K. Anne

1998 Smallholders in the Maya Lowlands: Homage to a Garden Variety Ethnographer. *Human Ecology* 26:267–286.

Rosenswig, Robert M.

2012 Materialism, Mode of Production, and a Millennium of Change in Southern Mexico. *Journal of Archaeological Method and Theory* 19:1–48.

Sanders, William T.

1956 The Central Mexican Symbiotic Region. In *Prehistoric Settlement Patterns in the New World*, edited by Gordon R. Willey, pp. 115–127. Viking Fund Publication in Anthropology No. 23, New York.

Sanders, William T., Jeffrey R. Parsons, and Robert S. Santley

1979 *The Basin of Mexico: Ecological Processes in the Evolution of a Civilization*. Academic Press, New York.

Sanders, William T., and Barbara J. Price

1968 *Mesoamerica: The Evolution of a Civilization*. Random House, New York.

Santley, Robert S., and Kenneth G. Hirth (editors)

1993 *Prehispanic Domestic Units in Western Mesoamerica: Studies of Household, Compound, and Residence*. CRC Press, Boca Raton, Florida.

Scarborough, Vern L.

1991 Water Management Adaptations in Non-industrial Complex Societies. *Method and Theory in Archaeology* 3:101–154. University of Arizona Press, Tucson.

2006 An Overview of Mesoamerican Water Systems. In *Precolumbian Water Management: Ideology, Ritual, and Power*, edited by Lisa J. Lucero and Barbara W. Fash, pp. 223–235. University of Arizona Press, Tucson.

Schelling, Thomas C.

2006 *Micromotives and Macrobehavior*. W. W. Norton, New York.

Service, Elman R.

1962 *Primitive Social Organization: An Evolutionary Perspective*. Random House, New York.

Sewell, William H., Jr.
2005 *Logics of History: Social Theory and Social Transformation*. University of Chicago Press, Chicago.

Shaw, Leslie C.
2012 The Elusive Maya Marketplace: An Archaeological Consideration of the Evidence. *Journal of Archaeological Research* 20:117–155.

Sherratt, Andrew
1989 V. Gordon Childe: Archaeology and Intellectual History. *Past and Present* 125:151–185.

Smith, Michael E.
2004 The Archaeology of Ancient State Economies. *Annual Review of Anthropology* 33:73–102.
2009 V. Gordon Childe and the Urban Revolution: A Historical Perspective on a Revolution in Urban Studies. *Town Planning Review* 80:3–29.
2014 The Aztecs Paid Taxes, Not Tribute. *Mexicon* 36:19–22.

Smith, Michael E., and Frances F. Berdan (editors)
2003 *The Postclassic Mesoamerican World*. University of Utah Press, Salt Lake City.

Spencer, Charles S.
1990 On the Tempo and Mode of State Formation: Neoevolutionism Reconsidered. *Journal of Anthropological Archaeology* 9:1–30.
2000 Prehispanic Water Management and Agricultural Intensification in Mexico and Venezuela: Implications for Contemporary Ecological Planning. In *Imperfect Balance: Landscape Transformations in the Precolumbian Americas*, edited by David L. Lentz, pp. 145–178. Columbia University Press, New York.

Spores, Ronald
1965 The Zapotec and Mixtec at Spanish Conquest. In *Handbook of Middle American Indians*, vol. 3, part 2, edited by Gordon R. Willey, pp. 962–987. University of Texas Press, Austin.

Stark, Barbara L., and Christopher P. Garraty
2010 Detecting Marketplace Exchange in Archaeology: A Methodological Review. In *Archaeological Approaches to Market Exchange in Ancient Societies*, edited by Christopher P. Garraty and Barbara L. Stark, pp. 33–58. University Press of Colorado, Boulder.

Steward, Julian H.
1955 Some Implications of the Symposium. In *Irrigation Civilizations: A Comparative Study*, edited by Julian H. Steward, pp. 58–78. Social Science Monographs Vol. 1. Pan American Union, Washington, D.C.

Tarschys, Daniel
1988 Tributes, Tariffs, Taxes, and Trade: The Changing Sources of Government Revenue. *British Journal of Political Science* 19:1–20.

Taylor, Walter B.
1972 *Landlord and Peasant in Colonial Oaxaca*. Stanford University Press, Stanford.

Trigger, Bruce G.
1993 Marxism in Contemporary Western Archaeology. *Archaeological Method and Theory* 5:159–200.
2003 *Understanding Early Civilizations*. Cambridge University Press, Cambridge.
White, Leslie A.
1949 *The Science of Culture*. Grove Press, New York.
Wittfogel, Karl
1957 *Oriental Despotism*. Yale University Press, New Haven.
Wolf, Eric R.
1959 *Sons of the Shaking Earth*. University of Chicago Press, Chicago.
1982 *Europe and the People without History*. University of California Press, Berkeley.
1994 Explaining Mesoamerica. *Social Anthropology* 2:1–17.
Wolf, Eric R. (editor)
1976 *The Valley of Mexico: Studies in Pre-Hispanic Ecology and Society*. University of New Mexico Press, Albuquerque.

# 4

# MODERN STATES

# 12

## Colonialism, Articulation, and Modes of Production at an Early Seventeenth-Century English Colony in the Western Caribbean

CHARLES E. ORSER JR.

How are colonialism and the transplantation of modes of production related? And how can archaeology contribute to illustrating and interpreting their relationships in the past? These questions rest at the heart of any archaeological analysis of post-Columbian, New World colonialism, though both have received little treatment in the archaeological literature. The failure of archaeologists to investigate such questions is regrettable, since the capitalist mode of production, or at least its mercantilist predecessor, accompanied European colonists everywhere they went. An engagement with the mode of production concept provides archaeologists with an enlightening avenue into the socioeconomic realities of post-Columbian colonialism.

Three prominent reasons mandate the archaeological examination of the connections between colonialism and post-Columbian, New World modes of production. First, a substantial amount of archaeological research in the New World has focused on colonialist endeavors for at least the past four decades. Interest in the process of settler transplantation and contact between diverse cultures will likely grow in the foreseeable future. American historical archaeology, originally designed as historical anthropology, was developed largely with the intent of studying colonial encounters. In fact, one of the most well-cited definitions of historical archaeology stresses that it "is the archaeology of the spread of European culture throughout the world since the fifteenth century and its impact on indigenous peoples" (Deetz 1977:5). Many scholars have found justifiable reason to quibble with this definition, but few can deny its impact on the practice of contemporary historical archaeology. Secondly, all modes of production employ material culture, and since tangible evidence is the hallmark of archaeological research, the linkage between production and materiality is inherently relevant. No less a figure than V. Gordon Childe (1951 [1936]:13) enshrined this perspective in archaeology by observing that its practitioners study "the tools and instruments of production." And finally, the concept of mode of production forever links material objects with the social relations inherent in their comprehension and use. As Eric Wolf (1984:397) observes: "The engagement of the natural world is social—it always involves human beings in relation to one another; and that engagement, as well as these relations, always involve, simultaneously, head and hand. But these relations are not evident on the surface of things; they must be analyzed out." Modes of production are fertile ground for analysis and interpretation, because understanding past social relations rests at the core of socially oriented historical archaeology.

The linkage between colonialism and the transplantation of modes of production is often expressed by the concept of "articulation." In this chapter I explore the concept of articulation as it relates to colonialist encounters by foregrounding the role of conflict in the articulation process. I present an example from a small island in the western Caribbean on which a company of powerful Englishmen attempted to create a colony with capitalist principles embedded within three modes of production.

## Colonialism and Modes of Production

Philosophical attempts to link production with the definition and organization of social relations has a long history, extending back to descriptions of human history as a series of progressive, teleological steps ending with manufacturing, commerce, and a credit economy (Hodgen 1971:467). Late-eighteenth- and nineteenth-century scholars generally investigated the role of production in the transition of societies from one form to another, with the works of Karl Marx being prominent among them. Marx's writings, despite their controversial reception and inherent difficulties, are extremely useful when investigating post-Columbian capitalism, and his insights remain remarkably relevant today (Eagleton 2011; Patterson 2009; Yang 2012).

Marx's central scholarly intent, beyond his occasional ruminations about precapitalist societies, was to disassemble and explain the inner workings and practical realities of capitalism and capitalist practice. The mode of production concept was a key component of his analysis. The many complexities of this concept, and its various treatments and critiques, are far too numerous to detail here. Suffice to say, as an anthropological concept, it had great utility for many years. Since the 1980s, however, many scholars, even those identifying as Marxist-inspired, have tended to abandon it (Graeber 2006).

Abandoning the mode of production concept is problematic, because it remains pertinent to archaeological research, especially as it pertains to the analysis of capitalism and capitalist practice in the post-Columbian world. The concept of the capitalist mode of production is inescapable in the practice of modern-world archaeology, because capitalism is one of its primary topics of interest (Orser 2014).

At the outset, capitalism—as a general theory of political economy designed to maximize profit, minimize cost, and separate workers from the products of their labor—must be conceptually differentiated from capitalist practice—the day-to-day actions of individuals acting within a capitalist environment and accepting a capitalist mind-set. Modern-world archaeology, because of its explicit use of multiscalar analysis, is concerned with all levels of capitalism and capitalist practice in the post-1500 CE era. Its interest extends from an individual's actual use of capitalist ideas to the overarching theory itself. The mode of analysis is dialectical, such that "research begins with the whole, the system . . . and then proceeds to an examination of the part to see where it fits and how it functions, leading eventually to a fuller understanding of the whole" (Ollman 1993:12).

Marx often referenced modes of production in his writings about colonialism, but seldom directly. In the *Communist Manifesto*, for instance, Marx (1954 [1848]:22) describes how "civilization" compels all nations, "on pain of extinction, to adopt the bourgeois mode of production," by which he means capitalism. In this polemic he follows his brief outline of human economic change—situated within a sketch of the seeming triumphs of Western culture—with a devastating critique of capitalism as a soul-crushing, exploitative system (see also Anderson 2010:9–10).

Marx wrote about colonialism both as a theoretical construct (e.g., Marx 1967 [1887]: 1:765–774) and as a social process practiced in actual historical situations. Because his focus is so strongly centered on British capitalism, his comments largely concern colonialist situations in Ireland and India, two colonies directly confronting capitalist transformation during his lifetime. Writing about India, Marx observed in 1853 how "the British intruder," by destroying the indigenous domestic spinning and weaving industries, concurrently damaged the traditional union between the society's agricultural and manufacturing sectors and, as a byproduct, also harmed the village system (Avineri 1968:86–87). In Ireland, Marx (1967 [1887]:1:697–712), who called Ireland "only an agricultural district of England," focused on landlordism and the capitalist transfiguration of small farming into a market-based output system. Marx's critique was useful because many of his contemporaries defined a colony in the most harmless terms as "a country wholly or partially unoccupied, which receives emigrants from a distance" (Wakefield 1849:16). A few earlier writers had noted the dark side of colonialism. Adam Smith (1999 [1776]:145) observed that "civilised nations" carried with them "knowledge of agriculture and of other useful arts superior" to those of indigenous peoples, but also, "They carry out with them, too, the habit of subordination." Marx agreed that post-Columbian colonialism involved violence and oppression as one side of the equation. He took the analysis further than anyone at the time by interrogating the inner workings of capitalist practice while also disentangling capitalist theory. The concept of articulation rested at the center of the integration of capitalism into an indigenous social setting.

Marx saw articulation as a dark process hiding within colonialism, one that eventually transforms free people into entombed slaves (Naved 2008:33–34). He observed that the capitalist mode of production, when initially established in a region, does not simply supplant the existing noncapitalist mode of production. Rather, it retains components of the old system (and often the entire system) for some time, depending upon the sociohistorical context. When on the move to acquire more space, capitalism comes into direct conflict with already-existing producers who own their own "conditions of labor" and who work for personal enrichment rather than for capitalist profit (Marx 1967 [1887], 1:765). Rather than improving the condition of the encountered working class, the introduction of capitalism in the new area worsens the workers' lot by converting them into wage laborers and appropriating "their surplus labor on the basis of the old mode of production" (Marx 1967 [1887], 3:335). The incorporation of workers demonstrates the deceptive power of capitalist articulation to enmesh noncapitalist people into a fully capitalist system (Bradby 1975).

Articulation has been a subject of considerable debate and contention among anthropologists and other scholars. Marx (1967 [1887], 1:769) explains that the creation of wage laborers out of formerly free producers secured "an unmistakable relation of dependence" in colonial situations. Anthropologists interested in the realities of underdevelopment in noncapital environments have conducted fieldwork to assess how articulation actually operates in lived experience (Berman 1984). In one example, Nicholas Hopkins (1978) examines tailoring in an agricultural town in Tunisia. The sewing of a winter overcoat, a major craft industry in the small town he studied, was part of a domestic mode of production that began with the springtime shearing of sheep, long before any garments were sown. Men and women worked together throughout the long tailoring process, and only the final stages of production occurred outside the domestic sphere. At the time of his fieldwork, Hopkins saw that the home-based production process was slowly being transformed into factory manufacture. In the emerging process, tailors completed work for commercial garment dealers living in the city of Tunis, rather than as craftspersons serving a local market. Interestingly, Marx (1967 [1887]:3:334) had studied the same process in the seventeenth-century English cloth industry. Eric Wolf (1982:85–88) also notes the process, albeit in a vastly different time and place, when he examines the articulation of the "tributary mode of production." During the long era of articulation in Europe, people with little collective power continued to pay tribute to powerful overlords at the same time that a incipient merchant class created long-distance commerce. The process expanded to regions outside Europe to encompass the North American fur trade, transatlantic enslavement, and trade with Asia. These historical examples provide concrete proof of the structural stability of the articulation process regardless of location or period of existence.

In an analysis of articulation that takes a more critical position, Bruce Berman (1984) argues that many researchers have overstated the power of capitalism to annihilate indigenous economies. Teleologically inclined analysts have stressed capitalism's inevitability as an inexorable force against which local economies are entirely helpless. Arguing against this interpretation, Berman notes that the problem rests with the removal of conflict from the theory of articulation. In other words, in the teleological view, indigenous peoples can do nothing to resist the inevitable power of capitalism. To rehabilitate articulation, Berman (1984:410) proposes viewing it as "a process of struggle and uncertainty" taking place in defined sociohistorical locales. At the same time, he accepts that the penetration of capital into formerly noncapitalist settings may undermine "the ability of domestic forms of production to reproduce themselves." In this interpretation, one of the most meaningful contradictions of the articulation process involves the wealth disparities resulting from capitalist practice. Large wealth gaps have the potential to create new classes of resistors. In this view, the articulation process contains its own inherent weakness (Foster-Carter 1978). Struggles against the onslaught of capitalist practices are plentiful in history, including within rural Europe (e.g., Donnelly 2009; Hill 1991; Thompson 1993). These historical case studies offer ample evidence of protest and violence directed against capitalists who attempted to alter or destroy precapitalist modes of production.

It must be noted, however, that the power of noncapitalists to oppose the steady creep of unequal articulation may be less apparent when viewed from a broader perspective. Individual case studies may be more persuasive than long-term history, because one of the goals of capitalism is constant expansion (Ritzer 2003, 2007). As one scholar notes, "Capital needs the whole globe, although it itself may occupy only a small part of it" (Bradby 1975:136). When viewed only in the short term, concrete conclusions about the ultimate power of anticapitalists to be successful may be overly optimistic. The outcome of class struggle can never be predicted or assumed to be predetermined, because the opposition usually requires individuals with unceasing commitment, abundant resources, and copious amounts of time (Eagleton 2011:50).

In working to redefine the concept of the mode of production to be more palatable to anthropologists, David Graeber (2006) proposes expanding the concept of the capitalist mode of production to encompass more than simply a struggle for material surplus. Rather, he argues for the addition of the production of human beings—social production—into the mode of production concept. In this appealing view, the character of capitalism shares a strong resemblance to the institution of enslavement, because the extraction of surplus and the creation of bonded human beings are conceptually identical. Marx's "abstract labor," acquired when one purchases a slave because of his or her ability to work, becomes analogous to the situation wherein an employer obtains the labor of a person who is ostensibly free but who must sell his or her labor-power in order to live in a capitalist system (Marx 1967 [1887]:1:185).

The articulation required in post-Columbian, New World environments helps to explain the colonialist process and the expansion of capitalism in a broad way. Case studies focusing on specific times and places variously help to refine the process as it was lived by historical men and women. When united, the broad view and the narrow analysis further our comprehension of an infinitely complex process that has unfolded since about CE 1500.

In this chapter I examine articulation from the standpoint of the transplantation of colonists laboring within a capitalist mode of production. My case study derives from the settlement of English men (and a few women) on Providence Island at the direction of a company of prominent Stuart-age Puritans living in London. The modes of production established on the island experienced dramatic changes during the colony's brief existence. The colony was uprooted by a Spanish invasion, but the social fissures inherent in the juxtaposition of the modes of production doomed the colony from the start.

## Providence Island

In 1629 a group of wealthy Englishmen—Puritans who would become prominent leaders of the antiroyalist forces during the English Civil War—gathered to create "The Company of Adventurers of the Cittie of Westminster for the Plantation of the Island of Providence, Henrietta, and the Adjacent Islandes lying upon the Coast of America" (Records of the Providence Island Company [hereafter PIC], "Commission to Capt. Philip Bell," 2/7/1631; see Kupperman 1989, 1993a, 1993b; Newton 1914). Providence Island (also historically known as Old Providence and Santa Catalina, and today called Isla de Providencia) is located 750 km (466 mi) northwest of mainland Colombia (the country to which it today belongs) and about 250 km (155 mi) east of the Nicaraguan coast (Figure 12.1). The island measures only about 39 km$^2$ (15 mi$^2$) (Figure 12.2).

The charter members of the Providence Island Company, called "adventurers" or "undertakers," were either high-ranking members of the English aristocracy or leading gentry. Notable members who served in Parliament were Robert Greville, Lord Brooke; William Fiennes, Lord Saye and Sele; Henry Rich, Earl of Holland; and Robert Rich, Earl of Warwick. Many of these men had invested in several colonial companies, and many were related either by ancestry or marriage (Kupperman 1993b:357–360). Another charter member was John Pym. Though lacking a large estate and a title, he was an influential parliamentarian, staunch Puritan, and prominent orator against the autocratic actions of Charles I (Braddick 2008:92; Brenner 2003:244). In 1643, at Pym's death, an unnamed author described him in an elegy as: "the Pillar of the English State:/The Peoples violent love; their greatest hate./His Countreys Patriot; Religions friend:/Lawes Champion: one that dared to defend/Just Liberty against Prerogative" (Anonymous 1643). The line "liberty against prerogative" refers to the overreach of Charles I and Pym's role in curtailing it. Many royalists at the time directly linked the Providence Island Company with the agitation to overthrow and

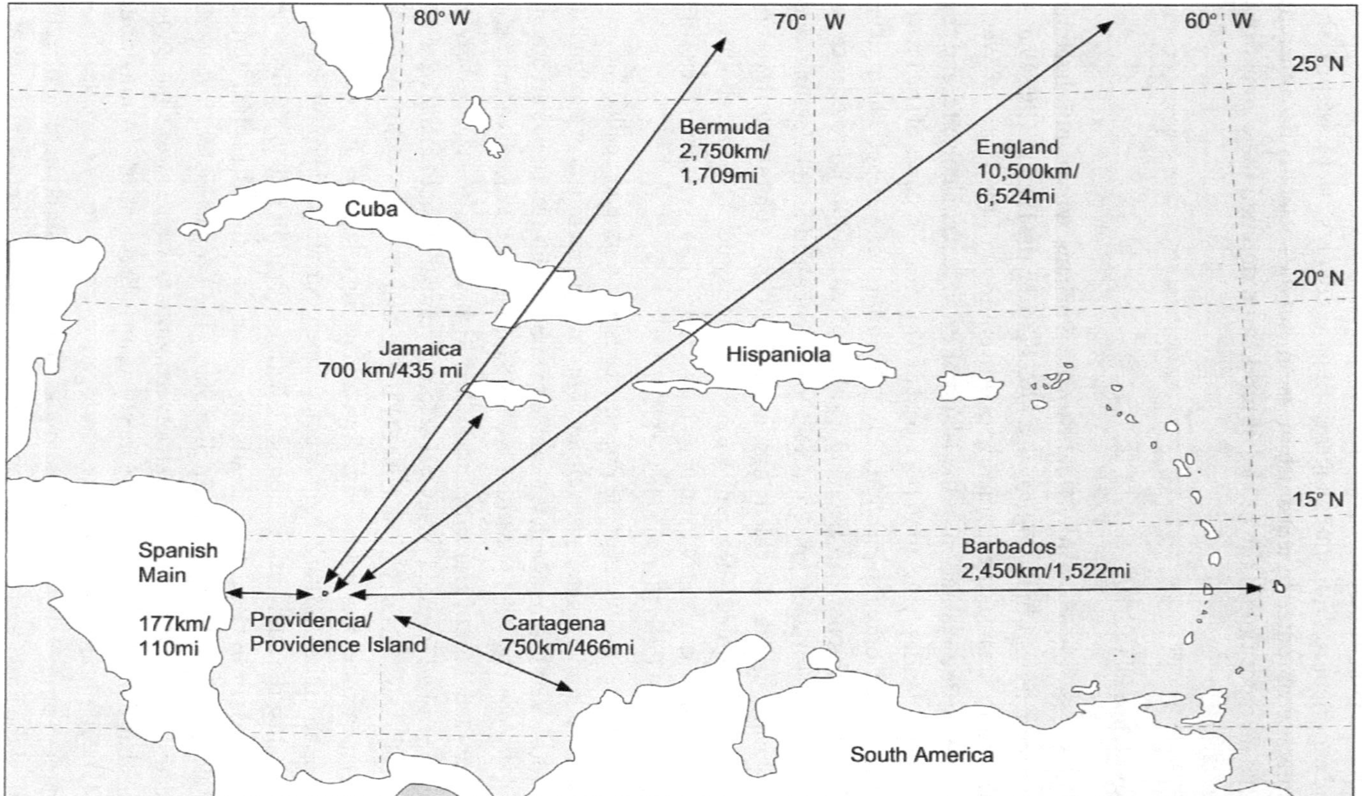


Figure 12.1. Straight-line distances between Providence Island and other notable places.

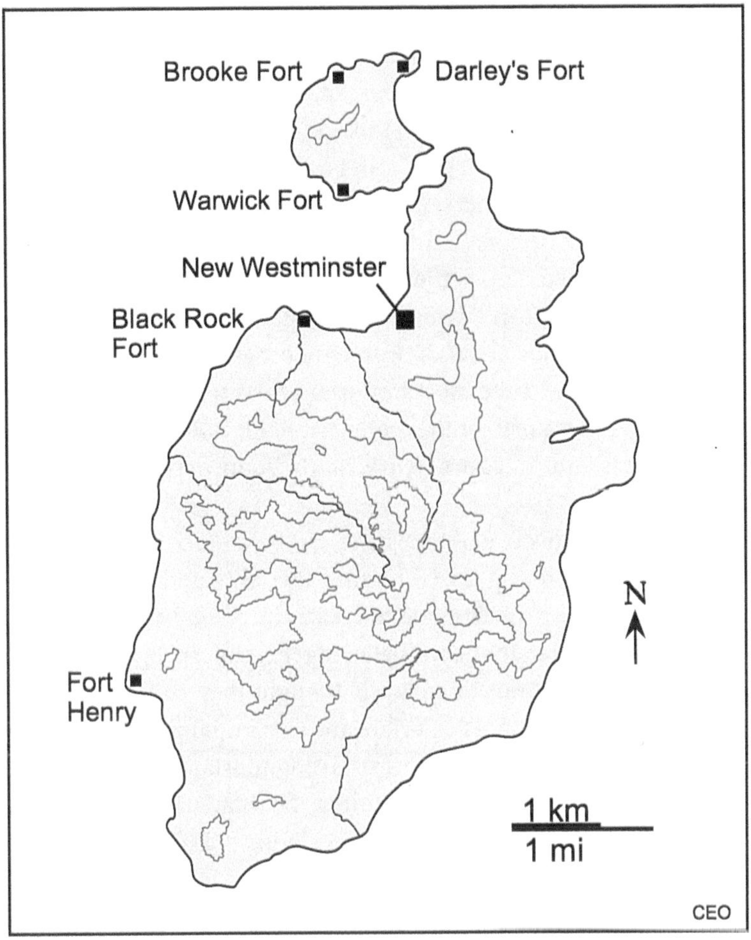


Figure 12.2. Providence Island, showing the locations of New Westminster and the most important forts.

eventually execute Charles I. In 1643 one writer observed that "though it [the rebellion against the king] were conceived (some say) neere Banbury, and shaped in Gray's-Inne Lane, where the undertakers for the Isle of Providence did meet and plot it, yet you know it was put out to nurse to London" (Butler 1810 [1643]:582). A footnote to this sentence reads, "The Puritanism of Banbury was famous." Thus, though Providence Island was a small and somewhat insignificant outpost of English colonialism when compared to Jamaica and Barbados, the men who created and funded the colonial design of Providence Island were important actors in English political history.

In designing their Providence Island colony, the charter members had three central goals: to develop a godly colony based on Puritan principles, to insert an English outpost into the heart of the Spanish Empire, and to recoup the costs of settlement from soil thought to be far richer than any to be found in rocky Massachusetts, then also being settled by Puritans (Levy 1960:85–86). The company owners ordered a town named New Westminster built on the island. Understanding the vital need for defense against the Spanish, they also required settlers to construct forts and earthworks at strategic locations to protect against anticipated attacks. At its height, New Westminster contained about 30 wooden houses, a brick church, and the governor's house. The three most important forts were Warwick Fort, located on the small islet north of the main island, Black Rock Fort, on the western side of the island, and Fort Henry, on the southwestern side of the island.

For convenience, the history of the island can be divided into three periods. The first era, beginning on Christmas Eve 1629 and extending to 1635, was characterized by the struggle to create the colony as a godly and profitable place. The Puritan founders, believing their own propaganda that the Spanish Empire was about to collapse, thought they could introduce an English wedge into the Spanish Caribbean. This initial period involved constructing the built environment and adjusting to island life in the Caribbean (for the colonists) and understanding the difficulties of directing operations from afar (for the Company owners living in London). The second period is characterized by privateering and piracy. During these years the founders decided to reap the financial benefits that could accrue from confiscating the cargoes of captured Spanish ships and beginning trade relations with the indigenous peoples of the Spanish Main. The association of Providence Island with privateering and piracy extended to its founding. The Earl of Warwick, a charter member of the Company, had a long history of supporting buccaneering (Craven 1930), and with time Providence Island became legendary as a refuge for pirates (Alcedo 1814; Jefferys 1775). It was partly this connection that spurred the Spanish attacks on the island in 1635 and 1640 (unsuccessfully) and in 1641 (successfully) (Milton 1847 [1655]:471–472). The third period, which extends from 1641 to the present, can be loosely designated the Spanish era. During this period, Spanish forces entered the island, renamed the fortifications, and built a town named Isabel (Collett 1837; Rowland 1935). The English settlers dispersed throughout the Caribbean or returned to England, and the enslaved were sold on the mainland. In 1666 the pirate Henry Morgan attacked and held the island but lost it again to the Spanish one year later. In 1787–1788, the captain of an English slaving ship obtained a grant to settle on the island with enslaved Africans. In 1822 the island was annexed to the Province of Cartagena, Colombia. In the nineteenth and twentieth centuries, the islanders exported coconuts to the international market (Parsons 1956). Several anthropologists have studied the island's society (e.g., Edwards 1970; Washabaugh 1981, 1986; Wilson 1973, 1974; Woodward 1975), but no systematic archaeological research has yet focused on the English colony (cf. R. Marx 1976:88–109).

## Providence Island's Social Organization and Modes of Production

The belief that Providence Island would be a profitable venture for the Company owners was at the forefront of their thinking about the colony's social composition. At the start they planned to populate the colony with independent English "middling" farmers (whom they called "planters"). In November 1630, early in the colony's history, the owners decided that each of them should find men willing to settle on the island. Concentrating on their home counties, the men found most of the planters in Essex, Northamptonshire, Oxfordshire, Cornwall, Devon, and Wales (Kupperman 1993b:46).

In addition to planters, the owners also recruited from three categories: laborers (men with "no particular handicraft"), artificers (men with skilled trades), and apprentices (boys over 14 years old) (PIC, "Meeting," 11/22/1630). Colonists were also allocated the labor of servants, depending upon their position in the hierarchy. A free planter was usually allowed six servants, and artisans (ministers, shipwrights, smiths, coopers) two. Planters were required to clothe and provide food for their servants, with the Company supplying the rest of the servants' needs. Servants typically served a term of three years. To entice "honest and able Artificers," the Company owners indicated that skilled men would have the same benefits as the freemen planters: they could "raise good profit" from any servants they took with them to the island, and they could make their own arrangements when doing work for other planters. They would be required to contribute labor on the island's fortifications, but only as much as required of the planters (PIC, "General Court for Providence," 2/9/1632).

All colonists regardless of social rank were expected to take an oath of fidelity stating that they would defend "the true religion . . . established in the Church of England," oppose Rome, be faithful to the king, the Providence

Island Company, and the island's governor and council, and do everything to further the success of the colony. The Company's owners also made it clear that they would be "the true owners" of the island, meaning that only they could direct its operations and make the most important decisions (PIC, "Instructions to Governor and Council," 2/7/1630).

Military men constituted a separate class of settlers. Defense against Spanish invasion was a paramount concern for the Company, and military men wishing to serve on the island could often make demands impossible for others. For example, in 1638, Thomas Scott, who was to be captain of Fort Henry, asked the Company to cover the cost of his voyage and to give him an allotment of tobacco and cotton in addition to six servants, fully furnished with clothing and arms (PIC, "Committee at Brooke House," 4/12/1638). In 1631 Captain Philip Bell, the island's first governor and captain general, being charged with the defense of the island, hired a gunner from the ship *Seaflower* for £40 per year. The Company owners thought the cost was "too great a proportion" but conceded the point, because the gunner would not stay on the island for any less remuneration (PIC, "Court for Providence," 12/3/1631). The Company owners usually required nonmilitary planters to repay the cost of their voyage to the island, but they completely understood the need to make allowances for each man's "abilities and merits and difference" (PIC, "Preparative Court," 2/6/1631). The importance of military men was made clear in the allocation of servants. In 1633 the Company owners allocated 10 men each to the captains of Black Rock Fort and Fort Henry, and eight men to the captain of Warwick Fort. The lieutenants received six men, and their ensigns three (PIC, "Letter to Governor and Council sent in *Golden Falcon*," 7/20/1633).

The mode of production originally instituted on Providence Island, and mandated in the Company's founding documents, required all freemen to work "on halves." This meant that half of their profits would go directly to the Company owners. The planters kept the other half but were to divide it according to the agreements they had made with their servants (PIC, "Letter to Bell," 2/1630). The Company required colonists to be divided into artificial "families" of about seven men each, to be led by a head who was the only person allowed to obtain goods from the Company storehouse.

The head, or "master," of each family was required "to build for themselves a substantial strong and well framed house, and conveniently large, so as they may lodge and entertain at least as many more people as now they have, and let them cover them with slike [mud]" (PIC, "Letter to Bell,

2/1630]. The families were also to plant potatoes and twice as much corn as they thought they would need for each household. They were to raise pigs and chickens, and to attempt to grow grapes, oranges, and lemons. The leader of each family was also responsible for the morality of the members in his charge and was to ensure that they faithfully performed their duties. The Company owners originally thought the spatial division of men into invented "families" would be beneficial, but in the May 10, 1632, instructions, they decided to let the planters "sort themselves as they shall see good" (PIC, "Instructions to Governor & Council," 5/10/1632). When new servants came to the island, however, the governor—the owners' leading representative—was "at liberty to dispose them into families" (PIC, "Letter to Bell," 4/10/1633).

The concept of a "family master," as it pertained to agricultural production, was similar to the medieval "tenant-in-chief," and the family members were akin to undertenants (Hilton 1975:118). By instituting a relatively straightforward and hopefully smoothly running agricultural system, the Company owners implemented a design consistent with the early Stuart "new rural economy," an important phase in the development of capitalist agriculture (Tawney 1967:177–230).

The Company owners had 25 acres (10 ha) of land set aside for them in case any of them or "a son, kinsman or near friend" might decide to settle on the island. No one was permitted to settle on this reserved land without the approval of the island's Company-appointed governor and council (PIC, "Instructions to Governor & Council," 5/10/1632). By reserving land specifically for their use, the Company's London owners made a powerful and unmistakable signal of their sole claim to the island.

The productive relations the Company owners mandated for the colony—working on halves within "families"—almost immediately caused tears to appear in the island's social fabric. As early as December 1631, only two years after initial settlement, planters objected "that to work on halves is too hard a condition." The Company answered the complaint by observing that half profit would be "a rich recompence" (PIC, "Court for Providence, 12/3/1631). Left unsaid but implied was the clause "if they worked diligently and faithfully." It became increasingly clear, however, that planters would find it extremely difficult to wrest profit from the soils of the island. Governor Bell reported to the Company owners in 1637 that, though the fortifications were in good order, all was not well on the island. Much of the ground was overrun with grass; many servants' terms of service had expired, leaving a shortage of laborers; and the soil was hard. In addition, the rain, which fell "three months together," chilled the ground and killed crops, especially the much-prized tobacco. The corn was susceptible to harsh winds, and the rats "increase[d] exceedingly through the people's negligence" (PIC, "Committee for Providence," 6/14/1637). Without question, the owners had overestimated and overstated the island's potential for substantial agricultural production.

The owners' failing mode of production was transformed when planters began using African slave labor. Bell had brought enslaved individuals with him when he came from Bermuda, where he had also served as governor, and Daniel Elfrith, captain of Black Rock Fort, had brought with him "a Muletto as you call him" (Kupperman 1993b:165; PIC, "Letter to Elfrith," 5/10/1632). As the Company became less committed to supplying the needs of the planters, given the high costs they bore, their need for labor increased. The enslaved—Africans captured from the Spanish or purchased from passing Dutch ships—made up for the shortfall. Even early in the colony's history, the owners of the Company, despite their Puritan morality, had no qualms about enslavement, because they deemed "English bodies not fit for that work" (PIC, "Ordinary Court for Providence and Association," 6/25/1632). Concerned by the apparent lack of progress on constructing the forts on the island, the Company owners recommended that Bell attempt to acquire "20 or 40 Negroes" to provide labor for the public works. They warned him, however, "that too great a number may as yet be dangerous in the Island" (PIC, "Letter to Bell," 4/10/1633). The settlers quickly adapted to the slave system, and the island had a slave majority when the Spanish conquered it in 1641. By one account made at the time, 381 enslaved individuals lived on the island, as compared to 350 free inhabitants (Games 1998:11). The islanders also acquired a few enslaved Massachusetts Pequots—whom they called "the Cannibal Negroes brought from New England"—captured during the war of 1636–1637 (Copeland 1871[1639]:277; Kupperman 1993b:178). With enslavement already established on the island, planters had no difficulty inserting Native Americans into the system.

Enslavement of imported Africans and indigenous Indians did not solve the owners' problems. On May 1, 1638, the first slave revolt in an English colony occurred. Enslaved individuals escaped into the island's mountainous interior, where they established at least one free community. Samuel Rishworth, one of the island's leading planters, may have been the first person in the English-speaking world to argue on humanitarian grounds against the institution of slavery (Kupperman 1993a:246, 1993b:168).

The Company owners, having adopted an Elizabethan, aristocratic model of colonization, were determined to keep all control firmly in their hands. But living so far away meant that the island's residents could simply disregard their directives. None of the Company owners ever visited Providence Island. What they had planned as an orderly, God-fearing agricultural system quickly became a multicultural society with three distinct, albeit intersecting, modes of production.

## Articulation

Much of the literature about the articulation of diverse modes of production concerns the interjection of capitalism into regions with preexisting noncapitalist productive systems. The preeminent questions take two forms: how does the capitalist mode of production transform and either destroy or operate alongside a preexisting system, and is capitalism really able to erase indigenous socioeconomic systems? The unique nature of the social organization of Providence Island—its small, bounded space and its short existence as an English colony—allows other questions to be posed, including: how do different modes of production articulate when operating under the dictates of the same authority, and what social structural problems may arise in such situations?

Providence Island was unique among English colonies, because it deviated from the small, family-based economy established in New England, and from the slave-based economies later developed in Barbados and Jamaica. The Providence Islanders quickly adapted to using enslaved African labor as the dominant mode of production, but the island was still incapable of producing a sustainable cash crop (Games 1998:3). Rather than having a single dominant mode of production of free planters, the island included two inherently oppressive modes: indentured servitude and enslavement. Thus, three agricultural modes existed side by side.

Even with the subtraction of the semifree and unfree laborers from the equation, the designed mode of production established by the Company owners was inherently flawed, because it was essentially a sharecropping system. As early as April 1632, the owners feared that the planters, despite ostensibly being members of the island's elite, would actually "revolt" (PIC, "Committee Meeting for Providence," 4/11/1632). When they read letters from planter John Essex, who had been killed in a Spanish attack during his unannounced and unauthorized return to England, they were outraged at the "spirit of Ingratitude" shown by the unhappy planters and said that such "ungreateful persons" should be "ashamed of their grudging." To demonstrate the depth of their commitment to the disgruntled planters, they added that whereas most owners of other plantations were usually out of pocket between only £25 and £50, each of them had spent "not less than 600 lb at least." They noted that over the first three years of the settlement's existence, they had collectively spent about £12,000–13,000 in support. In a further defense of their largesse, the owners reminded the island's governor and council members that they, not the colonists, had contributed most of the costs for the colony's maintenance. Whose fault was it that the planters' profits were not as expected, and who suffered the most—the men who had lived on good land on the island or the men who had provided the funding? After all, had they not established the system whereby the indentured servants gave half their produce to their masters? And anyway, did the planters not realize that one-half from Providence Island was more than a man could obtain in England in seven years (PIC, "Instructions to Governor & Council," 5/10/1632)? The owners' reaction to the planters' arguments verifies that they perceived the conflict between them and the unhappy planters to center on what the planters saw as unfair treatment. The sharecropping agreement was unquestionably central to the planters' quarrel with the Company.

Anthropologists, rural economists, sociologists, and public policy scholars have produced an abundant literature on sharecropping. At its most basic, sharecropping is an agricultural arrangement between a landowner and a farmer stipulating that the farmer agrees to pay the landowner a portion of his or her produced crop as rent. Historical evidence indicates that the system originated during the transition from feudalism to capitalism. Sometime during the sixteenth or seventeenth century, depending upon the region, poor farmers were stripped of their land ownership and reduced to working for someone else, often on the same land, as a sharecropper. Sharecropping was practiced in continental Europe well before the seventeenth century (e.g., Emigh 1999; Hoffman 1984; Pudney et al. 1998). At the time Providence Island was being settled, a number of factors had contributed to the deterioration of the Tudor agrarian order in England: rural population growth, a decline in real wages, enclosure of the landscape, and the development of commercially based agriculture. This transformational process fostered widening social gaps between farm laborers and landowners, and even between successful and less successful farmers (Everitt 1967:462).

Sharecropping inherently produces inequality, because it bestows to the landowner full ownership of the farmer-produced crop (Wells 1987). And despite differences in time and place, the realities of sharecropping remain the same. In the late-nineteenth- and early-twentieth-century American South, for example, arrangements allowing the landowner to divide the crop equally were termed "working on halves" (Langsford and Thibodeaux 1939:15; Rawick 1977:258). This is the same term used on Providence Island.

The inequality inherent in sharecropping is cogently expressed in the division of the crop. The central features of division are when it occurs and who makes it. In the nineteenth-century American South, landowners made the division, and sharecroppers did not legally own any part of the crop they had produced until after the division was made. Farmers, who contributed all the labor needed to produce the crop, received their physical share from the landowner. The rationale for this practice stemmed from the sharecropper having provided only the labor, while the landowner had supplied everything else (see Orser 1988:55–57). The Providence Island Company owners had used this same rationale 300 years earlier.

The difference on Providence Island, of course, was that the owners did not live on the island. They were far-distant absentee landlords. In this respect, the owners ironically shared the same fate as American sharecroppers, because they could not be certain they actually received one half of the crop. The planters on Providence Island made the crop divisions and consigned their share to friends in England, who then sold or warehoused it. To have a stronger role in the crop division, the owners commanded the governor and the council to "choose two honest and able men" who, once given an oath to be fair to both parties, would make the division" (PIC, "Instructions to Governor & Council," 5/10/1632).

The Company owners' design for Providence Island created a series of social fissures that disrupted the smooth articulation between the existing modes of production (Figure 12.3). The initial fault line appeared between the three categories existing among the elite free men: military officers (having the duty to build defenses and protect the owners' investment), planters (who sought a relaxation of the rigid rules of Puritanism and wished to own land rather than work on halves), and ministers (whose calling was to save souls and who, given their learned piety, believed their wisdom and advice should be consulted by the other two groups) (Kupperman 1993a:247–249).

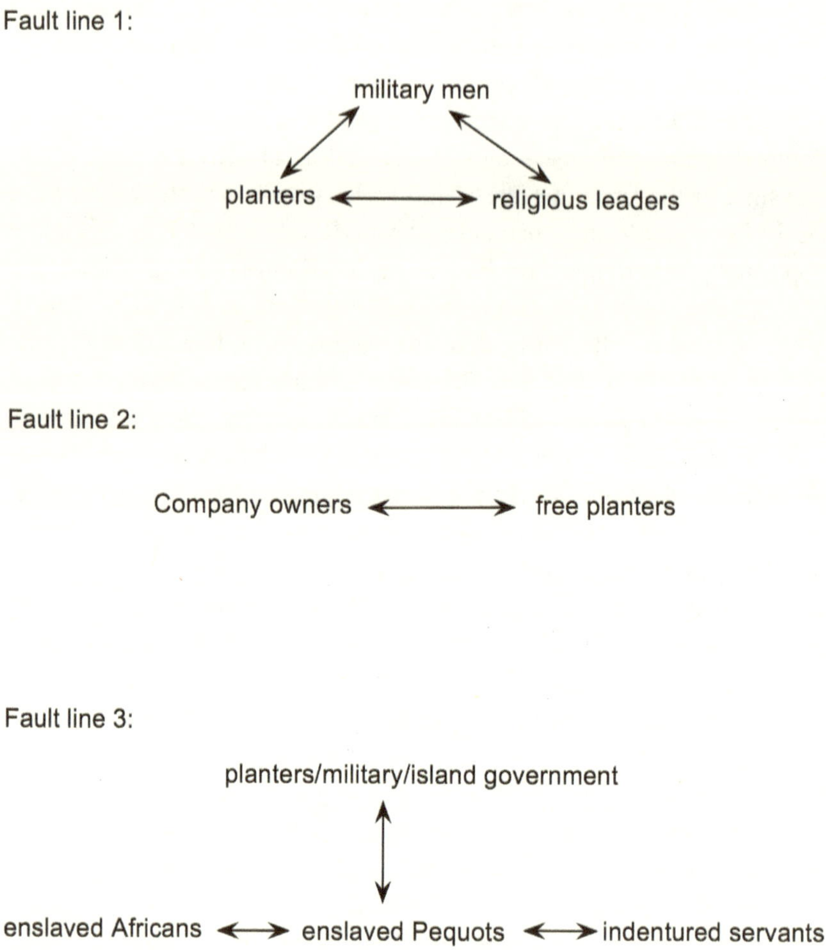


Figure 12.3. Three social fault lines on Providence Island.

Each group had a different reason for being on the island, and each had different responsibilities, some of which conflicted with those of the others.

A second important fault line appeared between the Company owners, who exclusively owned the island, and the free planters, who did not wish to work as sharecroppers. Their social position on the island was situated above the indentured servants, but they were not totally in control of their fates. The Company organized them into "families," put the Governor in charge of apportioning enslaved Africans and indentured English men and women, and limited their access to the Company's store. Planters were allotted only two acres (0.8 ha), their tenure was uncertain, and items available to them at the Company store were marked up 25 percent (Kupperman 1993b:42).

A third social fissure existed between the island's power structure (planters, military men, governor, and council) and the enslaved Africans, Pequots, and indentured English servants. By 1636 a number of enslaved Africans had run away from the sites of their bondage to live in the island's interior. The Company owners recognized the potential danger the self-liberated individuals represented, noting "it may cost some lives, much time and difficulty to bring them in" (PIC, "Committee for Providence, 3/26/1636). Self-liberation created a larger problem for the island's governor and council when indentured servants decided to join the runaways.

Added to this already tense social situation was the establishment of a trading post on the mainland at Cape Gracias à Dios at the mouth of the Rio Coco, which forms the boundary between today's Nicaragua and Honduras (PIC, "Committee for Providence," 5/30/1634). The Company owners planned this settlement to facilitate trade with the indigenous Miskitos, a venture the Spanish viewed as a serious affront. The English considered their settlement legal, because a Miskito "king" had approved it (Helms 1969:77). The Company owners notified the island council that the colonists were forbidden from trading or giving coastal Miskito "swords, pistols or materials of Iron of any kind, as hatchets, knives, hooks or the like." They were also not to trust any of the natives with any arms or to teach them "the use of powder and fire weapons." The owners made it known, however, that they had been advised that some islanders had already given weapons to the Miskitos, a fact they found "inconsiderate" and "inconvenient" (PIC, "Letter to Council at Providence, 4/10/1633).

## Archaeological Implications

The multicultural composition and close juxtaposition of three modes of production in such a small geographic space made the short-lived English colony on Providence Island unique. No sustained archaeological research has yet occurred on the island, so the material evidence documenting the modes of production is not yet available. Nonetheless, the richness of the historical record provides fertile ground for analyzing both the special nature of the island's settlement and the owners' attempted articulation between three capitalist-based modes of production. Several avenues of inquiry may be suggested, but here I concentrate on the complex relationships that existed between colonialism, the modes of production, and social unrest during the English history of the island.

One of the most remarkable features of Providence Island was the creation of a maroon community shortly after the English planters had arrived. Indigenous peoples are not known to have lived on the island, and the precise location of the island's fugitive settlement has yet to be identified. The placename Maroon Hill—in the far south of the island—is suggestive, however (Parsons 1956, map 3). This location makes sense, because this mountainous part of the island is as distant as possible from New Westminster, the seat of Puritan authority.

Archaeologists have been interested in maroonage for the past several years (e.g., Orser and Funari 2001; Sayers et al. 2007; Weik 2012). Self-liberation is an intriguing anthropological subject for numerous reasons, one of the most prominent being that it provides concrete examples of ethnogenesis, as different peoples united to create new cultural expressions. The union of escaped Africans with locally dwelling Native Americans characterizes many maroon communities, because runaways usually settled on lands already inhabited or claimed by indigenous peoples. Native inhabitants often taught newly arriving individuals about the natural environment, and newcomers, as community members, could provide assistance during violent hostilities. Europeans are also known to have assisted and even cohabited with maroons. Interactions between indigenous peoples and European colonists meant that maroon settlements were almost always multicultural establishments.

The settlement called Palmares, located in northeastern Brazil, provides a notable example. Enslaved individuals seeking freedom on their own terms created the settlement in response to the development of a string of hugely successful sugar plantations along the northeast coast of Brazil in the early seventeenth century (see Brandão 1987). During the time of Palmares' existence (1609–1694), over 520,000 Africans had been sold into northeast Brazil (Eltis 2015). These individuals provided the bulk of the plantations' labor. Population figures for Palmares vary widely, but the first European to describe their villages estimated the residents at around 11,000 individuals (Orser 1996:43).

Palmares was developed in reaction to European colonial slavery, but Europeans were always involved in the settlement in some capacity. At least one Dutchman lived in the fugitive community in the 1630s, and so prevalent was European involvement that in the 1670s and 1680s the Portuguese colonial governors threatened imprisonment to Portuguese colonists who assisted the people living at Palmares (Orser 1996:47). Despite the threat, many European settlers living on the edge of Portuguese settlement traded foodstuffs and weapons with Palmares and at times even notified them of impending Portuguese and Dutch attacks (Kent 1965:171; Ramos 1939:64).

As is true of all maroon communities, the runaways who built Palmares created it in response to the horrors and indignities of the slave regime. In removing themselves from enslavement, they practiced self-determination and threatened the stability of the coastal sugar plantations. Colonial Portuguese settlers assisted the fugitives because, as simple colonists unaffiliated with the coastal elites, they felt removed from the dominant mode of production. It made sense for them to find common cause with nearby Africans and Native South Americans.

Unlike Palmares, Providence Island was a small, bounded space with limited opportunities for true spatial isolation. Any successful maroon community would have to be situated within the small island space. Runaways who could acquire a boat could attempt to leave the island permanently, and some chose this risky route (PIC, "Letter sent in the *Blessing*, 5/1636). Those who could not take advantage of this option were restricted to the island. The physical environment thus played a huge role in the location of the settlement, a situation similar to what the enslaved faced when they first moved into the Great Dismal Swamp (Sayers et al. 2007). The small space of Providence Island determined that the establishment of a viable, island-based free community would have close spatial connections with the agricultural settlements—the "families" (which were composed of free planters and semi-free servants). This suggests that the island's social relations of production were intertwined, as free planters, enslaved Africans, and indentured Englishmen labored on the same plots of ground. This proximity meant that cross-ethnic associations could easily form, which in turn could lead to collaboration when individuals became unhappy with their particular situations. Cross-cultural collaborations were known on other seventeenth-century Caribbean islands. For example, in the late seventeenth century, enslaved Africans and indentured Irish servants banded together in an effort to overthrow English rule on Barbados (Shaw 2013:148–150). The first governor of English Providence Island, Philip Bell, later served in the same capacity on Barbados, and many of the English colonists who left Providence Island after the successful Spanish assault may also have settled on Barbados (Games 1998:18n5).

The English elite throughout the Caribbean feared associations between

Africans and non-African indentured servants, because it was a triple threat to stability. Cross-cultural associations simultaneously cast doubt on the dominant racial understanding (whites:non-whites), the social order (superiors:inferiors), and the agricultural productive system (owners:laborers). Unfree laborers were undoubtedly aware of how their "social betters" viewed the "lower orders." The equation of Irish indenture with African slavery has been a hotly debated issue (see, for example, Ellis 1975), but evidence for English anti-Irish sentiment is abundant in historical accounts. For instance, William Petty, scholar and surveyor-general of Ireland, compared the "value" of individual Irish men and women in terms of how "Slaves and Negroes are usually rated" (Petty 1691:21). No evidence exists that Irish servants settled on Providence Island, but many of the Company owners played important roles in suppressing the Irish rebellion of the 1640s (Kupperman 1993b:344).

Spatial proximity meant that the complaints of one Providence Island group—free, indentured, and enslaved—would be known and observable by members of the other two. The social fault lines created by the Company owners' design for the island were likely intensified as dissatisfaction grew. The social inequalities mandated by the Company owners and expressed in the modes of production produced a volatile situation on the island from the very beginning.

## Conclusion

Without question, modes of production can play an important role in archaeological research because the concept combines the material and the social worlds. All social archaeologists ground their interpretations in physical remains that help them to define, structure, and interpret how individuals united in social groups to sustain their ways of life. Human life is impossible without the production of material things, and a perspective sensitive to the modes of production helps archaeologists to foreground the relationships between social relations and the tangible things used to reproduce daily life.

The concept of the mode of production has an important place in the archaeological analysis of colonialism. The subject of articulation necessarily arises when people with a particular mode of production arrive in a place with a different, indigenous mode of production. The process of articulation begins when one mode of production is favored over another, or when the two attempt to exist in harmony alongside one another.

The subject of articulation is especially significant for archaeologists investigating the colonial New World. This immense area—often described as the Atlantic World—witnessed numerous examples of articulation between capitalist and noncapitalist modes of production. The myriad ways they were either linked together or kept separate has been a subject of considerable anthropological interest. Archaeological research has a special potential to contribute to this body of analysis by overtly focusing on the process of articulation. Modern-world archaeology, because of its overt interests in capitalism, capitalist practice, and its resultant globalization, offers a useful framework for investigating the colonial New World.

Providence Island provides a unique bounded space in which to inquire into the nature of articulation with the capitalist mode of production and to link it with concepts of racial identification and resistance. The spatial proximity of English indenture and non-English enslavement in such a small sphere invites interesting contrasts and comparisons perhaps more difficult to observe elsewhere.

## Acknowledgments

I wish to thank Karen Ordahl Kupperman for her willingness to share information about Providence Island. Her kindness represents the highest degree of professionalism. I also thank Jane Landers for helping me develop a proper appreciation for the significance of the island's Spanish era. I equally appreciate the willingness of Rob Rosenswig and Jerimy Cunningham to include me in the original session and in this book. As always, I must thank Janice for her careful reading of drafts and for her always-pertinent insights.

## References Cited

Alcedo, Antonio de
1814 *The Geographical and Historical Dictionary of America and the West Indies.* Vol. 4. Translated by G. A. Thompson. Carpenter and Son, London.

Anderson, Kevin B.
2010 *Marx at the Margins: On Nationalism, Ethnicity, and Non-Western Societies.* University of Chicago Press, Chicago.

Anonymous
1643 *An Elegie, Vpon the Much Lamented Death of that Renovvned and ever to be Honour'd Patriot of his Countrey John Pym Esquire: Lievtenant of the Ordnance, and a Member of the Honourable House of Commons.* n.p., London.

Avineri, Shlomo (editor)
1968 *Karl Marx on Colonialism and Modernization*. Doubleday, Garden City.

Berman, Bruce J.
1984 The Concept of "Articulation" and the Political Economy of Capitalism. *Canadian Journal of African Studies* 18:407–414.

Bradby, Barbara
1975 The Destruction of Natural Economy. *Economy and Society* 4:127–161.

Braddick, Michael
2008 *God's Fury, England's Fire: A New History of the English Civil Wars*. Penguin, London.

Brandão, Ambrósio Fernandes
1987 *Dialogues of the Great Things of Brazil, Attributed to Ambrósio Fernandes Brandão*. Translated and annotated by Frederick Holden Hall, William F. Harrison, and Dorothy Winters Welker. University of New Mexico Press, Albuquerque.

Brenner, Robert
2003 *Merchants and Revolution: Commercial Change, Political Conflict, and London's Overseas Traders, 1550–1653*. Verso, London.

Butler, Samuel
1810 [1643] A Letter from Mercurius Civicus to Mercurius Rusticus. In *A Collection of Scarce and Valuable Tracts on the Most Interesting and Entertaining Subjects*, vol. 4, edited by Walter Scott, pp. 580–598. T. Cadell and W. Davies, London.

Childe, V. Gordon
1951 [1936] *Man Makes Himself*. New American Library, New York.

Collett, C. F.
1837 On the Island of Old Providence. *Journal of the Royal Geographical Society of London* 7:203–210.

Copeland, Patrick
1871 [1639] Letter to John Winthrop, Dec. 4. *Collections of the Massachusetts Historical Society, Vol. 1, Fifth Series*, pp. 277–280. Massachusetts Historical Society, Boston.

Craven, W. Frank
1930 The Earl of Warwick, a Speculator in Piracy. *Hispanic American Historical Review* 10:457–479.

Deetz, James
1977 *In Small Things Forgotten: The Archaeology of Early American Life*. Anchor/Doubleday, Garden City.

Donnelly, James S., Jr.
2009 *Captain Rock: The Irish Agrarian Rebellion of 1821–1824*. University of Wisconsin Press, Madison.

Eagleton, Terry
2011 *Why Marx Was Right*. Yale University Press, New Haven.

Edwards, Jay D.
1970 *Social Linguistics of San Andres and Providencia Island, Columbia*. Doctoral dissertation, Tulane University, New Orleans.

Ellis, Peter Berresford
1975 *Hell or Connaught! The Cromwellian Colonisation of Ireland, 1652–1660.* Blackstaff, Belfast.

Eltis, David
2015 A Brief Overview of the Trans-Atlantic Slave Trade. Electronic document, *Voyages: The Trans-Atlantic Slave Trade Database*, http://www.slavevoyages.org/tast/assessment/essays-intro-01.faces, accessed January 29, 2015.

Emigh, Rebecca Jean
1999 Means and Measures: Property Rights, Political Economy, and Productivity in Fifteenth-Century Tuscany. *Social Forces* 78:461–490.

Everitt, Alan
1967 Farm Labourers. In *The Agrarian History of England and Wales, Volume IV, 1500–1640*, edited by Joan Thirsk, pp. 396–465. Cambridge University Press, Cambridge.

Foster-Carter, Aidan
1978 The Modes of Production Controversy. *New Left Review* 107:47–77.

Games, Alison
1998 "The Sanctuarye of Our Rebell Negroes": The Atlantic Context of Local Resistance on Providence Island, 1630–41. *Slavery and Abolition* 19:1–21.

Graeber, David
2006 Turning Modes of Production Inside Out. *Critique of Anthropology* 26:61–85.

Helms, Mary W.
1969 The Cultural Ecology of a Colonial Tribe. *Ethnology* 8:76–84.

Hill, Christopher
1991 *The World Turned Upside Down: Radical Ideas during the English Revolution.* Penguin, London.

Hilton, Rodney Howard
1975 *The English Peasantry in the Later Middle Ages.* Clarendon, Oxford.

Hodgen, Margaret T.
1971 *Early Anthropology in the Sixteenth and Seventeenth Centuries.* University of Pennsylvania Press, Philadelphia.

Hoffman, Philip T.
1984 The Economic Theory of Sharecropping in Early Modern France. *Journal of Economic History* 44:309–319.

Hopkins, Nicholas S.
1978 The Articulation of the Modes of Production: Tailoring in Tunisia. *American Ethnologist* 5:468–483.

Jefferys, Thomas
1775 *The West-India Atlas: Or, A Compendious Description of the West-Indies.* Robert Sayer and John Bennett, London.

Kent, Raymond K.
1965 Palmares: An African State in Brazil. *Journal of African History* 6:161–175.

Kupperman, Karen Ordahl
1989 *Papers Relating to the Providence Island Company and Colony, 1630–1660s.* Microform Academic, East Ardsley.

1993a A Puritan Colony in the Tropics: Providence Island, 1630–1641. In *Settlements in the Americas: Cross-Cultural Perspectives*, edited by Ralph Bennett, pp. 238–251. University of Delware Press, Newark.

1993b *Providence Island, 1630–1641: The Other Puritan Colony*. Cambridge University Press, Cambridge.

Langsford, E. L., and B. H. Thibodeaux

1939 *Plantation Organization and Operation in the Yazoo-Mississippi Delta Area.* Government Printing Office, Washington, D.C.

Levy, Babette M.

1960 Early Puritanism in the Southern and Island Colonies. *Proceedings of the American Antiquarian Society* 70, part 1, pp. 69–348.

Marx, Karl

1954 [1848] *The Communist Manifesto*. Henry Regnery, Chicago.

1967 [1887] *Capital: A Critique of Political Economy*. 3 vols. International, New York.

Marx, Robert F.

1976 *Still More Adventures*. Mason/Charter, New York.

Milton, John

1847 [1655] A Manifesto of the Lord Protector. In *The Prose Works of John Milton*, vol. 2, edited by Rufus Wilmot Griswold, pp. 464–477. John W. Moore, Philadelphia.

Naved, Shad

2008 The Colonial Encounter in Marxist Terms. *Social Scientist* 36:33–46.

Newton, Arthur Percival

1914 *The Colonising Activities of the English Puritans: The Last Phase of the Elizabethan Struggle with Spain*. Yale University Press, New Haven.

Ollman, Bertell

1993 *Dialectical Investigations*. Routledge, New York.

Orser, Charles E., Jr.

1988 *The Material Basis of the Postbellum Tenant Plantation: Historical Archaeology in the South Carolina Piedmont*. University of Georgia Press, Athens.

1996 *A Historical Archaeology of the Modern World*. Plenum, New York.

2014 *A Primer on Modern-World Archaeology*. Eliot Werner, Clinton Corners.

Orser, Charles E., Jr. and Pedro Paulo A. Funari

2001 Archaeology of Slave Resistance and Rebellion. *World Archaeology* 33:61–72.

Parsons, James J.

1956 *San Andrés and Providencia: English-Speaking Islands in the Western Caribbean*. University of California Press, Berkeley.

Patterson, Thomas C.

2009 *Karl Marx, Anthropologist*. Berg, Oxford.

Petty, William

1691 *The Political Anatomy of Ireland with the Establishment for that Kingdom when the late Duke of Ormond was Lord Lieutenant*. D. Brown and W. Rogers, London.

PIC [Providence Island, Records of]
1630–1660s National Archives, Kew.
Pudney, Stephen, Francesco L. Galassi, and Fabrizia Mealli
1998 An Econometric Model of Farm Tenures in Fifteenth-Century Florence. *Economica* 65:535–556.
Ramos, Arthur
1939 *The Negro in Brazil*. Translated by Richard Pattee. Associated, Washington, D.C.
Rawick, George P. (editor)
1977 *The American Slave: A Composite Autobiography: Volume 4, Part 1. Texas Narratives*. Greenwood, Westport, Connecticut.
Ritzer, George
2003 The Globalization of Nothing. *SAIS Review* 23:189–200.
2007 *The Globalization of Nothing 2*. Pine Forge Press, Thousand Oaks.
Rowland, Donald
1935 Spanish Occupation of the Island of Old Providence, or Santa Catalina, 1641–1670. *Hispanic American Historical Review* 15:298–312.
Shaw, Jenny
2013 *Everyday Life in the Early English Caribbean: Irish, African, and the Construction of Difference*. University of Georgia Press, Athens.
Smith, Adam
1999 [1776] *The Wealth of Nations, Book IV*. Penguin, London.
Sayers, Daniel O., P. Brendan Burke, and Aaron M. Henry
2007 The Political Economy of Exile in the Great Dismal Swamp. *International Journal of Historical Archaeology* 11:60–97.
Tawney, Richard Henry
1967 *The Agrarian Problem in the Sixteenth Century*. Harper and Row, New York.
Thompson, E. P.
1993 *Customs in Common*. New Press, New York.
Wakefield, Edward Gibbon
1849 *A View of the Art of Colonization*. John W. Parker, London.
Washabaugh, William
1981 Sign Language in Its Social Context. *Annual Reviews in Anthropology* 10:237–252.
1986 *Five Fingers for Survival*. Karoma, Ann Arbor, Michigan.
Weik, Terrance
2012 *The Archaeology of Antislavery Resistance*. University Press of Florida, Gainesville.
Wells, Miriam J.
1987 Sharecropping in the United States: A Political Economy Perspective. In *Farm Work and Fieldwork: American Agriculture in Anthropological Perspective*, edited by Michael Chibnik, pp. 211–243. Cornell University Press, Ithaca.
Wilson, Peter J.
1973 *Crab Antics: The Social Anthropology of English-Speaking Negro Societies of the Caribbean*. Yale University Press, New Haven.

1974 *Oscar: An Inquiry into the Nature of Sanity?* Waveland, Long Grove, Illinois.

Wolf, Eric R.

1982 *Europe and the People without History*. University of California Press, Berkeley.

1984 Culture: Panacea or Problem? *American Antiquity* 49:393–400.

Woodward, James C.

1975 Attitudes toward Deaf People on Providence Island. *Sign Language Studies* 18:49–68.

Yang, Manuel

2012 Specter of the Commons: Karl Marx, Lewis Henry Morgan, and Nineteenth-Century European Stadialism. *Borderlands* 11(2):1–31. Electronic document, www.borderlands.net.au/vol11no2_2012/yang_specter.pdf.

# 13

# The Plantation Mode of Production

JAMES A. DELLE

Most social theorists agree that in any given historical context, there exists some underlying logic binding individual human beings into coherent social groups. The nature of this underlying logic has been debated for centuries, and, perhaps because social phenomena are so complex, no consensus has yet been reached on just how to define the forces that bind individuals into groups and shape the nature of human relationships within and between recognized groups. Marx proposed that societies formed when human beings worked together to acquire and distribute the necessities of life; to Marx this meant that human society had a material, or physical, base (Marx 1979; Engels 2007). Because Marx argued that the production of goods and services was the primary force binding societies together, he defined the various social formations that historically developed as "modes of production" (Marx 1979, 1992).

While Marx himself proposed that capitalism was a single mode of production that developed directly out of what is generally referred to as the feudal mode of production (Marx 1979, 1992), some more recent theorists have suggested that multiple variants of the capitalist mode of production developed over time, particularly following the introduction of industrialized production (Bagchi 2004; Cowie 2011; Sen 1984). In cases where the economic and social interests of elite classes in a colonial metropolis or core differ from the interests of regional elites in the colonial periphery, variants of the capitalist mode of production will develop (Wallerstein 1979). Such was the case in much of the New World, including Jamaica, when systems of temporary bondage known as indentured servitude were replaced with chattel slavery (Epperson 1999, 2000), resulting in the formation of the plantation mode of production, a variant of the capitalist mode of production.

Defining the plantation mode of production as a distinct variant within capitalism provides a useful mechanism to understand how slavery was incorporated into the capitalist hegemony that emerged in the eighteenth century. A prevailing assumption about the operation of the capitalist mode of production asserts that the primary class relationship is defined and mediated by wages. The logic goes something like this: as members of the working class are increasingly alienated from the means of production, they are forced to sell their labor for a wage; wealth therefore accumulates in the hands of the capitalist class, who co-opt the products of labor and pay wages less than the value of what they produce. While this relationship can be easily understood in the context of industrial factory production—a key focus of Marx's original critique—the absence of a wage relationship within the capitalist system is difficult to interpret. This chapter explores one way to reconcile the long-standing existence of slave labor within the capitalist system in a way that does not merely dismiss slavery as a vestige of a previously existing mode of production or a system in which absent wages were somehow totally withheld from the working class. Rather, here I consider this labor system as an integral component within a coherent variant of the capitalist mode of production. In doing so, this chapter defines the plantation mode of production as it was manifested in early nineteenth-century Jamaica, providing an exemplar for other scholars of the relationship between slavery and capitalism to consider.

## The Plantation Mode of Production

Modes of production arise through a complex, historically contingent process through which humans organize labor and social relations, and develop tools and technologies, in order to transform what exists in nature into objects that fulfil physical and social needs. In the seventeenth and eighteenth centuries, the European markets developed needs for addictive agricultural products, including tobacco, tea, sugar, and coffee. Those that lived and worked on plantations both created and were created by the relations and forces of production operating within the plantation mode of production, which existed to supply the European markets with the tropical commodities so demanded.

A mode of production is composed of the tools and techniques used to produce and distribute commodities, and by the social relationships that emerge from the production and use of those commodities, generally referred to as the social relations of production (Marx 1992). Although the social relations of production are often equated with class structure, other operative principles of social organization can be considered as constituent elements of the social relations of production. Under the plantation mode of production, for example, slavery was a key element of the social relations of production. While enslavement on plantations was clearly related to the classification of people within the labor structure of the mode of production, and can thus be considered a class relationship, slavery was also, clearly, closely tied to the development of a racialized social hierarchy in colonial Jamaica, which was based on the capitalization of laborers as elements of the means of production. Perceived racial identity, when used to define a person's place within the hierarchy of production, can thus be considered a constituent element of the social relations of production.

Nevertheless, the social relations of production within the plantation mode of production were structured by a strict hierarchy defined by the relationship one had to the productive forces required to produce export crops. Existing at the top of the social pyramid, the members of the agrarian elite who controlled Jamaica's land base and directed the production of commodities referred to themselves as "planters." The planters were not a homogeneous group free from internal division but included members of the landed oligarchy, their estate staff, and other members of Jamaican society involved in the commodities trade and service industries required to maintain it, including merchants, attorneys, and financiers (Butler 1995; Checkland 1957; Davis 1975; Lobdell 1972; Pares 1950; Stinchcombe 1995). In part because ownership of a plantation allowed one to ascend to the status of "planter," many merchants and attorneys purchased estates, ensuring them access to planter status.

At the apex there was a significant variance in wealth and power among the proprietors; social standing within the planter class was largely dependent on the type(s) of plantations one owned, the amount of land one held, and the number of laborers one kept in bondage. The most valuable type of plantation was a sugar plantation. In 1823 John Stewart, a Jamaican planter himself, estimated that one would require an investment of approximately £43,000 in Jamaican currency to acquire the land, construct the buildings, and purchase the slaves required to run a profitable sugar plantation; this would amount to approximately £1,280,000 in modern sterling, or about $2,000,000 U.S. Coffee plantations and cattle breeding pens, the second and third most-important type of plantations on Jamaica, required a significantly smaller investment (Shepherd 2009). Although many of Jamaica's pens were owned by wealthy planters who operated them in support of their sugar estates, the relatively low start-up costs of a cattle pen or coffee plantation provided opportunities for people of relatively modest means to become proprietors. For example, Thomas Thistlewood, a famous diarist of eighteenth-century Jamaica, owned a cattle pen that was worth only £600 in 1789; at the time of his death in 1786, his 34 enslaved workers were valued at £1,500. Although £2,100 was a lot of money in the late eighteenth century, it was nothing near £43,000. Thistlewood's example demonstrates that a cattle pen could be established for a fraction of the cost of setting up a sugar estate (Burnard 2004).

Many of the wealthiest plantation owners did not reside on their estates. Some were investors who lived in Great Britain; they were known as absentee proprietors. Many plantations were owned by proprietors choosing to live in one of Jamaica's urban centers, or else by a planter who owned multiple plantations and chose one for a principal residence. Absentee proprietors depended on the managerial skills of agents residing on Jamaica, many of whom lived primarily in Kingston (Higman 2005). Such attorneys, or island factors as they were sometimes known, would correspond with the proprietors and would accumulate wealth by taking a percentage of the profits realized by the estates they managed. The more successful attorneys would manage multiple estates, creating great opportunities for the accumulation of wealth through a mixture of good management and clever fraud.

The daily operation of a plantation was supervised by a salaried estate employee known as an overseer, who could earn a salary of as much as £200 per year. Although the majority of overseers probably never rose above this station, some, through a combination of thrift and luck, could accumulate enough wealth to acquire property (Burnard 2004; Hall 1989). Overseers supervised one or more lower-level plantation managers, known in Jamaica as "bookkeepers." Bookkeepers tended to be young men of modest means trying to get a start in plantation society. Their primary responsibility was keeping the daily "book," which did not involve accounting as in the modern usage of the word *bookkeeper*, but rather referred to the plantation daybook, which logged daily activities.

Although the greatest wealth was controlled by the proprietors and attorneys of Jamaica's many vast sugar estates, there were also a significant number of small plantation owners who primarily owned cattle pens or coffee plantations. While a significant minority of wealthy coffee plantation owners held in excess of 1000 acres, nearly the same number held less than 100 acres (Smith 2002:103). At 699 acres, the average size of a coffee plantation was just over two-thirds the size of the average sugar plantation, and even this number may be skewed by the few truly large estates. Far fewer people were enslaved on an average coffee plantation than on a sugar estate; 128 to 223. As a middling class of plantation proprietors, coffee planters tended to live on the island; only about 9 percent of coffee plantations were owned by absentees.

Civil and political rights were granted in colonial Jamaica based on a racial hierarchy created and imposed by the planter class. The European population of Jamaica was not gender-balanced; for much of the eighteenth and early nineteenth century, European men outnumbered European women. This gender imbalance resulted in many sexual unions between European men and women of African descent; the ensuing pregnancies resulted in a large mixed-race population on Jamaica, some of whom remained enslaved, others of whom were either born into freedom or were manumitted by their white fathers. During the colonial era, this population was known as "free colored" or "free people of color."

Prior to the abolition of slavery, by far the greatest percentage of Jamaica's colonial population was composed of enslaved Africans and their descendants; in colonial terms this encompasses both the enslaved black population and those people of color who remained enslaved. Barry Higman, the noted demographer of colonial Jamaica, has estimated that there were some 313,000 enslaved people on Jamaica in the year 1832 (Higman 1995:16), of whom about 90 percent were black and 10 percent people of color (Higman 1995:142).

The social structure and complex relationships that developed among proprietors, attorneys, overseers, bookkeepers, whites, free people of color, and enslaved workers were products of the organization of plantation production yet simultaneously worked to shape and reproduce the plantation mode of production. Marx imagined that any mode of production is structured by historically contextual interactions between the forces and relations of production; the social relationships we have explored would not exist outside of the context of the material realities of the plantation system.

## The Forces of Production

The materials, tools, knowledge, and techniques used to transform raw materials into saleable commodities are collectively known as the forces of production (Marx 1992). While human labor can be considered an element of the forces of production, the nonhuman elements of the forces of production, including land, tools, machinery, and infrastructure, are known

Figure 13.1. A stonemason's chisel found in situ at Marshall's Pen, a nineteenth-century coffee plantation. Enslaved masons would have used this tool to build and maintain stone structures on the plantation. Photograph by James A. Delle.

as the means of production. The analysis of the means of production is a general goal of archaeological fieldwork, as the means of production tend to leave readable imprints on the archaeological record. Plantation production required a variety of tools, techniques, and knowledge specific to the agriculture needs of tropical produce, as well as tools and technologies of more general application, including coopering (barrel making), masonry and carpentry for the construction and repair of plantation buildings and infrastructure, blacksmithing for the creation and repair of iron tools, transportation technologies for the movement of goods by water and by land, and animal husbandry to raise and care for beasts of burden (Figure 13.1). Each of these activities required tools and training; each was an integral part of the plantation mode of production.

The techniques used specifically to produce coffee were a key factor in the development of the other means of production specific to Jamaican coffee plantations. Although there was some variation, the primary techniques used to produce coffee were generally similar throughout the island. After a parcel of undeveloped land, referred to in nineteenth-century Jamaica as a "run," was acquired, that land would need to be cleared for

Figure 13.2. This tool, known as a socketed bill, was found in situ at Marshall's Pen. This tool would have been used to prune coffee trees. Wooden handles of various lengths would have been inserted in the socket to enable enslaved workers to prune branches at various heights off the ground.

coffee production. Once cleared, the ground would be developed for a series of uses, including coffee fields, known as "pieces," where the coffee trees would be planted, provision grounds for growing foodstuffs for the plantation workforce, grass pieces for pasture and fodder for horses, mules, and cattle, residential quarters for the white plantation staff, industrial buildings for the processing and storage of coffee for export, and villages to house the enslaved workforce.

The economic purpose of a coffee plantation was to produce a profitable export crop, which in the case of coffee quite literally grows on trees. In Jamaica, coffee trees would bear fruit after three to five years, requiring careful pruning done primarily with hand tools (Figure 13.2). Coffee trees bear a red fruit known as a cherry; cherries were picked by hand, with each coffee tree needing to be picked more than once per season, as the cherries on a given branch will not all ripen simultaneously; it was thus impossible to strip a branch of its entire fruit without wasting a number of unripe cherries.

Once picked, the coffee fruit would be transformed into an exportable form, a process that required several steps. Jamaican planters preferred a wet process for pulping, which included the use of a mill to break up the skin and pulp of the cherries; the pulping mill or pulper would separate the pulp and skin from the beans through the action of a perforated copper-sheathed cylinder. The resulting material was then placed in a suspension tank filled with water. The pulp would float to the surface, while good beans would sink to the bottom. The pulpy waste product would be skimmed out of the tank, and the wet beans would be collected for curing.

After pulping, the wet beans would be cured or dried on a large drying platform known as a barbecue. Once laid out, the beans would be turned several times to ensure thorough drying so as to prevent the growth of mold. While the beans were drying, the barbecues would be monitored to ensure the beans would not get soaked by rain. Should the barbecues be threatened by rain, the beans would either be moved into small shelters incorporated into the barbecue complex or else be covered by tarpaulins (Laborie 1798; Lowndes 1802; Montieth 2002).

The dried beans have a thin membrane called parchment, which is removed by a separate dry process known as peeling or grinding. The beans would be placed in a grinding mill, and a wooden wheel would be lightly turned over the beans to separate them from the dry parchment; once ground, the parchment waste would be winnowed from the beans either by hand or through a fanning mill. The final stage in the process is the separation of beans into qualities. Inferior beans, including those damaged in the process, were sold as triage in local markets or consumed on the estate. The majority of the high-quality beans were shipped in bags or barrels to any one of the numerous wharves on the Jamaican coast. Once at a wharf or other transhipment point, the crop was consigned to merchants for transport and sale in the European markets.

The means of production on a Jamaican coffee plantation thus included arable land suited for coffee production, a mill complex suited to both the wet process of pulping and the dry processes of grinding and fanning, drying platforms for the pulped beans, a sorting room, and storage facilities to hold the sorted beans prior to shipping. A variety of hand tools would also be required for coffee production, including axes and saws for felling trees while clearing coffee fields, hoes to weed the coffee trees, sharp tools for pruning trees, and baskets and bags for collecting coffee cherries as they were picked from the trees. The means of production would also include the housing required for overseers, bookkeepers, and the enslaved laborers, as well as the tools and knowledge to build and maintain these structures. Technologies required to distribute coffee to market can also be considered part of the means of production; enslaved laborers on plantations built roads within the estate boundaries, and each planter was required to pay a labor tax for maintaining the roads leading from enclaves of plantations to the wharves on the coast. Enslaved artisans on the plantations were skilled in these technologies, from making barrels for storage and transport of coffee beans, to building and maintaining carts, to knowing how to finesse mule trains down the sometimes treacherous mountain roads to the wharves.

## The Division of Labor

In defining how modes of production were structured, Marx argued that the forces of production could be subdivided into objective forces and subjective forces, the former including the means of production, and the latter a variety of socially constructed phenomena. The objective forces of production include strategies for training specific members of the workforce to complete specific productive tasks, a process often referred to as the technical division of labor. It can thus be argued that the relations and forces of production converge in the division of labor structuring a mode of production.

The life experiences of people living under a mode of production are largely shaped by the roles they play in the organization of production; as productive tasks become increasingly specialized, the range of actions for workers becomes more and more constrained. Similarly, as the productive process becomes more complex, it is increasingly difficult for workers to control all of the means of production required to produce commodities for sale. As we have seen, one of the primary tenets of Marxism holds that social relationships are in large measure defined by one's position in the hierarchy of productive tasks. This hierarchy of tasks was defined by what Marx called the technical division of labor. The roles and social positions people held in a given society emerging from the technical division of labor are collectively called the social division of labor. The technical division of labor is considered to be part of the forces of production, as it is largely a mechanical division of the tasks needed to be performed as part of the productive process. The social division of labor, on the other hand, is a component of the relations of production, as status and wealth bestowed on individual people are directly correlated with the task they complete within the technical division of labor. In many modes of production, social categories are created or reinforced when members of defined groups are assigned to specific tasks within the technical division of labor. In the case of the plantation mode of production, for example, clearing forests and picking coffee were tasks assigned to enslaved laborers, who were people of African descent. Thus, the social division of labor that emerged was defined by enslavement and racialization of the population, and these categories of social relationship were tied to the specific manifestation of task specialization that emerged in eighteenth-century Jamaica.

The technical division of labor is a key element in the organization of any mode of production. Modes of production can be characterized by varying levels of task specialization, which allows for the development of expertise in a specific set of tasks required in the productive process. In Marxist analysis, what is known as the technical division of labor is considered to be part of the objective forces of production, objective inasmuch as the range of actions required to complete a specific task is specific but standardized, and so can be learned and completed by anyone trained to carry out that task (Marx 1992). In terms of the plantation mode of production, the technical division of labor refers to the way that tasks were divided up on the plantation and how specific roles within the labor force were defined. Because the technical division of labor is an objective force of production, what is really referred to is the categorization of work, rather than the talents of any specific workers.

Jamaica plantation managers kept sometimes detailed records of the operations of the estates; a few of these records have survived into the twenty-first century. Among those documents are plantation journals kept by the overseers and/or bookkeepers of Maryland Plantation in the parish of St. Andrew, New Forest Plantation in the parish of Manchester, and Radnor Plantation in St. David. In addition to these journals, a detailed correspondence between the Earl of Balcarres (a Scottish nobleman and the absentee owner of several Jamaican plantations) and his attorneys in Kingston documents the workings of three of his coffee estates, including Martins Hill and Marshall's Pen in Manchester, and Balcarres Plantation in St. George.

The records of these six early-nineteenth-century coffee plantations indicate that each maintained a similar technical division of labor. In each case the workforce was divided into specific occupation groups, including field work, artisan trades, domestic service, healthcare service, watchmen, and supervisory positions (e.g., drivers or head people). On average, approximately one half of the population (49.2 percent with a standard deviation of 2.9 percent) were field workers; this percentage ranged but little, with a low of 46.6 percent on Martins Hill and a high of 54.7 percent on

Balcarres. Field workers on these coffee estates would engage in a variety of tasks, from felling trees and clearing fields for coffee production, to picking coffee from the trees, to processing the coffee for export. On average, 6.6 percent (with a standard deviation of 2.2 percent) of the enslaved population of the six estates were artisans, with a low of 4.7 percent on Balcarres and a high of 9.5 percent on Marshall's Pen.

About an equal number of enslaved workers were employed as domestic servants, watchmen, and stock keepers, with averages of 3.6 percent, 3.2 percent, and 3.1 percent respectively. Domestic servants were engaged in a variety of tasks, primarily in support of the white estate staff. Each of the estates also employed people to mind the variety of species of animals on the estates, including poultry, swine, cattle, and horsekind (i.e., horses, donkeys, and mules). Not surprisingly, New Forest and Martins Hill, both of which raised livestock for sale, had the highest number and percentage of stock keepers; more surprising is the relatively few number of people engaged in this activity. At New Forest 12 of the 181 enslaved workers were stock keepers, accounting for 6.6 percent of the population; at Martins Hill 10 of 232, or 4.3 percent of the people, were engaged in these activities. In contrast, 2.3 percent and 2.5 percent of the population at Balcarres and Maryland, respectively, were stock keepers; at Radnor only 1.9 percent (4 people) and at Marshall's Pen only 0.9 percent (1 person) were stock keepers.

Health care was an important concern on tropical plantations. Plantation managers would arrange to have a white doctor visit the enslaved population at least once per year. Such doctors would make regular rounds through a number of plantations, being paid by the head for the enslaved workers they visited on each plantation. Many plantations had enslaved doctors and nurses who would minister to the sick and tend to wounds and infections caused by work-related (and other) accidents. Most plantations also counted one or more midwives among the enslaved population, who helped women through pregnancies and childbirth. Some plantations also employed enslaved nurses to care for infants and young children while their mothers were engaged with field work or domestic chores for the estate staff. All of the coffee plantations in our sample, with the exception of New Forest, had between one and five health care specialists among the enslaved population: Balcarres with one, Martins Hill and Marshall's Pen each with two, and Maryland and Radnor each with five.

When task specialization emerges in a mode of production, the potential exists for this technical division of labor to become a basis both for how people working within these tasks are treated, and who is given access to the various jobs. In Marxist terms, the objective technical division of labor is the material basis for the development of social identity through the negotiation of what is called the social division of labor (Marx 1992). Even within working communities, a person's status, position, and overall quality of life can be affected by the job to which he or she is assigned. Furthermore, in Marxist terms, the technical division of labor in large measure defines these categories. Under the plantation mode of production, the productive process was partitioned into the various tasks we have seen defined as the technical division of labor; who actually performed those specialized tasks led to a subjective division of labor, which nevertheless affected quality of life; this subjective division is what is known as the social division of labor.

The social division of labor on plantations was structured not only by task, but by age, gender, and racial and ethnic assignation. While it was certainly in the planters' interests to enslave as many able-bodied young adults as possible, the realities of life result in babies being born, small children growing up, and young adults growing older and, sometimes, becoming elderly. The plantation workforce comprised children, adolescents, adults, and the elderly; boys, girls, men, and women; Africans abducted to Jamaica and island-born creoles; blacks, people of color, and whites.

## Age

Age is one of the primary structuring principles for most societies, and this was certainly true within the plantation mode of production. On Jamaican plantations children would be introduced to the workforce at age five or six (Delle 2000; Higman 1995), often in a separate children's gang. In young adolescence, at about age 12, boys and girls would be elevated from the children's gang to the second gang, and when they reached young adulthood at about age 18, they would become part of the first or great gang, which was responsible for most of the heavy work to be done on a plantation. While there was no predetermined retirement age for enslaved workers, many would become incapacitated by age, accident, or disease, often by their mid-forties; such people were listed by estate managers as invalids. The percentage of nonworking children at the six coffee plantations examined here was fairly consistent; on average 17 percent of the plantations' population was composed of nonworking children, with a standard deviation of 3.2 percent. Balcarres (15.6 percent), Maryland (16.9 percent), and Martins

Hill (16.4 percent) had very comparable percentages, as did Marshall's Pen (20.7 percent) and Radnor (20.4 percent). New Forest, with 12.2 percent of the population being composed of nonworking children, had a relatively smaller percentage of nonworking children. The population of working children on all of the estates was very comparable, with an average of 8.7 percent, with a standard deviation of 1.4 percent. With the exception of Marshall's Pen (11.2 percent), each of the plantations had a population of working children constituting between 7.2 percent and 8.8 percent of the overall population.

Looking in more detail at the age structure of Marshall's Pen gives us a more thorough understanding of the nature of how chronological age was intertwined with the social relations of production. The Marshall's Pen community was divided into age grades through which people would pass; as plantation workers, in the eyes of the planters, members of these age grades were differentially assigned tasks and relative status on the plantation. When first born, any individual was defined as a child; this status was sometimes referred to in plantation documents as "unserviceable children," clearly reflecting that, from the perspective of plantation management, very small children performed no useful service in the organization of production. Members of this age grade were allowed some measure of freedom; no work was expected of them, and social rules separating the various racial groups and genders did not apply. At Marshall's Pen individuals passed out of the "unserviceable children" age grade at age six or seven, when they would enter a more highly gendered age grade, which the planters sometimes referred to as "serviceable children." The third age grade was what is commonly referred to as adolescence; boys and girls would usually enter adolescence at 10 or 11; Jamaicans generally refer to members of this age grade as "youth." Adult status was attained between ages 18 and 19, and elder status attained between the ages of 45 and 60.

Although there was some overlap with the youngest age grade, most children aged six to 11 were assigned to the third or children's gang, responsible for light work around the plantation, like weeding coffee trees. In 1832 at Marshall's Pen, the third gang was composed of 43 children aged between 6 and 13 (five 6-year-olds, two 7-year-olds, eleven 8-year-olds, eleven 9-year-olds, seven 10-year-olds, four 11-year-olds, one 12-year-old, and two 13-year-olds). At the age of 11 or 12, most members of the third age grade moved into the second or small gang, where they would work alongside several adults. While in this age grade, gender-specific tasks would reinforce emerging gender identities. For example, while in this age grade, Frances Adams and Peggy Powell became "house girls" or domestics, while Joe Logan and William Learmond became apprentice carpenters.

At age 17 or 18, able-bodied people were assigned to the first gang, sometimes referred to as the great gang, where they would do the heaviest plantation work, so long as they remained healthy, until their late forties or fifties. There was no specific age at which elders "retired;" those too infirm or old to work were defined by the crass descriptor of "invalid." In 1834, of the 342 people enslaved at Marshall's Pen, 20 people over the age of 39 were defined as invalids and thus were not assigned work tasks on the estate; these included one woman in her late thirties, six women and two men in their forties, three women and one man in their fifties, five women and one man in their sixties, and the 86-year-old John Noble, by far the oldest member of the community. Some elders were assigned lighter tasks when they reached their forties. Older men would become watchmen, while older women would mind small children while their mothers worked in the fields, or were cooks for the plantation community.

## Gender

Although it may seem counterintuitive, the social division of labor on Jamaican coffee plantations was organized such that the majority of field labor was conducted by women. The plantation records of five of the six plantations indicate that the majority of field workers were women or girls (Radnor 56 percent, Maryland Plantation 57 percent, New Forest 58 percent, Balcarres 64 percent, and Martins Hill 67 percent). At Marshall's Pen the genders were equally split. Although the numbers are much smaller, a similar trend can be observed for domestic service at each estate; at both Maryland and New Forest, there were seven female and two male domestics; at Marshall's Pen and Martins Hill, the ratios were 3:1 and 6:1 respectively; Balcarres employed only one domestic servant who was a woman. At each of the plantations, including Marshall's Pen, there were a greater number of exclusively male occupations. Cumulatively, 82 artisans were identified on the six plantations, including blacksmiths, masons, coopers, saddlers, carpenters, and sawyers. All 82 were male. Similarly, all 45 watchmen were male, and 29 of the 36 stock keepers were male, with the women generally being assigned to tend fowl, while men tended the breeding and working stock on the estates. Health care and cooking were two occupations that tended to be heavily female. Between the six plantations, 18 women were identified as midwives, doctresses, hospital attendants, or nurses, though this latter category likely included women tending to young children rather than to the sick. Nevertheless, most women born on or purchased by coffee plantations could expect to spend much of their lives doing manual labor in the fields, as 403 of the 474 able-bodied working women and girls on the six plantations, 85 percent of the females, were field laborers. In contrast, only 63 percent of the able males were field laborers, meaning that more than one in three working men were doing something other than manual labor.

## Race

In early nineteenth-century Jamaica, racial assignation was based on the genealogical distance one had from "whiteness." The terms "negro" and "black" were used to describe a person solely descended from African ancestors; people of mixed African and European heritage were racially defined as "mulatto" (one white parent, one black parent); "sambo" (one mulatto parent, one black parent); "quadroon" (one white parent, one mulatto parent); "mustee" or "mestee" (one white parent, one quadroon parent); "mustifini (one white parent, one mustee parent), "quintroon" (one white parent, one mustifini parent), and "octaroon" (one white parent, one quintroon parent); the child of a white man and an octaroon woman was considered legally white. In theory at least, the British West Indian racial structure recognized eight races of African-descent people, as well as a variety of other racial groups, including whites, "coolies" (South Asians), Chinese and Indians (indigenous people, not those from the subcontinent).

Racial hierarchy was clearly evident at Marshall's Pen and Martin's Hill. In 1825 the so-called valuation list for these two plantations identified people by name, age, "color," whether African or creole, occupation, and gender. The vast majority enslaved on these two plantations, 401 people, were identified as black; 18 were identified as mulatto, two as quadroon, 15 as sambo, and one 18-year-old woman simply as "colored." Racial assignation had a real effect on the lives of the people. While a number of blacks (74) held skilled positions (e.g., driver, cooper, mason, midwife, doctress, cook) or were assigned lighter duties (house servants, cattleman, penkeeper, watchman, fowl keeper), the majority, 257, were field hands; the remaining people were either young children or aged or infirm. Thus, of the 351 able-bodied workers recognized as black, 73 percent were field workers. In contrast, none of the 18 mulattos were field hands; of the seven adults assigned to this category, one was a carpenter, one a stableman, one a mason, three were house servants, and one was sick with yaws. Of those 15 defined as sambo, one was a driver, one a cattleman, one a house servant, one a penkeeper, five were children, and six—fewer than half—were field hands. Both quadroons were under the age of three and thus had not yet been assigned duties on the plantations.

## Landscapes of the Plantation Mode of Production

In this discussion of the means of production, we have considered the various kinds of buildings and other elements of plantation infrastructure that were required by Jamaican coffee planters to produce their export commodity. However, we have not yet touched on how these various elements of the means of production were related to one another. Buildings, machines, coffee fields, and villages did not independently float in space but were connected physically and cognitively. The network of spaces and objects that tied the various elements of the plantation infrastructure together is what we can call the plantation landscape. Buildings, roads, bridges, coffee fields, provision grounds, slave villages, and overseers' houses were all connected together in a unified spatial phenomenon, but one that was experienced differently by the various people who lived, worked, and were bound together within the plantation landscape. It is by examining how the landscapes tied the material and social together—the way that the forces and relations of production were linked—that we can understand how the mode of production operated to create the habitus of coffee plantation landscapes (Delle 2008, 2009).

Because they occupied different positions within their social structure, planters and enslaved workers perceived and experienced the material and social realities of coffee plantation landscapes differently. The planter class who designed the estate landscapes actively constructed plantation spaces—or, more accurately, had enslaved workers create the plantation spaces according to the planters' designs—as an active part of their strategy to control the lives and labor of enslaved workers and thus maximize their ability to accumulate surplus value from the production of plantation commodities. Similarly, those who were enslaved within these landscapes created social meanings of their own, sometimes quite different from those anticipated by the planters when they designed the landscapes.

It has long been thought that the majority of enslaved plantation workers lived in nucleated villages located on the estates to which they were attached. From the perspective of the planters, villages were a necessary component of plantation infrastructure. Composed of numerous small houses, many villages were abandoned following the abolition of slavery,

Figure 13.3. The barbecues at Sherwood Forest. In the early nineteenth century, the overseer would walk directly onto this barbecue from his veranda. Photo by James A. Delle.

while others developed into towns or villages that are still occupied. In the former case, the small houses located in the villages have become part of the archaeological record and tend to exist now as scatters of artifacts and construction debris. In the latter case, few of the eighteenth- or nineteenth-century houses still exist, having been rebuilt and replaced over the decades.

An example of this spatiality is a coffee plantation known as Sherwood Forest. The original pulping mill at Sherwood Forest was located in the overseer's house. The mill was housed in one room of this structure, while the overseer occupied the other. The Sherwood Forest pulping mill was water powered. However, Sherwood Forest is not situated below a river, but rather is located above the Negro River. To compensate for the lack of river-fed water power, the mill complex is attached to a spring-fed cistern, which serves as a sort of "mill pond." During the pulping process, water from the cistern was channeled to the mill by means of a small aqueduct, which survives today but is not functional.

The barbecues at Sherwood Forest were terraced into a hillside (Figure 13.3). Above the terraced barbecues is a series of smaller terraces, which are currently used as a coffee nursery. It is possible that this is the original purpose of these terraces, as coffee plants require careful nurturing for several years before they can be transplanted into the coffee fields. It is likely that each plantation had some kind of nursery facility.

The overseer's house at Sherwood Forest also survives into the twenty-first century. This particular structure exhibits two phases of construction, with the older house actually serving as part of the foundation for the later house. The earlier overseer's house is a relatively small structure built with massive stone walls. This structure is divided into two rooms, containing the domestic space of the overseer as well as the pulping mill. In this case the overseer would be in direct contact with the first stage of the industrial processing of coffee. The other key architectural feature of this building is a veranda, oriented toward the barbecues. From this vantage point, the overseer would have the capability to be in direct surveillance of the drying beans. At Sherwood Forest the domestic space of the overseer, at least during the first phase of the plantation's existence, was inseparable from the space of production. An archaeological survey conducted in 1998 confirmed the location of the slave village at Sherwood Forest. It is likely that the village occupied about three acres of land, and contained between 15 and 25 houses (Delle 1998, 1999, 2014; Higman 1986).

The plantation landscape at Sherwood Forest was designed to create a spatiality of control. From the side entrance to the house, the overseer had a vantage point from which he could survey the flats below the coffee works, where archaeological testing confirmed the village had once been located. The original overseer's house at Sherwood Forest was massively built, with 21-in-thick stone walls. A veranda provided the overseer with a southern view encompassing the coffee barbecues while an 18-in-thick interior wall separated the overseer's room from the pulping mill. Although contained within an imposing fortresslike structure, as long as he was in his room or on his veranda, the overseer could directly supervise the production of coffee. From the veranda the overseer could monitor the coffee crop as it dried, while from his room he could watch the coffee as it was pulped and channeled to the barbecues. This spatial arrangement created an intensive capacity for surveillance over production while simultaneously socially and physically segregating the overseer from the workforce (Figure 13.4).

The overseer could also view the slave village from the veranda of his house. The coffee works and barbecues were located downhill and within the viewscape of this vantage point. Thus, from the comfort of his veranda, the overseer could supervise the coffee works, and any activity occurring on the barbecues. During those times when the overseer wanted to exert the greatest measure of control over the workers, he could practice

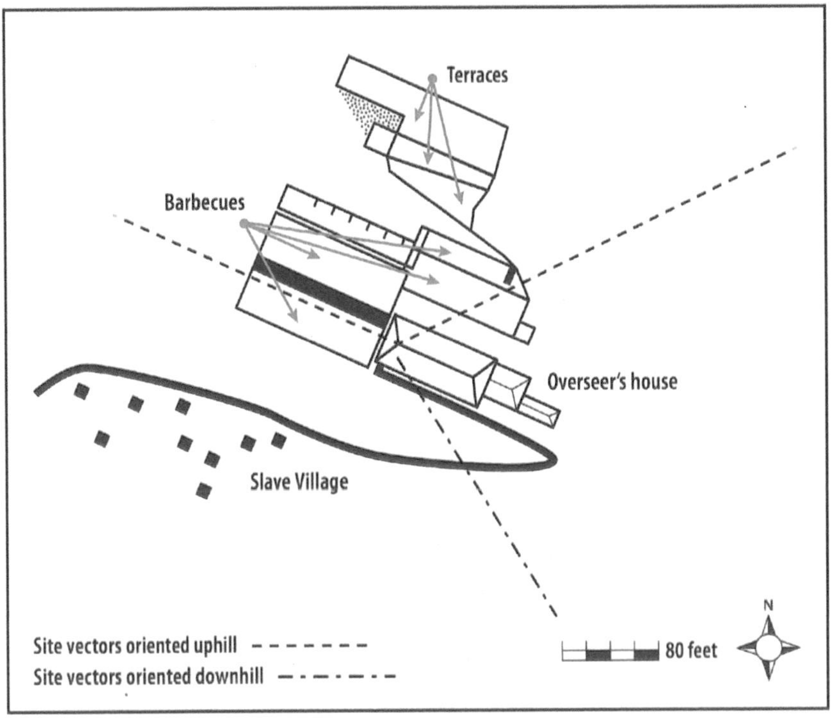


Figure 13.4. The plantation landscape at Sherwood Forest.

panoptic surveillance over the population in the village. By locating the overseer's house in such a way that the overseer could be surveying the village and works from the veranda, or even by gazing out of one of the house's windows, the workers could never be entirely sure whether they were being watched. The purpose behind the construction of this spatiality was the construction of discipline in the workforce; the logic of the panopticon dictated that the workers would cooperate if they thought they were being watched. Through this mechanism the actual physical layout of the plantation influenced behavior among the enslaved and thus linked the forces and relations of production into a material and social whole: the plantation mode of production.

## Conclusion

The production of agricultural commodities on colonial plantations resulted in the construction of material and social realities that defined how landscapes were built and lived; these plantation landscapes were in turn created to produce export commodities for European markets. Unlike sugar, tea, and tobacco, however, coffee was never consumed in great quantities in Great Britain; at least not as in as great a quantity as tea. Nevertheless, by the turn of the nineteenth century, there was a thriving coffee industry in the British West Indies, most notably in Dominica and Jamaica. If, as the historian S. D. Smith argues (Smith 1996), the consumption of coffee in Great Britain remained stagnant until the middle of the nineteenth century, how can one account for the rapid rise and seeming success of coffee planters in pre-emancipation Jamaica?

The answer lies in two places. First, according to Smith's research on the history of coffee consumption in Great Britain, much of the coffee crop that was imported into British ports was re-exported to continental Europe, where there was a much greater market for coffee than there was in England (Smith 1996). Prior to 1790 the largest suppliers to the European markets were the planters of the French Antilles, notably the colony of St. Domingue, which in the late 1780s was the world's leading exporter of both sugar and coffee (Geggus 1993). When the Haitian revolution broke out, the export of plantation commodities from the erstwhile colony of St. Domingue came to a screeching halt. The British, having a re-export system already in place, were more than happy to fill the void left by the destruction of the St. Domingue coffee economy. Jamaican coffee planters were relatively quickly able to step into the breach, as Jamaica coffee could fulfill the needs of European coffee drinkers when St. Domingue coffee could not.

Second, as coffee grows best in tropical highlands and thus did not compete directly with sugar for land use in Jamaica, and because coffee plantations require a relatively low initial investment, many would-be planters eagerly invested in coffee production on lands that had not previously been developed for export production. At the turn of the nineteenth century, the number of monocrop coffee plantations skyrocketed in the highland parishes. The Jamaican historian Kathleen Montieth has calculated that prior to 1790 there was virtually no coffee sector in the Jamaican economy. By 1799 a rapid escalation of coffee production resulted in there being some 519 coffee plantations on the island; by 1808 there were more than 600 (Montieth 1991:34–35; Shepherd and Montieth 2002; see also Delle 1996:201–208, 1998). New to the production of coffee, Jamaican planters adapted the existing plantation mode of production, which had been thoroughly developed for the production of sugar, to the requirements of coffee cultivation.

Unlike sugar cane, which needs to be replanted each year and produces best on coastal lowlands, coffee grows on trees, which can bear for years and thrive in cool, humid, tropical highlands. Nevertheless, despite these significant differences in the ecology of crop production, Jamaican coffee planters were closely tied into the existing economic and social structures of the island. When coffee production was introduced, it was not introduced into a historical vacuum; planters thus adapted the existing plantation mode of production that had developed primarily in the sugar industry to the physical and social realities of highland tree husbandry. Although different in many ways from sugar production, coffee production was organized through the development of a plantation mode of production. The forces of production, like the relations of production, were thus similar in their organization to those developed for sugar production.

The plantation mode of production in operation in Jamaica at the turn of the nineteenth century was complex. It was a web of social relations that defined the nature of class and gender relations, structured relationships between people of various social standings with the hierarchy of the island, and, more than anything, defined who would collect the surplus value produced on the coffee plantations of Jamaica.

Because the mode of production was dependent on the brutal use of enslaved labor to work the land, it was by its nature unstable. Plantation theorists, as well as the actual planters on the ground, developed a series of strategies to ensure that the mode of production would be reproduced from year to year and generation to generation. The key to this for the planter class was to maintain control over the labor force. Violence was commonly used to terrify people into subservience, but other, more subtle strategies were employed, including the creation of landscapes within plantations that allowed planters to create and maintain systems of surveillance over the labor force, surveillance that was designed to maintain order, if not full control over the lives of the enslaved.

## References Cited

Bagchi, Amlya Kumar
2004 The Axial Ages of the Capitalist World System. *Review* 27(2):93–134.
Burnard, Trevor
2004 *Mastery, Tyranny, and Desire: Thomas Thistlewood and His Slaves in the Anglo-Jamaican World.* University of North Carolina Press, Chapel Hill.

Bush, Barbara
1990 *Slave Women in Caribbean Society, 1650–1838*. Indiana University Press, Bloomington.
Butler, Kathleen M.
1995 *The Economics of Emancipation: Jamaica and Barbados, 1823–1843*. University of North Carolina Press, Chapel Hill.
Checkland, S. G.
1957 Finance for the West Indies, 1780–1815. *Economic History Review* 10:461–469.
Cowie, Sarah
2011 *The Plurality of Power: An Archaeology of Industrial Capitalism*. Springer, New York.
Davis, David B.
1975 *The Problem of Slavery in the Age of Revolution, 1770–1823*. Cornell University Press, Ithaca.
Delle, James A.
1996 *An Archaeology of Crisis: The Manipulation of Social Spaces in the Blue Mountain Coffee Plantation Complex, 1790–1865*. Ph.D. dissertation, Department of Anthropology, University of Massachusetts, Amherst.
1998 *An Archaeology of Social Space: Analyzing Coffee Plantations in Jamaica's Blue Mountains*. Plenum, New York.
2000 The Material and Cognitive Dimension of Creolization in Nineteenth-Century Jamaica. *Historical Archaeology* 34(3):56–72.
2008 An Archaeology of Modernity in Colonial Jamaica. *Archaeologies: The Journal of the World Archaeology Congress* 4(1):87–109.
2009 The Governor and the Enslaved: Archaeology and Modernity at Marshall's Pen, Jamaica. *International Journal of Historical Archaeology* 12(4): 488–512.
2011 The Habitus of Jamaican Plantation Landscapes. In *Out of Many, One People: The Historical Archaeology of Colonial Jamaica*, edited by James A. Delle, Mark Hauser, and Douglas V. Armstrong pp. 122–143. University of Alabama Press, Tuscaloosa.
2014 *The Colonial Caribbean: Landscapes of Power in the Plantation System*. Cambridge University Press, Cambridge.
Engels, Frederick
2007 *Socialism: Utopian and Scientific*. Pathfinder, Atlanta.
Epperson, Terrence
1999 Constructing Difference: The Social and Spatial Order of the Chesapeake Plantation. In *"I, Too, Am America": Archaeological Studies of African American Life*, edited by Theresa Singleton, pp. 159–172. University Press of Virginia, Charlottesville.
2000 Panoptic Plantations: The Garden Sights of Thomas Jefferson and George Mason. In *Lines That Divide: Historical Archaeologies of Race, Class, and Gender*, edited by James A. Delle, Stephen A. Mrosowski, and Robert Paynter, pp. 58–77. University of Tennessee Press, Knoxville.
Geggus, David
1993 Sugar and Coffee Cultivation in Saint Domingue and the Shaping of the Slave

Labor Force. In *Cultivation and Culture: Labor and the Shaping of Slave Life in the Americas*, edited by Ira Berlin and Philip D. Morgan, pp. 73–98. University Press of Virginia, Charlottesville.

Hall, Douglas
1989 *In Miserable Slavery: Thomas Thistlewood in Jamaica*. Macmillan, London.

Higman, Barry W.
1995 *Slave Population and Economy in the British Caribbean, 1807–1834*. University of the West Indies Press, Kingston.
2005 *Plantation Jamaica, 1750–1850: Capital and Control in a Colonial Economy*. University of the West Indies Press, Kingston.

Laborie, P.J.
1798 *The Coffee Planter of Saint Domingo*. Cadell and Davies, London.

Lobdell, Richard A.
1972 Patterns of Investment and Sources of Credit in the British West Indian Sugar Industry. *Journal of Caribbean History* 4:31–53.

Lowndes, John
1802 *The Coffee Planter*. C. Lowndes, London.

Marx, Karl
1979 *A Contribution to the Critique of Political Economy*. International, New York.
1992 *Capital*. Volume 1. International, New York.

Pares, Richard
1950 *A West-India Fortune*. Longmans, Green, New York.

Montieth, Kathleen
1991 The Coffee Industry in Jamaica, 1790–1850. Master's thesis, University of the West Indies, Mona, Jamaica.
2002 Planting and Processing Techniques on Jamaican Coffee Plantations during Slavery. In *Working Slavery, Pricing Freedom: Perspectives from the Caribbean, Africa, and the African Diaspora*, edited by Verene A. Shepherd, pp. 112–129. Palgrave, New York.

Sen, Asok
1984 Transition from Feudalism to Capitalism. *Economic and Political Weekly* 19(30)51–69.

Shepherd, Verene A.
2009 Land, Labor, and Social Status: Non-sugar Producers in Jamaica in Slavery and Freedom. In *Working Slavery, Pricing Freedom: Perspectives from the Caribbean, Africa, and the African Diaspora*, edited by Verene A. Shepherd, pp. 153–178. Palgrave, New York.

Shepherd, Verene A., and Kathleen E. A. Montieth
2002 Pen-Keepers and Coffee Farmers in a Sugar-Plantation Society. In *Slavery without Sugar: Diversity in Caribbean Economy and Society since the 17th Century*, edited by Verene A. Shepherd, pp. 82–101. University Press of Florida, Gainesville.

Smith, S. D.
1996 Accounting for Taste: British Coffee Consumption in Historical Perspective. *Journal of International History* 27(2):183–214.

2002 Coffee and the "Poorer Sort of People" in Jamaica during the Period of African Enslavement. In *Slavery without Sugar: Diversity in Caribbean Economy and Society since the 17th Century*, edited by Verene A. Shepherd, pp. 102–128. University Press of Florida, Gainesville.

Stinchcombe, Arthur L.

1995 *Sugar Island Slavery in the Age of Enlightenment: The Political Economy of the Caribbean World.* Princeton University Press, Princeton.

Wallerstein, Immanuel

1979 *The Capitalist World Economy.* Cambridge University Press, Cambridge.

# Contributors

Guillermo Acosta Ochoa is associate investigator at the Instituto de Investigaciones Antropológicas of the Universidad Nacional Autónoma de México. His research focuses on subsistence practices of Paleoindian, Archaic, and Formative peoples of Mexico. He has collaborated on projects in Chiapas, Veracruz, and Tabasco, and his current research focuses on the Basin of Mexico. He has over 40 publications, including three books.

Myrian Álvarez is a researcher at the National Scientific and Technical Research Council (CONICET-CADIC-Argentina). Her line of research has been focused on technological practices developed by hunter-gatherer societies from Tierra del Fuego and on the role of tool-using and consumption patterns for unveiling substantial modifications in human action. Currently she is carrying out a project on coastal hunter-gatherers on the Atlantic coast of Tierra del Fuego, and her interests center on pursuing the material correlates and cultural markers of social relations and on the rhythms of social innovations in broad time spans.

Bill Angelbeck is an archaeologist and anthropologist who focuses on cultures of Salishan peoples of the Northwest Coast and interior. He acquired his doctorate at the University of British Columbia in Vancouver in 2009, researching warfare in the Coast Salish past through an anarchist analysis. Other research interests include archaeological theory, sociopolitical organization, ideation, and ideology. He has published his work in *Current Anthropology*, *Ethnohistory*, and *the Journal of Anthropological Archaeology*. He is faculty member of the Department of Anthropology and Sociology at Douglas College in New Westminster, B.C.

Per Cornell is professor in archaeology at the University of Gothenburg, Sweden, and has taught in Sweden, Argentina, Bolivia, Nicaragua, Spain, and Sri Lanka. He has organized sessions at international congresses and is currently the co-organizer of the AACCP workshops on architecture and archaeology. His recent research projects have been financed by the Swedish Research Council (VR) and include the early modern town, field research in Argentina, and his current work in Quintana Roo in collaboration with the INAH-Chetumal, México, and a study of the sixteenth-century town of Nya Lödöse in present-day Gothenburg, Sweden. He has also worked on Bronze Age rock art in Scandinavia and developed with Fredrik Fahlander the "microarchaeological approach" in Scandinavian archaeology. His research interests include socioeconomic process in a comparative perspective, time and archaeology, built environments, aesthetics, imagery, and ideology.

Jerimy J. Cunningham is associate professor in the Department of Anthropology at the University of Lethbridge. His research interests focus on the areas of archaeological epistemology, material culture studies, political economy, sociocultural evolution, and the history of archaeological theory. His past research projects include an ethnoarchaeological analysis of ceramic exchange and consumption in the Inland Niger Delta of Mali that highlighted the connections between women's ceramic production systems, domestic political economies, and capitalism. His new project is exploring the emergence of social and political complexity in the southern periphery of the Casas Grandes Regional System in what is now Chihuahua, Mexico. Currently he is writing a book on ethnographic analogy and archaeological interpretation.

James A. Delle is associate dean of the College of Arts and Sciences at Shippensburg University. His research focuses on historical archaeology of the Caribbean. He has published widely, including *Lines That Divide: Historical Archaeologies of Race, Class and Gender* and *The Colonial Caribbean: Landscapes of Power in Jamaica's Plantation System*.

Ivan Briz Godino is researcher at the National Scientific and Technical Research Council (CONICET-Argentina), professor at the National University of Tierra del Fuego, Antártida e Islas del Atlántico Sur (Argentina), and associated researcher of the University of York (United Kingdom). He has undertaken different research projects about coastal hunter-gatherer societies and shell middens, from an ethnoarchaeological perspective. His research interests have been focused on the socioeconomic dimension of lithic technology and the role of cooperation in small-scale societies. He has worked in Tierra del Fuego (Argentina), Nicaragua, and Northern England.

Bradley E. Ensor is professor of anthropology at Eastern Michigan University. His research emphasizes adapting archaeology to address political economic theory in social anthropology, which includes Marxist and kinship analyses. Having extensive archaeological experience in Mesoamerica and the U.S. Southwest and Southeast, he has most recently conducted long-term field research at Islas de Los

Cerros in coastal Tabasco, Mexico, since 2001, and along the Lower Huron River in Southeast Michigan since 2005. He is the author of numerous published works, including *The Archaeology of Kinship: Advancing Interpretation and Contributions to Theory* and *Crafting Prehispanic Maya Kinship*.

Gary M. Feinman is MacArthur Curator of Mesoamerican, Central American, and East Asian Anthropology at the Field Museum of Natural History, Chicago. He has directed long-term archaeological field programs in Oaxaca, Mexico, and Shandong, China, and has also studied in the U.S. Southwest. His research interests include comparative studies of leadership, cooperation, and inequality, preindustrial economics, and the complex relations between humans and environments over time. Feinman is a Fellow of the American Association for the Advancement of Science and received the Presidential Recognition Award from the Society for American Archaeology. He is the founding and contact coeditor for the *Journal of Archaeological Research*.

Kristian Kristiansen is professor of archaeology and chair at the University of Gothenburg. His main research is the Bronze Age, but archaeological theory and archaeological heritage are also central research interests. His books include *Europe before History* and *The Rise of Bronze Age Society*.

Johan Ling is associate professor in archaeology in the Department of Archaeology and Ancient History at the University of Gothenburg. Ling has worked with topics in rock art and landscape but also on aspects of provenancing Scandinavian Bronze Age artifacts by lead isotope and elemental analyses. His recent books are *Rock Art and Seascapes in Uppland* and *Elevated Rock Art: Towards a Maritime Understanding of Rock Art*.

Linda M. Nicholas is adjunct curator of anthropology at the Field Museum of Natural History, Chicago. She has codirected long-term archaeological field projects in Oaxaca, Mexico, and Shandong, China. Her research interests include settlement pattern studies, household archaeology, and processes associated with early urbanization. She has published extensively on her fieldwork in Mexico and China.

Charles E. Orser Jr., research professor at Vanderbilt University, is an anthropological historical archaeologist who investigates the modern world as it was created after about 1492. He gained experience in historical archaeology in the United States (eastern and southern), Europe (Ireland), and South America (Brazil). He is the author of over 90 professional articles and a number of books, including *Historical Archaeology*; *A Historical Archaeology of the Modern World*;

*The Archaeology of Race and Racialization in Historic America*; *Race and Practice in Archaeological Interpretation*; *Unearthing Hidden Ireland: Historical Archaeology at Ballykilcline, County Roscommon*; *A Primer on Modern-World Archaeology*; and *Archaeological Thinking*. He is the founder and editor of the *International Journal of Historical Archaeology*. His research interests include post-Columbian historical archaeology; practice, network, and socio-spatial theory; globalization and consumerism; and social inequality, discrimination, and poverty. His regional interest is the Atlantic World.

Thomas C. Patterson joined the University of California, Riverside, Department of Anthropology in 2000. He conducted archaeological and ethnohistorical research in Peru during the 1960s. Since the 1970s he has studied complex organizations in the United States. His current research focuses on the historical development of anthropology and archaeology in the political-economic, social and cultural contexts shaped by nation-states, especially the United States, Peru, and Mexico; critical analyses of contemporary trends in social and cultural theory; comparative political economy; class and state formation; the intersection of class, race, and gender; theories of change and development, especially the political-economic, social, and cultural changes associated with imperialism and the processes of globalization; and critical investigations of how the realities of past societies are constituted and appropriated into the fabric of everyday life today.

Robert M. Rosenswig is associate professor at the University at Albany-SUNY. He has directed research in Mexico, Belize, and Costa Rica investigating the origins of agriculture and the development of political complexity. His publications include over three dozen journal articles and the books *The Beginnings of Mesoamerican Civilization: Inter-Regional Interaction and the Olmec* and *Early New World Monumentality*.

# Index

Page numbers in *italics* refer to illustrations and tables.

www.ingramcontent.com/pod-product-compliance
Lightning Source LLC
LaVergne TN
LVHW091534200926
848483LV00002B/392
*9780813054308*